WHAT IS JUSTICE?

WHAT IS JUSTICE?

JUSTICE, LAW, AND POLITICS
IN THE MIRROR OF SCIENCE

Collected Essays by HANS KELSEN

UNIVERSITY OF CALIFORNIA PRESS
BERKELEY, LOS ANGELES, LONDON: 1971

UNIVERSITY OF CALIFORNIA PRESS
BERKELEY AND LOS ANGELES, CALIFORNIA

UNIVERSITY OF CALIFORNIA PRESS, LTD.
LONDON, ENGLAND

©, 1957, BY
THE REGENTS OF THE UNIVERSITY OF CALIFORNIA

SECOND PRINTING, 1960
CALIFORNIA LIBRARY REPRINT SERIES EDITION 1971
ISBN: 0-520-01925-3
LIBRARY OF CONGRESS CATALOG CARD NUMBER: 56-8474

PRINTED IN THE UNITED STATES OF AMERICA
DESIGNED BY JOHN B. GOETZ

PREFACE

T HE essays collected in this book deal with the problems of justice and their relations to law, philosophy, and science. Some are published here for the first time, some were published before, but are presented in a revised version. The author wishes to thank the editors of the following publications for permission to republish articles: *The American Political Science Review* ("Absolutism and Relativism in Philosophy and Politics" and "Science and Politics"), *The University of Chicago Law Review* ("The Law as a Specific Social Technique"), *Ethics* ("Platonic Justice" and "Causality and Imputation"), *The Journal of Science, Philosophy, and Jurisprudence* ("Value Judgements in the Science of Law"), *Philosophy of Science* ("Causality and Retribution"), *The Yale Law Journal* ("Law, State, and Justice in the Pure Theory of Law"), the *Harvard Law Review* ("The Pure Theory of Law and Analytical Jurisprudence"), *Rivista Jurídica de la Universidad de Puerto Rico* ("The Idea of Justice in the Holy Scriptures"), *Louisiana Law Review* ("A 'Dynamic' Theory of Law"), and *The Western Political Quarterly* ("The Natural-Law Doctrine Before the Tribunal of Science").

H.K.

Berkeley, January, 1957

CONTENTS

WHAT IS JUSTICE?

1

THE IDEA OF JUSTICE IN THE HOLY SCRIPTURES

25

PLATONIC JUSTICE

82

ARISTOTLE'S DOCTRINE OF JUSTICE

110

THE NATURAL-LAW DOCTRINE BEFORE THE
TRIBUNAL OF SCIENCE

137

A "DYNAMIC" THEORY OF NATURAL LAW

174

ABSOLUTISM AND RELATIVISM IN
PHILOSOPHY AND POLITICS

198

VALUE JUDGMENTS IN THE SCIENCE OF LAW
209

THE LAW AS A SPECIFIC SOCIAL TECHNIQUE
231

WHY SHOULD THE LAW BE OBEYED?
257

THE PURE THEORY OF LAW AND ANALYTICAL
JURISPRUDENCE
266

LAW, STATE, AND JUSTICE IN THE PURE
THEORY OF LAW
288

CAUSALITY AND RETRIBUTION
303

CAUSALITY AND IMPUTATION
324

SCIENCE AND POLITICS
350

NOTES
376

WHAT IS JUSTICE?

When Jesus of Nazareth was brought before Pilate and admitted that he was a king, he said: "It was for this that I was born, and for this that I came to the world, to give testimony for truth." Whereupon Pilate asked, "What is truth?" The Roman procurator did not expect, and Jesus did not give, an answer to this question; for to give testimony for truth was not the essence of his divine mission as the Messianic King. He was born to give testimony for justice, the justice to be realized in the Kingdom of God, and for this justice he died on the cross. Thus, behind the question of Pilate, "What is truth?" arises, out of the blood of Christ, another still more important question, the eternal question of mankind: What is justice?

No other question has been discussed so passionately; no other question has caused so much precious blood and so many bitter tears to be shed; no other question has been the object of so much intensive thinking by the most illustrious thinkers from Plato to Kant; and yet, this question is today as unanswered as it ever was. It seems that it is one of those questions to which the resigned wisdom applies that man cannot find a definitive answer, but can only try to improve the question.

I

Justice is primarily a possible, but not a necessary, quality of a social order regulating the mutual relations of men. Only second-

This essay is based on the author's farewell lecture as an active member of the University of California, Berkeley, May 27, 1952.

1

arily it is a virtue of man, since a man is just, if his behavior conforms to the norms of a social order supposed to be just. But what
does it really mean to say that a social order is just? It means that
this order regulates the behavior of men in a way satisfactory to all
men, that is to say, so that all men find their happiness in it. The
longing for justice is men's eternal longing for happiness. It is
happiness that man cannot find alone, as an isolated individual,
and hence seeks in society. Justice is social happiness. It is happiness
guaranteed by a social order. In this sense Plato, identifying justice
with happiness, maintains that only a just man is happy, and an unjust man unhappy. The statement that justice is happiness is evidently not a final answer; it is only shifting the question. For, now,
we must ask: What is happiness?

It is obvious that there can be no "just" order, that is, one af-
fording happiness to everyone, as long as one defines the concept
of happiness in its original, narrow sense of individual happiness,
meaning by a man's happiness, what he himself considers it to be.
For it is then inevitable that the happiness of one individual will,
at some time, be directly in conflict with that of another. For example, love is one of the most important sources of happiness as
well as of unhappiness. Let us suppose that two men are in love with
one and the same woman, and each believes, rightly or wrongly,
that he cannot be happy without having this woman exclusively for
his own wife. However, according to law and perhaps also according to her own feelings, a woman can be only the wife of one of
them. Hence, the happiness of the one is inevitably the unhappiness
of the other. No social order can solve this problem in a satisfactory,
that is to say, in a just way, guaranteeing the happiness of both—
not even the famous judgment of the wise King Solomon. He decided, as will be remembered, to divide into two parts a child which
each of two women claimed as her own; but he was willing to attribute the child to the one who should withdraw her claim in
order to avoid the death of the child, because—so the king assumed
—she truly loved the child. If the Solomonic judgment was just at
all, it was so only under the condition that one woman only loved
the child. If both loved the child, which is quite possible and even
probable since both wished to have it, and if both had withdrawn
their claim, the dispute would have remained undecided; and if,
despite the fact that both women waived their claim, the child had

been awarded one of them, the judgment would certainly not have been just, since it would have made one party unhappy. Our happiness very often depends on the satisfaction of needs which no social order can satisfy.

Another example: The commander in chief of the army shall be appointed. Two men are in competition, but only one can be appointed. It seems to be evident that it is just to appoint the one who is more fit for the office. But what if the two are equally fit? Then, no just solution is possible. Let us suppose that the one is considered to be better than the other because he is tall and handsome, and has an impressive personality, whereas the other, although professionally absolutely equal, is small and plain and looks insignificant. If the first one gets the job, the other will not feel that the decision was just. He will ask, "Why am I not tall and handsome as the other, why has nature given me a less attractive body?" And, indeed, if we judge nature from the point of view of justice, we must admit that nature is not just; it makes the one healthy, and the other sick, the one intelligent, the other stupid. No social order can compensate completely for the injustice of nature.

If justice is happiness, a just social order is impossible if justice means individual happiness. But a just social order is impossible even on the supposition that it tries to bring about, not the individual happiness of each, but the greatest possible happiness of the greatest possible number of individuals. This is the famous definition of justice formulated by the English philosopher and jurist Jeremy Bentham. But Bentham's formula is not applicable, if by happiness is meant a subjective value, and if, consequently, different individuals have different ideas of what constitutes their happiness. The happiness that a social order is able to assure cannot be happiness in a subjective-individual sense; it must be happiness in an objective-collective sense, that is to say, by happiness we must understand the satisfaction of certain needs, recognized by the social authority, the lawgiver, as needs worthy of being satisfied, such as the need to be fed, clothed, housed, and the like. There can be little doubt that satisfaction of socially recognized needs is very different from the original meaning which the idea of happiness implies. That idea has, by its very nature, a highly subjective character. The desire for justice is so elementary, and so deeply rooted in the human mind, because it is a manifestation of man's indestructible desire for his own subjective happiness.

In order to become a social category—the happiness of justice—the idea of happiness must radically change its significance. The metamorphosis of individual happiness into satisfaction of socially recognized needs as the meaning of justice, is similar to the transformation which the idea of freedom must undergo in order to become a social principle; and the idea of freedom is sometimes identified with the idea of justice, so that a social order is considered just if it guarantees individual freedom. Since genuine freedom, that is, freedom from any kind of social authority or government, is incompatible with any kind of social organization, the idea of freedom must cease to mean absence of government; it must assume the meaning of a special form of government: government exercised by the majority—if necessary, against the minority of the governed individuals. The freedom of anarchy turns to the self-determination of democracy. In the same way and for the same reason, the idea of justice is transformed from a principle guaranteeing the individual happiness of all subjects, into a social order protecting certain interests socially recognized by the majority as worthy of being protected.

But which human interests are worthy of being satisfied and, especially, what is their proper order of rank? That is the question which arises when conflicting interests exist, and it is with respect to the possible conflict of interests that justice within a social order is required. Where there is no conflict of interests, there is no need for justice. A conflict of interests exists when one interest can be satisfied only at the expense of the other; or, what amounts to the same, when there is a conflict between two values, and when it is not possible to realize both at the same time; when the one can be realized only if the other is neglected; when it is necessary to prefer the realization of the one to that of the other; to decide which one is more important, or in other terms, to decide which is the higher value, and finally: which is the highest value. The problem of values is in the first place the problem of conflicts of values, and this problem cannot be solved by means of rational cognition. The answer to these questions is a judgment of value, determined by emotional factors, and, therefore, subjective in character—valid only for the judging subject, and therefore relative only. Some examples will illustrate this statement.

II

According to a certain ethical conviction, human life, the life of every human being, is the highest value. Consequently it is, according to this ethical conviction, absolutely forbidden to kill a human being, even in war, and even as capital punishment. This is, for instance, the opinion of so-called conscientious objectors who refuse to perform military service; and of those who repudiate in principle, and in any case, the death penalty. However, there is another ethical conviction, according to which the highest value is the interest and honor of the nation. Consequently, everybody is, according to this opinion, morally obliged to sacrifice his own life and to kill other human beings as enemies of the nation in war if the interest or the honor of the nation requires such action, and it is justified to kill human beings as criminals in inflicting capital punishment. It is impossible to decide between these two conflicting judgments of value in a rational scientific way. It is, in the last instance, our feeling, our will, and not our reason; the emotional, and not the rational element of our consciousness which decides this conflict.

If a man has been made a slave or a prisoner in a Nazi concentration camp, and if it is impossible to escape, the question of whether suicide is justifiable in such a situation arises. This is a question which has been again and again discussed, since Socrates drank his poison cup. The decision depends on the answer to the question of which is the higher value: life or freedom. If life is the higher value, then suicide is not justifiable; if freedom is the higher value, if life without freedom is worthless, suicide is morally justified. It is the question of the order or rank of the values, life and freedom. Only a subjective answer is possible to this question, an answer valid only for the judging subject; no objective statement, valid for everybody, as for instance the statement that heat expands metallic bodies.

Let us suppose that it is possible to prove that the economic situation of a people can be improved so essentially by so-called planned economy that social security is guaranteed to everybody in an equal measure; but that such an organization is possible only if all individual freedom is abolished. The answer to the question whether planned economy is preferable to free economy depends on our decision between the values of individual freedom and social security. A man with strong self-confidence may prefer individual freedom, whereas one suffering from an inferiority complex may prefer social security. Hence, to the question of whether individual freedom is a higher value than social security or vice versa, only a subjective answer is possible, no objective judgment, as for instance, the statement that iron is heavier than water, and water heavier than wood. This is a judgment about reality verifiable by experiment, not a judgment of value which defies such verification.

A doctor, after a careful examination of a patient, diagnoses an incurable disease of which the patient shall probably die within a short time. Must the doctor tell the truth, or is he allowed, or even obliged, to lie and tell the patient that his disease is curable and that there is no imminent danger? The decision depends on the order of rank we recognize in the relationship between the value of truth and the value of freedom from fear. To tell the truth means to cause the patient's fear of death; to lie means to free him from fear. If the ideal of truth stands above the ideal of freedom from fear, the doctor has to tell the truth; if the ideal of freedom from fear stands above the ideal of truth, he has to lie. But the answer to the questions as to whether truth or freedom from fear is the higher value is not possible on the basis of a rational scientific consideration.

Plato advocates the opinion that a just man—that means in this connection, a man who obeys the law—and only a just man, is happy; whereas an unjust man—a man who violates the law—is unhappy. Plato says, that "the most just life is the most pleasant." [1] Plato, however, admits that perhaps in one case or another the just man may be unhappy and the unjust man happy. But, asserts the philosopher, it is absolutely necessary that the individuals, subject to the legal order, believe in the truth of the statement that only the just man is happy, even if it should not be true; for otherwise nobody would obey the law. Consequently the government has, according to Plato, the right to spread among the people by means of propaganda the doctrine that the just is happy and the unjust unhappy, even if this doctrine be a lie. If this is a lie, says Plato, it is a very useful lie, for it guarantees obedience to the law. "Could a lawgiver, who was worth his salt, find any more useful lie than this, or one more effective in persuading all men to act justly in all things willingly and without constraint? . . . If I were a legislator, I should endeavour to compel the poets and all the citizens to speak in this sense [that the most just life is the happiest]." The government, then, is fully justified in making use of a useful lie. Plato places justice— and that means here, what the government considers to be justice, namely, lawfulness—above truth; but there is no sufficient reason not to place truth above lawfulness and to repudiate as immoral a governmental propaganda based on lies, even if it serves a good purpose.

The answer to the question concerning the rank of the different values such as freedom, equality, security, truth, lawfulness, and others, is different according to whether the question is answered by a believing Christian, who holds his salvation—the fate of his soul in the hereafter—more important than earthly goods; or by a materialist who does not believe in an after life. And it will be just as different according to whether the decision is made by one who considers individual freedom as the highest good, that is by a liberal, or by one for whom social security and the equal treatment of all men is rated higher than freedom, by a socialist. The answer has always the character of a subjective, and therefore only relative, judgment of value.

III

The fact that value judgments are subjective and that very different value judgments are possible, does not mean that every individual has his own system of values. In fact, very many individuals agree in their judgments of value. A positive system of values is not an arbitrary creation of the isolated individual, but always the result of the mutual influences the individuals exercise upon one another within a given group, be it family, tribe, clan, caste, profession, and under certain political and economic circumstances. Every system of values, especially a system of morals and its central idea of justice, is a social phenomenon, the product of a society, and hence different according to the nature of the society within which it arises. The fact that there are certain values generally accepted in a certain society in no way contradicts the subjective and relative character of these judgments of value. That many individuals agree in their judgments of value is no proof that these judgments are correct, that is to say, valid in an objective sense. Just as the fact that most people believe or used to believe that the sun turns around the earth, is, or was, no proof of the truth of this idea. The criterion of justice, like the criterion of truth, is not dependent on the frequency with which judgments about reality or judgments of value are made. In the history of human civilization quite generally accepted value judgments have often been replaced by quite different value judgments no less generally accepted. In ancient times, blood revenge based on collective responsibility was generally considered as a just institution; but in modern times the opposite idea obtains that only individual responsibility is just. Nevertheless, it is not incompatible with the feeling of justice of most people that in some fields, as, for example, in international relations, the principle of collective responsibility is established; and in religious belief the idea of an original sin—which, too, implies collective responsibility—is still prevailing. And it is by no means impossible that in the future, if socialism should become victorious, a kind of collective responsibility again may generally be considered as adequate.

Although the question as to whether the individual or the nation, the material or the spiritual, freedom or security, truth or justice, represent the highest value, cannot be answered rationally, yet the subjective, and hence relative, judgment by which this question actually is answered, is usually presented as the assertion of an objective and absolute value, as a generally valid norm. It is a peculiarity of the human being that he has a deep need to justify his behavior, that he has a conscience. The need for justification or rationalization is perhaps one of the differences which exist between human beings and animals. Man's external behavior is not very different from that of animals. The big fish swallow the small ones, in the kingdom of animals as well as in that of men. But if a human fish, driven by his instincts, behaves in this way, he wishes to justify his behavior before himself as well as before society, to appease his conscience by the idea that his behavior in relation to his fellow man is right.

If man is more or less a rational being, he tries to justify his behavior, motivated by the emotions of his fear and desire, in a rational way, that is to say, through the function of his intellect. This, however, is possible only to a limited extent—only to the extent that his fear or desire refers to means by which some end is to be achieved; for the relationship of means to end is a relationship of cause and effect, and this can be determined on the basis of experience, which means in a scientific rational way. To be sure, even this is frequently not possible, if the means to achieve a certain end are specifically social measures. For the actual status of social science is such that we have no adequate insight into the causal nexus of social phenomena, and hence no sufficient experience which enables us to determine how certain social aims may best be attained. This is, for example, the case, when a legislator has to decide the question of whether he should provide capital punishment or only imprisonment in order to prevent certain crimes. This question may be formulated as the question of whether capital punishment or imprisonment is a "just" punishment. To decide this question the legislator must know the effect which the threat of these different penalties has on the mind of men inclined to commit the crimes the legislator wishes to prevent. But unfortunately, we have no exact knowledge of this effect and are not in a position to acquire such knowledge, since this is possible only by experiment, and experiment in the field of social life is possible only to a very limited extent. Hence, the problem of justice even as thus restricted to a question of the appropriate means to a presupposed end, cannot always be rationally answered. And even if it could be answered, the answer could not constitute a full justification of our behavior, that justification which our conscience requires. By most appropriate means, most inappropriate ends may be achieved. Think of the atomic bomb. The end— it is true—justifies the means, but the means do not justify the end; and it is the justification of the end, the end which is not itself a means to a further end, the ultimate end, which is the final justification of our behavior.

If something, especially a pattern of human behavior, is justified as means to a certain end, the inevitable question arises whether this end is justifiable. This train of ideas must finally lead to the assumption of an ultimate end, which is the very problem of morality in general and justice in particular. If some human behavior is justified only as an appropriate means to a presupposed end, this behavior is justified only conditionally—under the condition that the presupposed end is justifiable. Such a conditional—and in this sense relative—justification does not exclude the possibility of the opposite. For if the ultimate end is not justifiable, the means to this end is also not justifiable. Democracy is a just form of government only because it is a form of government by which individual freedom is preserved. That means that it is a just form of government under the condition that individual freedom is presupposed as an ultimate end. If instead of individual freedom, social security is presupposed as the ultimate end and if it can be proved that social security cannot be established under a democratic form of government, then not democracy, but another form of government may be considered as just, since another end requires another means. Hence democracy can be justified only as a relatively—not as an absolutely—just form of government.

Our conscience may not be satisfied with such a conditional—and that means relative—justification; it may require an unconditional—an absolute—justification, that is to say, our conscience may be appeased only if our behavior is justified not merely as an appropriate means to an end whose justification is doubtful, but as an end, an ultimate end, or, what amounts to the same, as an absolute value. However, such a justification is not possible in a rational way, because a rational justification is justification as an appropriate means; and an ultimate end is—by definition—not itself a means to a further end. If our conscience requires absolute justification of our behavior—and that means the validity of absolute values—human reason is not able to fulfill this requirement. The absolute in general, and absolute values in particular, are beyond human reason, for which only a conditional, and in this sense relative, solution of the problem of justice, as the problem of justification of human behavior, is possible.

But the need for absolute justification seems to be stronger than any rational consideration. Hence man tries to attain the satisfaction of this need through religion and metaphysics. That means that absolute justice is transferred from this world into the transcendental world. It becomes the essential quality, and its realization the essential function, of a superhuman being, of God, whose qualities and functions are, by definition, inaccessible to human cognition. Man must believe in the existence of God, and that means in the existence of absolute justice, but he is unable to understand it. Those who cannot accept this metaphysical solution of the problem of justice and nevertheless maintain the idea of absolute values in the hope of being able to determine them in a rational-scientific way deceive themselves with an illusion—namely, that it is possible to find in human reason certain fundamental principles from which absolute values may be deduced. But these values are, in truth, determined, in the last analysis, by the emotional elements of their mind. The determination of these absolute values, and in particular the definition of the idea of justice, achieved in this way, are but empty formulas by which any social order whatever may be justified as just.

Hence the many doctrines of justice that have been expounded from the oldest times of the past until today may easily be reduced to two basic types: a metaphysical-religious and a rationalistic or —more exactly formulated—a pseudorationalistic one.

IV

The classical representative of the metaphysical type is Plato.[2] The central problem of his whole philosophy is justice, and for the solution of this problem he developed his famous doctrine of ideas. The ideas are transcendental entities, existing in an ideal world; they represent the absolute values which should be, but never can be, realized entirely in this world. The main idea, the one to which all others are subordinated and from which they all receive their validity, is the idea of the absolute good. This idea plays in Plato's philosophy exactly the same role as the idea of God in the theology of any religion. The idea of the absolute good implies the justice, at whose cognition almost all Platonic dialogues aim. The question as to what is justice coincides with the question as to what is good. Plato makes numerous attempts to approach this problem in a rationalistic way, but none of them leads to a final result. If some definition seems to be reached, Plato immediately declares that it cannot be considered as definitive; that further investigations are necessary. Plato speaks frequently of a specific method of abstract thinking, the so-called dialectic, which, as he maintains, enables those who master it, to grasp, or rather to get a sight or vision of, the ideas. But he himself does not apply this method in his dialogues, or at least does not let us know the results of this dialectic cognition. Of the idea of the absolute good, he even says expressly that it is beyond all rational cognition. In one of his epistles—*Epistle VII,* where he gives an account of the inner motives of his philosophy—he declares that the vision of the absolute good is possible only through a specifically mystic experience, which only very few are able to attain by divine grace; but that it is impossible to describe the object of their mystic vision, the absolute good, in words of human language. Hence there can be no answer to the question of what is justice. For justice is the secret which God reveals, if at all, only to a few select persons who cannot communicate it to others.

It is interesting to note how near Plato's philosophy of justice is to the teaching of Christ, whose main concern, too, was justice. After having rejected the rationalistic answer of the Old Testament, that justice is retribution—the principle of an eye for an eye, a tooth for a tooth—he proclaimed as the new justice the principle of love: Don't requite evil with evil, don't resist injury, pass no judgment upon others, love the wrongdoer, love even your enemy.[3] This justice is beyond any social order to be established in reality; and the love which is the essence of this justice is evidently not the human instinct we call love. Not only because it is against human nature to love one's enemy, but also because Jesus emphatically rejected human love uniting man with woman, parent with children. He who wants to enter the Kingdom of God must give up home and wife and brothers and sisters and parents and children.[4] Jesus goes even so far as to say: "If anyone comes to me without hating his own father and mother and wife and children and brothers and sisters, and his very life too, he cannot be a disciple of mine." [5] The love taught by Jesus is not human love. It is the love through which man shall become as perfect as his Father in heaven, who makes his sun rise on bad and good alike and makes the rain fall on the upright and the wrongdoer.[6] It is the love of God. It is supposed to be compatible with the cruel and even eternal punishment of the sinner in the Last Judgment, and hence with the deepest fear, the fear of God. Jesus did not and could not explain these contradictions; for contradictions they are only for the limited human reason, not for the absolute reason of God, which is incomprehensible to man. Hence, Paul, the first theologian of the Christian religion, taught that this world's wisdom is foolishness to God,[7] that philosophy—that is logical-rationalistic cognition—is no way to the divine justice hidden in the mysterious wisdom of God,[8] that justice comes from God through faith,[9] faith acting through love.[10] Paul maintains Jesus' teaching of the new justice, the love of God. But he admits that the love taught by Jesus is far beyond our understanding.[11] It is a secret, one of the many secrets of faith.[12]

V

The rationalistic type, the one which tries to answer the question by defining the concept of justice by the means of human reason, is represented in the popular wisdom of all nations as well as in some famous philosophical systems. To one of the seven sages of ancient Greece, the well-known saying is attributed that justice is to give to each his own. This definition has been accepted by many outstanding thinkers and especially by legal philosophers. It is easy to show that this is an empty formula, because the decisive question, what is that which is everybody's own, is not answered, and hence the formula is applicable only under the condition that this question is already decided by a social order—legal or moral —established by custom or legislation, that is to say, by positive morality or positive law. Hence the formula can be used to justify any such order, whether it be capitalistic or communistic, democratic or autocratic—which probably explains its general acceptance, but which shows that it is useless as a definition of justice as an absolute value, different from the merely relative values guaranteed by positive law or positive morality.

The same holds true with respect to the principle which probably is most often presented as the essence of justice: like for like, that is, good for good and evil for evil, the principle of retribution. This principle is meaningless unless the answer to the question, what is good and what is evil, is presupposed as self-evident. But the answer to this question is not at all self-evident, since the ideas of good and evil are very different among different peoples and at different times. The principle of retribution expresses only the specific technique of the positive law, which reacts against the evil of the delict with the evil of the sanction. Hence, any positive legal order corresponds to this principle. The question of justice, however, is the question of whether a positive legal order, attaching to the evil of the delict the evil of the sanction, is just, whether that which the lawmaker considers as an evil to society is indeed a behavior against which society should justly react, and whether the sanction with which society actually reacts is appropriate. To this question, which is the very question of the justice of the law, the principle of retribution is no answer at all.

So far as retribution means like for like, it is one of the many varieties of the principle of equality, which, too, is presented as the essence of justice. This idea of justice starts from the presupposition that men are by their very nature equal, and results in the postulate that all men shall be treated in an equal way. Since, however, the presupposition is evidently wrong, men being in fact very different, no two men being really equal, the only possible meaning of the postulate is that a social order, in conferring rights and imposing duties on men, should ignore certain differences—only certain, not all differences. It would be absurd to treat children in the same way as adults, insane people in the same way as mentally normal ones. But which are the differences that should, and those that should not be taken into consideration? This is the decisive question; and to this question the principle of equality is no answer. In deciding this question, the existing legal orders differ essentially. They all, it is true, agree in ignoring certain differences. But in the differences they do not ignore—the differences they take into consideration in conferring rights and imposing duties on men—there are hardly two legal orders that are completely in harmony. According to one law, only men have political rights, not women; according to another, both, but only men have the duty to do military service; whereas under a third one, the difference of sex has no legal effect in this respect. Which of these legal orders is just? If somebody is indifferent with regard to religion, he will be inclined to consider the difference of religion as irrelevant; if, however, he has a deeply rooted religious conviction, he will certainly consider the difference between those who share his faith—which, for him, is the only true faith—and all others, whether they believe in another religion or are atheists, as more important than any other difference. He will interpret the principle of equality to mean that only equals shall be treated equally. This is indeed the meaning of the principle of equality. Then, the decisive question is: "What is equal?" and this question is not decided by the principle of equality. Hence a positive legal order may make any difference whatever between human beings the basis of a different treatment of its subjects, without getting in conflict with the principle of equality, which is too empty to have practical consequences.

The principle of equality as a postulate directed at the authority creating the law meaning equality in the law, should not be confused with the principle of equality before the law, which is directed at the authorities applying the law to concrete cases. It means that the law-applying organs shall not, in deciding a case, make a difference that is not provided for in the law to be applied, that is to say, they shall apply the law as it should be applied according to its own meaning. It is the principle of legality, of lawfulness, which is immanent in every legal order. It is presented sometimes as justice under the law. But, in truth, it has nothing to do with justice at all.

The principle of equality, if applied to the relationship between labor and product, leads to the maxim: "For an equal quantity of labor an equal quantity of the product." This is according to Karl Marx the idea of justice which is at the basis of the capitalist social order, the allegedly "equal law" of this economic system. It is, in reality, a violation of equality and hence an unjust law. For people who are actually unequal are treated equally. If a man who is strong and a man who is weak get both for the same quantity of labor the same quantity of product, an equal quantity of product is given for a factually unequal quantity of labor. True equality, and hence true, not merely apparent, justice can be realized only within a communist economic system where the principle prevails: "Each according to his capacities and to each according to his needs." [13] If this principle is to be applied within a system of planned economy, which presupposes that the process of production is regulated by a central authority, the questions arise: "What are the capacities of each, what kind of labor is he fit for, what quantity of labor may be ex-

pected from him?" It stands to reason that this question cannot
be answered by each individual according to his own subjective
judgment, but must be decided upon by the competent organ of
the community according to general rules adopted by the social
authority. And then the next question arises: "Which are the
needs that shall be satisfied?" Evidently only those for whose
satisfaction the process of production, planned and directed by a
central authority, is working. Even if, as Marx affirms, in the
communist society of the future the production forces should
grow and all springs of social wealth should pour forth a full
flow, the choice of the needs to be satisfied and the extent to
which they are to be satisfied could not be left entirely to the
subjective wishes of the single individual. This question too,
must be decided by the social authority according to general
norms. Thus, the communist principle of justice—like the formula "To each his own"—presupposes the answer to questions
essential for its application to be given by an established social
order. It is true, not by any such order whatever, but by an order
of which nobody can foresee how it will answer the questions
concerned. This fact taken into consideration, the communist
principle of justice—so far as it claims to be such a principle at
all—amounts to the rule: "Each according to his capacities recognized by the communist social order, to each according to his
needs likewise recognized by that social order." It is a utopian
illusion that this social order will recognize the capacities of each
individual in complete conformity with his own subjective judgment and guarantee the satisfaction of all his needs according to
his own subjective wishes, so that there will be full harmony of
the collective and individual interests and, hence, unrestricted
individual freedom within the society constituted by this order.
It is the typical utopia of a Golden Age, a paradise where not
only—as Marx prophesied—the "narrow horizon of bourgeois
law" but—since there will be no conflicts of interests—also the
much wider horizon of justice will be completely overcome.

Not very different from the principles of equality and retribution is the golden rule—to do, or not to do, to others as we
would, or would not, have them do to us. What everybody wants
others to do to him, is to give him pleasure; and what everybody
wants others not to do, is to give him pain. Hence the golden rule

amounts to the norm: "Give pleasure to others, do not inflict pain upon them." However, it frequently occurs that it is somebody's pleasure to inflict pain upon another. If this is a violation of the golden rule, then the question arises: "What shall be done to the violator in order to prevent such violation as far as possible?" This is the question of justice. If nobody would inflict pain upon another, no problem of justice would exist. It is quite evident that the golden rule, if applied to cases of its violation, must lead to absurd consequences; for nobody wants to be punished, even if he has committed a crime. Hence, according to the golden rule, nobody should punish a criminal. Somebody might not mind at all that others tell lies to him, since he—rightly or wrongly—thinks himself to be clever enough to find out the truth and thus to protect himself against the liar. Then, according to the golden rule, he is allowed to lie. The golden rule, taken literally, results in the abolition of law and morality. But its intention is evidently not to abolish, but to maintain, the social order. If interpreted according to its intention, the golden rule cannot, as its wording pretends, establish a merely subjective criterion of the right behavior, the right behavior of the individual being the behavior that he wishes to get from others; such criterion is incompatible with any social order. The golden rule must establish an objective criterion. Its true meaning is: "Behave in relation to others as the others shall behave in relation to you." But how shall they behave? This is the question of justice. The answer to this question is not given, but presupposed by the golden rule; it is given by an established social order—by any such order, whether just or unjust.

VI

If the subjective criterion of the right behavior—implied in the wording of the golden rule—is replaced by an objective criterion; if the meaning of the golden rule is that each individual shall behave toward the others as the others shall behave toward him, then this rule amounts to the principle: "Behave in conformity with the general norms of the social order." It was evidently the golden rule, interpreted in this way, which inspired the German philosopher Immanuel Kant [14] to his formulation of the categorical imperative, which is the essential result of his moral philosophy, and his solution of the problem of justice. It runs as follows: "Act only on that maxim whereby you can at the same time will that it should become a universal law." Its meaning is that one's acts should be determined only by principles that one shall wish to be binding on all men. But which are these principles of which we shall wish that they be binding upon all men? This is the decisive question of justice. To this question the categorical imperative, just as the golden rule—its model—is no answer.

The concrete examples by which Kant tries to illustrate the application of his categorical imperative, are precepts of the traditional morals and the positive law of his time. They are not, as the doctrine of the categorical imperative pretends, deduced from this principle—for nothing can be deduced from this empty formula. They prove only to be compatible with it; and any precept of any established social order is compatible with the principle that says nothing else but that the individual shall act in conformity with general norms. Thus the categorical imperative, just as the rule "To each his own" or the golden rule, can serve as a justification of any social order. This possibility explains why these formulas in spite of—or rather because of—their emptiness, are still, and probably always will be, accepted as satisfactory answers to the question of justice.

VII

Another characteristic example of a futile attempt to define justice in a scientific or quasiscientific way based on reason, is the ethics of Aristotle.[15] He aimed at a system of virtues of which justice is the "chief of the virtues," the "perfect virtue." Aristotle assures us that he has detected a mathematical-geometrical, a scientific, method of defining virtue, and that means the morally good. The moralist, Aristotle maintains, can find the virtue he is looking for just as the geometrist can find the point equidistant from the two ends of a line. Hence virtue is a mean state between two extremes, which are vices (one of excess and one of deficiency).[16] Thus, for example, the virtue of courage is a mean between the vice of cowardice, as too little, and the vice of audacity, as too much confidence. This is his famous doctrine of the mean (*mesótes*). A geometrist can divide a line into two equal parts only if the two extreme points of the line are given, and if these two points are given, the middle point of the line is predetermined by them. Thus Aristotle can find by his geometrical method the virtue he is looking for only if the two vices are given. But if we know what the vices are, we know also what the virtues are, because a virtue is the opposite of a vice. If deceitfulness (falsehood) is a vice, veracity is a virtue. And indeed the existence of the vice, Aristotle takes for granted. He presupposes as self-evident that vices are what the traditional morality of his time stigmatizes as such. This means that the ethics of the *mesótes* doctrine only pretends to solve its problem—the determination of what is evil or a vice and, consequently, also the determination of what is good or a virtue, because the latter is implied in the former. It leaves the solution of this problem to another authority—to the authority of the positive morality and the positive law, the established social order. By presupposing in his *mesótes* formula the given social order, the *Ethics* of Aristotle justifies the positive morality and the positive law, and it is this positive morality and positive law, not the philosophy of Aristotle, which, as a matter of fact, determines what is "too much" and what is "too little," what are the extremes of evil or wrong, and thereby determines what is the mean, that is, good and right. In this justification of the given social order lies the true—the highly conservative—function of the empty tautology which a critical analysis of the *mesótes* formula reveals.

In its application to the problem of justice the tautological character of the *mesótes* formula is still more evident. Aristotle says that "just conduct is a mean between doing and suffering injustice, for the former is to have too much and the latter to have too little." [17] Here the formula that a virtue is the mean between two vices is useless even as a mere figure of speech, for the injustice done, and the injustice suffered, are not two different evils; they are one and the same evil, of which justice is simply the opposite. The decisive question: "What is injustice?" is not answered by the formula. Instead, the answer is presupposed, and Aristotle presupposes as unjust what is unjust under the then existing moral and legal order. The true function of the *mesótes* doctrine is not, as pretended, to determine the concept of justice, but to confirm the validity of the established social order; and this politically highly important achievement protected it against a critical analysis which proves its scientific futility.[18]

VIII

The metaphysical as well as the rationalistic type of legal philosophy is represented in a school of thought which was prevalent during the seventeenth and eighteenth centuries, and which, although repressed more or less during the nineteenth century, has again gained influence in our time. It is the doctrine of natural law.[19] This doctrine maintains that there exists a perfectly just regulation of human relations, emanating from nature—nature in general; or human nature, the nature of man as a being endowed with reason. Nature is conceived of as a legislator. By an analysis of nature we find the immanent norms prescribing the just conduct of men. If nature is supposed to be created by God, the norms immanent in nature, natural laws, are the expression of the will of God. Then the natural-law doctrine has a metaphysical character. If, however, the natural law is to be deduced from the nature of man as a being endowed with reason, if the principle of justice is supposed to be discoverable by an analysis of human reason (in which this principle is immanent), then the natural-law doctrine pretends to assume a rationalistic character. From the point of view of science, neither the one nor the other view is tenable.

Nature as a system of facts, connected with one another according to the law of causality, has no will and hence cannot prescribe a definite behavior of man. From facts, that is to say, from that which is, or actually is done, no inference is possible to that which ought to be or ought to be done. So far as the natural-law doctrine tries to deduce from nature norms of human behavior, it is based on a logical fallacy.

The same holds true with respect to human reason. Norms prescribing human behavior can emanate only from human will, not from human reason; hence the statement that man ought to behave in a certain way can be reached by human reason only under the condition that by human will a norm has been established prescribing this behavior; human reason can understand and describe such behavior but cannot prescribe it. To detect norms of human behavior in human reason is the same illusion as to deduce them from nature.

Hence it is not astonishing that the various followers of the natural-law doctrine deduced from nature, or found in human reason, the most contradictory principles of justice. According to one leading representative of this doctrine, Robert Filmer, the autocracy of an absolute monarchy is the only natural, and that means just, form of government. But another likewise outstanding philosopher, John Locke, proved by the same method that absolute monarchy is no form of government at all, and that only democracy can be considered as such, because only democracy corresponds to the intention of nature. Most writers of this school maintained that individual property, the basis of the capitalistic system, is a natural and consequently sacred right, because it is conferred directly by nature or reason upon man; and that, consequently, communism is a crime against nature or reason. But the propaganda for the abolition of private property and the establishment of a communistic society as the only just social organization was based during the eighteenth and the beginning of the nineteenth century on the same natural-law doctrine.

IX

If the history of human thought proves anything, it is the futility of the attempt to establish, in the way of rational considerations, an absolutely correct standard of human behavior, and that means a standard of human behavior as the only just one, excluding the possibility of considering the opposite standard to be just too. If we may learn anything from the intellectual experiences of the past, it is the fact that only relative values are accessible to human reason; and that means that the judgment to the effect that something is just cannot be made with the claim of excluding the possibility of a contrary judgment of value. Absolute justice is an irrational ideal or, what amounts to the same, an illusion— one of the eternal illusions of mankind. From the point of view of rational cognition, there are only interests of human beings and hence conflicts of interests. The solution of these conflicts can be brought about either by satisfying one interest at the expense of the other, or by a compromise between the conflicting interests. It is not possible to prove that only the one or the other solution is just. Under certain conditions the one, under others the other may be just. If social peace is supposed to be the ultimate end—but only then—the compromise solution may be just, but the justice of peace is only a relative, and not an absolute, justice.

X

What then is the moral of this relativistic philosophy of justice? Has it any moral at all? Is relativism not amoral, or even immoral, as it is sometimes maintained? Is relativism incompatible with moral responsibility? On the contrary! The view that moral principles constitute only relative values does not mean that they constitute no value at all; it means that there is not one moral system, but that there are several different ones, and that, consequently, a choice must be made among them. Thus, relativism imposes upon the individual the difficult tasks of deciding for himself what is right and what is wrong. This, of course, implies a very serious responsibility, the most serious moral responsibility a man can assume. If men are too weak to bear this responsibility, they shift it to an authority above them, to the government, and, in the last instance, to God. Then they have no choice. It is easier to obey a command issued by a superior than to be morally one's own master. The fear of personal responsibility is one of the strongest motives of the passionate resistance against relativism. Relativism is rejected and—what is worse—misinterpreted,[20] not because it morally requires too little, but because it requires too much.

The particular moral principle involved in a relativistic philosophy of justice is the principle of tolerance, and that means the sympathetic understanding of the religious or political beliefs of others—without accepting them, but not preventing them from being freely expressed. It stands to reason that no absolute tolerance can be commended by a relativistic philosophy of values; only tolerance within an established legal order guaranteeing peace by prohibiting and preventing the use of force among those

subjected to the order, but not prohibiting or preventing the peaceful expression of ideas. Tolerance means freedom of thought. Highest moral ideals have been compromised by the intolerance of those who fought for them. On the stakes which the Spanish Inquisition set on fire for the defense of the Christian religion, not only the bodies of the heretics were burned, but also one of the noblest precepts of Christ was sacrificed: "Pass no judgment upon others so that you may not have judgment passed on you." During the religious struggles of the seventeenth century, when the persecuted church agreed with the persecuting church only in the wish to destroy the other, Pierre Bayle, one of the great liberators of the human mind, said, with regard to those who thought it best to defend an established religious or political order by persecuting dissenters: "It is not tolerance, it is intolerance that causes disorder." If democracy is a just form of government, it is so because it means freedom, and freedom means tolerance. If a democracy ceases to be tolerant, it ceases to be a democracy. But can a democracy be tolerant in its defense against antidemocratic tendencies? It can—to the extent that it must not suppress the peaceful expression of antidemocratic ideas. It is just by such tolerance that democracy distinguishes itself from autocracy. We have a right to reject autocracy and to be proud of our democratic form of government only as long as we maintain this difference. Democracy cannot defend itself by giving itself up. But to suppress and prevent any attempt to overthrow the government by force is the right of any government and has nothing to do with the principles of democracy in general and tolerance in particular. Sometimes it may be difficult to draw a clear boundary line between the mere expression of ideas and the preparation of the use of force; but on the possibility of finding such a boundary line depends the possibility of maintaining democracy. It may be that any such boundary line involves a certain risk. But it is the essence and the honor of democracy to run such risk, and if democracy could not stand such risk, it would not be worthy of being defended.

Because democracy, by its very nature, means freedom, and freedom means tolerance, there is no other form of government which is so favorable to science. For science can prosper only if it is free; and it is free if there is not only external freedom, that

is, independence from political influence, but if there is also freedom within science, the free play of arguments and counter arguments. No doctrine whatever can be suppressed in the name of science, for the soul of science is tolerance.

I started this essay with the question as to what is justice. Now, at its end I am quite aware that I have not answered it. My only excuse is that in this respect I am in the best of company. It would have been more than presumptuous to make the reader believe that I could succeed where the most illustrious thinkers have failed. And, indeed, I do not know, and I cannot say what justice is, the absolute justice for which mankind is longing. I must acquiesce in a relative justice and I can only say what justice is to me. Since science is my profession, and hence the most important thing in my life, justice, to me, is that social order under whose protection the search for truth can prosper. "My" justice, then, is the justice of freedom, the justice of peace, the justice of democracy—the justice of tolerance.

THE IDEA OF JUSTICE IN THE
HOLY SCRIPTURES

THE TRANSCENDENTAL CHARACTER
OF DIVINE JUSTICE

ONE of the most important elements of Christian religion is the idea that justice is an essential quality of God. Since God is the absolute, his justice must be absolute justice, that is to say, eternal and unchangeable. Only a religion whose deity is supposed to be just can play a role in social life. To attribute justice to the deity in order to make religion applicable to human relations implies a certain tendency of rationalizing something which, by its very nature, is irrational—the transcendental being, the religious authority, and its absolute qualities.

From the point of view of rational cognition the absolute justice of God must necessarily be in conflict with another absolute quality, as essential as the former, namely, his omnipotence. If God is omnipotent nothing which actually happens can happen against or without his will. Since injustice actually exists—if it would not exist, the idea of justice were meaningless—how is God's omnipotence compatible with his justice? This is the problem of theodicy, insoluble for rational cognition. It is, however, no valid argument against a religious belief in an almighty and at the same time absolutely just God, because the facts of faith are outside of rational cognition. The transcendental nature of God in general and his absolute justice in particular are inaccessible to human knowledge, based on sensual experience controlled by reason and hence subjected to the principles of logic. What is incompatible for rational cognition is by no means incompatible for religious faith.

From *Rivista Jurídica de la Universidad de Puerto Rico*, Sept., 1952–April, 1953.

If the idea of absolute divine justice shall be applicable to the social life of men, that is to say, if divine justice shall serve as a standard of the justice which men are seeking for the regulation of their mutual relations, theology must attempt to proceed from its starting point, the incomprehensibility of absolute justice, to a less rigid position—to the assumption that God's will, although incomprehensible by its very nature, may nevertheless be comprehended by man in one way or another. The inconsistency of the position makes it inevitable that this turn of thought must ultimately result in a re-turn to the starting point. Since God exists, absolute justice exists; and as man must believe in the existence of God though he is not able to comprehend his nature, man must believe in the existence of absolute justice, though he cannot know what it really means. Justice is a mystery—one of the many mysteries—of the faith.

JUSTICE IN DIVINE REVELATION AND MODERN CHRISTIAN MORALITY

The specific means of theology in its attempt to let the incomprehensible appear comprehensible is its doctrine of revelation. God reveals himself in two ways: in his acts and in his word. If God has created the universe, the whole creation is a manifestation of his will. Then it is possible to find the answer to the question as to what is just and what unjust in nature as well as in history. The natural-law doctrine is based on the one, the Hegelian philosophy of history on the other assumption.[1] However, both manifestations of God show to the human mind facts which, if interpreted as being in conformity with divine norms, lead to contradictory statements. In nature as well as in history we see a pitiless struggle in which the stronger destroys the weaker; and at the same time mutual help. The most careful analysis of nature and history cannot furnish a criterion to distinguish good and evil; and our reason tells us that it is not possible to conclude from that which is, that which ought to be. Natural and historical reality seem to be a manifestation of God's omnipotence rather than God's justice, and their mutual relation remains an

open question. Revelation of God's will in creation is evidently
not sufficient to solve the problem of justice.

The other revelation—God's word in the Scriptures—seems to
be a much clearer manifestation of his justice. But many institutions presented in the Scriptures as directly approved, or at least
not disapproved of, by God or the men inspired by him—polyg-
amy, slavery, blood revenge—are in open opposition to the feeling of justice of modern Christians. Lamech married two wives
(Genesis IV:19); Abraham, Isaac, and Jacob had each more than
one wife; Deuteronomy XXI:15 refers to a man having two wives
as to a legally recognized relationship. In view of these facts Luther
and Melanchthon declared in their famous opinion justifying, by
divine law, the bigamy of Philip of Hesse, "What is permitted
concerning matrimony in the Mosaic law is not prohibited in
the Gospel." [2] Not only in the Old but also in the New Testament slavery is recognized as a legal and just institution, although
there are also prescriptions aiming at restricting the right of the
owner and thus to soften the situation of the slave. In Leviticus
XXV:6 slavery is presented as ordered by Yahweh or at least as
not incompatible with the law he gave on Mount Sinai through
Moses. Exodus XXI:2 ff. shows that it was not unlawful to make
even an Israelite a slave and that it was permitted to sell one's own
daughter as a slave. In the Epistle which Paul wrote to Philemon
concerning the slave Onesimus who ran away and was sent back
to his master by the Apostle, the latter did not at all deny the
justice of the institution; in his Letter to the Ephesians (VI:5–9)
he even declared the obligation of the slave toward his master a
sacred duty, whose fulfillment is also a duty toward God.

Although Yahweh's Law shows a tendency to restrict blood
revenge, this custom appears as firmly established among the Jews
and recognized by God. Cain, after having killed Abel, says, "Anyone who comes across me will kill me," whereupon Yahweh says,
"In that case, sevenfold vengeance shall be taken on anyone who
kills Cain" (Genesis IV:14 f.).[3] And to Noah Yahweh commands,
"Whoever sheds the blood of man, by man shall his blood be
shed" (Genesis IX:6). Yahweh does not forbid blood revenge. He
only orders to set apart three cities in the land which he is giving
to his people, "that any homicide may flee there, so that the

avenger of blood may not pursue the homicide in the heat of his anger, and overtake him, because the way is long, and take his life, when he did not deserve to die, since he had no standing feud with him" (Deuteronomy XIX:1 ff.).

There is a procedure directly ordered by Yahweh, which aims at determining whether a woman suspected of adultery has committed it. In this rite a "water of bitterness that causes a curse" plays the decisive part. The priest performing the rite has to put into this water "dust that is on the floor of the tabernacle. Then he must have the woman take an oath, saying to her: 'If no man has lain with you, and if you have not turned aside to indecent acts while married to your husband, be immune to this water of bitterness that brings a curse; but if you have gone wrong while married to your husband and if you have defiled yourself, and some man besides your husband has lain with you . . . then may Yahweh make you an execration and an oath among your people by making you have miscarriages, along with a womb easily fertilized; may this water that brings a curse enter your bowels causing your womb to be easily fertilized, but making you have miscarriages'; and the woman must say, 'So be it; so be it.' " Then "the priest must write the curses in a book [that is, on a slip of parchment] and then wash them [that is, the ink with which the curses have been written] off into the water of bitterness, and must make her drink the water." If she is innocent, the water will do her no harm, if she is guilty, the water will have the effect indicated in the curse. "This is the law in case of suspicion, when a woman while married to her husband goes wrong and defiles herself, or when a fit of suspicion comes over a man and he becomes suspicious of his wife" (Numbers V:11 ff.). This procedure prescribed by Yahweh as law is hardly different from the magic operations known as poison ordeal and practiced among primitive tribes.[4] It is doubtful whether the "water of bitterness" contained any poison. But this is of no importance as to the magic character of the rite. This character is evident from the fact that the written curse must be put into the water, which presupposes the belief that the curse, imagined as a powerful substance, has the desired effect. It is just the magic element of the rite which is highly repulsive to the religious feeling as well as to the idea of due process of law prevailing among modern Christians. The same is true with respect to the belief in demons or "foul spirits" entering the bodies of men and causing mental diseases, of which the Gospels report. According to them Jesus himself believed in the existence of these demons and used his divine power to exorcise them, as in the strange story of the Gerasa demoniac (Mark V:1 ff.).

SCRIPTURAL REVELATION CONTRADICTORY IN ITSELF

Scriptural revelation is not only in some parts in direct opposition to the morality of modern Christianity, it is also contradictory in itself, no less contradictory than revelation in creation.

Sarah, Abraham's wife, is his half sister, the daughter of his father though not of his mother (Genesis XX:12). But in Leviticus (XVIII:9; XX:17) and Deuteronomy (XXVII:22) intercourse of a man with his half sister is absolutely forbidden and a great sin. Jacob married two sisters, Rachel and Lea, the daughters of Laban (Genesis XXIX:1 ff.); but in Leviticus (XVIII:18) it is written: "You must not marry a woman in addition to her sister as a rival wife having intercourse with her as well as with the other, while she is alive." [5]

As to divorce, the code of Deuteronomy, which presents itself as an act of divine legislation, contains the rule: When a man takes a wife and marries her, if it turns out that she does not please him, because he has found some indecency in her, he may write her a bill of divorce, and, putting it into her hand, may dismiss her from his house. And when she has left his house she may go and marry another man (Deuteronomy XXIV:1 ff.). But when the Pharisees asked Jesus whether it is lawful for a man to divorce his wife, Jesus answered that husband and wife "shall become one, so that they are no longer two, but one. What therefore God has joined together, let not man put asunder." "Whoever divorces his wife and marries another, commits adultery against her; and if she divorces her husband and marries another, she commits adultery" (Mark X:2 ff.). Jesus' answer implies the principle that a man must have only one wife. There can be little doubt that two totally different ideas, incompatible with each other, are at the basis of the divine law instituting the polygamous and separable marriage, revealed by Moses, and the divine law instituting the monogamous and inseparable marriage revealed by Jesus.

Another contradiction exists in the Old Testament itself with respect to the question as to whether individual or collective, and especially hereditary, responsibility is just. In Exodus XX:5 ff., where Yahweh proclaims his Ten Commandments, we read: "I, Yahweh, your God, am a jealous God, punishing children for the sins of their fathers, to the third or fourth generation of those who hate me, but showing kindness to the thousandth generation of those who love me and keep my commands." But in Deuteronomy XXIV:16, it is written: "Fathers are not to be put to death with their children, nor are children to be put to death with their fathers. Everyone is to be put to death for his own sin."

All these contradictions may easily be explained from a historic point of view as different stages of a legal evolution. But a historic interpretation is inapplicable if the Scriptures are to be taken as the revelation of God's absolute and hence unchangeable justice. Besides, the contradiction between collective and individual responsibility is to be found within one and the same document, namely, in the Book of Ezekiel, where the principle of individual responsibility is proclaimed (XIV:12–20), but where we also read that Yahweh said to sinful Israel: "Behold, I am against you, and I will draw my sword from its sheath—and will cut off from you righteous and wicked alike" (XXI:1 f.).

RETRIBUTION AND LOVE—LAW AND JUSTICE

There are, however, within the Scriptures not only contradictions as to the justice of concrete institutions—there is an antagonism between two fundamentally different principles of justice. And this antagonism exists not only between the Old and the New Testament as between the teaching of Moses and that of Jesus, but also within the New Testament as between the teaching of Jesus and that of Paul, and especially within the teaching of Jesus itself. It is the antagonism between the principle of retribution and the principle of love, between the rule: requite evil with evil and good with good, and the rule: love your enemy and requite evil with good. In close connection with this antagonism there are two totally different views of the relationship which exists between justice and positive law. According to the one, justice and law are identical, according to the other, they may conflict with one another.

Yahweh as king and legislator.—The idea, prevailing in the Old Testament, that the positive law of the Jewish people is identical with divine justice is the consequence of the theocratic character of its political ideology. Yahweh is considered to be the head of the state. After Moses led Israel out of the land of the Egyptians, he declares in his thanksgiving: "Yahweh shall reign for ever and ever" (Exodus XV:18). God is addressed as "King of Israel" (Numbers XXIII:21; Deuteronomy XXXIII:5; Isaiah XLIV:6). "As I live—is the oracle of Yahweh—with a strong hand, with an outstretched arm and with outpoured fury, will I be king over you," announces the prophet Ezekiel (XX:33); and the prophet Zephaniah (III:15) says: "The king of Israel, Yahweh, is in the midst of you." In the so-called Psalms of Solomon (XVII:1 ff.) we read: "Lord, you, yourself, are our king for ever and ever." "Yahweh as the king of Israel" is not to be understood as a figure of speech. It is in the belief of the Jewish people the expression of an indubitable reality. According to Deuteronomy (XVII:14), Moses said to all Israel: "When you reach the land that Yahweh, your God, is giving you, and occupy it, and then declare 'I must place a king over me like all the nations surrounding me,' you must be sure to make him king over you whom Yahweh, your God, chooses." When the Israelites said to Gideon, "Rule over us, you, your son, and then your grandson; for you have saved us from the power of Midian," Gideon said to them, "I will not rule over you, nor shall my son rule over you, since Yahweh rules over you" (Judges VIII:22 f.).

As king of Israel Yahweh is the supreme legislator, judge, and commander-in-chief. "Yahweh is our judge, Yahweh our commander, Yahweh is our king; he will save us" (Isaiah XXXII:22). "Yahweh is king. . . . O king, who lovest justice, thou hast established equity" (Psalms XCIX:1; 4). That the law has its origin in a divine being, is an idea prevailing among many nations. But the Jewish people, as no other nation, did consider its law as a direct emanation of God's will. It was Yahweh himself who, according to Exodus XXIV:12, XXXI:18, wrote his "instructions and commands on the stone tablets," which were "inscribed by God's own finger." According to Deuteronomy V:22, Moses said to the Israelites of the Ten Commandments: "These words, and nothing more, Yahweh spoke to all your assemblage at the mountain with a loud voice out of the midst of the fire, cloud, and gloom; and he wrote them on two stone tablets, which he gave to me." But not only the Ten Commandments, the whole law of the Jewish people is presented by Moses as communicated to him directly by God who appears as the actual legislator. "Praise Yahweh, O Jerusalem, extol your God, O Zion. . . . He declares his word to Jacob, his statutes and judgments to Israel. He has not acted thus with any other nation" (Psalms CXLVII:12, 19 f.). The law comes from the "mouth" of Yahweh (Psalms CXIX:72). Consequently the positive law is absolutely just and as such perfect, sacred, and eternal. Psalm CXIX expresses in poetical form the idea the Jewish people had of their law: "Thou art just, O Yahweh, and thine ordinances are right. Thou hast issued thy decrees in justice and in exceeding faithfulness" (137 f.). "Thy decrees are eternally right" (144). "The sum of thy word is truth; and all thy just judgments are everlasting" (160). This divine law, given by Yahweh to his chosen people, is the best law ever established on earth. Moses says to Israel: "Heed the statutes and ordinances which I am teaching you to observe . . . Be careful, then, that you observe them; for that will demonstrate your wisdom and intelligence to the nations, who, when they hear of all these statutes, will say, 'This great nation is indeed a wise and intelligent people.' For what great nation is there that has a God so near it as is Yahweh, our God, whenever we call on him? And what great nation is there that has statutes and ordinances so just as all this code that I am putting before you today?" (Deuteronomy IV:1 ff.)

Yahweh as judge.—Even more characteristic than Yahweh's legislative function is his judiciary power. When Moses takes "capable and experienced men" and sets them as judges for the various tribes, he charges them saying: "You must never show partiality in a case; you must hear high and low alike, standing in fear of no man; for the judgment is God's" (Deuteronomy I:15 ff.). It is God who renders judgment through human instruments. In Exodus XXII:9, we read: "In every case of dispute,

whether it concerns ox, or ass, or sheep, or clothing, or any article
at all that has disappeared, concerning which claim is made . . .
the case of both parties shall come before God; he whom God
convicts must make twofold restitution to the other." In Numbers
XV: 32 ff. the story of a man is reported who was gathering wood
on the Sabbath day. He was brought to Moses and Aaron. "Then
Yahweh said to Moses: 'The man must be put to death by having
the whole community stone him outside the camp.' So the whole
community took him outside the camp, and stoned him to death,
as Yahweh had commanded Moses." Another incident where
Yahweh in person renders judgment is that of the daughters of
Zelophehad, who died without leaving sons. "So Moses laid their
case before Yahweh, and Yahweh said to Moses: 'The daughters of
Zelophehad are right in their statements; you must certainly give
them the possession of a heritage along with their father's kins-
men, transferring their father's heritage to them" (Numbers
XXVII: 3 ff.). Hence it is not a mere metaphor when Yahweh is
called "judge." Already in Genesis XVIII: 25, Abraham, asking
God not to let perish in Sodom the good together with the bad,
says: "Shall not the judge of the whole earth himself act justly?"
And Hannah, in her song of praise exclaims: "Yahweh will judge
the ends of the earth" (1 Samuel II: 10). The whole Psalm LXXV
is a glorification of God as judge; and in Psalms L:6 we find:
"The heavens declared his justice, that God was giving judgment."
Here are some additional passages: "Behold, Yahweh abides forever. He has established his throne for judgment, and he judges
the world in justice. He passes sentence on peoples with equity"
(Psalms IX: 7 f.). "Tell among the nations that Yahweh is king;
the world also is established that it cannot be moved. He judges the
peoples in equity" (Psalms XCVI: 10).

Yahweh is an ideal judge because he is omniscient and knows
the most secret thoughts and feelings of men. The prophet Jeremiah let Yahweh say: "I, Yahweh, am a searcher of the heart, a
tester of the conscience; that I may give to every man according
to his ways, according to the fruits of his doings" (Jeremiah
XVII: 10). "Yahweh judges the peoples: do me justice, O Yahweh,
in accordance with my righteousness and my integrity. May the
evil of the wicked come to an end, and establish thou the righteous, since he who tries heart and mind is the just God. My shield

is with God, who saves the upright in heart. God is a just judge"
(Psalms VII:8 ff.). That Yahweh frequently is called a god of
vengeance means in the first place that he is a judging god: "O
Yahweh, thou avenging God, O thou avenging God, shine forth!
Rise up, O judge of the earth" (Psalms XCIV:1 f.) In one of his
sermons, which are but a passionate cry for justice, Isaiah says:
"Yahweh saw with displeasure that there was no justice; and when
he saw that there was no man—when he saw with amazement that
there was none to interpose—his own arm helped him, his justice
upheld him. He put on justice as a coat of mail. With the helmet
of salvation on his head, he put on garments of vengeance for
clothing, and wrapped himself in fury as a cloak. According to
men's deserts shall he recompense them—wrath to his enemies,
shame to his foes" (Isaiah LIX:15 ff.). God's "vengeance" means:
the retributory function of his just judgment.

Yahweh as "witness" and party to a contract.—The forensic
character of the justice of God manifests itself also in the fact
that Yahweh is sometimes presented as "witness." Since this function is decisive in the procedure against an evildoer, it is identified
with that of the judge. Zephaniah (III:8) speaks of the day of
judgment as of the day when Yahweh will "arise as a witness,"
and Malachi (III:5) let Yahweh say: "I will draw near to you for
judgment, and I will be a swift witness against the sorcerers and
adulterers." Micah (VI:2) speaks of a dispute between Yahweh
and Israel; and Isaiah (LIV:5 f.) compares their relationship to a
marriage: he calls Yahweh the "husband" of Israel and Israel the
"wife of his youth"; and through the mouth of Ezekiel (XVI:32,
38) Yahweh says to Israel: "You adulterous wife, preferring stran-
gers to your husband . . . I will judge you as women are judged
who break wedlock."

In this metaphor, one of the basic ideas of Jewish theology is expressed: that the relationship between God and man is constituted
by a contract, the covenant Yahweh has concluded with his people, represented—at the beginning of each of the various periods
—by Adam, Noah, Abraham, Moses, David, and which Yahweh
will finally conclude again when the future Kingdom of God will
be established for ever.

The idea that God has concluded a contract with men and that
he, just as the other partner to this contract, is bound by it, is

very characteristic of the tendency to rationalize what by its very nature is irrational—the relationship between God and men.

By this contract Yahweh assumes the obligation to protect his people, and Israel to be faithful to Yahweh and obey his law. The conclusion of this contract is described in Exodus XXIV and XXXIV, as a procedure in which an offer was made by Yahweh to Israel through Moses, which offer was accepted by Israel; whereupon the contents of the contract was written down in the book of the covenant. Israel as well as Yahweh himself were supposed to be bound by this contract. According to Deuteronomy VII:7 ff., Moses said to the people: "It was not because you were the greatest of all peoples that Yahweh set his heart on you and chose you (for you were the smallest of all peoples), but it was because Yahweh loved you and would keep the oath that he swore to your fathers . . . Be assured then that Yahweh your God is God, a trustworthy God, who to a thousand generations keeps loving faith with those that love him and keep his commands . . . So be careful to observe the charge, the statutes and ordinances that I am enjoining on you today." "I will remember my covenant," says Yahweh (Leviticus XXVI:42); "He remembers his covenant for ever" (Psalms CV:8); "Yahweh swore to David an inviolable oath from which he will not swerve" (Psalms CXXXII:11).

That Yahweh is called a "jealous" God (for example, Exodus XX:5), means that he rightly insists upon the other party's fulfilling the stipulations of the contract. Such fulfillment is rewarded by Yahweh's fulfilling his own obligation under the contract. But its violation by his people entitles Yahweh to punish the breaker of the covenant. This is Yahweh's justice. Justice is his most essential quality and the principle of this justice is retribution.

Yahweh as god of justice.—"Yahweh is a God of justice," says Isaiah (XXX:18). This is the meaning of numerous turns of expression with the prophets and in the Psalms. "Thy justice is like the highest mountains" (Psalms XXXVI:6); "Yahweh's justice will endure forever" (Psalms CXII:3); "Yahweh will bring forth your right like the light and your just cause like the noonday" (Psalms XXXVII:5); "Righteousness and justice are the foundations of thy throne" (Psalms LXXXIX:14). Hence it is Yahweh's justice that is to be exercised by the earthly king. "Give the king thy justice, O God, and thy righteousness to the king's son" (Psalms LXXII:1). So essential is justice to Yahweh that he is sometimes identified with this quality. To "seek Yahweh" is—according to Zephaniah II:3—equivalent to "seek justice." In the future Kingdom of God the name of the king will be "Yahweh is our justice" (Jeremiah XXIII:6). To do justice means: to know Yahweh. Through Jeremiah Yahweh says to Judah's king: "Did not your father . . . do justice and righteousness? . . . Then all went well. Is not that how to know me?" (XXII:15 f.) If one has the law in his heart one knows Yahweh. "Behold, days are coming, is the oracle of Yahweh, when I will make a new covenant with the house of Israel and with the house of Judah not like the covenant which I made with their fathers . . . I will put my law within them, and will write it on their hearts; and I will be their God and they shall be my people. And they shall teach no more every one his neighbor and every one his brother, saying, 'Know Yahweh'; for all of them shall know me, from the least of them to the greatest of them" (Jeremiah XXXI:31 ff.). And not only to know Yahweh, but also to serve Yahweh requires nothing but to be just. This is the meaning of the admonition: God prefers justice to offerings and prayers. "The doing of right and justice is more acceptable to Yahweh than sacrifice" (Proverbs XXI:3); "Bring no more worthless offering: The odor of sacrifice is an abomination to me. New moon and Sabbath, the holding of assemblies, fasting and festival I cannot endure . . . Even though you make many a prayer, I will not listen. Your hands are full of bloodshed—wash yourselves clean; put away the evil of your doings from before my eyes; cease to do evil, learn to do good; seek justice" (Isaiah I:13 ff.); "I hate, I spurn your feasts, and I take no pleasure in your festal gatherings. Even though you offer me burnt-offerings, and your cereal-offerings, I will not accept them; and the thank-offerings of your fatted beasts I will not look upon. Take away from me the noise of your songs, and to the melody of your lyres I will not listen. But let justice roll down like waters, and right-eousness like a perennial stream" (Amos V:21 ff.).

Since God personifies justice, the longing for God is the long-ing for justice. This is the keynote of the Psalms and the Prophets. The Psalmist prays: "O Lord, be not far from me! Bestir thy-self and rise up to do me justice, my God and my Lord, to plead my cause! Do me justice in accordance with thy righteousness, O Lord, my God!" (Psalms XXXV:23 f.). And the Prophet exclaims: "Pour down, O heavens, from above, and let the clouds rain righteousness; let the earth open her womb and bring forth salvation; let her cause righteousness also to spring up, since I, the Lord, have created it" (Isaiah XLV:8). The center of the postexilian literature is the hope for the coming of the Messiah, the Kingdom of God, whose main, if not only, function is the realization of divine justice on earth.

YAHWEH'S JUSTICE: RETRIBUTION

Before the teaching of Jesus it was self-evident to the Jewish people that justice means retribution. Like all primitive peoples, the Hebrews in the earliest stages of their evolution considered nature as part of society and hence explained its phenomena in terms of social life; that means, in the first place, according to the principle of retribution. Any event primitive man fears, he interprets as punishment; any event he desires, as reward from a superhuman authority. This personalistic and therefore social interpretation of nature may be based on animism, that is, on the belief that all things are animated, endowed with indwelling souls; but it may also be the consequence of true monotheism, according to which nature is the creation of an omnipotent God and hence the manifestation of his all-just will. The divine act of creation as described in Genesis is a command of God, and, in coming into existence, nature obeys this command. "God said, 'Let there be light' and there was light . . . Then God said, 'Let there be a firmament' . . . and so it was . . ." (Genesis I:1 ff.). Since nature obeys the commands of God as man obeys the commands of his king, any natural event that affects man must be interpreted as being sent by God; and since God is just, any such event must be interpreted as being deserved by man; if it is an evil, as punishment for his evil conduct, and if it is a good, as reward for his good conduct.

Interpretation of nature according to the principle of retribution.—The Jews, as so many other peoples, explain the greatest of all evils, death, as punishment for sin. But as an evil they consider also the necessity of labor and the suffering of the pangs of childbearing. Hence these evils too, are brought in connection with the fall of man. God said to Adam: "Because you followed your wife's suggestion, and ate from the tree from which I commanded you not to eat, cursed shall be the ground through you, in suffering shall you gain your living from it as long as you live . . . By the sweat of your brow shall you earn your living, until you return to the ground, since it was from it that you were taken. For dust you are, and to dust you must return." And to Eve God says: "I will make your pain at childbirth very great; in pain shall you bear children and yet you shall be devoted to your husband while he shall rule over you" (Genesis III:16 ff.).

In Genesis, as in the myths of many peoples, the great flood is explained as punishment. "When Yahweh saw that the wickedness of man on the earth was great and that the whole bent of his thinking was never anything but evil, Yahweh regretted that he had ever made man on the earth and he was grieved to the heart. So Yahweh said, 'I will blot the men that I have created off the face of the ground'" (Genesis VI:5 ff.).

In the story of the tower of Babel (Genesis XI:1–9), the fact that mankind does not speak one language but is split into many peoples which "do not understand one another's speech," is justified as a punishment for man's haughtiness. The plagues of Egypt which all are natural phenomena harmful to man, such as the water of the Nile becoming undrinkable, the plagues of frogs, of lice, of flies, of the murrain of cattle, of boils, of hail, of locusts, of the thick darkness, of the death of the first-born—all are explained as punishments for nonobedience of a command of Yahweh (Exodus VII:14 ff.). Diseases, especially the dreaded leprosy, are typical signs of God's dissatisfaction with a man's conduct. In this way Miriam, the sister of Moses (Numbers XII:10), and King Uzziah (2 Chronicles XXVI:21) were punished. The same explanation is given to the sting of venomous serpents (Numbers XXI:4 ff.). Among the evils with which Yahweh threatens his people if they should disobey his law are diseases, such as consumption, fever, inflammation, sunstroke, ulcers, scurvey, itch, madness, blindness, dismay, malignant sores on the knees, legs, the sole of the foot, the crown of the head; but also bad harvest, harvest consumed by locusts, cattle plague; and catastrophies, such as the sky becoming bronze and the earth iron, the turning of the rain into powder and dust (Deuteronomy XXVIII:19 ff.). It is through nature that God punishes the evil-doers, it is the evil deeds of man which turn the good order of nature into a bad one. The prophet Jeremiah says: "Let us reverence Yahweh, our God, who gives us both winter and spring rain in its season, and keeps for us the weeks appointed for harvest. Your crimes have upset this order, and your sins have withheld the blessings from you" (Jeremiah V:24 f.).

Punishment and reward in the Old Testament.—In the Pentateuch incidents are recorded where Yahweh punishes evildoers. Thus Cain is cursed for having killed his brother (Genesis IV:9 ff.). Sodom and Gomorrah must perish in a rain of sulphur and fire because of the sins of their inhabitants (Genesis XIX:23 ff.); Nadab and Abihu, the sons of Aaron, were consumed by fire because they offered improper fire before Yahweh (Leviticus X:1 ff.). Moses and Aaron themselves were punished because they once did not trust Yahweh: "That is why you shall not bring this community into the land which I have given them," says Yahweh (Numbers XX:12). Even to animals does this law of retribution apply: "If an ox gores a man or woman to death, the ox must be stoned to death, but its flesh is not to be eaten" (Exodus XXI:28).

There are also cases where merits find their rewards. When Abraham shows himself willing to obey Yahweh's command to sacrifice his son Isaac, Yahweh says to him: "Since you have done this and have not withheld your son, your only son, I will indeed bless you and will surely make your descendants as numerous as the stars of the sky or the sands that are on the seashore, so that your descendants shall take possession of the cities of their enemies, and through your descendants all the nations of the earth shall invoke blessings on one another—just because you heeded my injunction" (Genesis XXII:16 ff.). When an Israelite, in violation of the law, introduced a Midianite woman into his family, Phinehas, the son of Eleazar, the son of Aaron the priest, killed both of them. Then Yahweh said to Moses: "I hereby give him [Phinehas] my pledge of friendship, which shall serve him and his descendants after him as the pledge of a perpetual priesthood, because he was jealous for his God, and made atonement for the Israelites" (Numbers XXV:6 ff.).

Again and again Yahweh promises Israel his blessing if they obey his law. Moses says: "There shall be no poor among you; for Yahweh will be sure to bless you in the land which Yahweh, your God, is giving you as a heritage to occupy, if you but heed the injunctions of Yahweh your God by being careful to observe all this charge which I am enjoining on you today. When Yahweh, your God, blesses you, as he has promised you, you shall have many nations obligated to you, but you shall never be obligated to them; you shall rule over many nations, but they shall never rule over you" (Deuteronomy XV:4 ff.). "If you will but heed the commands that I am giving you today to love Yahweh, your God, and serve him with all your mind and heart, he will give you rain for your land in due season, the winter rain and the spring rain, so that you will gather in your grain and wine and oil, and he will produce grass in your fields for your cattle and you will eat your fill" (Deuteronomy XI:13 ff.).

Yahweh a god of vengeance.—Even more frequent and more emphatic are the threats of Yahweh to punish Israel severely if they do not obey his law; and the penalties are the most cruel ones human imagination can invent. Thus, for example, we read in Leviticus XXVI:14 ff.: "But if you will not listen to me, nor observe all these commands; if you reject my statutes, and treat my ordinances as abhorrent by not observing all my commands, by breaking my covenant, I on my part will do this to you: I will inflict consumption and fever upon you as terrors, exhausting your eyes and depressing your spirits; you shall sow your seed in vain, since your enemies shall consume it. I will set my face against you, so that you shall be laid low before your enemies, and your foes shall rule over you, and you shall flee when no one is pursuing you. If you will not listen to me even for these things, I will punish you seven more times for your sins; I will shatter your vaunted power; I will make your sky like iron, and your earth like bronze, so that your strength shall be spent in vain, since your land shall not yield its crops, nor the trees of the land yield their fruit. If you live at enmity with me, and will not listen to me, I will bring seven more afflictions upon you, as your sins deserve; I will let wild beasts loose among you, that shall rob you of your children, destroy your cattle, and reduce you in numbers, so that your roads shall be desolate. And if by this discipline you are not turned to me, but live at enmity with me, then I in turn will live at enmity with you, and I will afflict you seven times for your sins; I will bring a sword upon you that shall wreak vengeance for the covenant, so that you shall huddle together in your cities; I will send pestilence among you, and you shall be delivered into the power of the enemy. When I deprive you of the sustenance of bread, there will be ten women to bake your bread in a single oven, and your bread shall be doled out in rations, and you shall not have enough to eat to satisfy you. And if you will not listen to me for all this, but live at enmity with me, I will live at fierce enmity with you, and I on my part will punish you seven times for your sins; you will have to eat the flesh of your sons, and the flesh of your daughters, too, you will have to eat; I will destroy your high places, cut down your incense altars, and cast your carcasses on the ruins of your idols; I will abhor you; I will make your cities a waste, and desolating your sanctuaries; I will not smell your soothing odors; I will also desolate the land, so that your enemies who come to live in it shall be amazed at it; while you yourselves I will scatter among the nations, and unsheathe the sword on you, so that your land shall become a desolation and your cities a waste. Then shall the land enjoy its sabbaths, as long as it lies desolate, and you remain in your enemies' land; then shall the land have rest, and enjoy its sabbaths; as long as it lies desolate, it shall have rest, which it did not have on the sabbaths when you lived in it. As for those of you that may be left, I will inject faintness into their hearts in the lands of their enemies, so that the sound of a driven leaf shall chase them, and they shall flee as from the sword, and fall when there is no one in pursuit; they shall trip over one another, as if in flight from the sword, although there is no one in pursuit. You shall have no power to stand before your enemies; you shall perish among the nations; and the land of your enemies shall consume you. Those of you that may be left shall pine away in their enemies' lands because of their iniquity, and also because of their father's iniquities shall they pine away." A true God of vengeance is Yahweh, a punishing God, not only in relation to his own people, but even more so in relation to other peoples, the enemies of Israel, for whom the "day of revenge and requital" is imminent: "For Yahweh will vindicate his people" (Deuteronomy XXXII:35 f.); "I will whet my flashing sword, and my hand shall lay hold on justice; I will wreak vengeance on my foes, and punish those who hate me; I will drench my arrows with blood, with the blood of captives slain; and my sword shall devour flesh from the shaggy heads of the enemy" (Deuteronomy XXXII:41 ff.).

Jus talionis.—The principle of retribution—as the essence of Yahweh's justice—is expressed by Moses in this short formula: "See, I am putting before you today a blessing and a curse: a blessing if you heed the commands of Yahweh your God which I am giving you today; and a curse, if you do not heed the command of Yahweh your God, but swerve from the way that I am appointing you today, by running after alien gods of whom you have had no experience" (Deuteronomy XI:26 ff.). As in almost all religions, punishment and reward are not of equal importance. Punishment is in the foreground, reward in the background of this system of justice, especially if it is to be applied—not directly by God in a transcendental way but—by men in the way of socially organized sanctions. That justice as retribution means in the first place punishment, is the consequence of the fact that the threat of punishment for undesired conduct—not the promise of reward for the contrary conduct—is the specific technique of positive law, and the idea of justice always more or less reflects the social reality as it appears in positive law. Hence the principle of retribution is presented also as *jus talionis:* [6] "You shall eradicate the wicked persons from your midst; and when those that are left hear of it, they will be afraid, and never again do such a wicked thing as this in your midst. So you must show no mercy— life for life, eye for eye, tooth for tooth, hand for hand, foot for foot" (Deuteronomy XIX:19 ff.). The same principle is proclaimed in Exodus XXI:23–25, Leviticus XXIV:19–21.

In the Book of Judges I:4 ff., it is told that the Israelites vanquished the Canaanites and captured their king, Adoni-bezek. Then "they cut off his thumbs and great toes; whereupon Adoni-bezek said, 'Seventy kings with their thumbs and great toes cut off used to pick up crumbs under my table; as I did, so has God requited me.' " And Psalm CXXXVII, which begins so poetically:

> By the rivers of Babylon,
> There we sat down, and wept,
> When we remembered Zion,

ends with the cry for retaliation:

> O daughter of Babylon, destructive one,
> Blessed be he who requites to you
> The treatment that you dealt out to us!
> Blessed be he who seizes your little ones,
> And dashes them to pieces upon a rock!

In the book of Job, one of the most characteristic documents of the Jewish belief in the justice of God, the doubts concerning this quality of the Almighty aroused by undeserved suffering, are removed by God himself. He redeems Job, the perfect, upright, God-fearing man, who repents his doubts; and thus the principle of retribution is finally maintained.

Take Vengeance, But Love Your Neighbor

It seems as if this principle of retaliation is not quite consistent with the rules laid down in Leviticus XIX:18 and 33 f., translated in the King James version: "Thou shalt love thy neighbor as thyself"; and: "If a stranger sojourn with thee in your land ye shalt not do him wrong. The stranger that sojourneth with you shall be unto you as the home-born among you, and thou shalt love him as thyself." But since by "neighbor" only a member of the Jewish community is to be understood, the true meaning of the first sentence is: "You must love your fellow as one of your own." This is a command of national solidarity and quite compatible with the principle of retribution. The correct translation of the second sentence is: "If a proselite is residing with you in your land, you must not mistreat him; you must treat the proselite who resides with you like the native-born among you, and love him as one of your own." The latter sentence means hardly more than: treat proselites in the same way as native-born persons. The first sentence (Leviticus XIX:18) is preceded by the command, "You must not avenge yourself, nor bear a grudge against the members of your own race." The general prohibition of revenge is certainly in contradiction to the institution of blood revenge recognized in other parts of the Scripture; but it is quite compatible with the *jus talionis* if exercised, not by the injured person himself, but by courts. That a Jew shall love his fellow as one of his own, and that he shall treat proselites like native-born, are political principles, which have nothing to do with the rule of justice "like for like, evil for evil, good for good." There are, however, some passages in the Proverbs and the Wisdom of Sirach which indeed seem to advocate a higher principle. "Rejoice not when your enemy falls, nor exult when he stumbles; lest the Lord see it and be displeased, and turn back his anger from him." "Say not, 'I will do to him as he has done to me, I will requite the man according to his work'" (Proverbs XXIV:17, 18, 29). "The man who takes vengeance will have vengeance taken on him by the Lord, and he will keep close watch of his sins. Forgive your neighbor his wrongdoing; then your sins will be forgiven when you pray" (The Wisdom of Sirach XXVIII:1 ff.). But these sporadic manifestations of a morality of forgiveness are not symptomatic of the Old Testament which is dominated by the justice of "like for like."

The Rejection of the Principle of Retribution by Jesus: The New Justice of Love

The principle of love in opposition to positive law.—It is just this rule which Jesus solemnly rejects. In the Sermon on the Mount he says: "You have heard that they were told 'An eye for an eye and a tooth for a tooth.' But I tell you not to resist injury, but if any one strikes you on your right cheek, turn the other to him too, and if anyone wants to sue you for your shirt, let him have your coat too. And if anyone forces you to go one mile, go two miles with him" (Matthew V:38 f.). It is the essence of positive law to resist injury, to react against the injury of the delict with the injury of the sanction—the sanction being of the same nature as the delict according to the principle "evil for evil." It is the specific technique of the law to inflict upon the evildoer the evil of punishment, if necessary by the employment of force. The state is the organization of this force, replacing self-help of the injured by judgment of courts. But Jesus teaches: "Pass no more judgments upon other people, so that you may not have judgment passed upon you. For you will be judged by the standard you judge by, and men will pay you back with the same measure you have used with them. Why do you keep looking at the speck in your brother's eye and pay no attention to the beam that is in your own?" (Matthew VII:1 ff.); and: "Do not judge others and they will not judge you. Do not condemn them and they will not condemn you. Excuse others and they will excuse you" (Luke VI:37). In rejecting the principle of requiting evil with evil, in denying the right of man to judge man, Jesus refuses recognition of the positive law and the established state. This is the negative side of his idea of justice. The positive side appears in his word: "You have heard that they were told, 'You must love your neighbor and hate your enemy.' But I tell you, love your enemies and pray for your persecutors, so that you may show yourselves true sons of your Father in heaven, for he makes his sun rise on bad and good alike, and makes the rain fall on the upright and the wrongdoers" (Matthew V:43 f.). Instead of retribution—love, which makes no difference between the wrongdoer and the one who abides by the law. Love, not as a return to those who love you: "If you love only those who love you, what merit is there in that?" (Luke VI:32.) You must love also your enemy, and that means, also the wrongdoer. You must not requite evil with evil, but evil with good. Hence punishment of the evildoer, provided by the law and applied by the judge, cannot be in conformity with divine justice, the new justice: the love of God.[7]

This is indeed a revolutionary doctrine; not only because it is incompatible with the existing law but because the demand to love one's enemy is beyond human nature, and the love of God is justice only in a transcendental sense, far above any rational ideal. From the point of view of human reason, Jesus' teaching is not a solution of the problem of justice as a problem of a social technique for the regulation of human relations; it is rather the dissolution of this problem. For it implies the request to abandon the desire for justice as conceived of by man. And Jesus is quite aware that his teaching on justice is totally different from the traditional view. According to Matthew (V:20) he said: "Unless your justice (δικαιοσύνη) is far superior to that of the scribes and Pharisees, you will never enter the Kingdom of Heaven." But it is understandable that the Gospels try to hide the conflict between the existing Jewish law and the teaching of Jesus. Thus Matthew let Jesus say: "Do not suppose that I have come to do away with the Law or the Prophets. I have not come to do away with them but to enforce them" (Matthew V:17). But Mark and Luke report the word of Jesus: "No one pours new wine into old wine skins; or if he does, the wine bursts the skins, and the wine is lost, and the skins too. New wine has to be put into fresh skins" (Mark II:22; Luke V:37). This parable is Jesus' answer to the question why he and his disciples did not keep the fast. It is followed by the story of his disciples passing through the fields and picking the heads of wheat on the Sabbath, which was evidently against the law (Mark II:18, 23; Luke V:33, VI:1 ff.). The parable can hardly mean anything else but the admission that the new justice revealed by Jesus is no longer compatible with the law of Moses. According to Luke XVI:16, Jesus said to the Pharisees: "Until John came, it was the Law and the Prophets. From that time the Kingdom of God has been proclaimed, and everyone has been crowding into it." This word, too, expresses the idea that a new justice is replacing the old law. In the next sentence, it is true, Luke let Jesus say, "But it is easier for heaven and earth to pass away than for one dotting of an *i* in the Law to go unfulfilled" (Luke XVI:17). But the subsequent sentence (Luke XVI:18) brings Jesus' teaching on divorce, which is in direct opposition to the law.

Jesus' teaching on family.—This opposition is manifested quite openly not only in that Jesus does not respect certain ritual prescriptions such as concerning food (Mark VII:20 f.), washing (Matthew XV:3 ff., 20), fasting (Mark II:18), the Sabbath (Matthew XII:10; Mark II:23 ff.; Luke VI:5 f., XIV:1 f.; John V:10 f., IX:14 f.), but also in his nonrecognition of some fundamental institutions established by the existing law. He not only declared divorce, although permitted by the Law, a crime equivalent to adultery (Matthew V:31 ff; Mark X:2 ff.), but he taught that it was better not to marry at all. After he answered the question of the Pharisees, "Is it right for a man to divorce his wife for any cause?" by the famous saying, "Whoever divorces his wife on any ground but her unfaithfulness, and marries another woman, commits adultery," his disciples said to him, "If that is a man's relation to his wife, it is better not to marry!" Which statement he did not reject, but said, "It is not everyone who can accept that but only those who have a special gift. For some are incapable of marriage from their birth, and some have been made so by men, and some have made themselves so for the sake of the Kingdom of Heaven. Let him accept it who can" (Matthew XIX:3 ff.). In this statement he approved even self-castration. That it was better not to marry was certainly his own opinion; for he himself did not marry. Although celibacy "was disapproved by the rabbis, who taught that a man should marry at eighteen, and that if he passed the age of twenty without taking a wife he transgressed a divine command and incurred God's displeasure." [8] But Jesus' attitude toward marriage was in complete conformity with the idea of the human relations in the Kingdom of God where, according to his teaching, there will be "no marrying or being married" (Matthew XXII:30). This view of Jesus is in close connection with his belief that in the Kingdom of God there will be no death. According to Luke XX:34 ff. he said: "The people of this world marry and are married, but those who are thought worthy to attain that other world and the resurrection from the dead, neither marry nor are married. For they cannot die again." Hence no propagation is necessary. Since according to his belief the Kingdom of God has already begun to exist or was perceptibly near, and since this kingdom was to be established in this world, the rule of celibacy is to be understood as immediately applicable. It is also in conformity with other sayings of Jesus, which, directly or indirectly, amount to a nonrecognition of the family bond. When Peter said to him, "We have left home and followed you," Jesus said, "I tell you, there is no one who has given up home or wife or brothers or parents or children for the Kingdom of God who will not receive many times more in this time, and in the coming age eternal life" (Luke XVIII:28 f.). He even says: "If anyone comes to me without hating his own father and mother and wife and children and brothers and sisters, and his very life too, he cannot be a disciple of mine" (Luke XIV:26). Not only the legal relationship between husband and wife but also the natural relationship between parents and children, brothers and sisters, is incompatible with the following of Christ. Hence Jesus did not recognize one of the most sacred obligations of a son, to bury his dead father: "He said to another, 'Follow me.' But he said, 'Let me first go and bury my father.' Jesus said to him, 'Leave the dead to bury their own dead; you must go and spread the news of the Kingdom of God' " (Luke IX:59 ff.). His followers are even not allowed to call their progenitor father: "You must not call anyone on earth your father, for you have only one father, your heavenly Father" (Matthew XXIII:9).

Jesus said to his disciples to be aware that their teaching might have the effect of dissolving the family: "It is not you who will speak, it is the spirit of your Father that will speak through you. One brother will give up another to death, and a father his child, and children will turn against their parents and have them put to death" (Matthew X:20 f.). Jesus did not regret this effect of his teaching; he even declared it as its purpose: "Do not think that I have come to bring peace to the earth. I have not come to bring peace, but a sword. For I have come to turn a man against his father and a daughter against her mother, and a daughter-in-law against her mother-in-law, and a man's enemies will be in his own household. No one who loves father or mother more than he loves me is worthy of me, and no one who loves son or daughter more than he loves me is worthy of me" (Matthew X:34 ff.); "I have come to bring fire down to the earth, and how I wish it were kindled already! I have a baptism to undergo, and how distressed I am till it is over. Do you think I have come to bring peace to the earth? Not peace, I tell you, but discord! For from now on if there are five people in a house they will be divided three against two and two against three. Father will be against son and son against father, mother against daughter and daughter against mother, mother-in-law against her daughter-in-law and daughter-in-law against her mother-in-law" (Luke XII:49 ff.). The love of God he is teaching is not the natural instinct which unites the members of a family. And again he gives an example by his own attitude toward his family. Matthew, Mark, and Luke, all three report accordingly that Jesus ignored any relation with his mother and his brothers. "And his mother and his brothers came. And they stood outside the house and sent word in to him to come outside to them. There was a crowd sitting around him when they told him 'Your mother and your brothers are outside asking for you.' He answered, 'Who are my mother and my brothers?' And looking around at the people sitting about him, he said, 'Here are my mother and my brothers! Whoever does the will of God is my brother and sister and mother' " (Mark III:31 ff.; Matthew XII:48 ff,; Luke VIII:19 ff.). When "a woman in the crowd raised her voice and said to him, 'Blessed is the mother who bore you and nursed you,' " he—openly ignoring the command to honor father and mother—rejected the honoring of his mother and said, " 'You might better say: Blessed are those who hear God's message and observe it' " (Luke XI:27 ff.).

Jesus' teaching on taxes.—That Jesus' teaching was—at least—not in favor of the existing law, shows in his answer to the question of the Pharisees whether it was "right to pay the poll tax to the emperor." " 'Why do you put me to such a test? Bring me a denarius to look at.' And they brought him one. He said to them, 'Whose head and title is this?' And they told him, 'The emperor's.' And Jesus said, 'Pay the emperor what belongs to the emperor, and pay God what belongs to God' " (Mark XII:14 ff.). Jesus did not say that it is right to pay the poll tax to the emperor—he did not answer the question of the Pharisees. According to the opinion prevailing within the Roman Empire, the coin, in that the portrait and the name of the emperor was stamped on it, was marked the property of the emperor; it "belonged" to the emperor. The statement that the money "belongs" to the emperor has nothing to do with the obligation to pay the poll tax. If Jesus had been of the opinion that it was right to pay the tax, he had had no reason to withhold the answer.[9] According to Luke XXIII:1 f., the charge under which the council of the elders of the people, the high priests and scribes, took him to Pilate was: "Here is a man whom we have found misleading our nation, and forbidding the payment of taxes to the emperor and claiming to be an anointed king himself." The council asserts that Jesus has been found forbidding the payment of taxes to the emperor. It may be that this accusation was not without foundation, for Jesus considered himself to be the Messianic king of Israel and consequently believed that the Kingdom of God has already come; he also believed that the existing political organization of the world, the Roman Empire, was a kingdom of Satan and would necessarily disappear after the Kingdom of God will be fully established. He did not recognize the authority of the Roman state, incompatible with the Davidic kingdom of the Messiah established on this earth.[10] How could he believe that it was right to pay taxes to the emperor?

The obligation to pay taxes to the emperor, it is true, was not established by the Jewish Law; and therefore Jesus' answer to this question may be considered to be not conclusive as to the relation of his teaching to the Law. But the Temple tax was prescribed by the Jewish Law (Exodus XXV:1 ff.; Nehemiah X:32); and when the question arose whether this tax should be paid by Jesus and his disciples, he said to Simon, "What do you think, Simon? From whom do earthly kings collect duties and taxes? From their own people, or from aliens?' He said, 'From aliens.' Jesus said to him, 'Then their own people are exempt. But rather than give offense to them, go down to the sea and throw in a hook. Take the first fish that comes up, open its mouth and you will find in it a dollar. Take that and pay the tax for us both.' " (Matthew XVII:24 ff.) Jesus obviously does not recognize an obligation to pay that tax; only to avoid to give offense to the authorities he orders Simon to pay. But, in truth, it was not Simon and Jesus who paid the tax out of their property—the money was procured by a miracle.

Jesus' teaching on property.—This is highly significant. Those who follow Jesus' teaching cannot pay taxes, for they have no property and especially no money, and cannot earn money by working, for they must not work at all. They are supposed to live as beggars. Just as family, property is incompatible with the following of Christ. When Jesus sent the Twelve out to preach "that the Kingdom of God is at hand," he expressly forbade them to carry money with them. He said to them, "Cure the sick, raise the dead, heal lepers, drive out demons. Give without payment, just as you received without payment. Do not accept gold or silver or copper money to put in your pockets, and do not take a bag for your journey, nor two shirts, nor shoes, nor a staff, for the workman deserves his food!" (Matthew X:5 ff.) "Workmen" they were not in an economic sense of the term; for to follow Jesus they had to give up their professional work: "As he was walking by the Sea of Galilee, he saw two brothers, Simon, who was afterward called Peter, and his brother, Andrew, casting a net into the sea, for they were fishermen. He said to them, 'Come and follow me, and I will make you fish for men!' They immediately dropped their nets and went with him. And he went on a little farther and saw two other men who were brothers, James, the son of Zebedee, and his brother, John, in the boat with Zebedee, their father, putting their nets in order, and he called them. And they immediately left the boat and their father, and went with him" (Matthew IV:18 ff.). Peter said to Jesus, "We have left all we had, and have followed you." And Jesus again asserts that nobody can follow him who does not give up his family as well as his "land" (Mark X:28 f.). A young man said to Jesus: " 'I have obeyed all these commandments. What do I still lack?' Jesus said to him, 'If you want to be perfect, go! Sell your property and give the money to the poor, and you will have riches in heaven. Then come back and be a follower of mine' " (Matthew XIX:20 f.).

Neither property nor any kind of economic consideration has a place in this doctrine. This is the meaning of the parable of the employer who paid the laborer who worked in his vineyard a whole day on the same footing as those who worked only one hour (Matthew XX:1 ff.); this is why Jesus preferred Mary to her sister Martha, although the latter did all the housework alone, whereas the former "seated herself to the Master's feet and listened to what he was saying" (Luke X:38 ff.). His antieconomic attitude Jesus showed in the Sermon on the Mount where he taught: "Do not store up your riches on earth, where moths and rust destroy them, and where thieves break in and steal them, but store up your riches in heaven, where moths and rust cannot destroy them, and where thieves cannot break in and steal them. For wherever your treasure is, your heart will be also. The eye is the lamp of the body. If then your eye is sound, your whole body will be light, but if your eye is unsound, your whole body will be dark. If, therefore, your very light is darkness, how deep the darkness will be! No slave can belong to two masters, for he will either hate one and love the other, or stand by one and make light of the other. You cannot serve God and money" (Matthew VI:19 ff.). Money is the adversary of God, money—the mammon —is the devil. Hence Jesus preferred the poor to the rich. In the Sermon on the Mount, he said, "Blessed are you who are poor for the Kingdom of God is yours. Blessed are you who are hungry now, for you will be satisfied" (Luke VI:20 f.). And according to Mark X:23 ff., Jesus said to his disciples: " 'How hard it will be for those who have money to enter the Kingdom of God!' But the disciples were amazed at what he said. And Jesus said to them again, 'My children, how hard it is to enter the Kingdom of God! It is easier for a camel to get through the eye of a needle than for a rich man to get into the Kingdom of God!' " Highly characteristic is the parable of the rich man and poor Lazarus (Luke XVI:19 f.). The rich man, after he died and was buried, was tormented in Gehenna, whereas poor Lazarus after death "was carried away by the angels to the companionship of Abraham." But of the rich man it is not said that he committed any wrong, and to the poor man no particularly good deeds are attributed. The vice of the former is to be rich, and the merit of the latter to be poor. Hence it is quite in the spirit of Jesus' teaching that in the Letter of James (V:1 ff.) being rich is identified with being unjust, being poor with being just.

Jesus is against money, not because he is for a primitive economy based on direct exchange of goods. He is against any kind of economy, against any production of goods for the satisfaction of human needs. "Therefore, I tell you, do not worry about life, wondering what you will have to eat or drink, or about your body, wondering what you will have to wear. Is not life more important than food, and the body than clothes? Look at the wild birds. They do not sow or reap, or store their food in barns, and yet your heavenly Father feeds them. Are you not of more account than they? But which of you with all his worry can add a single hour to his life? Why should you worry about clothing? See how the wild flowers grow. They do not toil or spin, and yet I tell you, even Solomon in all his splendor was never dressed like one of them. But if God so beautifully dresses the wild grass, which is alive today and is thrown into the furnace tomorrow, will he not much more surely clothe you, you who have so little faith? So do not worry and say, 'What shall we have to eat?' or 'What shall we have to drink?' or 'What shall we have to wear?' For these are all things the heathen are in pursuit of, and your heavenly Father knows well that you need all this. But you must make his kingdom, and uprightness before him, your greatest care, and you will have all these other things besides" (Matthew VI:25 ff.).

This antieconomic attitude of Jesus is the result of his idea of the Kingdom of God which was—in his opinion—imminent, nay, even present. For in the Kingdom of God no work is necessary, since God will feed, clothe, and house his people directly. The miraculous feeding of a great crowd, first with five loaves and two fish, and then with seven loaves, reported in the Gospel according to Mark (VI:41 ff.; VIII:1 ff.) shows how Jesus and his disciples imagined the solution of these problems in the Kingdom of God.

Jesus' teaching on the right of man to judge man.—The most evident conflict between the teaching of Jesus and the Jewish Law lies in his command to pass no more judgments upon other people (Matthew VII:1 ff.; Luke VI:36 f.). That Jesus himself has practiced this principle is reported in Luke XII:13 ff.: "Someone in the crowd said to him, 'Master, tell my brother to give me my share of our inheritance.' But he said to him, 'Who made me a judge or arbiter of your affairs?' " And in John VIII:1 ff. we read the beautiful story of the adulteress: "And the scribes and the Pharisees brought a woman taken in adultery; and having set her in the midst, they said unto him, 'Teacher, this woman hath been taken in adultery, in the very act. Now in the law, Moses commanded us to stone such: what then sayest thou of her?' And this they said, trying him, that they might have whereof to accuse him. But Jesus stooped down, and with his finger wrote on the ground. But when they continued asking him, he lifted up himself, and said unto them, 'He that is without sin among you, let him first cast a stone at her.' " This passage may be a later interpolation. But Jesus' answer to the question of the Pharisees as reported here, is in complete conformity with the new principle of justice proclaimed by him in the Sermon on the Mount: no retribution, but love. If no more retribution, then, the positive law is no more applicable. That the love of God is incompatible with judgment is clearly expressed in John III:16 f.: "For God loved the world so much that he gave his only Son, so that no one who believes in him should be lost, but that they should all have eternal life. For God did not send his Son into the world to pass judgment upon the world, but that through him the world might be saved." But in the following sentences the antagonism between love of God and judgment is somewhat attenuated, for it is evidently incompatible with Jesus' mission as Messiah and judge in the last judgment, punishing the sinners and rewarding the upright.

THE MESSIANIC IDEA

That Jesus, the preacher of the new justice of love, is the Messiah and judge of the world, constitutes, indeed, an unsurmountable contradiction in the doctrine of justice as presented in the Gospels; and there can be no doubt that Jesus' followers believed in him as the Messiah, king of Israel, whose coming was predicted by the Prophets, and that he never rejected this belief.

The Kingdom of God as a realm of justice in this world.—The Messianic idea of the Kingdom of God was the center of Jesus' teaching. The belief in the Kingdom of God, as it prevailed among the Jews at the time of Jesus, was the belief in the coming of a realm of perfect justice and happiness, the hope for a second paradise. The paradise lost through the fall of man at the beginning of this evil age, will be restored at its end, but this time for ever.[11] Just as the first paradise, the second one, the Messianic paradise, will be established in this world.[12] Palestine, the Holy Land, is the center of the Kingdom of God, but finally it will comprise the whole world. Peace and prosperity will reign, the soil will be fertile, men will no more gain their living in suffering, and death will no more threaten mankind. Men will live eternally or at least reach patriarchal age. The curse which God had pronounced after the fall of man will be annulled.

It is highly significant that the happiness of the coming golden age is essentially connected with its perfect justice.[13] In the Book of Enoch the paradise is called the "garden of justice" (1 Enoch XXXII:3; LXXVII:3).[14] Isaiah describes this state of justice in the future paradise as follows: "And on that day shall the deaf hear the words of a book, and out of gloom and darkness shall the eyes of the blind see; and the humble shall find new joy in the Lord, and the poorest shall exult in the Holy One of Israel. For the tyrant shall have vanished, and the scoffer shall have ceased, and all who are on the outlook for evil shall have been cut off— those who bring condemnation upon a man by a word, those who lay traps for the upholder of justice at the gate, and those who thrust aside the innocent on an empty plea" (XXIX:18 ff.); and: "Then will the steppe become garden land, and the garden land be counted an orchard. And justice will dwell in the steppe, and righteousness abide in the garden land; and the effect of righteousness will be peace, and the product of justice quietness and confidence forever" (XXXII:15 ff.); and: "A shoot will spring from the stem of Jesse, and a sprout from his roots will bear fruit. And the spirit of the Lord will rest upon him, the spirit of wisdom and understanding, the spirit of counsel and might, the spirit of knowledge and the fear of the Lord—and his delight will be in the fear of the Lord. He will not judge by that which his eyes see, nor decide by that which his ears hear; but with justice will he judge the needy, and with fairness decide for the poor of the land; he will smite the ruthless with the rod of his mouth, and with the breath of his lips will he slay the wicked. Righteousness will be the girdle round his loins, and faithfulness the girdle round his waist. Then the wolf will lodge with the lamb, and the leopard will lie down with the kid; the calf and the young lion will graze together, and a little child will lead them. The cow and the bear will be friends, their young ones will lie down together; and the lion will eat straw like the ox. The suckling child will play on the hole of the asp, and the weaned child will put his hand on the viper's den. They will do no harm or destruction on all my holy mountain; for the land will have become full of the knowledge of the Lord, as the waters cover the sea" (XI:1 ff.). A fundamental change of human nature must take place in order to make the golden age of justice possible.[15] Ezekiel announces as a word of Yahweh: "I will give you a new heart, and will put within you a new spirit; I will remove the heart of stone out of your flesh, and will give you a heart of flesh; and I will put my spirit within you, and make you follow my statutes and be careful to observe my ordinances" (XXXVI:26 f.).

The Kingdom of God was—at least originally—imagined as a community established on this earth. It was considered to be a political organization of the Jewish people either under the direct leadership of Yahweh or of his deputy, the Messiah, a descendant of David. But later the idea prevailed that the Messiah,

endowed with extraordinary powers, will rule. In the **Psalms
of Solomon**, which were written in the middle of the first century
B.C., we read (XVII:23 ff.): "Behold, O Lord, and raise up unto
them their king, the son of David, at the time in the which Thou
seest O God, that he may reign over Israel Thy servant. And gird
him with strength, that he may shatter unrighteous rulers, and
that he may purge Jerusalem from nations that trample her down
to destruction. . . . And he shall have the heathen nations to
serve him under his yoke; and he shall glorify the Lord in a place
to be seen of all the earth; and he shall purge Jerusalem, making
it holy as of old: so that nations shall come from the ends of the
earth to see his glory, bringing as gifts her sons who had fainted,
and to see the glory of the Lord, wherewith God hath glorified
her. And he shall be a righteous king, taught of God, over them,
and there shall be no unrighteousness in his days in their midst,
for all shall be holy and their king the anointed of the Lord." In
general, the Messiah was thought of as a human being. But there
was also the conception of the Messiah as a superhuman being
coming down from heaven and hence preëxistent, chosen by God
before the world was created. In both cases, his essential characteristic is justice. In the Book of Enoch it is said of the Messiah:
"This is the Son of Man who has righteousness, with whom righteousness dwells" (1 Enoch XLVI:3); "He is mighty in all the secrets
of righteousness, and unrighteousness shall disappear as a shadow,
and have no continuance"; "And he shall judge the secret things
and none shall be able to utter a lying word before him" (1
Enoch XLIX:2, 4).

No belief in the immortality of the soul.—The mission of the
Messiah was to realize justice in this world.[16] This justice was
not conceived of as retribution exercized in another world on
the immaterial and immortal souls of men after death. Such idea
was—at least originally—impossible among the Jews of Palestine. For among them the view prevailed that body and soul are
inseparably connected, so that the idea of a human soul living
without its body was foreign to them.[17] The belief that the soul
continues its existence after the dissolution of the body, is no-
where taught in the Old Testament; it is directly rejected in
Job XIV:10 ff. and Psalms XXVII:13; XLIX:12, 20; LXXXVIII:
10 ff.; and met with scepticism in Ecclesiastes III:21. When the

prophets or the psalmists speak of the soul or spirit of man they mean life or the living man. There are good reasons to assume that the ancient Hebrews, like other primitive peoples, originally believed in powerful and dangerous souls of the dead; that cult of the dead, especially ancestor worship, preceded the Yahweh religion. Relics of this pre-Yahweh religion can be found in the Pentateuch; thus, for example, in Deuteronomy XXVI:14, where the Israelite whose produce was being tithed, had to confess: "I have not eaten thereof in my mourning . . . nor given thereof to the dead." [18] The Yahweh religion was strongly opposed to the cult of the dead, and degraded them—like the religion of the Olympic gods the souls of the dead of the pre-Homeric religion— to powerless shades dwelling in a kind of Hades. In the Old Testament the idea prevails that the dead exist in the Sheol (Numbers XVI:33), a place of darkness and dust, that the dead are "sleeping" there, without real life, work, subsistence, or knowledge (Lamentations III:6; Job X:22; XIV:12; Ecclesiastes IX:10). The Sheol is the generalization of the grave. It is of importance that originally Yahweh's jurisdiction was limited to the upper world; it did not extend to the Sheol,[19] which was not created by him.[20] When a man dies he is "cut off from the hand of Yahweh" (Psalms LXXXVIII:5); there is no relationship between God and the land of the dead (Isaiah XXXVIII:11, 18; Psalms VI:5; XXX:9; CXV:17). Consequently the Sheol has nothing to do with justice. In this "land of oblivion" there is no difference between the just and unjust; there is one fate for all. God's justice is not made known in the Sheol (Psalms LXXXVIII:12). There is no retribution in Hades (Wisdom of Sirach XLI:4). That Yahweh and his justice was originally excluded from the Sheol may be explained as a relic of the pre-Yahweh religion,[21] in which the dead were gods and as such the agents of retribution exercised upon the living.

The belief in resurrection of the dead.—Although there was no idea of justice in Sheol there was, nevertheless, a belief in God's justice to be realized after death. The instrument of this belief was not the idea of the immortality of the soul but the idea of the resurrection of the body. Since there was no belief in the existence of an immortal soul, the longed-for justice could not be imagined as realized in another, transcendental world. It was conceived of as realized in this world, by the final judgment inaugurating the Messianic kingdom to be established on earth. The belief in bodily resurrection was an essential element of this conception.[22] Originally, resurrection of the just only was expected, as their reward; the punishment of the unjust was: not to rise from the dead but to remain in Sheol. But later the idea prevailed that in order to be judged in the last judgment all the dead must rise from the Sheol and come to the place where the judgment is held. In the Book of Daniel, XII:2 f., it is predicted: ". . . there shall be a time of trouble such as there has never been since there was a nation; but at that time your people shall be delivered, even everyone whose name is found written in the book. And many of those who sleep in the land of dust shall awake, some to everlasting life, and others to everlasting reproach and contempt." And in the Book of Enoch, we read: "And in those days shall the earth also give back that which has been entrusted to it, and Sheol also shall give back that which it has received, and hell shall give back that which it owes. For in those days the Elect One shall arise, and he shall choose the righteous and holy from among them: for the day has drawn nigh that they should be saved." (1 Enoch LI:1 f). That a bodily resurrection was meant, shows Ezekiel XXXVII:1 ff.: "The hand of the Lord was upon me; and the Lord carried me out by the spirit, and set me down in the midst of a valley which was full of bones. He led me all round them, and lo! there were very many of them on the surface of the valley, and lo! they were very dry. Then he said to me, 'O mortal man, can these bones live?' And I answered, 'O Lord God, thou knowest.' Then he said to me, 'Prophesy over these bones, and say to them, O dry bones, hear the word of the Lord! Thus says the Lord God to these bones: Behold, I am causing breath to enter you, and you shall live. I will put sinews upon you, and will clothe you with flesh, and cover you with skin; then I will put breath into you, and you shall live; and you shall know that I am the Lord.' So I prophesied as I had been commanded; as I prophesied, there was a sound; and lo! there followed a rustling; and the bones came together, bone to its bone. And as I looked, lo! there were sinews upon them, and flesh came up, and skin covered them over, but there was no breath in them. Then he said to me, 'Prophesy to the breath; prophesy, O mortal man, and say to the breath, Thus says the Lord God: Come from the four winds, O breath, and breathe into these slain men, that they may live!' So I prophesied as he had commanded me; and the breath came into them, and they lived, and stood upon their feet—an exceedingly great host."

Since the hope for national liberation played a decisive role in the belief in the coming Messiah and consequently the Kingdom of God was conceived of as the restoration of the Davidic kingdom—a kingdom on this earth—only bodily resurrection could fit in this scheme. The spiritualization of the belief in resurrection and the Kingdom of God is a later transformation.

The last judgment.—The Psalmists and the Prophets were convinced that the Kingdom of God was to come in the near future, and will be inaugurated by a grandiose judgment. The original idea was that there will be a victorious fight of Yahweh against the enemies of Israel. Later the idea of a fight was replaced by that of a judgment. This judgment was considered to be directed not only against the heathen, the enemies and suppressors of Israel; it was conceived of as an individual judgment of all the living and—resurrected—dead, of the Jewish people as well as of the other nations. The general resurrection of the dead was an essential element of the belief in the last judgment, because the latter was imagined as a universal judgment of the whole mankind.[23] It has the true character of a judicial procedure. Everybody will be judged exactly according to his very deeds committed during lifetime, on the basis of heavenly books in which these deeds are registered. "And do not think in your spirit nor say in your heart that ye do not know and that ye do not see that every sin is every day recorded in heaven in the presence of the Most High. From henceforth ye know that all your oppression wherewith ye oppress is written down every day till the day of your judgment" (1 Enoch XCVIII:7 f.); "And a book of remembrance was written before him, concerning those who revere the Lord and think upon his name. 'So they shall be mine,' says the Lord of hosts, 'On the day that I am about to make —my very own; and I will spare them even as a man spares his son who serves him. Then shall you again distinguish between the righteous and the wicked, between him who serves God, and him who serves him not" (Malachi III:16 ff.).

According to one version Yahweh himself will be the judge, according to another the Messiah will exercise this office, and reward the just with eternal and happy life in the paradise of the Kingdom of God, the unjust with eternal pain in Hades. In the Syriac Apocalypse of Baruch XLIV:12 ff., it is predicted: "And the new world [comes] which does not turn to corruption those who depart to its blessedness, and has no mercy on those who depart to torment, and leads not to perdition those who live in it. For these are they who shall inherit that time which has been spoken of, and theirs is the inheritance of the promised time. These are they who have acquired for themselves treasures of wisdom, and with them are found stores of understanding, and from mercy have they not withdrawn, and the truth of the law have they preserved. For to them shall be given the world to come, but the dwelling of the rest who are many shall be in the fire." And in 4 Ezra VII:32 ff., we read: "And the earth shall restore those that sleep in her, and the dust those that are at rest therein, and the chambers shall restore those that were committed unto them. And the Most High shall be revealed upon the throne of judgment: and then cometh the End and compassion shall pass away, and pity be far off, and long suffering withdrawn; but judgment alone shall remain, truth shall stand, and faithfulness triumph. And recompense shall follow, and the reward be made manifest; deeds of righteousness shall awake, and deeds of iniquity shall not sleep. And then shall the pit of torment appear, and over against it the place of refreshment; the furnace of Gehenna shall be made manifest, and over against it the Paradise of delight."

Separation of the Eschatological Belief from the Messianic Idea

Originally the belief in resurrection and the Messianic kingdom, inaugurated by the final judgment, coincides with the eschatological belief as the belief in a future world. But later two ideas arose which ultimately led to a separation of the one from the other. The desire for justice necessitated the belief in a retribution to be established immediately after death. In the time between death and resurrection the fate of the just and that of the unjust was assumed not to be the same—a state of happiness being allotted to the former, a state of pain to the latter. There were two versions of this belief in retribution immediately after death.[24] In one, Sheol was divided in compartments, one of torment for the unjust, another of comfort for the just. The other version was that the just go immediately after death to heaven. The idea of a division of Sheol, made to separate the just from the unjust, we find in the Book of Enoch. There are hollow places in the Sheol, which have been made for the purpose "that the spirits of the souls of the dead should assemble therein . . . to receive them till the day of their judgment . . . till the great judgment comes upon them" (1 Enoch XXII:3, 4). To the question of Enoch why the "hollow places are separated one from the other," the Archangel Raphael answers: "Such division has been made for the spirits of the righteous, in which there is the bright spring of water. And such has been made for sinners when they die and are buried in the earth and judgment has not been executed on them in their lifetime. Here their spirits shall be set apart in this great pain till the great day of judgment and punishment and torment of those who curse for ever and retribution for their spirits. There he shall bind them for ever. And such a division has been made for the spirits of those who make their suit, who make disclosures concerning their destruction, when they were slain in the days of the sinners. Such has been made for the spirits of men who were not righteous but sinners, who were complete in transgression, and of the transgressors they shall be companions: but their spirits shall not be slain in the day of judgment nor shall they be raised from thence." Whereupon Enoch "blessed the Lord of glory and said: 'Blessed be my Lord, the Lord of righteousness, who ruleth for ever' " (1 Enoch XXII: 9–14). The same idea of a division of Sheol is presupposed in the parable of the rich man and Lazarus (Luke XVI:19 ff.): "There was once a rich man, who used to dress in purple and fine linen, and to live in luxury every day. And a beggar named Lazarus was put down at his gate covered with sores and eager to satisfy his hunger with what was thrown away from the rich man's table. Why, the very dogs came and licked his sores. And it came about that the beggar died and was carried away by the angels to the companionship of Abraham, and the rich man too died and was buried. And in Hades he looked up, tormented as he was, and saw Abraham far away, with Lazarus beside him. And he called to him and said, 'Father Abraham! Take pity on me, and send Lazarus to dip the tip of his finger in water and cool my tongue, for I am in torment, here in the flames!' And Abraham said, 'My child, remember that you received your blessings in your lifetime, and Lazarus had his misfortunes in his; and now he is being comforted here, while you are in anguish. Besides there is a great chasm set between you and us, so that those who want to go over from this side to you cannot, and they cannot cross from your side to us.' " It is evident that both the rich man and Lazarus, are in the same room, called Hades; the rich man can "see" Abraham with Lazarus beside him; it is true, they are "far away," but it is possible to speak to them. There is a "great chasm" between the place of torment where the rich man is, and the place of comfort where Lazarus is, "so that those who want to go over" from one side to the other "cannot cross"; apparently because the chasm dividing Sheol into two parts is too great. The idea that the just go to heaven whereas the unjust remain in Sheol is expressed in 1 Enoch XXXIX:4 ff. and CIII:7.

Retribution exercised immediately after death, could have only a provisional character as long as there was belief in the final judgment and resurrection. There was, however, on the other hand an increasing tendency of spiritualizing the idea of the world to come; and this tendency finally led to a transformation of the idea of the Messianic kingdom. It ceased to be conceived of as an ultimate stage. This kingdom, established on earth, was not supposed to bring final happiness; a still higher and heavenly happiness was expected in a transcendental state to be realized after the kingdom had come to its close. Hence the Messianic period was conceived of as limited in time and resurrection as well as the final judgment shifted from its beginning to its close. The transcendental state of blessedness, expected after the Messianic period, could not refer to the physical life in the Messianic paradise; it presupposed the belief in the immortality of the soul which, indeed, under the influence of Greek philosophy penetrated Jewish theology. The belief in the immortality of the soul must necessarily supersede the belief in the resurrection of the body, closely connected with the Messianic kingdom. As a matter of fact, this spiritual movement took place among the Hellenistic Jews.[25]

The Jews, however, to whom Jesus preached still believed in the resurrection of the dead and the Messianic paradise as a final stage. The Synoptic Gospels reflect this belief. As to the idea of the Kingdom of God which Jesus himself held, it was probably not very different from that of his disciples.

JESUS' IDEA OF THE KINGDOM OF GOD

It is hardly possible to separate in Jesus' teaching the Messianic from the eschatological sphere.[26] The future world of justice coincides with the Messianic kingdom. Jesus shared the Prophets' pessimistic evaluation of the present world; he spoke of "the present wicked age" (Matthew XII:45; Luke XI:29), of "this unfaithful and sinful age" (Mark VIII:38). But this age is near to its close (Matthew XIII:39) and to the beginning of the new age of justice, the Kingdom of God. Since this present age is by its very nature unjust, justice in the new age will be established by a complete reversal of the present social relations.

The principle of reversion.—This is the meaning of Jesus' saying that "many who are first now will be last then, and the last will be first" (Mark X:31). This principle of reversal is most clearly expressed in Luke VI:20 ff.: "Blessed are you who are poor, for the kingdom of God is yours! Blessed are you who are hungry now, for you will be satisfied!" "But alas for you who are rich, for you have had your comfort! Alas for you who have plenty to eat now, for you will be hungry!" "Blessed are you who weep now, for you will laugh." "Alas for you who laugh now, for you will mourn and weep!" And in John IX:39: "I have come into this world to judge men, that those who cannot see may see and those who can see may become blind." This principle of reversal is quite opposite to the command, "Love your enemies and pray for your persecutors"; it is an application of the law of retribution. It presupposes that in this evil age those who are happy do not deserve their happiness, because they are unjust and therefore will be punished by becoming unhappy; and those who are unhappy do not deserve their unhappiness because they are just and therefore will be rewarded by becoming happy. This is an idea of justice as conceived by those excluded from the good things of the earth, directed against those enjoying them; it is a justice of resentment, not the justice of the love of God.

The idea of retribution in Jesus' teaching.—The Gospels ascribe to Jesus some deeds and sayings which are not quite in conformity with his command not to resist evil and to love one's enemy. According to Matthew and Luke he expelled from the Temple the money changers and the pigeon dealers (Matthew XXI:12 f.; Luke XIX:45 f.); and according to Matthew he called the Pharisees "hypocrites," "blind fools," "serpents." "You brood of snakes! How can you escape being sentenced to the pit . . . on your heads may come all the innocent blood shed on the earth" (Matthew XXIII:14 ff.). And in Matthew XVI:27, we read: "The Son of Man . . . will repay everyone for what he has done."

Even when Jesus preaches the new justice of love in opposition to the old justice of retribution, he does not always emancipate himself of the latter. The love of God must not expect any reward (Luke VI:32). But Jesus says also, "If you love only those who love you, what reward can you expect?" (Matthew V:46); and "If you forgive others when they offend you, your heavenly Father will forgive you" (Matthew VI:14); he even says that the heavenly Father will punish you "if you do not each forgive your brothers from your heart" (Matthew XVIII:35). He says further, "No one who will give the humblest of my disciples even a cup of cold water because he is my disciple, I tell you, can ever fail of his reward" (Matthew X:42); and "When you pray, you must not be like the hypocrites, for they like to pray standing in the synagogues and in the corners of the squares, to let people see them. I tell you, that is the only reward they will get. But when you pray, go into your own room, and shut the door, and pray to your Father who is unseen, and your Father who sees what is secret will reward you" (Matthew VI:5). According to Luke VI:22 ff., he said: "Blessed are you when people hate you and exclude you and denounce you and spurn the name you bear as evil, on account of the Son of Man. Be glad when that happens, and leap for joy, for you will be richly rewarded in heaven, for that is the way their forefathers treated the prophets." When forbidding to one of the men who were with him to use the sword against those who came to arrest him, he said: "All who draw the sword, will die by the sword" (Matthew XXVI:52). It is the very principle of retribution which Jesus applies in saying: "Everyone who will acknowledge me before men I will acknowledge before my Father in heaven; but any one who disowns me before men, I will disown before my Father in heaven" (Matthew X:32). According to Matthew VII:12, Jesus taught: "You must always treat other people as you would like to have them treat you." This is the positive formulation of the principle attributed to Rabbi Hillel: "What is odious to you do not inflict upon others." The negative as well as the positive formula presuppose the principle of retribution—like for like.

Jesus' teaching on the last judgment.—It is especially the judgment at the close of the unjust age, and the beginning of the just one which is announced by John the Baptist as well as by Jesus himself as a day of retribution and of merciless and cruel punishment. According to Matthew III:7 ff., John said to the Pharisees and Sadducees: "You brood of snakes! Who warned you to escape from the wrath that is coming? Then produce fruit that will be consistent with your professed repentance! Do not suppose that you can say to yourselves, 'We have Abraham for our forefather,' for I tell you God can produce descendants for Abraham right out of these stones! But the axe is already lying at the roots of the trees. Any tree that fails to produce good fruit is going to be cut down and thrown into the fire. I am baptizing you in water in token of your repentance, but he who is coming after me is stronger than I am, and I am not fit to carry his shoes. He will baptize you in the Holy Spirit and in fire. His winnowing fork is in his hand, and he will clean up his threshing-floor, and store his wheat in his barn, but he will burn up the chaff with inextinguishable fire"; and according to Luke III:16: "I am only baptizing you in water, but someone is coming who is stronger than I am, whose shoes I am not fit to untie. He will baptize you in the Holy Spirit and in fire. He has his winnowing fork in his hand, to clean up his threshing-floor, and store his wheat in his barn, but he will burn up the chaff with inextinguishable fire."

And Jesus said to the Twelve when he sent them out: "Whatever town or village you come to, inquire for some suitable person, and stay with him till you leave the place. And as you go into his house, wish it well. If the house deserves it, the peace you wish it will come over it, but if it does not deserve it, your blessing will come back upon yourselves. And where no one will welcome you, or listen to you, leave that house or town and shake off its very dust from your feet. I tell you, the land of Sodom and Gomorrah will fare better on the Day of Judgment than that town" (Matthew X:11 ff.). When he "reproached the towns in which his numerous wonders had been done, because they did not repent," he said, "Alas for you . . . you will go down among the dead . . . I tell you that the land of Sodom will fare better on the Day of Judgment than you will!" (Matthew XI:20 ff.) When the Pharisees accused Jesus of driving out demons "by the aid of Beelzebub, the prince of the demons," Jesus said that he was driving the demons out by the aid of God's spirit: "But if I am driving the demons out by the aid of God's spirit, then the Kingdom of God has overtaken you. How can anyone get into a strong man's house and carry off his property unless he first binds the strong man? After that he can plunder his house. Anyone who is not with me is against me, and anyone who does not join me in gathering, scatters. Therefore, I tell you, men will be forgiven for any sin or abusive speech, but abusive speech about the Spirit cannot be forgiven. And whoever speaks against the Son of Man will be forgiven for it, but whoever speaks against the holy Spirit cannot be forgiven for it, either in this world or in the world to come" (Matthew XII:24 ff.).

"The Kingdom of God in the midst of you."—Jesus' statement "the Kingdom of God has overtaken you" implies that according to his opinion, the Kingdom of God has already come, that its harbingers can already be seen. According to Mark I:15, Jesus said, "The time has come and the reign of God is near; repent and believe this good news"; according to Matthew XVII:12: "Elijah [the precursor of the Messiah] does come and is to reform everything, but I tell you Elijah has come already." Again and again he inculcated upon his disciples to "be on the alert," to "be on the watch," to "be ready," for the Kingdom of God may come at any moment (Mark XIII:33 ff.; Matthew XXV:13; Luke

XII:35 ff.). He even said to his disciples, "I tell you, it [the Kingdom of God] will all happen before the present generation passes away" (Luke XXI:32); and "I tell you, some of you who stand here will certainly live to see the reign of God come in its might" (Mark IX:1). When the Pharisees asked him, "when the Kingdom of God would come," he answered, "The Kingdom of God is in the midst of you" (Luke XVII:21),[27] which has about the same meaning as the above-quoted words, "the Kingdom of God has overtaken you." And the opinion that the Kingdom of God is imminent, nay, already present, is the inevitable consequence of the belief that he is the Messiah, whose mission is to establish this realm of justice on this earth.

The Kingdom of God as realization of justice on earth.—There can be little doubt that the Kingdom of God as described in the Synoptic Gospels was imagined, in conformity with the Jewish tradition, as an earthly community of men physically living.[28] Jesus repeatedly speaks of eating and drinking in the Kingdom of God. He said to his disciples: "So just as my Father has conferred a kingdom on me, I confer on you the right to eat and drink at my table in my kingdom" (Luke XXII:29 f.). It is true that there will be no marriage, no sexual intercourse in the Kingdom of God. When the Sadducees, who did not believe in resurrection, asked Jesus to which of the several brothers a woman will be married after resurrection when she, during life, was married after the death of one of them to the other, Jesus answered: "You are wrong, because you do not understand the Scriptures nor the power of God. For after resurrection there is no marrying or being married, but they live as angels do in heaven" (Matthew XXII:23 ff.). This was not quite in conformity with the traditional idea according to which in the Kingdom of God the soil as well as the women will be fertile and the women will give birth to children without pain (1 Enoch X:17; 2 Baruch LXXIII:7). The elimination of sexual intercourse from the Kingdom of God might be interpreted as a tendency toward spiritualization. But the complete transfer of the Kingdom of God to a transcendental sphere is not yet achieved in the Synoptic Gospels. The spiritualization of the Kingdom of God is the result of an intellectual process which, under the influence of political necessities and philosophical speculation, was accomplished only after the death of Jesus. The Messianic restoration of the Davidic kingdom was incompatible with the Roman Empire.[29] Hence the tendency is quite understandable to reinterpret this ideology, in order to make it politically acceptable to the established authorities. That the Kingdom of God which Jesus, or at least his followers, had in mind was an earthly political organization results from the fact that they believed in him as the Messianic king of Israel, the predicted ruler in the restored Davidic kingdom. Since the legitimate king must descend from David, the Gospels try to prove this descendance in spite of the fact that Jesus himself declared that the Messiah need not be the son of David (Matthew XXII:45). They prove it by the descendance of his father Joseph, the husband of his mother Mary, although, at the same time, they assert that Mary conceived him through the influence of the Holy Spirit (Matthew I:20), that the Most High overshadowed her (Luke I:35). Jesus did not reject his disciples' belief that he was the Messiah, king of Israel (Matthew XI:2 f., XVI:13 ff., XXIV:3 ff.; Mark VIII:29 ff.; Luke IX:20 f.; John I:49, VI:69, X:24 ff.). When the high priest asked him: "I adjure you by the living God, tell us if you are the Christ, the Son of God," his answer was "You have said so" (Matthew XXVI:64). He entered Jerusalem riding an ass in order to fulfill the prophecy, "Lo, your king comes to you; vindicated and victorious is he; humble and riding on an ass" (Zechariah IX:9); and he was acclaimed with the cry "hosanna" (Matthew XXI:9), which was the salute due to the king. Jesus even promised his disciples that they will become in the Kingdom of God the rulers of the twelve tribes of Israel: "In the new world, I tell you, when the Son of Man takes his seat on his glorious throne, you who have followed me will also sit upon twelve thrones, and judge the twelve tribes of Israel!" (Matthew XIX:28.) To "judge the twelve tribes of Israel" means to rule over them. According to Acts I:6, the disciples asked Jesus, "Master, is this the time when you are going to re-establish the kingdom for Israel?" By this they meant the Kingdom of God. And in his answer Jesus by no means contradicted their hope. He finally admitted to the high priest as well as to Pilate to be the Messiah and king of Israel (Matthew XXVI:63; XXVII:11; Mark XV:2, 26; Luke XXIII:2 f.). And it was on the basis of this confession that he was condemned to death.[30]

On the other hand, it is true, the author of the Gospel according to John let Jesus declare before Pilate: "My kingdom is not of this world" (John XVIII:36). But this statement does not mean —as it is sometimes interpreted—that his kingdom is beyond this world, that it has nothing to do with dominion over this real world. It only means that his kingdom originates in heaven and that it will be established in this world by a direct and miraculous intervention of God.[31]

Any attempt to interpret the Kingdom of God in the teaching of Jesus as a merely spiritual realm, is incompatible with the fact that an essential element of this teaching was the belief in resurrection. That the rise from the dead was imagined, at least by his followers, as a resurrection of the body, is evident from the story of his own resurrection presented in all three Synoptic Gospels; especially the description of his appearance after death, told in Luke XXIV:36 ff.: "While they were still talking of these things, he himself stood among them. They were startled and panic-stricken, and thought they saw a ghost. But he said to them, 'Why are you so disturbed, and why do doubts arise in your minds? Look at my hands and feet, for it is I myself! Feel of me and see, for a ghost has not flesh and bones, as you see I have.' But they could not yet believe it for sheer joy and they were amazed. And he said to them, 'Have you anything here to eat?' And they gave him a piece of broiled fish, and he took it and ate it before their eyes."

Resurrection of the body is an essential element of Jesus' teaching on the Kingdom of God not only because this kingdom is a community of human beings living in this world, but, above all, because the last judgment with which this kingdom begins, is a judgment "of the living and the dead" (Acts X:42). Since in this evil age many died without having got the punishment or the reward they deserved, they must rise from the dead in order to be brought to justice at the day of the last judgment. According to Matthew, "The Son of Man is going to come with his angels in his Father's glory, and then he will repay everyone for what he has done" (XVI:27). The same idea is expressed in Matthew XXV:31 ff. That it was prevailing among his followers is shown by statements in the Acts and even in the Letters of Paul. Peter says: "He also directed us to announce to the people and bear solemn testimony that he is the one whom God has appointed to the judge of the living and the dead" (Acts X:42 f.); and in Paul's Second Letter to Timothy we read: "I charge you in the sight of God and Christ Jesus who is to judge the living and the dead, and by his appearing and his kingdom, preach the message" (2 Timothy IV:1).

To carry out the judgment, the Messiah, Son of Man, will come down from heaven on the clouds of the sky: "Then the sign of the Son of Man will appear in the sky, and all the nations of the earth will lament when they see the Son of Man coming on the clouds of the sky, in all his power and splendor" (Matthew XXIV:30). It is significant that the Kingdom of God comes from the sky onto this earth, and not that men come—after death—to a kingdom in heaven. This is the idea expressed in the prayer, "Thy kingdom come! Thy will be done on earth as it is done in heaven!" (Matthew VI:10.) The kingdom comes like a bridegroom to his bride (Matthew XXV:1 ff.). It is as if the kingdom would descend from heaven to earth,[32] and the kingdom of Satan, which reigns now on earth would descend to the underworld. Since there will be heaven on earth, the antagonism of this imperfect world and another, perfect, world will disappear. The Kingdom of God as established after the last judgment is a perfect, and that means in the first place, an absolutely just and in this respect superhuman, world on this earth.

It is very characteristic of the Kingdom of God that the dualism of an empirical human and a transcendental divine sphere is abolished. Those who live in the Kingdom will see God;[33] and that means: will experience absolute justice.

The justice of the last judgment: retribution.—However, the justice to be realized by the last judgment is nothing but retribution: merciless punishment of the bad, generous reward for the good; and the punishment is in the foreground. Jesus announces the last judgment as the "days of vengeance" (Luke XXI:22), as a time like that of Sodom (Luke XVII:22 ff.); even worse than the day of Sodom: "There will be greater misery than there has ever been from the beginning of creation until now" (Mathew XXIV:21). At the imminent close of this age, the Messiah, Son of Man, "will send out his angels, and they will gather up out of his kingdom all the causes of sin and the wrongdoers and throw them into the blazing furnace; there they will wail and grind their teeth. Then the upright will shine out like the sun, in their Father's kingdom" (Matthew XIII:41 f.); "That is what will happen at the close of the age. The angels will go out and remove the wicked from among the upright, and throw them into a blazing furnace. There they will wail and grind their teeth (Matthew XIII:49 f.). Nobody will escape punishment (Matthew XXIII:33). The retributory function of the last judgment appears quite clearly in the vision of Jesus: "When the Son of Man comes in his splendor, with all his angels with him, he will take his seat on his glorious throne, and all the nations will be gathered before him, and he will separate them from one another, just as a shepherd separates his sheep from his goats, and he will put the sheep at his right hand and the goats at his left. Then the king will say to those at his right, 'Come, you whom my Father has blessed, take possession of the kingdom which has been destined for you from the creation of the world. For when I was hungry, you gave me food, when I was thirsty you gave me something to drink, when I was a stranger, you invited me to your homes, when I had no clothes, you gave me clothes, when I was sick, you looked after me, when I was in prison, you came to see me.' Then the upright will answer, 'Lord, when did we see you hungry and give you food, or thirsty, and give you something to drink? When did we see you a stranger, and invite you home, or without clothing, and supply you with it? When did we see you sick or in prison, and go to see you?' The king will answer, 'I tell you, in so far as you did it to one of the humblest of these brothers of mine, you did it to me.' Then he will say to those at his left, 'Begone, you accursed people, to the everlasting fire destined for the devil and his angels! For when I was hungry, you gave me nothing to eat, and when I was thirsty you gave me nothing to drink, when I was a stranger, you did not invite me home, when I had no clothes, you did not supply me, when I was sick and in prison, you did not look after me.' Then they in their turn will answer, 'Lord, when did we see you hungry, or thirsty, or a stranger, or in need of clothes, or sick, or in prison, and did not wait upon you?' Then he will answer, 'I tell you, in so far as you failed to do it for one of these people who are humblest, you failed to do it for me.' Then they will go away to everlasting punishment, and the upright to everlasting life" (Matthew XXV:31 ff.). There can be no doubt that in this passage of the Gospel according to Matthew the "Son of Man" presented as the judge in the last judgment is Jesus, the Messiah, himself. That he considered himself as the judge of the world is confirmed in John V:22, where he says, "The Father passes judgment on no one, but he has committed the judgment entirely to the Son." The judgment is the execution of the justice of retribution. The "everlasting punishment" of this divine retribution is quite consistent with the God of vengeance of the Old Testament; but incompatible with the new justice, the love of God in the Sermon on the Mount.

The principle of retribution is even at the basis of the mystic idea of Christ's vicarious death. He says that "the Son of Man has come . . . to give his life to ransom many others" (Matthew XX:28), that his blood "is to be poured out for many people, for the forgiveness of their sins" (Matthew XXVI:28). His death is interpreted as punishment of the sins of others. To justify as just what seems to be the most unjust happening, the deadly suffering of the absolutely innocent, no other principle is used but the rule that the evil of wrong must be requited by the evil of punishment.

Many attempts have been made to eliminate the contradictions in the teaching of Jesus, by more or less artificial interpretations. The most successful method is to differentiate between authentic and nonauthentic sayings of Jesus on the basis of an historical-critical analysis of the sources. Thus, for instance, the decisive passage in Matthew XXV:31 where Jesus is presented as the judge in the last judgment sentencing the evildoers to the everlasting fire, has been declared to be a "Matthean construction." [34] Such historical-critical method, however, is hardly compatible with the concept of the New Testament as a divine revelation. By this method one can reconstruct a more or less consistent system of morality in the teaching of Jesus, but one cannot eliminate the fact that the New Testament contains contradictory ideas of justice. This is especially true with respect to the relation which exists between the Synoptic Gospels and the Letters of Paul.

THE TEACHING OF JESUS AS COMPARED WITH THE TEACHING OF PAUL

Paul's rejection of the Jewish Law.—It has often been stressed that there is a difference between the teaching of Jesus and that of Paul. This difference is evident with respect to the idea of justice and its relation to positive law. As to the Jewish Law, Paul goes much further than did Jesus, who tried to maintain the appearance as if he were—at least in principle—not against the Law. But Paul openly declared, "Now the Law no longer applies to us" (Romans VII:6); "Man is not made upright by doing what the Law commands but by faith in Christ Jesus. . . . By doing what the Law commands no one can be made upright" (Galatians II:16 ff.); "There is a curse upon all who rely on obedience to the Law. . . . That no one is accepted as upright by God for obeying the Law is evident, because the upright will have life because of his faith, and the Law has nothing to do with faith" (Galatians III:10 ff.). Consequently, "If you are guided by the spirit [not by your physical cravings], you are not subject to law" (Galatians V:18).

However, the "Law" against which Paul raised his voice was rather the ritual provisions of the Jewish code. For he recognized and confirmed, as in conformity with God's will, the main legal institutions of the positive law of his time: family based on marriage, property based on work, and government firmly established in the state.

Paul's teaching on marriage and property.—As to marriage it might seem as if Paul had permitted it only as the lesser of two evils. For he said, "It is an excellent thing for a man to remain unmarried; but there is so much immorality that every man had better have a wife of his own, and every woman a husband of her own. The husband must give his wife what is due her, and the wife must do the same by her husband" (1 Corinthians VII:1 ff.). But in the First Letter to the Thessalonians, he teaches: "It is God's will . . . that each of you learn to take a wife for himself from pure and honorable motives" (1 Thessalonians IV:3 f.); and in the Letter to the Ephesians he declares marriage as an institution so sacred that he compares it with the relation between Christ and the Church: "You married women must subordinate yourselves to your husbands, as you do to the Lord, for a husband is the head of his wife, just as Christ is the head of the Church, which is his body, and is saved by him. Just as the Church is in subjection to Christ, so married women must be, in everything, to their husbands. You who are husbands must love your wives, just as Christ loves the Church and gave himself for her, to consecrate her" (Ephesians V:22 ff.). As to the relationship between parents and children, he teaches: "Children, as Christians obey your parents, for that is right. 'You must honor your father and mother'—that is the first commandment accompanied with a promise—'so that you may prosper and have a long life on earth!' You fathers, too, must not irritate your children, but you must bring them up with Christian training and instruction" (Ephesians VI:1 ff.).

Jesus taught: Give up your profession, do not work for the satisfaction of your bodily needs, for God will take care of you. Since after Jesus' death, the new Christians believed that the Kingdom of God was near at hand, there was a certain danger that the believers would consider labor superfluous, which might have caused serious political difficulties. Consequently Paul taught: "If any one refuses to work, give him nothing to eat" (2 Thessalonians III:10). He said: "We do entreat you, brothers, to surpass yourselves in striving to live quietly and mind your own affairs, and work with your hands, as we directed you, so that you may have the respect of the outsiders, and not be dependent upon anybody" (1 Thessalonians IV:11 f.); and "we hear that some of you are living in idleness, mere busybodies, not doing any work. Now with the authority of the Lord Jesus Christ we charge and exhort such people to keep quiet and do their work and earn their own living" (2 Thessalonians III:11 f.). Paul himself gained his living as a tentmaker, whereas Jesus, when he became a preacher seems to have ceased to exercise his profession as a carpenter. Jesus ordered his disciples to take no money and to carry no money in their pockets; but Paul made organized collections of money for "God's people," that is for the community of the first Christians in Jerusalem (1 Corinthians XVI:1 ff.; 2 Corinthians VIII:1 ff.; IX:1 ff.; Galatians II:10; Romans XV:25 ff.; Philippians IV:10 ff.). Jesus taught that a rich man cannot get into the Kingdom of God, but Paul only asked "the rich of this world" to be also "rich in good deeds, open-handed and generous, storing up a valuable treasure for themselves for the future, so as to grasp the life that is life indeed" (1 Timothy VI:17 ff.). Paul even recognized slavery as a legal institution not incompatible with the new justice of love. Thus he says: "You who are slaves, obey your earthly masters, in reverence and awe, with sincerity of heart, as you would the Christ, not with mere external service, as though you had only men to please, but like slaves of Christ, carrying out the will of God. Do your duties heartily and willingly, as though it were for the Lord, not for men, for you know that everyone, slave or free, will be rewarded by the Lord for his good conduct. You who are masters, too, must treat your slaves in the same way, and cease to threaten them, for you know that their Master and yours is in heaven, and that he will show no partiality" (Ephesians VI:5–9). And in 1 Timothy VI:1 ff., we read: "All who are under the yoke of slavery must treat their masters with the greatest respect, so that the name of God and our teaching may not be abused. Those who have Christian masters must not think lightly of them because they are brothers; they must serve them all the more faithfully, because those who benefit by it are believers and hence dear to them."

Paul's teaching on established authority.—Jesus did not teach to pay taxes and he did not recognize any earthly authority. But Paul expressly ordered the Christians to "pay taxes to the man entitled to receive them." He gave this order in connection with the solemn recognition of any established authority: "Everyone must obey the authorities that are over him, for no authority can exist without the permission of God; the existing authorities have been established by him, so that anyone who resists the authorities sets himself in opposition to what God has ordained, and those who oppose him will bring down judgment upon themselves" (Romans XIII:1 f.). The existing authorities of the Roman Empire—which were to Jesus Satan's realm—are God's agents. Consequently: "The man who does right has nothing to fear from the magistrates, as the wrongdoer has. If you want to have no fear of the authorities, do right, and they will commend you for it, for they are God's agents to do you good. But if you do wrong you may well be afraid, for they do not carry swords for nothing. They are God's servants, to execute his wrath upon wrongdoers. You must obey them, therefore, not only to escape God's wrath, but as a matter of principle, just as you pay your taxes; they are God's ministers, devoting themselves to this service. Pay them all what is due them—tribute to the man entitled to receive it, taxes to the man entitled to receive them, respect to the man entitled to it, and honor to the man entitled to it" (Romans XIII:3 ff.). The last sentence is the application of the principle: to each his own, according to the existing law. Paul's doctrine not only implies a recognition without reservation of the positive law of the Roman Empire and the established authority of this state, it is the highest possible justification of any positive law and any established state authority, and hence of the principle of retribution as a manifestation of God's will.

PAUL'S MYSTIC IDEA OF JUSTICE

Paul's interpretation of the justice of love.—After having insisted upon unconditional obedience to the law of the state and thus having recognized retribution as the principle of justice, Paul states: "Owe nobody anything—except the duty of mutual love, for whoever loves his fellow men has fully satisfied the Law. For the commandments, 'You must not commit adultery, You must not murder, You must not steal, You must not covet,' and any other commandments there are, are all summed up in one saying, 'You must love your neighbor as you do yourself.' Love never wrongs a neighbor, and so love fully satisfies the Law" (Romans XIII:8 ff.). But is this love really compatible with the Law based on the principle of retribution, is it the love which Jesus opposed to the rule, Eye for eye, tooth for tooth? In his Letter to the Hebrews (XII:6) Paul refers to a passage in the Book of Proverbs (III:11), "Whom Yaweh loves he punishes." But he is quite aware of the problem whether the love of God is compatible with punishment. He asks, "Is it wrong in God—I am putting it in ordinary human terms— to inflict punishment?" And he answers, "By no means! For then how could he judge the world?" (Romans III:5 f.) Paul maintains, it is true, Jesus' new idea of justice, the love of God; he has even expressed this idea in the most beautiful poetical form, in the famous Love's song of songs (1 Corinthians XIII:1 ff.) and he thinks it necessary to distinguish between the "justice based on the law" taught by Moses and the justice "based on faith" which "comes from God" and is taught by Jesus who is "the end of the law" (Romans X:1–5).

In Paul's Letters God's vengeance, anger, and wrath are no less referred to than God's love (Romans I:18, II:5, V:9; 1 Thessalonians II:16, IV:6). "Before the tribunal of the Christ each is to be repaid with good or evil for the life he has lived in the body" (2 Corinthians V:10). "God considers it only just to repay with suffering those who are making you suffer and give rest to you who are suffering and to us, when our Lord Jesus appears from heaven, with his mighty angels in a blaze of fire, and takes vengeance on the godless who will not listen to the good news of our Lord Jesus" (2 Thessalonians I:6 f.); "The man who wrongs anyone will be paid back for the wrong he has done; there will be no exceptions" (Colossians III:25). In his second Letter to Timothy (IV:14) Paul mentions that "Alexander the metal worker did me a great deal of harm." But Paul does not say that he will pray for him; he finds consolation in the hope that "the Lord will repay him for what he did." Paul says, "Your love must be genuine," but he adds, "You must hate what is wrong" (Romans XII:9). He writes to the Corinthians: "I am prepared to punish any trace of disobedience" (2 Corinthians X:6); and to the Galatians: "A curse upon him," who contradicts the good news, and: "I wish the people who are upsetting you would go on and have themselves emasculated" (Galatians I:9, V:12). Paul repeats Jesus' commands, "Do not pay back with evil for evil"; "Do not take your revenge"; but he adds, "Leave room for God's anger, for the Scripture says, 'Vengeance belongs to me, I will pay them back, says the Lord.' " (Romans XII:17 ff.). And immediately after proclaiming the justice of love he presents his doctrine that the established authorities of the state are instituted by God and that consequently it must be considered to be God's will that wrongdoers be punished by these authorities.

The spiritualization of the Kingdom of God in the teaching of Paul.—When Jesus stood before the Roman procurator under the charge of "misleading the Jewish nation, forbidding the payment of taxes to the emperor and claiming to be an anointed king himself," and when the Roman magistrate asked him, "Are you the king of the Jews?" his answer was simply "Yes" (Luke XXIII:1 ff.). When Paul was arrested by a Roman colonel and bound to be examined under the lash, he protested, referring to his Roman citizenship: "Is it legal for you to flog a Roman citizen?" (Acts XXII:23 ff.) And when he stood before the Roman governor under the charge of being a disturber of the peace among the Jews, he pleaded not guilty: "I have committed no offense against the Jewish Law or the Temple or the emperor" and, exercising his right as a Roman citizen, he declared: "I appeal to the emperor" (Acts XXV:1 ff.).

As a Roman citizen, recognizing the legal authority of the emperor, Paul could not maintain the belief in the Kingdom of God as the restoration of the Jewish state established in this world. The Kingdom of God was to be transformed into a purely religious, completely unpolitical ideology by being transferred from this into another, transcendental world, in order to appear harmless to the Roman police. This spiritualization of the Kingdom of God and especially of its most essential element, the resurrection from the dead, is the most important contribution of Paul to the Christian belief: [35] "Someone will say, 'How can the dead rise? What kind of a body will they have when they come back?' You foolish man, the very seed you sow never comes to life without dying first; and when you sow it, it has not the form it is going to have, but is a naked kernel, perhaps of wheat or something else; and God gives it just such a form as he pleases, so that each kind of seed has a form of its own. Flesh is not all alike; men have one kind, animals another, birds another, and fish another. There are heavenly bodies, and there are earthly bodies, but the beauty of the heavenly bodies is of one kind, and the beauty of the earthly bodies is of another. The sun has one kind of beauty, and the moon another, and the stars another; why, one star differs from another in beauty. It is so with the resurrection of the dead. The body is sown in decay, it is raised free from decay. It is sown in humiliation, it is raised in splendor. It is sown in weakness, it is raised in strength. It is a physical body that is sown, it is a spiritual body that is raised. If there is a physical body, there is a spiritual body also. This is also what the Scripture says: 'The first man Adam became a living creature.' The last Adam has become a life-giving Spirit. It is not the spiritual that comes first, but the physical, and then the spiritual. The first man is of the dust of the earth; the second man is from heaven. Those who are of the earth are like him who was of the earth, and those who are of heaven are like him who is from heaven, and as we have been like the man of the earth, let us also try to be like the man from heaven. But I can tell you this, brothers: flesh and blood cannot share in the Kingdom of God, and decay will not share in what is imperishable. I will tell you a secret. We shall not all fall asleep, but we shall all be changed in a moment, in the twinkling of an eye, at the sound of the last trumpet. For the trumpet will sound, and the dead will be raised free from decay, and we shall be changed. For this perishable nature must put on the imperishable, and this mortal nature must put on immortality. And when this mortal nature puts on immortality, then what the Scripture says will come true—'Death has been triumphantly destroyed!' " (1 Corinthians XV:35 ff.). If flesh and blood cannot share in the Kingdom of God, if it is not a physical but a spiritual body which is raised from the dead, then the destruction of death means the immortality of the soul and then "the Kingdom of God is not a matter of what we eat or drink but of justice, peace, and happiness through possession of the holy Spirit" (Romans XIV:17).

Justice: the secret of faith.—The belief in the immortality of the soul—and that means in a justice to be realized in another, transcendental world—has a conservative character. It feeds man, suffering injustice in this world, with the hope that those who inflict evil on him will be punished after death. Hence nothing need to be done against them in this world. But the belief in the resurrection of the body as an essential element of the Kingdom of God to be realized in this world has rather a revolutionary tendency, even if the realization of this Kingdom—quite incompatible with the established state—is believed to be an act of God, and not a human enterprise.

Paul's attempt to spiritualize the Kingdom of God is certainly not caused only by the intention to avoid a direct conflict with the Roman authorities. It is closely connected with a general tendency of Paul's religious feelings, his inclination for irrationalism and mysticism. As pointed out, he was quite aware of the contradiction between the principle or retribution and the principle of love. But such contradiction exists only from the point of view of human understanding; it is relevant only within the wisdom of this world, not within the mysterious wisdom of God. And "this world's wisdom is foolishness to God" (1 Corinthians III:19). Referring to a word of Isaiah (XXIX:14), he says: "It was written: 'I will destroy the wisdom of the wise, and the cleverness of the clever I will thwart.' Where is the wise man? Where is the scribe? Where is the debater of this age? Has not God made foolish the wisdom of the world? For since, in the wisdom of God, the world did not know God through wisdom, it pleased God through the folly of what we preach to save those who believe. . . . God chose what is foolish in the world to shame the wise, God chose what is weak in the world to shame the strong" (1 Corinthians I:19–27). "Yet there is a wisdom that we impart when we are with people who have a mature faith, but it is not what this world calls wisdom, nor what the authorities of this world, doomed as they are to pass away, would call so. But it is a mysterious divine wisdom that we impart, hitherto kept secret, and destined by God before the world began for our glory. It is a wisdom unknown to any of the authorities of this world, for otherwise they would never have crucified our glorious Lord. . . . For what human being can understand a man's thoughts except the man's own spirit within him? Just so no one understands the thoughts of God but the Spirit of God. But the Spirit we have received is not that of the world, but the Spirit that comes from God, which we have to make us realize the blessings God has given us. These disclosures we impart, not in the set phrases of human philosophy, but in words the Spirit teaches, giving spiritual truth a spiritual form. A material man will not accept what the Spirit of God offers. It seems mere folly to him, and he cannot understand it, because it takes spiritual insight to see its true value. But the spiritual man is alive to all true values, but his own true value no unspiritual man can see. For who has ever known the Lord's thoughts, so that he can instruct him? But we share the thoughts of Christ" (1 Corinthians II:6 ff.). Reason and rational science are against God, and God is against reason and rational science. Hence Paul warns the Christians of the delusions of philosophy: "Take care that nobody exploits you through the pretensions of philosophy, guided by human tradition, following material ways of looking at things, instead of following Christ" (Colossians II:8). Not on human philosophy, but on faith we must rely. "When I came to you, brothers," Paul says in the First Letter to the Corinthians: "I did not come and tell you the secret purpose of God in superior, philosophical language, for I resolved, while I was with you, to forget everything but Jesus Christ and his crucifixion. For my part, I came among you in weakness and with a great deal of fear and trembling, and my teaching and message were not put in plausible, philosophical language, but they were attended with convincing spiritual power, so that your faith might rest, not on human philosophy, but on the power of God" (1 Corinthians II:1 ff.).

God's wisdom—which implies his justice—is a mystery; and faith, nothing but faith, enables us to get hold of this justice. Again and again Paul emphasizes that "God's way of justice is disclosed through faith and for faith" (Romans I:17; III:22); that "a man is made just by faith" (Romans III:28); that "justice comes from God through faith" (Philippians III:9). In the Letter to the Galatians Paul writes: "But we, by the Spirit, through faith wait for the justice we hope for. For in union with Christ Jesus, neither circumcision nor the want of it counts for anything, but only faith acting through love" (Galatians V:5 f.). This love, however, is "beyond human understanding." In the Letter to the Ephesians Paul exhorts the Christians "to let Christ in his love make his home in your hearts. Your roots must be deep and your foundations strong, so that you and all God's people may be strong enough to grasp what breadth, length, height, and depth mean, and to understand Christ's love, so far beyond our understanding, so that you may be filled with the very fullness of God" (Ephesians III:17 ff.). To human understanding the justice of love remains a secret. The same idea is expressed in the Book of Enoch, which frequently refers to the "secret of justice." At the final judgment "it shall be said to the holy [that is, the righteous] in heaven that they should seek out the secrets of justice, the heritage of faith" (1 Enoch LVIII:5).

The final result of Paul's teaching, which is the basis of the Christian theology of justice, may be formulated as follows: There is a relative, human, justice which is identical with the positive law, and an absolute, divine, justice which is the secret of faith. Hence, there is in this theology no answer to the question as to what is justice, as a question of human reason referring to an ideal which is not necessarily identical with every positive law and which can be realized in this world.

PLATONIC JUSTICE

THE mark of Platonic philosophy is a radical dualism. The Platonic world is not one of unity; and the abyss which in many ways results from this bifurcation appears in innumerable forms. It is not one, but two worlds, which Plato sees when with the eyes of his soul he envisages a transcendent, spaceless, and timeless realm of the Idea, the thing-in-itself, the true, absolute reality of tranquil being, and when to this transcendent realm he opposes the space-time sphere of his sensuous perception—a sphere of becoming in motion, which he considers to be only a domain of illusory semblance, a realm which in reality is not-being. This dualism manifests itself also in the opposition between true knowledge (*epistéme*) and mere opinion (*dóxa*), the limit (*péras*) and the unlimited (*ápeiron*), the immortal and the mortal, the divine and the human.

This multiform, protean dualism is, in the final analysis and in its most primitive sense, the opposition of good and evil. This ethical connotation is not the only one possible; but it is the primary aspect of the Platonic dualism; it is the deepest layer of Platonic thought in which all others take root as in a nourishing soil. The ethical dualism of good and evil is, as it were, an inner ring which is enveloped by the ontological and epistemological dualism which grew out of and beyond the ethical dualism itself.

It is evident that the key to all the oppositions in which Platonic thought moves, the real meaning of Platonic dualism, is to be found in the basic treatment of good and evil; but this is true not

From *Ethics*, April 1938. Translated by Glenn Negley from "Die platonische Gerechtigkeit," *Kantstudien*, 1933. (The author corrected the translation in 1957.)

merely because of the fact that, whenever this opposition between the two worlds occurs in Plato's thought, it appears as an opposition of values, as a separation between a higher and a lower world, between a realm of value and a realm of disvalue. The situation is evident first of all in the fact that the ethical maintains a position of unmistakably primary importance in the Platonic philosophy. It is only in the sphere of ethics, wherein pure thinking, freed from all sensuous experience is possible; for this thinking is, by its very nature, directed at the ethical ideal. Throughout all the manifold speculations concerned with such a vast variety of objects as we meet in the Platonic dialogues, through the many deviations from the main subject under consideration, the moral idea remains ever steady, fixed as a polestar. It alone points the way through the frequently involved trains of thought to the final goal; and this goal of the entire Platonic philosophy, the goal toward which Plato strives from the most diverse points of view and with the greatest energy from the first to the last of his works—that goal is the absolute good. The good, however, is inconceivable apart from evil. If good is to be the object of cognition, then cognition must also recognize evil; and this is true in the Platonic philosophy, which is by no means a doctrine of the good as it is usually represented, but a speculation concerning good-evil.

It is true that the idea of the good in the Platonic representation stands out more clearly than the conception of evil; the reflections concerned with good are developed with more force and clarity than are those which have evil as their object. For it is not only the thought of the moralist, it is in the first place his will which is directed at the good. Evil would not be thought of at all were it not for the necessity of conceiving it as the antithesis of the good; but it remains as subordinate—merely tolerated in the glorious apotheosis of the good. As it is only a shadow in the light of the good, it must remain a shadow in all representations of the good. Only in the last of the Platonic writings does evil assume a more solid form and become established like the good in the form of a particular substance. Only in a late period of his creativity did evil become for Plato a reality, a being, and then only after he had been forced to attribute to *becoming,* the representative of evil in the ontological dualism, originally disqualified as not being, a kind of real existence or *being.* This is the reason why the original conception of Platonic dualism holds that only the world of the Idea which is the world of the good, partakes of real existence; whereas the world of things, of becoming, must be regarded as not-being: because this world of becoming, the empirical world of sensuous, perceptible reality, the temporal world of factual events is the world of evil, in so far as it is in opposition to the world of the good. It can be none other than a world of evil, although Plato did not explicitly designate it as such. By definition, only the good ought to be; evil ought not to be; and for this reason, evil is not-being, and only the good is being. For ethical thought, the *ought* implies the *is;* because the moralist intends that evil ought not to be, it becomes for him not-being. In this manner he satisfies will by cognition; and this primacy of the will over cognition, which is decisive for moral character, appears as the primacy of the *ought* over the *is,* of value over reality.

In the pure system of the good there is no place for evil. This is expressed in the Platonic, as well as in other good-evil speculations, by denying the quality of being to evil or its ontological representative. What *ought* to be, *is;* it has "real" existence; consequently that which ought not to be cannot be, can only appear to us as being. For this reason, it is necessary that a distinction be made between true or real being and apparent being; that which has being from an ordinary point of view must be reduced to the status of a mere semblance of being. Thought which is directed toward true being must be placed above the sensuous perception of this semblance of being; ethics must take precedence over natural science in order that the good, that which ought to be, can be asserted as really being. On the other hand, that which appears as being for ordinary perception ought not to be, because it is not the good; it is evil, and as evil it is not-being. Similarly, every attempt to explain the world in ethical terms, every speculation concerning good and evil, has done—more or less—violence to the naturalistic conception. The view established by scientific cognition directed at the reality of sensuous experience, that is, at an explanation of the world, is radically turned upside down by the ethical view directed at value and justification of the world.

Because evil is the complete negation of good, ethical dualism in its original sense is absolute. The tendency to give absolute form to conceivable oppositions is a rather sure sign of normative ethics, of contemplation directed finally to value rather than upon reality, to the transcendental *ought* rather than upon the empirical *is*. In contrast to normative ethics, empirical investigation will if possible avoid working with absolute opposites. Rather will it endeavor to relate what oppositions are presented, that is, to assume degrees of difference, gradual passages from one to another, arranging the abundance of phenomena in a series according to quantitative differences so that each passes over into the other. It is, therefore, concerned above all with the notion of evolution. Even the history of Greek thought shows us how the cognition of nature undertook to free itself of religious and ethical speculation by making relative the opposites upon which such speculative views of the world are based. In general, all such opposites of religious and ethical specu- lation are derived from the fundamental opposition between good and evil. Thus, the process of making relative this fundamental opposition of good and evil is one of the bridges over which human thought passes on from ethics to natural science. The decisive point in this process is this: Not only the good, but evil also, is conceived as being, as reality; consequently, empirical reality is perceived not only as evil, but also as good, as a mixture of good and evil. This process of making relative the opposition between good and evil is the first step toward the abandonment of an exclusively normative interpretation of the world by the good-evil speculation; that spec- ulation is driven backward in favor of an objective cognition of empirical reality.

In the original Platonic conception of world structure, there is clearly present an inclination to make absolute this fundamental dualism of good and evil. Between the two worlds into which the whole universe is split, between the realms of *dóxa* and *epistéme*, Plato assumes an unmitigated opposition. If the path which leads from the world of mere appearance to the cognition of true be- ing is to be followed, it is necessary that there be a complete liberation from the world of sensuous experience, a radical "about- face"; but this complete turning-away from the world of sensuality to the spiritual world would be incomprehensible if it did not at the same time signify a turning-away from evil and a turning- toward the good. What Plato means by the famous image of the cave is "that the true analogy for this indwelling power in the soul and the instrument whereby each of us apprehends is that of an eye that could not be converted to the light from the darkness except by turning the whole body. Even so this organ of knowledge must be turned around from the world of becoming together with the entire soul . . . until the soul is able to endure the contemplation of essence and the brightest region of being. And this, we say, is the good, do we not?" In this connection, however, we are told that the soul which, although possessing good power of perception, cannot completely achieve this "turning-around," it is "forcibly enlisted in the service of evil, so that the sharper its sight the more mischief it accomplishes"; it is burdened by "the leaden weights, so to speak, of our birth and becoming, which . . . turn downwards the vision of the soul." [1] Only if the sphere of sensuous perception signifies the evil, and that of thought indicates the good, can one understand the refusal to unite sensuous perception and thought. In this doctrine of complete reversal there is expressed no epistemological insight. Only the ethical experience of a sinner who has become a saint can approach awareness of the typical adventure of such an overwhelming conversion. It is the speculation on good and evil which coördinates the opposite of sensuous perception and thought with that of the particular and the idea, respectively; and thus the opposition is maintained right into the absolute itself.

On the other hand, there is evidence in Plato's doctrine of a tendency to make these opposites relative. His thought is as divided as the world which it reflects. Thus one sees in his work a rugged dualism which tolerates no bridges over which cognition might proceed from one world to the other, and a profound pessimism which denies this world and the possibility of knowing it in order to affirm that other world in being and knowing. Plato expresses a pessimistic dualism which is as extreme as any ever dared by a genius who scorned nature and natural science. It is extreme in that he denies the possibility of empirical science and proclaims the only object of true cognition to be that which lies beyond experience. At the same time, he is obviously striving to fill up in some manner the chasm between the two worlds by introducing in a middle term—a mediator for the implacable opposition of these products of dualistic speculation. This doctrine of *metaxý* appears in many forms; but always it is the symptom of a turning-away from pessimistic dualism to an attitude which recognizes also the reality of the empirical world.

II

The intellectual activity of great moralists is rooted in their personal life to a greater extent than is true of other thinkers, because all speculation of good and evil arises out of profound moral experience. So the compelling pathos which appears in the work of Plato, his tragic dualism and the heroic effort to overcome it, are deeply grounded in the particular character of Plato as an individual, as well as in circumstance and in the conditioning of his personal attitude toward life by these factors.

The course of Plato's life is essentially determined by the passion of love, the Platonic Eros. The image of Plato's life which can be made out from the documents left by him does not picture the cold, contemplative nature of a scholar who is content to look upon the world merely as an object of knowledge. Here is no philosopher whose meditation and endeavor are directed solely to the observation and penetration of the machinery of human and external phenomena merely to the end of attaining an explanation of the perplexities of experience. Rather, there appears here a soul shaken by the most violent passions, a human soul in which lives, in intimate and inextricable union with his Eros, an indomitable will to power, the power over men. To love men and at the same time to shape them, to love them in the very shaping itself, and to make their community into a community of love—this is the aspiration of Plato's life. His aim was to form men and to reform their community. Thus, there is nothing with which his thought is more concerned than with education and the state; and, as a consequence, his greatest problem becomes that of the good or justice, which in itself constitutes the only justification for the government of men over men, the only legitimate aspect of education and the state. The pedagogical and political passion of Plato, however, has its origin in his Eros. Having once recognized that this Eros is the dynamic source of the Platonic philosophy, we cannot then ignore a consideration of the peculiar nature of that Eros, for it is the nature of the Eros which determines Plato's personal relation to society in general and to the democratic society of Athens in particular. It is likewise the explanation of his flight from the very world he desires to dominate, in order that he may the better model it according to his own desire.

This Eros, the love of youths, set Plato in opposition to society and to the world in general, for it does not appear in him as an extension and enrichment of the normal sex' life as was usual in the aristocratic Athenian society (but only in this, and not in the lower social levels). Plato's nature excludes the normal sex life. As a rule, those who loved beautiful youths had also a wife and child at home, as did Socrates; but no woman played any part in Plato's life. Marriage, which was surrounded with a halo of sanctity by Greek religion, and the family, which was a fundamental element of the Greek state, remained foreign to Plato, who spent his life in a circle of men. He felt himself unable to fulfil the most important patriotic duty—that of providing the state with new citizens by begetting legitimate offspring; and this must have been all the more painful to him because his entire intellectual attitude was directed against the moral decline of the time and aimed at the reëstablishment of ancestral morality. In this complete singularity lies the danger of a profound conflict with social reality, the laws of which are strange to the philosopher's temperament. Outside of the realm of Dorian culture, and especially in Athens, pederasty was looked upon with contempt; Aristotle stigmatized it in his *Nicomachean Ethics* as an unnatural vice. No trace of it is to be found in Homer. The great tragedians, Aeschylus and Sophocles, in spite of their personal inclinations, appear not to have dared to declare themselves publicly in favor of it. Euripides directly disapproved of it; comedy, especially the works of Aristophanes, scourged it with the sharpest scorn and irony; the Sophists attacked it decisively. Even the Athenian penal law shows a clear tendency of opposition to pederasty.[2]

The severe attitude of condemnation which Athenian society took against this Eros is indicated, although indirectly, in the Platonic dialogues *Symposium* and *Phaedrus,* wherein Plato defended this boy-loving Eros against the official view, confessing to it himself, although only in its spiritualized form. But this Eros was characterized by the old Plato in his last work as dangerous for the state, as the source of "countless evils both to individuals and to whole States."[3] This was undoubtedly written at a time when Plato had been freed from the tyranny of this Eros. As a youth and as a man he avoided open conflict only by the endeavor which he made from the very beginning with unparalleled energy and great moral strength to spiritualize this Eros. Forcing his Eros into the service of his philosophy, Plato explains the vision of beloved boys as the first step on the road to knowledge of the good. In doing this he strips his Eros of the sensuality which is its very nature, completely sublimating it under the pressure of social views and his own moral convictions. He thereby achieves for himself the desired justification of the Eros. It is in the *Symposium,* that supreme song of Platonic love, that the philosopher justifies his Eros (from which he may have suffered more than the dialogue indicates), thereby justifying himself and at the same time justifying the world itself. To Socrates' question concerning the real nature of the Eros, Plato has the prophetess Diotima answer: "He is a great spirit [*daimon*], and like all spirits he is intermediate between the divine and the mortal . . . the mediator who spans the chasm which divides them, and therefore in him all is bound together." [4] What had originally split the Platonic world unites it once again. Eros produced the separation; Eros is responsible for the reunion.

With this the Platonic dualism takes an optimistic turn. With the tendency to make the opposition of good and evil relative, the Platonic philosophy turns its attention to this world and aims at a unified world view which will comprise nature. The nature which it comprises will not be considered merely from an ethical point of view, that is, as something that *ought* to be or *ought* not to be, but will be conceived as something that *is,* because it is no longer conceived as absolutely evil and hence as not being but as participating —in different degrees—in real being. This new direction of his thought leads him back to society and the state. In this connection it is of the greatest importance to note that Plato, in the speech of Diotima—as in the speeches of all guests at the banquet—emphasizes the social nature of his Eros as a defense against the usual reproach that it is inimical to society and dangerous to the state. Plato affirms repeatedly that the boy-loving Eros, if it is spiritualized (and it is the only love capable of spiritualization), is a procreative force. Through the prophetess he makes it known that the most beautiful children propagated by this spiritual Eros include not only poetry and the works of sculpture but also the arts of social order, of constitutions, laws, and works of justice. Among these "immortal children," who are more valuable than mortal offspring,

Plato names the laws of Solon and the children "Lycurgus left behind him to be the saviour, not only of Lacedaemon, but of Hellas." [5] This is a most personal confession of Plato's, for these are the children which his Eros desired: the best laws, the just order of the state, the right education of youth. Here is revealed most clearly the inner connection which existed between the Platonic Eros and his will to power over men, between his erotic and his pedagogico-political passions.

III

Recent investigation of Plato has shaken the opinion that Plato was a theoretical philosopher whose aim was the establishment of rigorous science. Today it is known that Plato was by temperament more a politician than a theorist. One considers him today as a *Herrenmenschen* of an imperious temperament; one sees in him primarily the educator and founder. Whether he really was such a person, whether he actually possessed the characteristics which accompany the will to power, whether he had the capacity of a genius of action, one may perhaps doubt. We can be certain only that his personal ideal lay in this direction: He desired to be what for reasons of external and internal circumstances was denied to him. His entire intellectual position is less a view of the *is* than a regard for the *ought* which always is directed to will rather than to cognition; and since his ethical political will was thoroughly grounded in metaphysics and consequently expressed in an outspoken religious ideology, his works give not so much the impression of a learned system of moral science as of a prophecy of the ideal state. Plato is revealed less as a psychologist or a sociologist concerned with social reality than as a preacher of justice.

Testimony of this is to be found primarily in Plato's autobiography, the so-called *Epistle VII*, in which the now old man, in one of his most serious moments, gives to the world an account of his life. Here Plato confesses that his real desire, from youth onward, has been politics, and that he has waited all his life for the opportune moment to act. But even if we did not have this confession of Plato, it is nonetheless clear from his dialogues themselves that there existed for him this primacy of political will over theoretical knowledge. The fact that the principal problem of his philosophy to which all others are subordinated is the question concerning justice, betrays the fact that above all he is interested in finding a moral foundation for activity. From an abundance of detail in Plato's writings it appears that the keynote in the chord of this great life is political passion, that his most ardent desire is for mastery of the state. Even though it had not been expressed in direct and indirect intimations, yet it is betrayed by the principal thesis of the Platonic philosophy that it is to be the task of the philosophers to rule. He is stubborn in this demand that all power in the state be vested in philosophy, but not in just any philosophy. Power is to reside in the one true philosophy which alone leads to the knowledge of justice and makes legitimate the claim of mastery: Plato's philosophy.

Further, it is not only in Plato's work that indications are to be found of this political passion but likewise in his very life. His life stands in the shadow of a political undertaking that dated from his first journey to Sicily, when he was about forty years old, an undertaking which concerned him almost until his death, and which made unhappy the latter days of his life. This was the effort of Plato to win over to his ideas the tyrant of Syracuse, Dionysius II. Plato was driven to this fatal step by his demonic Eros, by his passionate love for Dion, a young relative of the tyrant. Dion, animated perhaps by the best of intentions, perhaps only to realize the political ideals of Plato, attempted to seize control of Syracuse. This effort however only succeeded in involving the Platonic Academy, or at least some of its prominent members, in a bloody civil war, in the course of which was destroyed the great Sicilian empire founded originally by Dionysius I—one of the strongest state organizations achieved by Hellenism, and perhaps its last stronghold in the ancient world. The name of the Platonic Academy was not exactly covered with honor in this catastrophe.

The role which the Platonic Academy played in the questionable undertaking of Dion—a role which Plato tacitly tolerated—is not the only ground for suspecting that the Academy was not, as it has so long been considered, merely a school of learning, peaceful, withdrawn from the cares of the world, and devoted to pure science. The Academy which Plato had founded soon after his return from his first voyage to Sicily, and which received encouragement especially from aristocratic circles, was a conventicle patterned upon the Pythagorean societies, a community founded upon the Platonic religion and the Platonic Eros. It is particularly in the political function of the Academy, in its character as a preparation for the vocation of statesmanship, that one recognizes its primary object. The decided antidemocratic, aristocratic tendencies of the Academy made it a stronghold of reactionary thought; but it was not only the center of education of conservative politicians—it was likewise the center of political activity as is indicated by the adventure in Syracuse. The attitude of the Academy corresponded to the fundamental intellectual position of Plato for whom education was the compensation for politics and school the virtual cell of the ideal state. The work of the Academy was not directed so much upon exact science as upon ethical and mystical speculation. Thus the school has correctly been termed a "metaphysical sect"; it indicates the final conclusion of the Platonic attitude as exemplified in the last years of Plato's life. This position is marked by a complete turning away from Socratic rationalism through a continually increasing insight into the transcendental nature of the object of all ethical cognition, together with a conviction of the impossibility of representing its result rationally. Because the irrational does not lend itself to rational expression, Plato resorts more and more to myths when he wishes to explain that which he considers essential. No man of science would do that. Plato discovers something higher and more important than exact theory lying close to his heart, and in attempting to give it expression he speaks in dark prophetic words like a seer of the world beyond, rather than as a scientist of this world.

Plato has perplexed his readers by the declaration that his published works are not to be taken as expressing his true thought, that in fact they are not even to be considered as his own work. If one may consider *Epistle II* as genuine, then Plato has said that he wrote nothing upon the real subject of his philosophy nor upon the ultimate or highest problem thereof. In this letter, the statement is made: "No treatise by Plato exists or will exist, but those which now bear his name belong to a Socrates become fair and young." [6] This is not the attitude of a scholar whose thought is directed to scientific knowledge; it is not the act of a man of science defending his theory simply to shake off the responsibility for works published over a period of years and to refuse to rise in their defense. That is rather the way of a politician for whom the theory is not an end in itself, but the means to an entirely different end: namely, to an end which seeks, not to quench man's thirst for knowledge, but rather to determine his will, to form his character, to educate and to govern him. We must then admit that there is no specific Platonic theory anywhere, that is, no doctrine which is inseparably connected with the name of Plato, at least none of which we have knowledge. This is as Plato wished.

There is a profound significance in the peculiar fact that Plato never appears as the representative of the opinions developed in the works which bear his name; he first presents these views through the person of Socrates, later through another, the Athenian Stranger. That is the real reason why he chose the dialogue form. Doubtless this literary form appealed to his disunited nature, torn as it was with a tragic conflict; it was more appealing to him than the monologue form of a scientific treatise in which only one opinion appears, and which thus can present only one side of a given problem. Who could feel more keenly than Plato the necessity of allowing his adversary as well as himself an opportunity to speak? Plato had this very adversary in his own breast, and it was only by allowing him to speak that Plato could be delivered of his internal conflict.

Plato found, however, another and even greater value than that of catharsis in the dialogue form; he discovered in this kind of presentation a possible escape from the necessity of identifying himself positively with any theory, however well founded it might be. The dialogues are dramatic, and in drama none of the opinions expressed by the persons acting can positively be taken as the opinion of the dramatist; and this is true even though the dramatist allows the actor to develop an opinion with all the force of persuasive rhetoric, or even to attest it by his activity. In the same manner Plato is unwilling in the last resort to take upon himself the doctrine which he expresses through Socrates. Because the metaphysical-religious character of his philosophy precludes expression in words, he will not even agree that what Socrates has said is the substance of his thought. It has repeatedly been said that Plato is not only a philosopher, but also, indeed even more, a poet; and that many of his works present beautiful dramas rather than the results of scientific research. Indeed, Plato is a poet in the sense that he is little concerned with what his characters say; whether their declarations are more or less true is a matter of little consequence to him. That to which Plato does attach the utmost importance is the effect produced by these speeches, their dialectical movement to a breath-taking climax, and the descending relief; but this technique is not productive of scientific conclusions. Plato is indeed a dramatist, except that his desired effect is not aesthetic, but of a religious and moral nature. Plato's knowledge is therefore not an end in itself. Science for him, as for the Pythagoreans, is only a means to an end. Man needs knowledge in order to act rightly; and just for this reason, the only real knowledge is that of the good, of divinity.

A world separates this Platonic conception from that of modern science, which rests upon the fundamental presuppositions that knowledge is to be sought for its own sake, that science be not directed toward an end outside itself, that its conclusions are not to be determined by the necessities of will and activity, that is, by ruling and being ruled, namely, by politics. Science is therefore primarily natural science; but it is likewise true that the science of man's will and activity and of the relations of men in society, even the modern science of the state, of law, and of society, rests upon an inexorable postulate of complete independence from politics and from religion. To know the world, either as nature or as society, is an entirely different end than that of determining the world by will, of forming or reforming it, of educating or dominating it. It is the vital law of all pure knowledge that it be carried on for its own sake. This law applies especially to the social sciences, for when these sciences are placed in the service of politics they can no longer serve the ideal of objective truth but must become an ideology of power. How great was the tendency of Platonic philosophy in this direction is indicated by Plato's conception of truth, Platonic truth, which is so characteristic that, together with Platonic love, it can be taken as an essential element of the Platonic thought.

IV

The Platonic conception of truth set forth in the *Republic* is the doctrine which justifies, even necessitates, the lie as a means to the best government; and this implies the further distinction of bad and "true" lies. A "true" lie is wholesome, a state truth, the *raison d'état*. Plato says that in the ideal state (which is the state governed by Platonic philosophy), government must use some frauds and deceits for "the welfare of the governed."

The necessity for lies on the part of government appears, to cite but one example, in the state regulation of birth control. The couples selected under state guidance for the purpose of propagation must be deceived in order that they will not consider themselves merely as instruments in the hands of the government. They must believe that fate (through the drawing of lots) has destined them for one another. According to Plato's device, parents whose children are not reared because of their inferior quality will be inclined to put the blame upon chance rather than upon government.[7] Plato excludes the painter, and also the poet who merely imitates, from his ideal state because these arts are "delusions" and not strictly true;[8] yet he has not the least scruple about this monstrous infringement upon the most intimate realm of man's life. In this personal sphere lies a vital state interest, and the interest of the state, which in the ideal state coincides with justice, is above all else in importance—even above truth itself. The maxim that "the end justifies the means" stands out quite clearly as a principle of Platonic political theory; and this maxim is a direct consequence of the primacy assumed by will over knowledge, by justice over truth. From the political point of view, which is of greater importance than all others, it is not so essential to know whether what the subjects believe is true as it is to know whether what they believe is useful to the state—whether it is to the interest of maintaining a just order in society. Therefore, Plato claims the right of government to determine the opinion of its citizens by any means which appear appropriate. In the dialogue *Laws*, Plato makes a number of surprising proposals in this connection.[9] To cite but one example, it will be remembered that Plato, in order to engender and guarantee a suitable attitude on the part of the citizens, proposes to divide them into three choruses: one for boys, one for youths, and one for old men. These choruses shall be required to sing the songs which are prescribed by the government—songs embodying teachings which are of use to the state; above all, they must proclaim the teaching that justice is conductive to happiness, injustice to unhappiness. Thus the belief in the truth of this teaching is propagated.

In this connection, Plato says: "And even if the state of the case were different from what it has now proved to be by our argument, could a lawgiver who was worth his salt find any more useful fiction than this . . . or one more effective in persuading all men to act justly in all things willingly and without constraint?" It is conceivable that there will be opposition to this program from the old men, for it is natural that with increasing years one feels a growing timidity about singing and dancing in public; thus it will be necessary to see that the members of the third or Dionysian chorus are induced to intoxication under the direction of a government official. In this drunken state they may be as easily managed as children. These statements are the more remarkable because Plato is clearly aware of the dangers of alcoholism and desires that the consumption of wine by the rest of the population be severely limited. He states here the famous simile of men as puppets in the hands of divinity, the divine operator of the puppet show.[10] In like manner government, which is the representative of divinity, may manipulate the wires while keeping itself invisible as far as possible. The only justification of this procedure is that it is for the best interests of man—that only in this manner can justice be realized. Plato makes other proposals which all aim at forcing science, poetry, and religion, in their function as producers of ideologies, into the service of the state. Indeed, he goes so far as to propose the suppression of all liberty of thought by instituting a state monopoly upon ideology—thus establishing a dictatorship to which not only the will and activity of men must submit, but also their opinions and beliefs.

It is perhaps not surprising to find that Plato as a politician or theorist of politics takes a position similar to that of pragmatism, that he declares that what is useful for the state, and therefore constitutes justice, likewise constitutes truth. One cannot escape the occasional impression, however, that Plato, in his capacity as an epistemologist and psychologist, is making the reservation of a possible duality of truth, although he does not say so directly. How else can we explain the fact that he develops, on the one hand, his theory of ideas with a pronounced monotheistic tendency, and, at the same time, affirms the official religion of the people which with its multiplicity of anthropomorphic gods was quite incompatible with this monotheism? Again in his theory of ideas, only the universal has eternal being, which is generally denied to particulars; yet the Platonic conception of the immortality of the soul attributes eternal being to the individual personality of man in its most particular form. Further, why is it that in a work which is so extremely personal in nature as the *Symposium*, no reference whatever is made to the immortality of the soul in the sense of a continuation of an individual soul substance, but only reference in a figurative sense to the continuation of name and glory?

One hesitates to suggest that only simple contradictions are to be found in the thought of such a powerful intellect as that of Plato. The inclination is rather to admit that Plato was well aware of these differences in his doctrine; that they represented for him different degrees of truth analogous to the different degrees of the Eros; that there appeared for Plato in particular a pedagogic, political, religious truth in addition to scientific rational truth. Plato considered the political religious truth to be the more important, and it therefore occupies a position of primacy in relation to rational truth. In describing how the soul reaches the other world after death, Plato says in the dialogue *Phaedo*:

A man of sense ought not to say, nor will I be very confident, that the description I have given of the soul and her mansions is exactly true. But I do say that, inasmuch as the soul is shown to be immortal, he may venture to think, not improperly or unworthily, that something of the kind is true. The venture is a glorious one, and he ought to comfort himself with words like these, which is the reason why I lengthen out the tale.[11]

When Plato teaches in the *Meno* that knowledge depends upon the recollection by the soul of what it has seen in the other world before its birth, he adds: "Some things I have said of which I am not altogether confident." [12] The decisive argument which he adduces in opposition to the Sophistic teaching of the impossibility of any knowledge is that the Platonic doctrine is to be preferred because that of the Sophists "will make us idle, and is sweet only to the sluggard; but the other saying will make us active and inquisitive." [13] Plato establishes the truth of his doctrine by reference to its vital utility. It is a pedagogical political truth which he characteristically supports, not by scientific explanation, but by reference to ancient teachings of religion.

These are the presuppositions which one must understand before his doctrine of justice can be fully comprehended.

V

The dialogues written by Plato in his youth while he was yet under the influence of Socrates, wherein he treats either directly or indirectly of the problem of justice, lose themselves in a sterile analysis of concepts, in empty tautologies; they are more or less without result. Especially characteristic of this early and wholly rationalistic period of Plato's creativity is the *Thrasymachus,* a work probably begun before Plato's first voyage to Syracuse. It was not entirely finished, at any rate it was not separately published; but it was later incorporated in the first book of the *Republic.* After a rather protracted discussion in which Socrates has tried by every available means to reach a definition of justice, this section of the *Republic* finally ends in Socrates' declaration that for him the result of the entire discussion is merely the information that he knows nothing, for the real and decisive question as to the essence of justice has not been discussed. As long as one does not know what the just is, one can hardly arrive at a decision as to whether or not it is a virtue, or whether the just man is happy. If the assumption about the time Plato started writing the first book of the *Republic* is correct, then the last words constitute a transition by means of which Plato has inserted the thought of a much earlier period into a work of his adult mature years. These words reveal to us the reason why the *Thrasymachus* remained unfinished: Socrates, with all his rationalistic speculation upon concepts, had not been able to lead Plato to a knowledge of the nature of justice. When Plato left his *Thrasymachus* unfinished, he stood at the turning point of his life, on the eve of a journey to southern Italy, where he became acquainted with the political and religious metaphysics of the

Pythagorean school. This Pythagoreanism became a new guide for him, a guide to which he remained faithful throughout the rest of his life. He believed that in Pythagoreanism he had found the answer to the most burning question—the mystery of justice.

The essence of the Pythagorean doctrine, which on this point agrees with the wisdom of the Orphic mysteries, is the belief that after death the soul of man will be punished for evil done and rewarded for the good. This punishment and reward may be accomplished in another world or by means of reincarnation in this world. The implication of this ethical religious conception, and it is the same wherever found, is a justification of the world as given, and especially of social phenomena. This results from the conviction that good will finally triumph over evil. From a political point of view, this metaphysics of a future world of souls, or of metempsychosis, indicates a doctrine of justice whose essence is retribution. In so far as this retribution is not realized in this world in the lives of good and bad men, it will be put off to the other world or to a second life in this world. This is the doctrine presented by Plato in his dialogue *Gorgias,* which was written either during his first voyage or immediately thereafter. The principal moral theses of this work are that it is better to suffer injustice than to commit it, and that it is better to submit to legal punishment than to evade it. The final proof of these theses does not rest upon the rather doubtful demonstration of Socrates, the principal figure in this dialogue also; rather, they depend upon the splendid myth which Plato relates in conclusion, wherein he describes how the good are rewarded and the evil punished in the other world. This prophetic belief, first set out in the *Gorgias,* the belief that justice is retribution in the other world, dominates the work of Plato from this point until his death. It constitutes the leitmotif of the second great dialogue devoted to the problem of justice, the *Republic,* Plato's masterpiece, which forms the center of his creativity.

This work begins [14] and ends with the myth of retribution in the other world; and this conception serves as the frame of reference for all that is to be said in the *Republic* about justice. It might appear that it is precisely in this dialogue that Plato shows an inclination to separate the idea of justice from that of retribution, for it is here that one of the speakers, Adeimantus, supports the view that justice is not adequately praised if one continues to refer only to

the reward of good and the punishment of evil. If one is to commend justice sufficiently, one must represent it without any reference whatever to retribution. Socrates does not contradict this assertion at the time; but at the end of the dialogue he expressly re-
pudiates this earlier tacit admission. Plato closes the *Republic* with
an account of a story by a mysterious stranger risen from the dead,
who reports the things which his soul has seen in the other world.
It is the same vision, with certain digressions, as is contained in the
final myth of his *Gorgias,* namely, the realization of divine justice
as retribution in the other world. Plato remained faithful to this
conception even in his last dialogue, the *Laws.*

The acceptance of retribution in the other world necessarily
implies a belief in the soul. In searching for justice in the other
world Plato found the soul in this world, indeed found it within
man. The soul must continue to live after death in a transcendental sphere in order that it be the object of retribution. The
intimate connection between Plato's doctrines of the soul and of
justice is obvious, not only in the fact that he always presents the
one in conjunction with the other, especially in his principal work
on the doctrine of the soul, in *Phaedo,* but likewise in the modifications through which the doctrine of soul passes. This is indicated
by the transition from the idea of the soul as a unity to the conception of the tripartite soul; and this transition is parallel to
corresponding modifications in the doctrine of justice. As the
problem of justice inevitably leads to the doctrine of the soul, so
this latter leads to the doctrine of ideas. The belief in the realization of justice in the other world compels the conception of a
future existence of the soul; the necessity of a cognition of the
nature of justice leads to the conception of a preëxistence of the
soul, to the theory of knowledge as reminiscence by the soul of
what it has seen in the other world before its birth to this world.
This theory is developed for the first time in *Meno;* and here lies
the germ of the doctrine of ideas. What the soul has seen in its
preëxistence is ideas, and above all, the idea of justice.

While Plato identifies justice with retribution, he does not only
take over the Orphic-Pythagorean doctrine, but he accepts a view
of the Greek people which has come down from antiquity. It might
appear, and it may so have seemed to Plato when he wrote the
Gorgias, that with the formula of retribution he has given the

54284

answer to the question concerning the nature of justice. But this answer is only an apparent one; it gives no real information as to the nature of justice. Fundamentally it describes only the actual function of positive law, which merely connects the evil of the delict with the evil of the sanction as its consequence. It only reflects the external structure of the existing social order which is a coercive order; and this order is justified by representing the mechanism of guilt and punishment as a special case of a general principle which—as the will of divinity—is the law of retribution. Taken by itself the concept of retribution is as empty as that of equality, which is usually considered to be the characteristic of justice. Indeed, retribution is itself a formula of equality, since it says nothing more than that the good will be for the good, evil for the evil; that like is for like, which, in its primitive meaning, amounts to saying "To each his due." But what is the good, what exactly is the nature of that good of which evil must be the negation? This decisive question remains unanswered. The question as to the nature of justice thus resolves into the question concerning the nature of the good.

This is exactly the turn taken by the problem of justice in the doctrine of ideas; for the central idea—the idea from which all other ideas derive their illumination, the idea which lies beyond the sphere of all other ideas as the realm of pure being—is the idea of the good. It appears thus in that representation of the doctrine of ideas given by Plato in his great dialogue on justice, the *Republic*. Here the relation between the good and the just is determined by the statement that the latter becomes useful and advantageous only by the use of the former; which is to say that the idea of justice derives its only value from the idea of the good.[15] The good is thus the substance of justice, and for this reason Plato frequently identifies them. If these two be distinguished, then justice, as retribution, is merely the technique for the realization of the good. Then justice, so far as it refers to earthly matters, is the state, functioning as the coercive apparatus of retribution. It is the state which must guarantee the triumph of good over evil in this world. Since the good is strictly a social category, it follows that it is only in the state that man can act in conformity with the good; indeed, it is only in the state that man as its organ can even know the good. Therefore, it appears that the work called *Republic* (actually *The State*) is designed to furnish an answer to the question concerning the substance of justice. Therefore, the central point of the *Republic* is in the explication of the problem of the good; and it is for this reason that the culmination of this work on the state is the theory of ideas, the highest of which appears to be the idea of the good.

What the good actually is, however, one does not learn from this dialogue, which confines itself to the affirmation that the good exists. The whole grandiose heaven of ideas which is erected beyond the earthly world is but the philosophical and poetical expression of this affirmation. Thus the construction of the ideal state which Plato outlines in the *Republic* is no solution of the material problems concerning the nature of justice. It is a misapprehension to assume that Plato's account of the true state furnishes the finished plan of a state order. Nor is this what Plato intended— at least in the first place. The description of an ideal state is not the principal problem of the *Republic;* indeed only a small part of the work is devoted to this subject. If Plato does present a state "arising in thought before our eyes," it is because he presumes an analogy between the state and man, and believes that one can find easier in the larger proportions of the state what he is seeking in man: the good constitution, the suitable relationship between the individual parts of the soul; and this, as later appears, is not itself justice, but the presupposition of man acting justly. Plato mainly represents the constitution of the state, its organization, not a complete order regulating material human relations. In the life of society, he shows only the conditions of organization under which life will presumably be shaped to the ends of justice; but he does not explicate this justly regulated life itself, nor does he indicate the multiplicity of norms which regulate human relationships, and themselves constitute the essence of justice. Further, the constitution of the ideal state, from a legal point of view, is scarcely more than a fragment which leaves all decisive questions in doubt. Especially is there no trace to be found of a solution of the social-political problem. The measure concerning the community of goods, of women and children, which is applicable only to the comparatively small social strata of warriors and philosophers, has significance only as an organizing factor. This measure has as its purpose the education and selection of leaders and has nothing at all to do with economic or political communism. No general norm is to be found for the regulation of the life of the people who submit to the two reigning classes. Here everything is left to the individual decisions of the government, which consists of the philosophers who, because of their education, know the good and therefore will it. But in what does this good consist that is to be realized in government? What is the substance of the acts of governing? Only from the answer to these questions can one learn the nature of justice.

Plato himself says that the description of the tripartite division of the social organism as the constitution of the true state shall in no wise be taken as an answer to the question concerning the nature of justice. This demonstrates the peculiarity of his method, the continual postponement of the solution of problems. At the very beginning of the conversation, Plato allows Socrates, who is to give the solution, to make a statement which in itself precludes all finality and certainty in anything that may follow: "Why how, my dear fellow, could anyone answer, if in the first place he did not know and did not even profess to know, and secondly, even if he had some notion of the matter, he had been told by a man of weight that he mustn't give any of his suppositions as an answer?" [16] This is not merely a statement dictated by modesty. The mysterious intimation of an obligation to silence means that what Plato might say concerning justice—apart from the refutation of false opinions—would not possess final truth, that his exposition could not penetrate to reality. That this is its meaning is confirmed by the content of the dialogue.

After the constitution of the ideal state and its three classes is set out, there is no statement: This is the justice for which we have been searching. The general principle which results from this constitution, namely, that each shall do only his own work, the principle of the division of labor (which is suitable here as in every constitution which distributes competence according to different organs)—this principle is not admitted unreservedly to be the principle of justice. Rather, there is proposed an examination as to whether this principle may be applied to a comparison between the state and the individual soul. "But if not," it is said, "then we will look for something else." [17] It is apparent that Plato is aware from the beginning that the attempt to arrive at the nature of justice by means of an analogy between state and individual will not succeed, at least not completely. This is indeed the case. After the parallel has been established and the three parts of the soul which correspond to the three parts of the state have been found, one might believe that the answer to the question of the nature of justice is obvious, even though not particularly significant. This answer would be that the three parts of the soul—the rational, the spirited, and that where the appetites are seated—each of these shall exercise its proper function and none other. In this connection Socrates declares: "In my opinion, we shall never in the world apprehend this matter from such methods as we are now employing in discussion. For there is another longer and harder way that conducts to this." [18] As a matter of fact he does not take this other way; he is satisfied for the present to continue with his inexact method. This leads to the conclusion that just action results in the true state when the philosophers, with the help of the warriors, rule over the working class in the same manner in which the individual man arrives at just action by governing his passions with the rational part of the soul, in which he is assisted by the spirited element. Just action thus results from activity which is directed by reason. The question of the substance of justice is referred to the substance of reason. There follows a comparison of justice with the well-being of the soul, which means nothing more than the right constitution of the soul, and is therefore not enlightening as to the analogy between the soul and state constitutions. After a rather long digression from the proper subject of justice, Socrates returns to his observation that actually a longer and more detailed way is necessary in order to understand the nature of justice. Thus at a somewhat advanced stage of the dialogue (we are already in the sixth book), the knowledge which has thus far been attained concerning the nature of justice is again disavowed.

The peculiarity of the method which Plato uses in treating of the problem of justice appears clearly here. Just as one appears to have arrived at an answer to the question, the position attained is abandoned; the result obtained is withdrawn as inexact or erroneous, and the end is again postponed. At this point of the discussion Plato makes use of his peculiar technique by substituting for the concept of justice that of the good, as he had earlier substituted the concept of reason. The question as to the nature of justice becomes then the question as to the nature of the good; but when Socrates finds it necessary to answer the question as to what he considers the good to be, he repeats the play begun at the beginning of the discussion when he was first asked the question as to the nature of justice. He declares again that he knows nothing, and seeks to evade the question, so that his companion in the discussion, Glaucon, exclaims: "In heaven's name, Socrates, do not draw back, as it were, at the very goal. For it will content us if you explain the good even as you set forth the nature of justice, sobriety, and the other virtues." Again the expected result is discredited as not final; and Socrates makes fertile use of the admission that the good can be defined only inexactly, for he declares: "Let us dismiss for the time being the nature of the Good in itself; for to attain to my present surmise of that seems a pitch above the impulse that wings my flight today." [19] Plato has left "the nature of the Good in itself" in this unsatisfactory state, not only for the present, but for eternity, and not only in the *Republic,* but in all other dialogues. He never answers the question.

Instead of speaking of the good, Socrates will only talk about the offspring of the good, of the son who is "most nearly made in its likeness." So the son takes the place of the father just as reason took the place of justice and was itself replaced by the good. This method of substitution has as its purpose the elevation of the object of the discussion, justice, to a degree of divinity in order that the question concerning its essential nature may thereby be evaded. Indeed, it appears in this passage that the good is for Plato the highest invisible divinity. In truth, that which we seek is divinity. Therefore questions about its essential nature are vain and impious. Discussion is thus cut short and the issue piously evaded. At the most, we can only speak of the visible son and thus perhaps gain an insight into the nature of the father. This son of the good is the sun, and as such is itself a god. Plato can say nothing of this god other than that he represents in the realm of the visible what the idea of the good represents in the realm of the conceivable. Again, nothing is said as to the nature or substance of the good, but only something concerning its position as the supreme authority. The good *is,* and is the highest of all. What it is, of what it consists, what is its criterion, how it can be recognized in human activities or in the social order, and thus what is its decisive nature for social theory and practice— these questions remain unanswered. The philosopher who rules in the ideal state will know the good. Others must be content to worship and obey.

To be sure, Plato prescribes a plan for the education of the philosophers appointed to rule. Under the proposed discipline dialectic is accorded the most important position. Dialectic is characterized by Plato as an art abstracted from all sensuous experience, which separates and relates concepts. It will lead the philosopher to the very boundary, but only to the boundary, of the knowable; it will not lead him to his specific goal—the idea of the good. The idea of the good lies beyond all being, and therefore beyond all rational or scientific knowledge. The realization of the good is reserved to another power of the soul. Considering what Plato has said in the *Symposium,* in *Phaedrus,* and especially in *Epistle VII,* one must represent the vision of the highest idea of the good as an intuitive act of sudden illumination which occurs in a moment of ecstasy. Plato describes the experience as follows: "As a result of continued application to the subject itself and communion therewith, it is brought to birth in the soul on a sudden, as light that is kindled by a leaping spark, and thereafter it nourishes itself." [20] What Plato here describes is a religious experience. The rational speculation about concepts affords no direct access to this experience; dialectic is rather to be understood as a spiritual exercise similar to that of prayer. The knowledge of the good does not follow as a logical conclusion of the dialectical process; but it is an allotment of grace to the soul which has purified itself of all sensuality by meditation.

Since Plato rejects all experience acquired through the outer senses as giving comprehension of the highest idea of the divine good, he must attain this comprehension through some experience other than that of the senses. It is not possible to have even an inner knowledge without any experience whatever; and there must therefore be an inner sense which makes this specific religious experience possible. This inner experience is specifically distinguished from the outer in that not everyone is capable of it as everyone is capable of the outer experience. Inner knowledge is possible only to a very small elite, perhaps only to a single person chosen by God. Such a person is elevated above other men because his particular experience brings him closer to divinity. This religious experience derived from such a rare inner sense cannot be expressed rationally in concepts as can the experience of the outer senses; nor can it be conveyed to others. Here it becomes self-evident that Plato can give no answer to the question concerning the absolute good which is the object of his religious experience. The essence of his God remains inexpressible. Thus may we understand Plato's paradoxical statement in *Epistle VII* that there have been no writings from him on these questions, nor will there be any, "for it does not at all admit of verbal expression like other studies."

It is not surprising that a philosopher should conceal his knowledge of the absolute good as inexpressible, or place it within the frame of an esoteric philosophy. Can this be admitted though when the philosopher is called upon to rule over the state and to be the maker of law? Plato, however, does not shrink from the consequences which this involves. As it is neither possible nor permissible to write anything concerning matters of final importance, so one must assume that a true lawgiver will not put into the laws all that is of supreme importance to him, but that he will keep this in the most sacred shrine of his heart. The secret of justice cannot be disclosed, not even in the laws of the best of lawgivers. The final conclusion of Platonic wisdom, the answer given to the question asked again and again throughout the dialogues, that is the question of the nature of justice, is this: It is a divine mystery.

Because there is no answer, the question itself must finally be rejected as inadmissible. If one may rely upon *Epistle II* as a source, Plato referring to the question concerning the nature of the good or divinity says here that the question as to the highest good is a question as to its qualities, and divinity has no qualities. This very question, Plato suggests, is the source of all unhappiness because of the pain it causes to the soul. Man must deliver himself from this query if he hopes to participate in truth.[21] This is the final consequence which results from the transcendentalism of the good and from its elevation to divinity; even the question concerning its nature becomes meaningless.

The Sophists had skeptically denied the existence of an absolute justice; Socrates had asserted it passionately and dogmatically, but was finally forced to confess that he did not know what it really was. Plato declares that one may attain this knowledge through his philosophy; but he also says that the result will be inexpressible, that the question will remain unanswered, indeed, that the question is not even admissible. Thus the road which was to lead from rationalistic relativism to the metaphysical absolute ends in religious mysticism.

It has been disputed that Plato was a mystic, and it may in fact be doubted. His philosophy has a pronounced social character; his doctrine of ideas, which culminates in the idea of justice, clearly has a political orientation. Genuine mysticism, on the other hand, is asocial; the mystical experience isolates the individual from all others. In as much as God and the world are absorbed in the subjective experience of an isolated individual, the presupposition of all society is lost, namely, the opposition of *I* and *You*. There remains in the mystical experience only the all-embracing *ego* which has been raised to the status of divinity. Therein lies the individual salvation sought by the mystic. He has no desire to reform the world, and especially not the social world, but endeavors to deliver himself from it. He must extinguish all will, and especially the will to power, in order that he may be enabled to receive divinity within himself. The experience which he seeks, the union of the *ego* with God, is for him the final goal—not the means to a social end.

In fact, Plato's teaching is a genuine mysticism at its most decisive point, for the vision of highest being is inexpressible—it is an experience which is not communicable and not the product of rational consideration. He who has seen the good, the chosen one, the object of grace, is isolated from the many who neither have, nor ever can, behold this vision. Just at the point in Plato's philosophy when one expects an objective solution, there appears merely a formula for personal salvation.

The aspect of Plato's thought which carries it beyond the frame of mystical speculation, raising it above the limits of a mere individual salvation, is the aim or goal of his mystical experience. Plato seeks the truth concerning good and evil; justice is the object of the vision which penetrates the mystery; and this vision, through which the visionary becomes a true philosopher, is the justification of the philosopher's exclusive right to rule. In *Epistle VII*, Plato so energetically emphasizes the esoteric character of his doctrine and the mystical nature of its secret that it appears he must deny to it any social function whatever. Yet here again he maintains his former demand that the philosopher, and only the philosopher, be appointed to rule. That appears to be a complete contradiction. How can a longing for individual salvation and a claim of recognition as ruler find a place in the same system? Well, they obviously found a place in the same breast, indicating a mutual endurance in some kind of compromise effected between their opposition.

The salvation of the chosen one—he who is blessed by grace—will be accomplished by the vision of the good; but this, the secret of the ruler, will also accomplish salvation for all others, i.e., for those who are ruled. These cannot follow their ruler along the path of salvation to a vision of the good, and for this reason they are excluded from ruling. They can find salvation only in complete submission to the authority of the ruler who alone knows the good and who thus wills it. Since the ruling philosopher has a knowledge of the divine good and is unique in the possession of this secret, he is entirely different from other men. The mass of the people, who have no political rights, have no choice but to believe in the wisdom and grace of the ruler. This belief is the ground of the unconditional obedience of subjects upon which the authority of the Platonic state rests. Plato's mysticism, the most complete expression of the irrational, is the justification of his antidemocratic political doctrine; it is the ideology of every autocracy.

ARISTOTLE'S DOCTRINE
OF JUSTICE

A

RISTOTLE tries to develop his moral philosophy, in his *Ethics,*
on a thoroughly rationalistic basis, in spite of the fact that his
philosophical system includes a true metaphysics which, in the last
analysis, is not without strong moral implications. It is true that
his metaphysics presents itself as an ontology, that is as a science
of being, a cognition of reality, a knowledge of the nature, the properties, and relations of being as such; it is concerned with that
which *is*—and not in the first place with that which *ought* to be or
to be done. He characterizes his metaphysics as a science which
deals with the primary causes and principles.[1] He says, "the things
which are most knowable are first principles and causes; for it
is through these and from these that other things come to be
known." But he adds that the science of first principles and causes
is supreme because it knows "for what end each action is to be done,
that is, the Good in each particular case, and in general the highest
Good in the whole of nature." Knowledge of the principles and
causes of that which *is* coincides with knowledge of that what *ought
to be or to be done,* that is the knowledge of the good, "for the
Good, that is, the end, is one of the causes." [2] Thus, in Aristotle's
metaphysics—as in any true metaphysics—the dualism of the *is*
and the *ought,* of reality and value, is abandoned. For Aristotle's—
as any true metaphysics—aims in its last instance at the concept of
God, who is at the same time the *first cause* and the ultimate end,
namely, the *absolute good.*

The starting point of the speculation leading to the Aristotelian
idea of God is the concept of motion, or, more exactly, the antago-

nism of the movable and the immovable. The movable is the realm of nature and hence the object of natural science; the immovable, so far as it exists apart, is the object of another science, the metaphysics, the "first philosophy," which Aristotle characterizes in another connection expressly as "theology," [3] that is, as the knowledge of God. This science is "the most honorable," the highest one, and as such superior to the other sciences; for its object is higher than that of the others. "The most honorable" (highest) science must deal with the "most honorable" (highest) class of subjects. Hence the antagonism of movable and immovable implies an order of values. The metaphysics or theology stands above the other sciences because the object of the former has a higher value than the objects of the latter. As the task of the first philosophy or theology Aristotle states here: "to consider being *qua* being—both what it is and the attributes which belong to it—*qua* being." [4] Thus the abstraction "being" is hypostatized as a separate entity and at the same time established as supreme, and that means as value. This ontology has the tendency to turn into an ethical theology.

If there is motion or change, there must exist something that is moved or changed and something that causes the motion or change. "Everything that changes is something, and is changed by something and into something." [5] "There is something which always moves the things that are in motion; and the first mover must itself be unmoved." [6] "There is, then, something which is always moved with an unceasing motion, which is motion in a circle. This is plain not in theory only but in fact. Therefore the first heaven must be eternal. There is therefore also something which moves it. And since that which is moved and moves is intermediate, there is a mover which moves without being moved, being eternal, substance, and actuality." [7] The first mover is the final cause of the motion and is itself unmovable. But it is at the same time the absolute good. "For the final cause is (a) some being for whose good an action is done, and (b) something at which the action aims. . . . The final cause, then, produces motion as being loved [and the object of rational love is the good], but all other things move by being moved. . . . The first mover, then, of necessity exists; and so far as it exists by necessity, its mode of being is good, and in this sense a first principle. For the necessary has all these senses—that which is necessary perforce because it is contrary to natural impulse; that without which the good is impossible; and that which cannot be otherwise but is absolutely necessary"; [8] which implies that the unmoved mover is the absolute good.

The Aristotelian metaphysics shows a clear tendency of personifying its first principle, presented as the unmoved mover and the absolute good. Life and happiness and activity are attributed to it, and its activity is characterized as thinking. "It is a life [the life of the unmoved mover, the first principle] such as the best which we [human beings] enjoy, and enjoy but for a short time. For it is ever in this state (which we cannot be) since its actuality is also pleasure." It is highly significant that Aristotle, in describing the happy life of the unmoved mover expressly speaks of it as of God. "If, then, God is always in that good state in which we sometimes are, this compels our wonder; and if in a better, this compels it yet more. And God *is* in a better state. And life also belongs to God; for the actuality of thought is life, and God is that actuality; and God's self-dependent actuality is life most good and eternal. We say therefore that God is a living being, eternal, most good, so that life and duration continuous and eternal belong to God; for this *is* God." [9]

Since God's actuality is thinking, the question arises: what is the contents of his thinking? Since God is the absolute good, this question is equivalent to the question: what is the contents of the absolute good? It is evident, says Aristotle, that God "thinks that which is most divine and precious." [10] Since the "most divine and precious" is only God himself, God can think only himself, or, what amounts to the same, his own thinking. "Therefore," says Aristotle, "it must be of itself that the divine thought thinks (since it is the most excellent of things) and its thinking is a thinking on thinking." [11] "The divine thinking will be one with the object of its thought." [12] That means that the question concerning the object of the divine thought, which in the Aristotelian metaphysics represents the absolute good, is not answered, but eliminated. The answer amounts to an empty tautology. The contents of the thinking is thinking, the good is the good.

At the end of book xii of his *Metaphysics*, which is the most informative part of this work, Aristotle raises the question "in which of two ways the nature of the universe contains the good and the highest good, whether as something separate and by itself, or as the order of the parts"; that means: whether the good is a value transcendent to empirical reality; or immanent in empirical reality. And his answer is: "Probably in both ways." [13] To illustrate this statement he compares the universe with an army, and states: "Its good is found both in its order and in its leader, and more in the latter." [14]

There can be no doubt that the leader of the army, in whom the highest good is found even more than in the army itself, is the unmoved mover. And Aristotle concludes: "The world must not be governed badly: 'The rule of many is not good; let one be the ruler.' " [15] The unmoved mover of the universe, the God of Aristotelian metaphysics is the personal ruler of the world. This ontology implies a monotheistic theology and as such a metaphysical ethics.

But this metaphysics has no essential influence on that part of Aristotle's system which is particularly devoted to the problem of morality and especially to that of justice, his treatise on moral science, his *Ethics*. We have three versions of his *Ethics*: the so-called *Nicomachean Ethics*, the *Eudemian Ethics*, and the *Great Ethics*. Nicomachus was Aristotle's son who fell in battle while still young; Eudemus was a pupil of Aristotle. The *Nicomachean Ethics* [16] is considered to be the authoritative statement of Aristotle's moral philosophy.

It is true that Aristotle starts his *Ethics* with the statement that "the good is that at which all things aim," [17] which is almost identical with the main thesis of his *Metaphysics*, that "the end for which each action is done is the good, the good in each particular case, and in general the highest good in the whole of nature"; [18] that he characterizes the good to which his *Ethics* refers as an "ultimate end," as "the supreme good," and that he defines the task of this science as: to "comprehend in outline what exactly this supreme good is." [19] This is the object of his *Metaphysics*. But he separates his *Ethics* from his *Metaphysics* by emphasizing that it is "the good for man," [20] and not the transcendent good of the unmoved mover, which his *Ethics* intends to determine. In opposition to Plato he rejects—for the purpose of his *Ethics*—the idea of an absolute good existing separately in another world. He states that "good is not a general term corresponding to a single idea." [21] He admits that different things are called good not merely by chance;

that they possibly are called good "in virtue of being derived from one good, or because they all contribute to one good." But he dismisses this question as belonging to another science [22]—the first philosophy, his *Metaphysics*. Of Plato's idea of the good he says: "If the goodness predicated of various things in common actually is a unity or something existing separately and absolute"—which definition applies also to the concept of God established in his *Metaphysics*—"it clearly will not be practicable or attainable by man." And he adds: "But the Good which we are now seeking is a good within human reach." [23] And in another connection he says: "We instinctively feel that the Good must be something proper to a man and not easily taken from him." [24]

Since the good which his *Ethics* has to define is a final end, something "for the sake of which everything else is done," [25] it must be happiness. For "happiness above all else appears to be absolutely final in this sense, since we always choose it for its own sake and never as a means for something else." [26] "To say, however, that the Supreme Good is happiness will probably appear a truism; we still require a more explicit account of what constitutes happiness." [27] The result of this inquiry is that happiness is identified with virtue.

This identification is a characteristic feature of a certain type of moral philosophy. Its starting point is man's desire for happiness as a definite state of mind, the unattainable state of complete satisfaction of all wishes. In order to induce those at whom the moral norms are directed to conform their behavior to these norms (and that means, to be virtuous) this moral philosophy maintains that through such behavior they will—in accordance with the principle of retribution—obtain the desired happiness. This happiness appears as the reward for virtue. If you are virtuous, that is to say, if you behave as you ought to behave, you will be happy. This is the teaching of this moral philosophy. However, since in reality the virtuous man is very often unhappy, and the wicked man happy, and since this philosophy is not able to change the reality of happiness, it is forced to change its concept. For this purpose, the happiness at which men actually aim, is distinguished, as a mere apparent, deceptive, and false happiness, from a real, genuine, and true happiness at which men ought to aim. Since this philosophy is not able and not willing to procure man the former, it promises him the latter; and it can do so without any risk, because it promises only that what it requires. For the true happiness is nothing else but virtue itself. Thus virtue—by its fictitious identification with happiness—becomes its own reward. The fundamental principle: If you are virtuous, that is to say, if you behave as you ought to behave, you will be happy, is still maintained. But since "to be happy" means now to be virtuous, to behave as one ought to behave, the principle amounts to the tautology: If you are virtuous, you are virtuous. However, it is a peculiarity of this ideology that the fiction on which it is based, may turn into reality. If somebody believes in the affirmation of this moral philosophy that virtue, and only virtue, makes man happy, then the consciousness of having behaved morally, of having fulfilled his moral duty, may produce in him the same feeling of satisfaction which is constituted by that happiness which the moral philosophy—because it cannot procure it to man as reward for his virtue—tries to replace by virtue itself.

When Aristotle takes happiness as the starting point of his ethics, because it is the supreme good, the good which is always chosen for its own sake, he first accepts this concept in its usual sense, as a real state of mind, as that condition of satisfaction which is actually desired by man. He is far from identifying it with virtue. He expressly rejects the doctrine that virtue is the end of life, "since it appears possible to possess virtue while you are asleep, or without putting it into practice throughout the whole of your life; and also for the virtuous man to suffer the greatest misery and misfortune—though no one would pronounce a man living a life of misery to be happy, unless for the sake of maintaining a paradox." [28] And when he characterizes happiness as something desired for its own sake, he opposes happiness to virtue: "Happiness," he says, "we choose always for itself and never for the sake of something else; but honor, pleasure, reason, and every virtue we choose, indeed, for themselves (for if nothing resulted from them we should still choose each of them) but we choose them also for the sake of happiness, judging that by means of them we shall be happy." [29] Happiness is here evidently conceived of as consequence or reward of virtue, and not at all as identical with it.

The transformation of happiness into virtue takes place while asking what happiness really is. Aristotle tries to answer this question "by ascertaining what is man's function." [30] By this he understands the specific function of man in general, in contradistinction to the function a man has in his capacity as a carpenter, a shoemaker, or the like. This specific function of man is, according to Aristotle, "the practical life of the rational part of man," the function of his rational faculty, the activity of his reason; and happiness is activity in conformity with reason. It is "an activity of soul which follows or implies a rational principle"; and "the function of a good man is to perform this activity well and rightly." Since a "good man" is a virtuous man, and to perform an activity "well and rightly" is to perform it in accordance with virtue, the just-quoted statement amounts to the redundancy: a virtuous man is the one who acts in accordance with virtue. On this, rather problematical, basis he arrives at the following definition of happiness as the supreme human good. It is "activity of the soul in accordance with virtue—if there is more than one virtue, in accordance with the best and most complete." [31] The good is happiness and happiness is virtue. "Our definition accords with the description of the happy man as one who 'lives well' or 'does well'; for it has virtually identified happiness with a form of good life or doing well." Aristotle expressly admits that his definition is in agreement "with those who pronounce happiness to be virtue, or some particular virtue." [32] He even declares, in fact, that "no supremely happy man can ever become miserable. For he will never do hateful or base actions, since we hold that a truly good and wise man will bear all kinds of fortune in a seemly way, and will always act in the noblest manner that the circumstances allow." [33] But he does not go so far as to ignore completely the importance of external goods for happiness. A revised definition of happiness reads as follows: That man is happy "who realizes complete virtue in action, and is adequately furnished with external goods, not for any casual period but throughout a complete lifetime." [34] But later Aristotle returns to the first definition of happiness as "a certain activity of the soul in conformity with perfect virtue" as a starting point of his investigation into the nature of virtue. And again he insists that "the virtue that we have to consider is clearly human virtue, since the good or happiness which we set out to seek is human good and human happiness." [35]

II

Thus the good, the moral value, is humanized; it is presented as virtue of man. Consequently the *Ethics* of Aristotle aims at a system of human virtues, among which justice is the "chief of the virtues," the "perfect virtue." [36] How to determine the moral value, or, in Aristotle's language, the moral virtues? At the beginnings of his *Ethics,* Aristotle emphasizes that "the same exactness must not be expected in all departments of philosophy alike, any more than in all the products of arts and crafts." In the field of ethics "we must be content if, in dealing with subjects and starting from premises thus uncertain [as the concepts of the good and of justice], we succeed in presenting a rough outline of the truth . . ." "It is the mark of an educated mind to expect that amount of exactness in each kind which the nature of the particular subject admits. It is equally unreasonable to accept merely probable conclusions from a mathematician, and to demand strict demonstration from an orator." [37] Nevertheless, Aristotle applies a mathematical-geometrical analogy to solve the central problem of his ethics, to answer the question as to what is virtue. It is his famous Doctrine of the Mean (*mesótes*). Virtue is a mean state between two extremes, which are vices, one of excess and one of deficiency. "Virtue is a mean state in the sense that it aims at hitting the mean . . . excess and deficiency are a mark of vice, and observance of the mean a mark of virtue." [38]

This formula is—as Aristotle himself admits—instigated by a commonplace, "the common remark about a perfect work of art: that you could not take from it nor add to it"; which—according to Aristotle—means "that excess and deficiency destroy perfection, whereas adherence to the mean preserves it." [39] Aristotle chooses this commonplace as starting point of his inquiry because in it the quality of value is presented as quantity; and the application of a mathematical-geometrical method in ethics is possible only if the moral value is transformed from a quality into a quantity. If the criterion of that what is good in a work is: that one cannot take away from it nor add to it, then the good is characterized in the same way as the point by which a line is divided into two equal parts. The moralist can find the virtue which he is looking for just as the geometrist can find the point equidistant from the two ends of a line. The tendency to quantify the moral value in order to render a mathematical-geometrical or quasi mathematical-geometrical method possible is very clear in the statement: "Now of everything that is continuous and divisible, it is possible to take the larger part or the smaller part, or an equal part, and these parts may be larger, smaller, and equal either with respect to the thing itself or relatively to us; the equal part being a mean between excess and deficiency. By the mean of the thing I denote a point equally distant from either extreme; which is one and the same for everybody; by the mean relative to us, that amount which is neither too much nor too little, and this is not one and the same for everybody." [40] In another connection Aristotle says of the two vices between which, as between two extremes, the virtue as the mean lies: "The greatest degree of opposition exists between the two extremes. For the extremes are farther apart from each other than from the mean, just as great is farther from small and small from great than either from equal." [41] That Aristotle intends to present his method of determining the moral good or virtue as a quasi mathematical-geometrical operation is shown by his saying that although it is possible to find what is good or a virtue, it is not easy: "It is a hard task to be good, for it is hard to find the middle point in anything: for instance, not everybody can find the center of a circle, but only someone who knows geometry." [42] To determine the good is, in principle, the same problem as to determine the middle point of a straight line or the center of a circle.

The quantification of the moral value, the three-partite scheme of "too much," "mean," "too little," the essential presupposition of a mathematical-geometrical method of determining the good, is a fallacy. In the realm of moral values there are no measurable quantities as in the realm of reality as object of natural science. Ethics deals with qualities only—with the qualities of good and evil, right and wrong, just or unjust, virtuous or vicious; that is to say, with conformity and nonconformity to a norm presupposed as valid. The statement that a definite human behavior is good or evil, right or wrong, just or unjust, virtuous or vicious, presupposes the assumption that something ought to be done. The statement that something ought to be or to be done, is a norm. It is a way to express the idea that something is an end, not a means to an end.

It is a value judgment. The statement that a human behavior is good or evil, right or wrong, just or unjust, virtuous or vicious, means that this behavior is in conformity with a presupposed norm, or is not in conformity with it, that is, in contradiction to the presupposed norm. If a man's behavior is in conformity with a norm presupposed to be valid, we say: he obeys the norm; if his behavior is not in conformity with the norm, because it contradicts the norm, we say: he violates the norm.

The statement that a virtue is the mean between a vice of deficiency and a vice of excess, as between something that is too little and something that is too much, implies the idea that the relationship between virtue and vice is a relationship of degrees. But, since virtue consists in conformity, and vice in nonconformity of a behavior to a moral norm, the relationship between virtue and vice cannot be that of different degrees. For with respect to this conformity or nonconformity no degrees are possible. A behavior can neither "too much" nor "too little" conform, it can only conform or not conform to a (moral or legal) norm; it can only contradict or not contradict a norm. If we presuppose the norm: men shall not lie, or—expressed positively—men shall tell the truth, a definite statement made by a man is true or is not true, is a lie or is not a lie. If it is true, the man's behavior is in conformity with the norm; if it is a lie, the man's behavior is in contradiction to the norm. But the behavior cannot be in different degrees in conformity with or in contradiction to the norm. It cannot be more or less and, hence, not too much or too little in conformity or contradiction to the norm. Aristotle's differentiation of three degrees or "amounts"—excess, mean, deficiency—does, in truth, not refer to the moral value, the quality of being good or evil, a virtue or a vice, but to a psychic reality. He says: Moral virtue "is concerned with feelings and actions, in which one can have excess or deficiency or a due mean. For example one can be frightened or bold, feel desire or anger or pity, and experience pleasure and pain in general, either too much or too little, and in both cases wrongly; whereas to feel these feelings at the right time, on the right occasion, toward the right people, for the right purpose, in the right manner, is to feel the best amount of them which is the mean amount—and the best amount is, of course, the mark of virtue." [43] Applied to the virtues of temperance and courage, the *mesótes* doctrine is presented as follows: "The observance of the mean of fear and confidence is courage. The man that exceeds in fearlessness is not designated by any special name (and this is the case with many of the virtues and vices); he that exceeds in confidence is Rash; he that exceeds in fear and is deficient in confidence is Cowardly. In respect of pleasures and pains—not all of them, and to a less degree in respect of pains—the observance of the mean is Temperance, the excess Profligacy. Men deficient in the enjoyment of pleasures scarcely occur, and hence this character also has not been assigned a name, but we may call it Insensible." [44] Cowardice is a "vice of deficiency," because it is characterized by too little confidence. Rashness is a "vice of excess," because it is characterized by too much confidence. Profligacy is a vice of excess, because it is characterized as too much indulgence in pleasure. Insensibleness is a vice of deficiency, because it is characterized by too little enjoyment of pleasure. The feeling which accompanies or causes a certain behavior may be capable of different degrees of intensity but not the conformity or nonconformity of this behavior with the moral norm which constitutes the virtue or the vice, the quality of being right or wrong. Neither of these degrees or amounts is, in itself, "too much" or "too little," or represents excess or deficiency. To be "too much" or "too little," are value judgments which are possible only if one presupposes that a certain degree or "amount" is the "right" one. And a certain degree or amount of feeling is "right" because the behavior accompanied or caused by this feeling is right, that is, in conformity with the moral norm. What is right or wrong is the behavior in its relation to the moral norm; and this relation is not capable of degrees. This is why Aristotle cannot consistently maintain his statement that the virtue is a mean, and, as such, opposed to the extremes, but has to admit that virtue is an extreme itself. He is compelled to modify his doctrine of the mean by saying that virtue is "the observance of the mean" only "in respect of its essence and the definition that states its original being," but "in point of excellence and rightness it is an extreme." [45] The point of excellence and rightness is in truth the only point which counts, for virtue is by its very nature "excellence and rightness." The ideas of "too much" and "too little," designating a quantitative distance from the good, are merely figures of speech, a special metaphor in presenting the relation of a human behavior to a moral (or legal) norm. Aristotle compares the fact that a certain behavior corresponds to a presupposed norm with the middle point of a line, and the fact that a behavior does not correspond to a presupposed norm with the two ends of the line. When the phenomenon is described without using a metaphor, the tripartite scheme of the *mesótes* formula must immediately be replaced by a bipartite scheme: the antagonism of good and evil, right and wrong, conformity and nonconformity. "Too much" and "too little" are not—as the doctrine of the mean presents them— two different quantities of the same moral substratum, but two different expressions designating one and the same quality, namely nonconformity—the fact that a certain behavior contradicts a norm. Virtue means: to comply with a moral norm, vice: to violate a moral norm.

To distinguish between two different vices as two different "extremes" is possible only if there are two different norms regulating human behavior. It seems that this is the situation at least in some cases to which the *mesótes* formula is applied. A typical example is the virtue of courage as a mean between the vice of cowardice as "too little" and the vice of rashness as "too much" (confidence). By characterizing the vice of cowardice as compared with the virtue of courage as "too little" we express figuratively the idea that the behavior in question contradicts the norm whose fulfillment constitutes the virtue that the coward violates, the norm prescribing courage. By characterizing the vice of rashness compared with the virtue of courage as "too much" we express the idea that the behavior contradicts a norm other than the one whose fulfillment constitutes the virtue concerned. Only rashness, the "too much," not cowardice, the "too little," is a violation of the norm prescribing courage. A rash man is courageous, whereas a coward is not. The former is courageous but he has too much confidence. In this sense he is "too" courageous; and that means that he, by being courageous, violates another norm, the one prescribing prudence, the duty to take into consideration the possibility of success, the principle that the value we risk to destroy should be in a certain proportion to the value we try to realize by our action. "Too" just is, according to a widespread opinion, he who applies a certain rule of international morality in a certain case even to the disadvantage of his own country, who in applying this rule violates the norm expressed in the well-known saying: "right or wrong, my country." In one of the two "too's" of the *mesótes* formula nonconformity to one norm, in the other nonconformity to another norm is expressed. In the spatial metaphor that virtue is the mean between two vices as two extremes, one conformity is brought in relation to two nonconformities, without expressing the fact that there are two different norms which the two patterns of behavior, characterized as "vices," are violating. The *mesótes* doctrine creates the appearance as if it were one and the same norm which one violates by, so to speak, remaining below, or by going beyond the line determined by it. The *mesótes* formula veils the problem it pretends to solve. Since the norms of a given moral system are very often in conflict with one another, it is necessary, in order to act morally, to restrict the sphere of validity of the different norms in the proper way. That "virtue" is the "mean" between two vices means that morally correct is only the behavior by which the one of the conflicting norms is obeyed without the other being violated. The true problem is to show how this is possible, how, for example, a man's behavior can conform to the norm of courage and at the same time to that of prudence. To this question the *mesótes* doctrine gives no answer; nor to any question aiming at a determination of the moral value.

It claims to be such an answer by pretending to furnish a method by which the moralist can find the good by finding the mid point between two vices, just as geometry furnishes a method to find the middle point between two extreme points of a line. If the *mesótes* formula is a determination of the good at all, it is it only if the virtue is a mean in the same sense as a line is bisected at a point equidistant from its two ends. But this Aristotle cannot maintain. For the two vices between which the virtue lies are not extremes in the same sense as the two ends of a line bisected at a point equidistant from them. This is shown by an example Aristotle himself presents. He says: "Suppose that ten pounds of food is too much for anybody and two pounds too little, it does not follow that a trainer will prescribe six pounds [which is the exact mean], for perhaps even this will be too much or too little for the particular athlete who is to receive it." [46] If the "extremes"—ten and two—can be characterized only as "too much" and as "too little," any quantity

greater than ten—that is, the one characterized as "too much"—
is also too much, and any quantity smaller than two—that is, the
one characterized as "too little"—is also too little, and the correct
quantity may be any of the infinitely many magnitudes between
ten and two. This is the reason why Aristotle distinguishes between
the mean in an objective sense and the mean in a subjective sense
of the term, between the "mean with respect to the thing" which
is the real mean, and "one and the same for everybody," and the
"mean with respect to us," which "is not one and the same for
everybody." That expresses that the "mean with respect to us"
is not determined and not determinable as the point equidistant
from the two ends of the bisected line. Virtue is a mean between
two vices in the sense of the "mean with respect to us." Since the
two "extremes" between which virtue lies as a "mean with respect
to us" are not so determined as the two extreme points of a line
must be determined in order that we can determine the point
equidistant from them—since the two vices are characterized only
as "too much" and "too little"—all we can say of the virtue we are
looking for is that it lies somewhere between them. There is no
reason to assume that the virtue lies exactly in the middle and not
nearer to the one or the other vice. Aristotle admits: "In some cases
the defect, in others the excess, is more opposed to the mean; for
example, Cowardice, which is a vice of deficiency, is more opposed
to Courage than is Rashness, which is a vice of excess; but Profligacy, or excess of feeling, is more opposed to Temperance than is
Insensibility, or lack of feeling." [47] Later he says: "Thus much
then is clear, that it is the middle disposition in each department
of conduct that is to be praised, but that one should lean sometimes
to the side of excess and sometimes to that of deficiency, since this
is the easiest way of hitting the mean and the right course." [48] If
one leans to the side of excess or to the side of deficiency, one does
not hit the mean, but one may hit the right course. Hence, virtue
is not the "mean" but the "right course." One of the definitions of
virtue runs as follows: "Virtue, then, is a settled disposition of
the mind as regards the choice of actions and feelings, consisting
essentially in the observance of the mean relative to us, this being
determined by a rational principle, that is, as a man of practical
wisdom would determine it." [49] According to the original formula
of the *mesótes* doctrine, the mean is determined by the two ex-

tremes. But the "mean relative to us" is not determined in this way and hence no "mean" at all. It is determined by "practical wisdom," and "practical wisdom issues commands, since its end is what ought to be done or not to be done" [50]—it coincides in Aristotle's ethics with the moral order. Hence virtue is that disposition of men that is in conformity with the moral order. This is the true meaning of the statement that virtue is the observance of the mean relative to us.

The statement that a virtue lies somewhere between two vices is a figure of speech. Its meaning, without the use of a metaphor, is: if we compare a virtue with two vices, the virtue is neither the one nor the other vice. The *mesótes* formula amounts to the tautology that: if something is correct it is not too much and not too little—or, in other words, that a virtue is not a vice, that good is not evil, right is not wrong.

But even if the two moral extremes were as completely determined as the two extreme points of a line bisected at a point equidistant from the two ends, and even if the moral mean were not a "mean with respect to us, but a mean with respect to the thing," and consequently as determined and determinable as the point equidistant from the two ends of the bisected line, the *mesótes* formula were no determination of the moral good. The alleged determination of the good consists in the statement that the virtue is a mean between two opposite vices. The existence of these vices Aristotle takes for granted. He does not prove that the two extremes, as for instance rashness and cowardice, are evils or vices; his ethics presupposes it as self-evident; just as a geometrist presupposes a circle or the two extreme points of a line as given in order to determine the center or the point by which the line is divided into two equal parts. The circle or the two extreme points being given, that is, predetermined, the determination of the center or the bisecting point is automatically implied. The center is determined by the given circle, the middle point of a line by the two given extreme points.

If an ethical doctrine presupposes all possible vices, it presupposes, together with those vices, all possible virtues. If we know what is evil, we thereby know what is good, and then nothing new remains to be determined. Even if the virtue determined according to the *mesótes* formula as a mean between two "given" vices, were "a mean with respect to the thing" and hence "one and the same for everybody," the formula could proclaim only a redundancy. For its meaning were, in this case too, nothing else but that the good is opposite to the evil; and the evil is not determined but presupposed by the formula.

Although the ethics of the *mesótes* doctrine pretends to establish in an authoritative way the moral value,[51] it leaves the solution of its very problem to another authority: the determination of what is evil or a vice, and, consequently, also the determination of what is good or a virtue. It is the authority of the positive morality and the positive law—it is the established social order. By presupposing in its *mesótes* formula the established social order, the ethics of Aristotle justifies the positive morality and the positive law which, as a matter of fact, determine what is "too much" and what "too little," what are the extremes of evil or wrong, and thereby what is the mean, that is, good and right. In this justification of the established social order lies the true function of the tautology which a critical analysis of the *mesótes* formula reveals.[52]

III

The book v of Aristotle's *Ethics*, devoted to the problem of justice, begins with the question: "In regard to justice and injustice (*dikaiosýne* and *adikía*) we have to inquire what sort of actions precisely they are concerned with, in what sense justice is the observance of a mean, and what are the extremes between which that which is just is a mean. Our inquiry may follow the same procedure as our preceding investigations." [53] It is the procedure of the *mesótes* doctrine. Aristotle first distinguishes justice in a general and justice in a particular sense. There are, he maintains, two concepts of justice: lawfulness and equality. "The term 'unjust' is held to apply both to the man who breaks the law and the man who takes more than his due, the unfair man. Hence it is clear that the law-abiding man and the fair man will both be just. 'The just' therefore means that which is lawful and that which is equal or fair, and 'the unjust' means that which is illegal and that which is unequal or unfair." [54] As to the relationship between lawfulness and equality, Aristotle says that the two concepts are not identical, lawfulness being the broader, equality the narrower concept: Not everything unlawful is unequal, though everything unfair is unlawful. Equality is related to lawfulness "as part to whole." [55] Consequently justice in the sense of lawfulness is "not a part of virtue but the whole of virtue"; [56] it is perfect virtue "with a qualification, namely that it is displayed toward others." [57] That means that justice in the sense of lawfulness is a social virtue. By lawfulness Aristotle undoubtedly understands conformity to positive law. He says: "We saw that the lawbreaker is unjust and the law-abiding man just. It is therefore clear that all lawful things are just in one sense of the word, for what is lawful is decided by legislature, and the several decisions of legislature we call rules of justice." The *nómimon* is identical with the *díkaion,* law identical with justice (in one sense of this term). But is *nómos,* the law, really to be understood as the positive law—any positive law? This question must certainly be answered in the affirmative. For Aristotle continues: "Now all the various pronouncements of the law aim either at the common interest of all, or at the interest of a ruling class determined either by excellence or in some other similar way; so that in one of its senses the term just is applied to anything that produces and preserves the happiness, or the component parts of the happiness, of the political community." [58] But the "happiness" may be the happiness "of all" or only of "a ruling class." It is this justice in the general sense of lawfulness which Aristotle characterizes as the "perfect virtue" and the "chief of virtues, and more sublime than the evening or the morning star." [59] Which amounts to an unconditional glorification of positive law. But Aristotle is not a positivist. He does not confine his inquiry to an analysis of positive law, he does not renounce the use of the two concepts of justice and law, the *díkaion* and the *nómimon;* he maintains the dualism, but only to identify positive law with justice, to justify the *nómimon* as *díkaion.*

Of the particular justice, which consists in equality, there are also two kinds: distributive and corrective justice. Distributive justice "is exercised in the distribution of honor, wealth, and the other divisible assets of the community which may be allotted among its members in equal or unequal shares" by the legislator. Corrective justice is "that which supplies a corrective principle in private transactions . . . those which are voluntary and those which are involuntary." [60] The corrective justice is exercised by the judge in settling disputes and inflicting punishments upon delinquents.

The principle of distributive justice is proportional equality. That "justice involves at least four terms, namely two persons for whom it is just and two shares which are just. And there will be the same equality between the shares as between the persons, since the ratio between the shares will be equal to the ratio between the persons: for if the persons are not equal, they will not have equal shares." [61] Thus the principle of distributive justice is expressed in a mathematical formula: If a right a is allotted to an individual A, and a right b to the individual B, the requirement of distributive justice is fulfilled if the ratio of value a to value b is equal to the ratio of value A to value B. If the individuals A and B are equal, the rights to be allotted to them must be equal too. However, there are in nature no two individuals who are really equal, since there is always a difference as to age, sex, race, health, wealth, and so forth. There is no equality in nature. Nor is there equality in society. Equality as a social category, the statement that two individuals are socially equal, does not mean that there are no differences between these individuals, but that certain differences which really exist, as for instance differences concerning age, sex, race, wealth, are considered to be irrelevant. The decisive question as to social equality is: Which differences are irrelevant? To this question Aristotle's mathematical formula of distributive justice has no answer. Nor to the other essential question as to which rights the legislator ought to allot to the individuals in order to be just. Is it just to confer upon the citizens the right of private property, or is it just to establish communism? Is it just to confer upon the citizens political rights, that is, to establish democracy, or is it just to confer upon the citizens no political rights at all, to establish autocracy? Aristotle's formula of distributive justice says only, that *if* rights are allotted, and *if* two individuals are equal, equal rights shall be allotted to them. According to this formula a capitalistic as well as a communistic legal order is just, and a legal order which confers political rights only to men who have a certain income, or who belong to a certain race, or are of noble birth is as just as a legal order which confers the same rights to all human beings who are of a certain age without regard to other differences. Any privilege whatever is covered by this formula. When a legal order reserves all possible rights to one single individual (the ruler) and assigns only duties to all others (the ruled), such a legal order too is just, since the difference between the ruler and the ruled is considered to be decisive, so that the ruled cannot be considered as equal to the ruler.

To illustrate his formula of distributive justice Aristotle refers to the "principle of assignment by desert." He says: "All are agreed that justice in distributions must be based on desert of some sort, although they do not all mean the same sort of desert; democrats make the criterion free birth; those of oligarchical sympathies, wealth or, in other cases, birth; upholders of aristocracy make it virtue." But his moral philosophy is not capable and considers itself not competent to answer the question which of these criteria is the just one. This, however, is the very question of justice.

The answer to this question Aristotle's *Ethics* leaves to the authority of positive law. Only if it is supposed that the positive law decides the question which rights shall be conferred upon citizens, and which differences between them are relevant, Aristotle's mathematical formula of distributive justice is applicable. As a postulate it means nothing else but that positive law shall be applied according to its own meaning. The equality of this justice is the equality before the law, which means merely legality, lawfulness. Aristotle's definition of distributive justice is but a mathematical formulation of the well-known principle *suum cuique,* to each his own, or to each his due. But this tautology has the important function of legitimizing the positive law which, as a matter of fact, fulfills the task, which legal philosophy is not capable of fulfilling—to determine what is everybody's due.

"Corrective" justice is exercised by the judge in deciding cases of "voluntary or involuntary transactions." "To go to a judge is to go to justice, for the ideal judge is, so to speak, justice personified." [62] Aristotle's distinction between "voluntary" and "involuntary" transactions probably coincides by and large with our distinction between civil and criminal law. He says: "Examples of voluntary transactions are selling, buying, lending at interest, pledging, lending without interest, depositing, letting for hire; these transactions being termed voluntary because they are voluntarily entered upon. Of involuntary transactions some are furtive, for instance, theft, adultery, poisoning, procuring, enticement of slaves, assassination, false witness. Others are violent, for instance, assault, imprisonment, murder, robbery with violence, maiming, abusive language, contumelious treatment." [63] All these acts are crimes which are punishable under positive law. Corrective justice, too, is equality; but it is equality not according to geometrical but according to arithmetical proportion; [64] it is not equality of two ratios, it is equality of two things, especially of two losses or two gains. A typical example is barter, which may stand for any voluntary transaction. Corrective justice requires that the service and counterservice constituting the barter should be equal. The loss of one party by doing a service to the other party ("doing a service" comprising also making a gift to the other party) shall be equal to the loss of the latter by doing a return service ("doing a return service" comprising also giving a return gift); and vice versa: the gain of one party in receiving service from the other should be equal to the gain of the latter by receiving a return service from the former. The same equality shall prevail in the relation between crime and punishment. To do a service to another without receiving from him an adequate return service amounts to the same injustice as to commit a crime without receiving the adequate punishment. The problem of this kind of justice is: what is the adequate, correct, just return service, the adequate, correct, just punishment? Aristotle tries to answer this question, too, by a mathematical-geometrical formula. He compares the situation when a man has done to another a service without receiving a return service, or when a man has committed a crime injuring another, with a line divided into unequal parts. "The unjust being here the unequal, the judge endeavors to equalize [the inequality] . . . the judge endeavors to make them [the two parts of the line] equal by the penalty or loss he imposes, taking away the gain." [65] "Now the judge restores equality: if we represent the matter by a line divided into two unequal parts, he takes away from the greater segment that portion by which it exceeds one-half of the whole line, and adds it to the lesser segment. When the whole has been divided into two halves, people then say that they 'have their own,' having got what is equal. . . . The equal is a mean by way of arithmetical proportion between the greater and the less. For when of two equals a part is taken from one and added to the other, the latter will exceed the former by twice that part, since if it had been taken from the one but not added to the other, the latter would exceed the former by once the part in question only. Therefore the latter will exceed the mean by once the part, and the mean will exceed the former, from which the part was taken, by once that part." [66] The two equal parts of a bisected line and the two halves of a whole are evidently only a metaphor for the relationship of equality which should be established between service and return service, crime and punishment. The metaphor is no solution of the problem of just return service and just punishment. It is only another way of presenting the problem. Aristotle, however, thinks that by stating that the judge has to find the mean in the same way a geometrist divides a given line into two equal parts, has solved the problem of corrective justice. He says with reference to the just quoted passage: "This process then will enable us to ascertain what we ought to take away from the party that has too much and what to add to the one that has too little." [67] That means: the process enables us to determine the just return service and the just punishment; "we must add to the one that has too little the amount whereby the mean between them exceeds him, and take away from the greatest of the three the amount by which the mean is exceeded by him." All this says nothing else but that service and return service, that crime and punishment should be equal. This equality is certainly not a mathematical quantitative equality. An exchange between two persons takes place if both need different things. Aristotle says: "An association for interchange of services is not formed between the physicians, but between a physician and a farmer, and generally between persons who are different [i. e., who are able to do different services] and who may be unequal [with respect to their services] though in that case they have to be equalized." [68] That means: service and return service have to be equalized, since they are in themselves not and cannot be, equal in the sense the two halves of a line are, nor can crime and punishment be equal in this sense.

This is why Aristotle is compelled finally to give up his mathematical formula according to which "equality" is established by corrective justice. In discussing the Pythagorean doctrine that justice is reciprocity (*antipeponthós*) he says that reciprocity is sometimes at variance with corrective justice. But he admits: "In the interchange of services justice, in the form of reciprocity, is the bond that maintains the association; reciprocity, that is, on the basis of proportion, not on the basis of equality. The very existence of the state depends on proportionate reciprocity, because men demand that they shall be able to requite evil with evil (if they cannot, they feel they are in the position of slaves) and to repay good with good (failing which, no exchange takes place, and it is exchange that binds them together)." [69] The principle of retribution, or—more, generally formulated, reciprocity—is the rule to return evil for evil, good for good, like for like. The punishment shall be equal to the crime, the reward equal to the merit. The decisive question, what is evil and what is good, is not answered by this formula; nor the question, what is "like" or equal. Positive law is, by its very nature, a coercive order. It provides coercive acts —forcible deprivation of life, freedom or property—as sanctions to be executed against the individual who commits a delict, that is, behaves in a way considered by the legislator to be harmful to society. The different legal orders differ very much in their determination of the delicts as well as the sanctions; but all correspond to the principle of retribution, which is at the basis of the social technique we call law. That retribution is considered as a principle of justice may be explained by the fact that it originates in one of the most primitive instincts of man, his desire for revenge. Aristotle's objection against the rule "like for like" as principle of justice, is that the relation between merit and reward, crime and punishment is not equality but proportionality. Return service shall not be equal to the service, the punishment not equal to the crime— this is impossible—but "proportional," which means that the one should be in an adequate proportion to the other. But this again is merely a presentation, not the solution, of the problem. The decisive question as to what is corrective justice remains unanswered. The pretended answer is a mere sham answer. It is again the tautology of the formula, "To each his own." [70]

Although the discussion of the problem of justice starts with the question in what sense justice is the observance of a mean, the *mesótes* doctrine plays but a subordinate role in Aristotle's legal philosophy. The application of the *mesótes* formula to the problem of justice is superficial and not very consistent. The sense of the statement that justice is a mean is not always the same. The main statement is: "Just conduct is a mean between doing and suffering injustice, for the former is to have too much and the latter to have too little." [71] It is evident that one of the two extremes (doing injustice and suffering injustice), namely, suffering injustice, is no vice. The *mesótes* formula has here a meaning different from that which it has in the discussion of the other virtues. This is admitted by Aristotle himself. He says: "Justice is a mode of observing the mean, though not in the same way as the other virtues are." [72] The difference is of no interest here, since the *mesótes* formula in their application to the problem of justice has the same character of a tautology as in its application to the other moral values. This character is here even more obvious. Doing injustice and suffering injustice are not two different degrees of one and the same substratum; they are not even two different facts between which a third fact can be situated. One man's doing injustice implies another man's suffering injustice. The one cannot be separated from the other. To say that justice is a mean between doing and suffering injustice, is a figurative expression of the judgment that justice is not injustice, neither the injustice which is done, nor the injustice which is suffered, which, however, are both one and the same injustice.

It might seem as if Aristotle himself was not completely satisfied with the result of his doctrine of justice. For in book viii of his *Ethics,* where he discusses the virtue of friendship, a certain tendency appears to complete the more or less empty idea of justice by the more substantial idea of peace. Here we read the astonishing passage: "Friendship appears to be the bond of the state; and lawgivers seem to set more store by it than they do by justice; for to promote concord, which seems akin to friendship, is their chief aim; while faction [discord], which is enmity, is what they are most anxious to banish. And if men are friends there is no need of justice between them; whereas merely to be just is not enough; a feeling of friendship also is necessary." [73] "Concord" means peace; and to establish peace rather than justice seems to be—according to this statement—the essence of the state. Aristotle does not disapprove that legislators aim chiefly at peace, not at justice; and where peace prevails there is no need of justice. Justice is not enough! Is that the same justice of which Aristotle so enthusiastically speaks at the beginning of his inquiry into the nature of this virtue, proclaiming it "the chief of virtue," and "more sublime than the evening or the morning star?" Since to establish peace is certainly a function of the law, the stress Aristotle lays on the idea of peace corresponds to his identification of justice with law. "Justice," says

Aristotle in his *Politics*, "is a function of the state. For the law is the order of the political community; and the law determines what is just." [74] If it is the law which determines what is just, justice is lawfulness; and if justice is equality, it is only equality before the law.[75]

This definition of justice as equality before the law implies the substitution of the logical value of truth for the moral value of justice.

Since a rationalistic moral philosophy is not capable of determining the content of a just order, of answering the questions what is good and what is evil, which differences between individuals are relevant and which irrelevant, who is equal and what is equal, it must presuppose these determinations. This means: leave it to the state (that is, to the positive legislator) who establishes a legal order, a system of general norms to be applied by the judge. When the legislator has established an order, when, for example, he has stipulated that every male citizen more than 24 years old may participate in the election of the magistrates, or that every individual more than 14 years old who commits theft shall be punished, and so on, then moral philosophy is in a situation to ascertain that it is just to allow not only A but also B to exercise a right of voting, provided that both are equal, that is, male citizens, 24 years of age; and that it is just for the judge to punish not only C but also D, provided that both individuals are equal, namely, both are more than 14 years old and both have committed theft. This is the principle of justice in the sense of lawfulness or in the sense of equality; this is equality before the law. And this kind of equality is established by any general norm. Equality before the law is maintained when the general norm is applied according to its own meaning. This is why this kind of equality is identical with lawfulness. If the judgment is valid that every individual more than 14 years old who has committed theft shall be punished, and if C and D are both individuals more than 14 years old who have committed theft, then the judgment is true that not only C but also D shall be punished. It is true as a conclusion from the general to the particular, which is implied in the application by a judge of a general norm to a particular case. If a judge, pretending to apply a general rule of law, states that C shall be punished and D shall not be punished, he presupposes in the first case the general judgment:

Every individual more than 14 years old who has committed theft shall be punished; and in the second case, the general judgment: Not every individual more than 14 years old who committed theft shall be punished. These two general judgments constitute a logical contradiction. The judgment that it is not just to decide that C shall be punished but D shall not be punished, only means: it is contradictory. The principle of justice in the sense of equality before the law or lawfulness is nothing but the logical law of contradiction with reference to the application of a general norm of positive law to particular cases. This is the only concept of justice which Aristotle's moral philosophy—as any other rational philosophy—is able to define.

It is obvious that this concept of justice, as a law of thought, is totally different from the original ideal of action we understand by justice. This ideal does not aim at a logically, but a morally satisfactory normative system. A totally noncontradictory order as a system of general rules may be totally unjust in the original sense of the ideal. The substitution of the logical value of noncontradiction for the moral value of justice, inherent in the definition of justice as equality before the law, is the result of the attempt to rationalize the idea of justice as the idea of an objective value. Although this substitution is no solution, but an elimination of the problem of justice, it seems that the attempt will never be abandoned—perhaps, because of its important political implication. This type of rationalistic philosophy, pretending to answer the question what is just, and hence claiming authority to prescribe to the established power how to legislate, ultimately legitimizes the established power by defining justice as equality before the law and thus declaring the positive law to be just.

Since the concept of justice produced by a rationalistic moral philosophy has no definite content, it must not necessarily be used in a conservative tendency, to legitimize the given social order, to justify the validity of positive law. It may be used—although the intellectual history of mankind shows that this is only exceptionally the case—in a reformatory, or even revolutionary, tendency, to deny the validity of a given social order by declaring it unjust. A very interesting example is the legal philosophy of Aurelius Augustinus, who was a bishop of the Christian Church in an African province of the Roman Empire at a time when this empire was not yet a firmly established province of Christianity. Augustine identifies law and justice, just as Aristotle identifies the *nómimon* and the *dikaion;* but he does so, not as Aristotle did, in order to strengthen the authority of the former by that of the latter. He propounds the thesis that a social order is law only if it is just, in order to destroy the authority of Roman law. "Where there is no true justice" [76] he says, "there can be no law. For what is done by law is justly done, and what is unjustly done cannot be done by law. For the unjust inventions of men are neither to be considered nor spoken of as laws; for even they themselves say that law is that which flows from the fountain of justice, and deny the definition which is commonly given by those who misconceive the matter, that right is that which is useful to the stronger party. Thus, where there is not true justice there can be no assemblage of men associated by a common acknowledgment of law," that is, a state. "If there is no law where there is no justice then most certainly it follows that there is no state where there is no justice." "Justice taken away, then, what are states but great robberies?" [77]

But what is justice? To this question Augustine answers with the same formula which Aristotle used to an exactly opposite purpose. "Justice is that virtue which gives everyone his due." But what is everyone's due? The Greek philosopher left the answer to the authority of the positive moral and legal order accepted by the majority of his society, the Christian bishop to the positive religious order of the minority to which he belonged. According to Augustine, justice is Christianity, injustice paganism. "Where, then, is the justice of man, when he deserts the true God and yields himself to impure demons? Is this to give every one his due? Or is he who keeps back a piece of ground from the purchaser, and gives it to a man who has no right to it, unjust, while he who keeps back himself from the God who made him, and serves wicked spirits, is just? . . . Hence, when a man does not serve God, what justice can we ascribe to him? . . . And if there is no justice in such an individual, certainly there can be none in a community composed of such persons." Consequently—and the Saint does not hesitate a moment to face this consequence—there never was a Roman State. Which amounts to saying: there never was a Roman law.

This is a very interesting result of a doctrine of justice based on the empty tautology of the formula "To every one his due." It is interesting not so much because this formula enables the one who is willing to use it, to deny to an empire (by which, during many hundred years, a great and the most civilized part of mankind, was organized) the character of a state, and to a law (which was so to speak the mother of all modern law) the character of law; it is so interesting because it shows the unlimited possibility of using this formula to any purpose whatever.

THE NATURAL-LAW DOCTRINE
BEFORE THE TRIBUNAL
OF SCIENCE

T HE natural-law doctrine undertakes to supply a definitive solution to the eternal problem of justice, to answer the question as to what is right and wrong in the mutul relations of men. The answer is based on the assumption that it is possible to distinguish between human behavior which is natural, that is to say which corresponds to nature because it is required by nature, and human behavior which is unnatural, hence contrary to nature and forbidden by nature. This assumption implies that it is possible to deduce from nature, that is to say from the nature of man, from the nature of society, and even from the nature of things certain rules which provide an altogether adequate prescription for human behavior, that by a careful examination of the facts of nature we can find the just solution of our social problems. Nature is conceived of as a legislator, the supreme legislator.

This view presupposes that natural phenomena are directed toward an end or shaped by a purpose, that natural processes or nature conceived of as a whole are determined by final causes. It is a thoroughly teleological view, and as such does not differ from the idea that nature is endowed with will and intelligence. This implies that nature is a kind of superhuman personal being, an authority to which man owes obedience. At the lowest stage of human civilization this interpretation of nature manifests itself in so-called animism. Primitive man believes that natural things—animals, plants, rivers, the stars in the sky—are animated, that spirits or souls dwell within or behind these phenomena, and that

From *The Western Political Quarterly,* Dec., 1949.

consequently these things react toward man like personal beings according to the same principles that determine the relations of man to his fellow men. It is a social interpretation of nature, for primitive man considers nature to be a part of his society. Since the spirits or souls animating the natural phenomena are believed to be very powerful and able to harm as well as to protect man, they must be worshipped. Animism is consequently a religious interpretation of nature. At a higher stage of religious evolution, when animism is replaced by monotheism, nature is conceived of as having been created by God and is therefore regarded as a manifestation of his all powerful and just will. If the natural-law doctrine is consistent, it must assume a religious character. It can deduce from nature just rules of human behavior only because and so far as nature is conceived of as a revelation of God's will, so that examining nature amounts to exploring God's will. As a matter of fact, there is no natural-law doctrine of any importance which has not a more or less religious character. Grotius, for example, defines the law of nature as a dictate of rational nature by which certain acts are forbidden or enjoined "by the author of nature, God." [1] He states that the law of nature proceeding from the "essential traits implanted in man can rightly be attributed to God, because of His having willed that such traits exist in us." [2] Hobbes declares that the law of nature is a dictate of reason, but the dictates of reason are "conclusions, or theorems concerning what conduces to the conservation and defense of themselves; whereas law properly is the word of him that by right has command over others. But yet if we consider the same theorems, as delivered in the word of God, that by right commands all things, then are they properly called laws." [3] Following Hobbes, Pufendorf states that if the dictates of reason—that is, the principles of natural law—are to have the force of law it must "under all circumstances be maintained that the obligation of natural law is of God." [4] Only thus can it be assumed that the law deduced from nature is an eternal and immutable law, in contradistinction to positive law which, created by man, is only a temporary and changeable order; that the rights established by natural law are sacred rights inborn in man because implanted in man by a divine nature; and that positive law can neither establish nor abolish these rights, but only protect them. This is the essence of the natural-law doctrine.

The first objection which must be made from the point of view of science is that this doctrine obliterates the essential difference which exists between scientific laws of nature, the rules by which the science of nature describes its object, and the rules by which ethics and jurisprudence describe their objects, which are morality and law. A scientific law of nature is the rule by which two phenomena are connected with each other according to the principle of causality, that is to say, as cause and effect. Such a rule is, for example, the statement that if a metallic body is heated it expands. The relation between cause and effect, whether it is considered as a relation of necessity or of mere probability, is not attributed to any act of human or superhuman will. If we speak of morality or law, on the other hand, we refer to norms prescribing human behavior, norms which are the specific meaning of acts of human or superhuman beings. Such a norm is, for instance, the moral norm issued by Christ enjoining that one help a fellow man in need, or a legal norm issued by a legislator prescribing punishment for a murderer. Ethics describes the situation which exists under moral norms by the statement: If a man is in need, his fellow men ought to help him; jurisprudence describes the situation under the legal norm: If a man commits murder, he ought to be punished. It is evident that a rule of morality or a rule of law connects the condition with its consequence not according to the principle of causality, but according to a totally different principle. A law of nature is a statement to the effect that if there is A, there *is* B, whereas a rule of morality or a rule of law is a statement to the effect that if there is A, there *ought* to be B. It is the difference between the "is" and the "ought," the difference between causality and normativity (or imputation).[5]

If we presuppose a general norm prescribing a certain type of human behavior, we may characterize concrete behavior which is in conformity with the presupposed norm as good, right, correct, and behavior which is not in conformity with the presupposed norm, as wrong, bad, incorrect. These statements are called value judgments, the term being used in an objective sense.[6] Value, in this sense of the term, is conformity with a presupposed norm. It is a positive value, in contradistinction to a negative value, which is nonconformity with a presupposed norm. Since the statement that the concrete behavior of a definite individual is good or bad (or, what amounts to the same, has a positive or negative value) means that his behavior is in conformity or not in conformity with a presupposed general norm, we may express this value judgment by the statement that the individual ought or ought not to behave as he actually does. Without presupposing a general norm prescribing (or forbidding) something, we cannot make a value judgment in the objective sense of this term. The value attributed to an object is not given with the properties of this object without reference to a presupposed norm. The value is not inherent in the object judged as valuable, it is the relation of this object to a presupposed norm. We cannot find the value of a real thing or of actual behavior by analyzing these objects. Value is not immanent in natural reality. Hence value cannot be deduced from reality. It does not follow from the fact that something is, that it ought to be or to be done, or that it ought not to be or not to be done. The fact that in reality big fish swallow small fish does not imply that the behavior of the fish is good, nor yet that it is bad. There is no logical inference from the "is" to the "ought," from natural reality to moral or legal value.

If we compare the rules by which ethics or jurisprudence describe their objects (rules referring to moral or legal norms) with the rules by which natural science describes its object, that is, causal rules, we must take into consideration the fact that the norms to which the rules of morality and the rules of law refer are, as previously stated, the meaning of acts of a moral or legal authority. So far as this authority is a human being, these norms are subjective in character, that is, they express the intention of their author. That which such a human authority prescribes or forbids depends on the end at which he aims. That at which somebody aims as an end is also called a value, but in a subjective sense of this term; and if it is an ultimate end, not a means to an end, it is called a highest value. There are great variances of opinion about ultimate ends or highest values in this subjective sense of the term, and frequently one highest value is in conflict with another, as, for instance, personal freedom with social security, the welfare of the single individual with the welfare of the whole nation, in situations where the one can be reached only at the expense of the other. Then arises the question which end is preferable, or which value is superior and which is inferior—which is in truth the highest value? This question cannot be answered in the same way as the question whether iron is heavier than water or water heavier than wood. This latter question can be resolved by experience in a rational scientific way, but the question as to the highest value in the subjective sense of the term can be decided only emotionally, by the feelings or the wishes of the deciding subject. One subject may be led by his emotions to prefer personal freedom; another, social security; one, the welfare of the single individual; the other, the welfare of the whole nation. By no rational consideration can it be proved that the one is right or the other wrong. Consequently there are, as a matter of fact, very different systems of morality and very different systems of law, whereas there is only one system of nature. What according to one system of morality is good may, under another system of morality, be bad; and what under one legal order is a crime may be under another legal order perfectly right. This means that the values which consist in conformity or nonconformity with an existing moral or legal order are relative values. Only if the authority issuing the norms is supposed to be God, an absolute and transcendental being, is there an exclusive moral and legal system, and then the values which consist in compliance with these norms are supposed to be absolute values.

The natural-law doctrine presupposes that value is immanent in reality and that this value is absolute, or, what amounts to the same thing, that a divine will is inherent in nature. Only under this presupposition is it possible to maintain the doctrine that the law can be deduced from nature and that this law is absolute justice. Since the metaphysical assumption of the immanence of value in natural reality is not acceptable from the point of view of science, the natural-law doctrine is based on the logical fallacy of an inference from the "is" to the "ought." The norms allegedly deduced from nature are—in truth—tacitly presupposed, and are based on subjective values, which are presented as the intentions of nature as a legislator. By identifying the laws of nature with rules of law, pretending that the order of nature is or contains a just social order, the natural-law doctrine, like primitive animism, conceives of nature as a part of society. But it can be easily proved that modern science is the result of a process characterized by the tendency of emancipating the interpretation of nature from social categories.[7] Before the tribunal of science, the natural-law doctrine has no chance. But it may deny the jurisdiction of this tribunal by referring to its religious character.

II

The natural-law doctrine is characterized by a fundamental dualism of positive and natural law. Above the imperfect positive law created by man, a perfect (because absolutely just) natural law exists, established by a divine authority. Consequently positive law is justified and valid only so far as it corresponds to the natural law.[8] If, however, the positive law is valid only so far as it corresponds to the natural law; if it is possible—as the natural-law doctrine asserts—to find the rules of natural law by an analysis of nature; if, as some writers assert, the law of nature is even self-evident,[9] then the positive law is quite superfluous. Faced by the existence of a just ordering of society, intelligible in nature, the activity of positive-law makers is tantamount to a foolish effort to supply artificial illumination in bright sunshine. This is another consequence of the natural-law doctrine. But none of the followers of this doctrine had the courage to be consistent. None of them has declared that the existence of natural law makes the establishment of positive law superfluous.[10] On the contrary. All of them insist upon the necessity of positive law.[11] In fact, one of the most essential functions of all natural-law doctrines is to justify the establishment of positive law or the existence of the state competent to establish the positive law. In performing this function most of the doctrines entangle themselves in a highly characteristic contradiction. On the one hand they maintain that human nature is the source of natural law, which implies that human nature must be basically good. On the other hand they can justify the necessity of positive law with its coercive machinery only by the badness of man. The only philosopher who avoids this contradiction is Hobbes, who proceeds from the assumption that man is by his very nature bad. Consequently, the natural law which he deduces from this nature is practically nothing else but the principle that a state endowed with the unlimited power to establish positive law is necessary and that, by natural law, men are obliged to obey unreservedly the positive law established by the state—a line of argument which amounts to the negation of natural law by natural law. If, however, natural law is considered to be a system of substantive rules, not a formalistic authorization of any positive law, then the contradiction between a human nature from which this natural law is deduced and a human nature which makes positive law necessary is inevitable. Thus Pufendorf emphasizes that there is "no more fitting and direct way to learn the law of nature than through careful consideration of the nature, condition, and desires of man himself." [12] If there is a law of nature as a dictate of reason which can be deduced from the nature of man, it is necessary that man "be sociable, that is, be willing to join himself with others like him, and conduct himself toward them in such way that, far from having any cause to do him harm, they may feel that there is reason to preserve and increase his good fortune." [13] But Pufendorf is aware that this is not the actual nature of man. He admits that man is "at all times malicious, petulant, and easily irritated, as well as quick and powerful to do injury." He admits "that the mass of men order their lives not by reason, but on impulse." [14] He does not go as far as Hobbes in his pessimistic evaluation of human nature, but he states:

There is, indeed, such perversity in most men, that, whenever they think they will secure a greater good from the violation than from the observance of laws, they violate them readily.[15]

Consequently he states that it is not possible to believe "that mere respect for natural law, which forbids every manner of injury, could have been able to make it possible for all mankind to live secure in natural liberty."

For the wickedness of man's character and his proneness to injure others can in no way be restrained more effectively, than by thrusting in his face the immediate evil which will await him upon his attacking another, and by removing every hope of impunity.[16]

Hence, the nature of man necessarily leads to the establishment of the state, and that means to positive law.

Yet, such is the stupidity of most men and the violence of their passions, that only a very few accord all these matters the consideration due them. Therefore, there remained no more effective remedy to curb the wickedness of men than what is supplied by states. . . .[17]

If the mass of men according to their nature do not order their lives by reason, if most men by their very nature are stupid and wicked, how can the law of nature, the dictates of reason, the absolutely just order of social life, be deduced from the nature of man? It is not from the nature of man as it actually is that Pufendorf—and all other writers—deduce what they consider to be the natural law; it is from the nature of man as it should be, and as it would be if it would correspond to the natural law. It is not the law of nature which is deduced from the nature, the real nature, of man—it is the nature of man, an ideal nature of man, which is deduced from a natural law presupposed in some way or another.[18]

III

If the positive law is, as all followers of the natural-law doctrine assert, valid only so far as it corresponds to the natural law, any norm created by custom or stipulated by a human legislator which is contrary to the law of nature must be considered null and void. This is the inevitable consequence of the theory which admits the possibility of positive law as a normative system inferior to natural law. The extent to which a writer abides by this consequence is a test of his sincerity. Very few stand this test. Some philosophers avoid the test by proving that a conflict between positive and natural law is impossible. Thus Hobbes maintains that positive law can never be against reason, and that means against the law of nature. It is impossible, he says, "for any civil [i. e., positive] law whatsoever, which tends not to a reproach of the Deity . . . to be against the law of nature." [19]

The law of nature and the civil law contain each other, and are of equal extent. . . . The law of nature . . . is a part of the civil law in all commonwealths of the world. Reciprocally also, the civil law is a part of the dictates of Nature . . . every subject in a commonwealth has covenanted to obey the civil law . . . and therefore obedience to the civil law is part also of the law of nature.[20]

Hobbes asserts that the lawyers agree that law can never be against reason. But he asks "whose reason it is that shall be received for law." And his answer is:

It is not meant of any private reason; for then there would be as much contradiction in the laws as there is in the schools.

It is the reason of the state, the commonwealth, which according to Hobbes determines the content of the law, and this law is at the same time the positive and the natural law.

The reason of this our artificial man, the commonwealth, and his command, that makes law: And the commonwealth being in their representative but one person, there cannot easily arise any contradiction in the laws; and when there does, the same reason is able, by interpretation or alteration, to take it away.[21]

Here it is evident that the natural-law doctrine has no other function than to justify the positive law—any positive law established by an effective government. Although it is not always so evident as in Hobbes's philosophy, this is the conscious or unconscious tendency of the overwhelming majority of the other writers. They do not deny that, in principle, a conflict between positive and natural law is possible; but they try to prove that such conflict can only exceptionally occur, and that if it occurs the validity of the positive law can almost never be doubted. Pufendorf's attitude on this question is typical. He rejects the opinion of those "who deny the possibility that even civil laws can be opposed to natural laws." [22] He emphasizes: "a civil law could, of course, be passed which is opposed to natural law"; but he adds: "yet none but an insane man, and one who had in mind the destruction of the state, would wish to pass legislation of this kind." [23] Hence a conflict between positive and natural law, although theoretically possible, is practically excluded. Consequently Pufendorf maintains that, as matter of fact, all positive laws are, at least in principle, in conformity with natural law.

And indeed, in all commonwealths most features of the law of nature, at all events such as those without which peace in the society itself cannot stand, have the force of civil law, or have been included in the body of civil laws.[24]
All civil laws, indeed, presuppose or incorporate the general principles at least of natural law, whereby the safety of the human race is maintained; and these latter are by no means done away with by the former, which are merely added to them as the distinct advantage of each state has required.[25]

Although Pufendorf decidedly opposes Hobbes's identification of positive with natural law, he accepts one of his arguments which inevitably leads to this result. Hobbes has no illusion about the subjective character of our judgments concerning good and civil. He says:

"Good" and "evil" are names that signify our appetites, and aversions; which in different tempers, customs, and doctrines of men are different and divers men differ not only in their judgment on the senses of what is pleasant and unpleasant to the taste, smell, hearing, touch, and sight; but also of what is conformable or disagreeable to reason, in the actions of common life. Nay, the same man, in divers times, differs from himself; and one time praises, that is, calls good, what another time he dispraises, and calls evil: From whence arise disputes, controversies, and at last war.[26]

Hence he admits: "what it is we call the law of nature is not agreed upon by those that have hitherto written." [27] Since from differences of value judgments arise quarrels and breaches of peace, a common measure of what is to be called right and wrong is necessary.

This common measure, some say, is right reason: with whom I should consent, if there were any such thing to be found or known *in rerum natura*. But commonly they that call for right reason to decide any controversy, do mean their own. But this is certain, seeing right reason is not existent, the reason of some man, or men, must supply the place thereof; and that man, or men, is he or they, that have the sovereign power . . . and consequently the civil laws are to all subjects the measures of their actions, whereby to determine, whether they be right or wrong, profitable or unprofitable, virtuous or vicious.[28]

It is not for the individual but for the state, represented by its government, to decide what the law of nature requires. Hobbes states:

The interpretation of the laws of nature, in a commonwealth, depends not on the books of moral philosophy. The authority of writers, without the authority of the commonwealth, makes not their opinions law, be they never so true. That which I have written in this Treatise, concerning the moral virtues, and of their necessity for the procuring and maintaining peace, though it be evident truth, is not therefore presently law; but because in all commonwealths in the world it is part of the civil law: For though it be naturally reasonable yet it is by the sovereign power that it is law; otherwise, it were a great error, to call the laws of nature unwritten law; whereof we see so many volumes published, and in them so many contradictions of one another, and of themselves.[29]

Following Hobbes in this respect, Pufendorf maintains

that is surely a seditious opinion, that "the knowledge of good and evil," that is, of that which is good or evil, advantageous or disadvantageous to the state, "belongs to individuals." That is, that each individual is empowered to pass judgment as to the aptitude of the means which a prince orders to be undertaken so as to secure the public good, with the effect that the obligation of each person to obedience depends upon that judgment.[30]

He states:

since the greatest diversity of judgments and desires is to be observed among men, because of which an infinite number of disputes can arise, the interests of peace also require that it be publicly defined what each man should consider his own, and what another's, what should be held lawful, and what unlawful, in the state, what honorable, and what dishonorable. So also what a man still retains of his natural liberty, or, in other words, how everyone should temper the use of his right to the tranquility of the state. And, finally, what every citizen can by his right require of another and in what manner.[31]

This means that if an individual considers a rule of positive law to be contrary to natural law, it is not the opinion of the private individual but the opinion of the competent authority of the state which prevails. In discussing the question as to whether a tyrant may be brought to order by the people Pufendorf expresses the highly characteristic view: "the presumption of justice stands always on the side of the prince"; [32] which means that there is always a presumption that the positive law is the natural law.

Another way of achieving the identification of the positive with the natural law starts from the definition of justice accepted by most followers of the natural-law doctrine: to each his own. Hobbes sees clearly that this formula presupposes a positive legal order determining what is one's own; and he concludes that where there is no positive law there can be no justice within the meaning of this formula. "Therefore where there is no commonwealth there nothing is unjust." [33] Pufendorf defines justice under natural law in conformity with Roman jurisprudence as the "perpetual will to give each man what is due him." [34] But he adds that something is due a person on the basis of a perfect right only if the person has the possibility of bringing an action in a human court against the injurer.[35] That means that justice as defined within the meaning of natural law is possible only under positive law. Hence Pufendorf makes the above-quoted statement that to avoid an infinite number of disputes, natural law requires that positive law determine "what each man should consider his own and what another's." In spite of his criticism of Hobbes, Pufendorf's natural-law doctrine aims, in the essential question of the relation between natural and positive law, at the same goal as that of the English philosopher: the justification of the positive by the natural law.

Finally, there is a principle advocated by all leading representatives of the natural-law doctrine, by which a conflict between the natural and the positive law—if at all admitted as possible—is deprived of any effect which could be dangerous to the established legal authority: it is the dogma that under the law of nature there is no or only a restricted right of resistance. It stands to reason, according to Hobbes, that "no man in any commonwealth whatsoever has right to resist him or them, on whom they have [obliged by the law of nature] conferred this [their] power coercive, or, as men used to call it, the sword of justice." [36] But also Grotius, who admits "that if the authorities issue any order that is contrary to the law of nature or the commandments of God, the order shall not be carried out," teaches that if "unjust treatment be inflicted upon us [by him who holds the sovereign power] we ought to endure it rather than resist by force." [37] He quotes a passage of Sophocles' *Antigone:* "You must obey him whom the state has placed in power, alike in small things and in things unjust as well as just"; [38] and concludes that "resistance cannot rightly be made to those who hold the sovereign power." [39] Pufendorf, it is true, rejects the thesis advocated by Hobbes that the state can do no wrong to a citizen, [40] but he states that "the lesser injuries of princes should be overlooked out of consideration for the nobility of their position and their other benefits, and, indeed, for the sake of our fellow-citizens and of the entire state." [41] As to the more serious injuries he says

that even when a prince with hostile intent threatens a most frightful injury, to leave the country, or protect oneself by flight, or seek protection in another state is better (than to take up arms against a harsh lord, it is true, and yet the lord of one's fatherland). But what if a prince undertakes with hostile intent to slay an innocent citizen, and there is left him no place to flee to? [42]

To this question he does not give a direct answer, but he states:

But since there are scarcely to be found any instances of princes who have undertaken to kill innocent citizens with an open profession of mere wantonness, a greater difficulty arises over what is permissible when a prince undertakes to vent his rage under a plea of right, on the excuse, for instance, that his citizens have failed to obey some unjust command. On this point we take it as established that . . . citizens . . . are not bound by any commands of the civil sovereignty, which are confessedly and openly repugnant to a command of God. . . . Yet in such a case there should be resort to flight, so far as possible, and the protection sought of some third person who lies under no obligation to that prince. Nay, if flight be not possible, a man should be killed rather than kill, not so much on account of the person of the prince, as for the sake of the whole commonwealth, which is usually threatened with great tumults under such circumstances.

He finally admits "that sometimes it is not wrong for some one citizen to defend his safety by force against the most open injuries of a superior," but he immediately adds: "yet it will not be allowable for the rest of the citizens on that account to drop their obedience and protect the innocent person by force." [43]

Locke goes relatively far in this question. He says:

May the commands, then, of a prince be opposed? May he be resisted as often as any one shall find himself aggrieved, and but imagine he has not a right done him? This will unhinge and overturn all polities, and, instead of government and order, leave nothing but anarchy and confusion.—To this I answer that force is to be opposed to nothing but to unjust and unlawful force; whoever makes any opposition in any other case draws on himself a just condemnation both from God and man; and so no such danger or confusion will follow, as is often suggested.[44]

Resistance is justifiable if the use of force by the government is not only unjust but also "unlawful"—that is, contrary not only to the natural but also to the positive law. But who is competent to decide this question? Not a private individual. For the effect of the establishment of a commonwealth is that

all private judgment of every particular member being excluded, the community comes to be umpire by settled standing rules, indifferent and the same to all parties, and by men having authority from the community for the execution of those rules, decides all the differences that may happen between any members of that society concerning any matter of right, and punishes those offences which any member hath committed against the society with such penalties as the law has established.[45]

Whenever, therefore, any number of men are so united into one society as to quit every one his executive power of the law of nature and to resign it to the public, there and there only is a political or civil society. . . . And this puts men out of a state of nature into that of a commonwealth by setting up a judge on earth, with authority to determine all the controversies and redress the injuries that may happen to any member of the commonwealth; which judge is the legislative, or magistrate appointed by it.[46]

This could be interpreted to mean that the question as to whether there exists an unjust and unlawful use of force by the government is to be decided by the authorities established by the positive law. But in another connection Locke advocates another view.

Who shall be judge whether the prince or legislative act contrary to their trust? This, perhaps, ill-affected and factious men may spread amongst the people, when the prince only makes use of his due prerogative. To this I reply: The people shall be judge; for who shall be judge whether his trustee or deputy acts well and according to the trust reposed in him but he who deputes him and must, by having deputed him, have still a power to discard him when he fails in his trust? If this be reasonable in particular cases of private men, why should it be otherwise in that of the greatest moment where the welfare of millions is concerned, and also where the evil, if not prevented, is greater and the redress very difficult, dear, and dangerous? [47]

But few writers on natural law went as far as Locke. Kant, for instance, whose philosophy of law is a typical application of the natural-law doctrine, emphasizes that "resistance on the part of the people to the supreme legislative power of the state is in no case legitimate," and that resistance is especially reprehensible if the "supreme legislative power is embodied in an individual monarch." [48]

The view that the interpretation of natural law is the prerogative of the authorities established by positive law and that there is no —or only a very restricted, practically ineffectual—right of resistance against these authorities amounts to a complete denaturation of the natural-law doctrine. A critical analysis of its classical works shows that its function was not—as the idea of a natural law superior to the positive law implies—to weaken, but to strengthen the authority of the positive law. The natural-law doctrine has, on the whole, a strictly conservative character. Its reformative tendency, of some importance in the field of international law, is rather overestimated as far as national law is concerned. It is highly characteristic that where such reformative tendency appears, the adaption of the positive law to what is presented as the natural law is not supposed to be the automatic effect of the latter, but is expected as the result of an act of the legislative authority. Moreover, there were followers of the natural-law doctrine who were decidedly opposed to legislative reforms. Thus, for example, a very influential representative of the Protestant natural-law doctrine, Benedictus Winkler, in his work *Principiorum Juris Libri Quinque* (1615) attacks *novatores*, those who introduce innovations in the field of law. "They dare," he says, "to shake the very foundations of justice." Sudden changes of the law are always dangerous.[49] This is only the consequence of his view, advocated also by almost all other writers, that not only the law of nature but also the positive law *jubet bona*, provides for the good.

IV

Since the judgment that a definite human behavior or a social institution is "natural" means, in truth, only that the behavior or the social institution is in conformity with a presupposed norm, based on a subjective value judgment of the particular writer presenting a natural-law doctrine, there is not one natural-law doctrine but many, advocating quite contradictory principles. According to Hobbes, reason teaches that the power of the government established in conformity with natural law is by its very nature absolute, which means unlimited.

The sum of these rights of sovereignty, namely the absolute use of the sword in peace and war, the making and abrogating of laws, supreme judicature and decision in all debates judicial and deliberative, the nomination of all magistrates and ministers, with other rights contained in the same, make the sovereign power no less absolute in the commonwealth, than before commonwealth every man was absolute in himself to do, or not to do, what he thought good . . . And therefore some have imagined that a commonwealth may be constituted in such manner, as the sovereign power may be so limited, and moderated, as they shall think fit themselves . . . wherein they deceive themselves.[50]

The sovereignty is indivisible; and that seeming mixture of several kinds of government, not mixture of the things themselves, but confusion in our understandings, that cannot find out readily to whom we have subjected ourselves.[51]

But Locke deduces from nature that

the supreme power in every commonwealth . . . is not, nor can possibly be, absolutely arbitrary over the lives and fortunes of the people; for it being but the joint power of every member of the society given up to that person or assembly which is legislator, it can be no more than those persons had in a state of nature before they entered into society and gave up to the community; for nobody can transfer to another more power than he has in himself, and nobody has an absolute arbitrary power over himself, or over any other, to destroy his own life, or take away the life or property of another.[52]

It cannot be supposed that they [i.e., those who established in conformity with the law of nature a commonwealth] should intend, had they a power so to do, to give to any one or more an absolute arbitrary power over their persons and estates and put a force into the magistrate's hand to execute his unlimited will arbitrarily upon them. This were to put themselves into a worse condition than the state of nature wherein they had a liberty to defend their right against the injuries of others and were upon equal terms of force to maintain it, whether invaded by a single man or many in combination.[53]

And Rousseau, following Locke, writes:

To renounce liberty is to renounce being a man, to surrender the rights of humanity and even its duties. For him who renounces everything no indemnity is possible. Such a renunciation is incompatible with man's nature; to remove all liberty from his will is to remove all morality from his acts. Finally, it is an empty and contradictory convention that sets up, on the one side, absolute authority, and, on the other, unlimited obedience. Is it not clear that we can be under no obligation to a person from whom we have the right to exact everything? Does not this condition alone, in the absence of equivalence or exchange, in itself involve the nullity of the act?[54]

Since, according to this version of the natural-law doctrine, the power of the state is necessarily limited, absolute monarchy is against nature. Locke states:

it is evident that absolute monarchy, which by some men is counted the only government in the world, is indeed inconsistent with civil society, and so can be no form of civil government at all.[55]

The only form of government in accordance with the law of nature is democracy, that is, a government whose power is derived from the people:

Men being, as has been said, by nature all free, equal, and independent, no one can be put out of this estate and subjected to the political power of another without his own consent.[56]

Whosoever, therefore, out of a state of nature unite into a community must be understood to give up all the power necessary to the ends for which they unite into society to the majority of the community, unless they expressly agreed on any number greater than the majority. And this is done by barely agreeing to unite into one political society, which is all the compact that is, or needs be, between the individuals that enter into or make up a commonwealth. And thus that which begins and actually constitutes any political society is nothing but the consent of any number of freemen capable of a majority to unite and incorporate into such a society. And this is that, and that only, which did or could give beginning to any lawful government in the world.[57]

But by exactly the same method, Filmer proves that democracy is against the law of nature. His main thesis is: It is unnatural for the people to govern or to choose governors.[58] He objects to those who place supreme power in the whole people:

Was a general meeting of a whole kingdom ever known for the election of a prince? Is there any example of it ever found in the whole world? To conceive such a thing is to imagine little less than an impossibility, and so by consequence no one form of government or king was ever established according to this supposed law of nature.[59]

And of the majority principle he says:

Unless it can be proved by the law of nature that the major or some other part have power to overrule the rest of the multitude, it must follow that the acts of multitudes not entire are not binding to all but only to such as consent unto them.[60]

His most powerful argument is that "God did always govern his own people by monarchy only." [61]

The most crucial problem of our time is the principle of private property and the justice of the legal and economic system based on this principle. The fact that in recent jurisprudence and political theory a quite remarkable revival of the natural-law doctrine can be observed may to a great extent be explained by the idea, widespread among lawyers and politicians, that the capitalistic system in its fight against communism can effectively be defended only by that doctrine. And indeed, the most outstanding champions of natural law, from Grotius to Kant, have done their best to prove that private property is a sacred right conferred by divine nature upon man.

This result of the natural-law doctrine appears all the more remarkable when one considers that the Holy Scripture is interpreted by the Church as revealing that God gave all things to all men in common. Hence it was rather difficult to prove that private property, that is the dominion over a thing by one man to the exclusion of all the others, was in conformity with nature as created by God. But just as man, although created in the image of God and hence originally good, has in conformity with divine providence fallen into sin and thus become bad, so things, after the fall of man, have in accordance with the second, the post-lapsarian, nature, become the private property of man. Thus Grotius, for example, admits that God originally established a community of property; but he says that this state of things corresponded only to the "simplicity of the state of the first men," of whom Adam is the type. Among them there "was ignorance of vices," "incorruption." But men "did not continue to live this simple and innocent life"; men "degenerated into craftiness," and in the course of this degeneration "the primitive common ownership, first of movable objects, later also of immovable property, was abandoned." Grotius, referring to the authority of Cicero, insists that in this change "there is no conflict with nature." [62]

One of the most original attempts to deduce the right of private property from nature is the one made by Richard Cumberland, Bishop of Peterborough, the author of a well-known treatise on the law of nature.[63] He writes:

We have seen how the nature of things imprints on us . . . a knowledge of good and evil, even of that which is common to many, as is that by which we know the causes of generation and corruption. I now proceed to consider, that the matter and motion, in which the powers of a human body, as of all other parts of the visible world, do consist, have a finite quantity, and certain limits, beyond which they cannot extent themselves. Whence flow these most evident axioms concerning all natural bodies: That the same bodies cannot at the same time be in more places than one; that the same bodies cannot at the same time be moved toward several places (especially if contrary), so as to be subservient to the opposite wills of several men; but that they are so limited, that they can be determined by the will of one only, unless several conspire to one and the same effect or use.[64]

It follows, that men, who are obliged to promote the common good, are likewise necessarily obliged to consent, that the use of things and labour of persons, so far as they are necessary to particular men to enable them to promote the public good, should be so granted them, that they may not lawfully be taken from them, whilst the aforesaid necessity continues; that is, that those things should, at least during such time, become their property, and be called their own. . . . It is, therefore, evident, that the nature of things discovers, that it is necessary to the happiness, life, and health of every particular person, upon which all other advantages depend, that the uses of things should be limited, at least for a time, to particular persons exclusive of others.[65]

The law of nature not only establishes the right of individual property; it commands also the inviolability of this right:

The same reason and law of nature, which commands the establishing a distinct dominion over things and persons, commands also more evidently to preserve them inviolable, now that they are established and proved by experience to answer the designed end. For it is evident, that the division of dominion, which we find made by our ancestors, and established by the consent, or permission, of all nations and states, has been sufficient for the procreation and preservation of all that now exist, and to the procuring all that happiness, which we now see mankind possessed of; and, beside, that it affords such intercourse among men, such opportunities of mutual assistance, that all may attain greater degrees of happiness, both in this life and a future.[66]

The distribution of goods established in conformity with natural law by the positive law of property is just; it guarantees the greatest possible happiness. Consequently any attempt to change it and to replace it by another economic system is against the law of nature, and hence unjust:

It is beside manifest, that the happiness we now enjoy, and have the greatest reason to expect from the present division, is greater than any prudent man could hope to obtain, by violating and overturning all settled rights, divine and human, and endeavouring to introduce a new division of all property, according to the judgment, or affections, of any one man whatsoever.—For it is obvious, that this is an undertaking, to which the understanding of no one man, or assembly of men, is equal; and it is easy to foresee, that the opinions of so many men would differ so widely upon this head, that all would immediately be reduced to a state of war and misery. Wherefore, a desire of innovation in things pertaining to property is unjust, because it is inconsistent with this law, which is inseparable from the common good. I do, therefore, not only highly approve (with Grotius) of that sentence of Thucydides, "It is just for everyone to preserve that form of government in the state which has been delivered down to him." But I am of opinion, that what he has affirmed of one state only, ought to be extended to the great society of all rational beings (which I call the Kingdom of God); and that it ought not to be limited only to the form of government, which contains the division of the principal offices in the administration, but extended universally to the division of things: And in this latitude I assert it just, to preserve inviolably the antient division of dominion over things and persons, both among different nations, and in particular states. For experience has shewn it conducive to the best end, and no laws of nature can be conceived, which, consistently with this end, could prohibit such a division's being at first made; that, therefore, could be injurious to no one. But the same reason, which first obliged men to make this division (since they who rightly judge must unavoidably agree), will also oblige their successors to approve and confirm the same.[67]

Many of the followers of the natural-law doctrine argue that one of the essential purposes of the state, and that means of the positive law, is to protect the right of property established by natural law; and that it is beyond the power of the state, because against nature, to abolish this right, which exists independently of positive law. Locke's thesis that the power of the state is limited by natural law refers in the first place to property. He writes:

The supreme power cannot take from any man part of his property without his own consent; for the preservation of property being the end of government and that for which men enter into society, it necessarily supposes and requires that the people should have property, without which they must be supposed to lose that, by entering into society, which was the end for which they entered into it—too gross an absurdity for any man to own. Men, therefore, in society having property, they have such right to the goods which by the law of the community are theirs, that nobody hath a right to take their substance or any part of it from them without their own consent; without this, they have no property at all, for I have truly no property in that which another can by right take from me when he pleases, against my consent. Hence it is a mistake to think that the supreme or legislative power of any commonwealth can do what it will, and dispose of the estates of the subject arbitrarily, or take any part of them at pleasure. . . . And to let us see that even absolute power, where it is necessary, is not arbitrary by being absolute, but is still limited by that reason and confined to those ends which required it in some cases to be absolute, we need look no farther than the common practice of martial discipline; for the preservation of the army, and in it of the whole commonwealth, requires an absolute obedience to the command of every superior officer, and it is justly death to disobey or dispute the most dangerous or unreasonable of them; but yet we see that neither the sergeant, that could command a soldier to march up to the mouth of a cannon or stand in a breach where he is almost sure to perish, can command that soldier to give him one penny of his money; nor the general, that can condemn him to death for deserting his post, or for not obeying the most desperate orders, can yet, with all his absolute power of life and death, dispose of one farthing of that soldier's estate or seize one jot of his goods, whom yet he can command anything, and hang for the least disobedience. Because such a blind obedience is necessary to that end for which the commander has his power, viz., the preservation of the rest; but the disposing of his goods has nothing to do with it.[68]

There is no absolute right to life; but there is an absolute right to property. The right reason, implied in nature, teaches that property is even more valuable than life.

In view of such statements, made by generally recognized authorities, it is understandable that the natural-law doctrine is considered to be a strong bastion in the defense against communism. But we can hardly rely upon it. For on the basis of the natural-law doctrine, and with its specific methods, it has also been proved that private property is against nature and the source of all social evils. To eradicate these evils nothing else is necessary but to abolish private property and to establish communism, the only economic system dictated by nature. This is the main thesis of a work which under the title *Code of Nature, or the True Spirit of its Laws* was published anonymously in Paris in 1755.[69] Its author was a certain Morelly of whom we know very little. It is significant that the work was originally attributed to the famous encyclopedist Diderot. It became the "great book of socialism of the eighteenth century"; [70] Baboeuf, the leader of a communist movement within the French Revolution, frequently referred to the *Code of Nature,* which anticipated many ideas later developed by Fourier and other communists.[71] The *Code of Nature,* as its title indicates, is a legitimate child of the natural-law doctrine. It proceeds from the assumption that nature has definite intentions, that these intentions are intelligible and are directed at the happiness of mankind, and that justice can be established only by conforming our social institutions to the intentions of nature. Morelly maintains as an "incontestable principle" that "nature is one, constant, unchangeable"; that the laws of nature are implied in "the pacific inclinations by which nature animates its creatures"; and that "anything that deviates from these friendly affections is unnatural." [72] Hence Morelly—as many writers on natural law—believes that human nature is basically good. He assumes a "natural probity of creatures endowed with reason" [73] and proclaims as the "first law of nature" the law of "sociability." [74] The positive legislators "have only to recognize and to put into force this law of nature." [75] The law of sociability is interpreted to mean "that nature has distributed the human faculties among the individuals in different proportions, but that nature has left the ownership in the means of production (la propriété du champs producteur de ses dons) indivisible to all, and to everybody the use of its liberality. The world is a table sufficiently provided for all guests, to whom all the dishes belong; and they belong to all guests because all are hungry; to some of them only when the others are satisfied. Hence nobody is the owner (maître) exclusively, nor has anybody the right to pretend to be so." [76] Consequently individual property is against nature. The positive legislators, in establishing individual property, are guilty of a "monstrous division of the products of nature. They divide what according to nature ought to remain a whole or ought to be restored as a whole if by accident it has been divided. Thus they destroy all sociability"; [77] in so doing they work "against the reason of nature." [78] By establishing individual property the legislators recognize the individual interest of man and thus create a social situation where avarice, the worst of all vices and the source of all the others, must prevail. "Could this universal pestilence, this slow [lingering] fever, this consumption of the entire society, the individual interest, exist where it could find no nourishment or ferment? Hence it is evident that: Where there exists no property, there cannot exist any of its disastrous consequences." [79] If we want to realize the "wise intentions of nature" and create "a situation where man is as happy as he can be in this life," [80] we must "dash to the ground that monster, the spirit of property" [81] and establish a social order under which nothing in society belongs as private property to the individuals, except the things they need for immediate use to satisfy their needs, their pleasure, or for their daily work; where each citizen is a public servant, supported and occupied by society and obliged to contribute to the public welfare according to his forces, talents, and age.[82] This is the essence of communism.[83] Needless to say, the law of nature on which Morelly bases his communistic ideal has a thoroughly religious character. He confesses as his belief that "nobody will contest that in the general order of the universe everything is, in the eyes of its Author, infinitely wise, and as good as it possibly can be. Consequently there exists no physical evil in the presence of the Creator." [84] Under the constitution of his ideal state religious education of the children is obligatory. They are to learn that there exists a Supreme Being, the Author of the universe and beneficent Cause of all that is good.[85]

V

The reason why the natural-law doctrine, in spite of its obvious fallacies, has had, and probably always will have, great influence on social thinking is that it satisfies a deeply rooted need of the human mind, the need for justification. To justify the subjective value judgments which emerge from the emotional element of his consciousness, man tries to present them as objective principles by transferring to them the dignity of truth, to make them propositions of the same order as statements about reality. Hence he pretends to deduce them from reality, which implies that value is immanent in reality. But reality may be conceived of not only as nature but also as society or history, determined by laws analogous to the laws of nature. Then the attempt may be made to deduce from these laws the just order of human relations. This is the essential tendency of sociology and philosophy of history as developed in the nineteenth century. Although these two disciplines are directly opposed to the natural-law doctrine, they apply the same method and hence run into the same fallacy as the doctrine they intend to replace—the inference from the "is" to the "ought."

The most outstanding representatives of nineteenth-century sociology are Auguste Comte and Herbert Spencer. Both proceed from the assumption that the social life of men is determined by causal laws, just as nature is; and, under the influence of the theory of organic evolution developed in the field of biology first by Lamarck and later by Darwin, they arrived at the hypothesis of a social law of evolution. The main works of the two writers, Comte's famous *Cours de philosophie positive* [86] and Spencer's *Principles of Sociology* [87] are characterized by the confusion of a description and explanation of the actual social life and the proclamation of normative postulates, of statements about social reality and political value judgments. Both writers claim to have found a fundamental law of evolution by which not only can the past and present be explained but also the future, as the necessary result of the preceding evolution, can to a certain extent be predicted. Both writers maintain that this fundamental law of social evolution indicates a permanent progress of mankind from a lower to a higher and finally to a highest stage; and the highest stage—in the theories of both writers—coincides with their political ideal, which they deduce in this way from the fundamental law of progressive evolution, just as the natural-law doctrine deduces the right law from nature. The assumption that social evolution is progressive, that is to say that it leads from a lower to a higher stage of civilization, implies that a social value is immanent in social reality—the characteristic presupposition of the natural-law doctrine. Comte as well as Spencer operates on this presupposition as self-evident. But since value is not and cannot be immanent in reality and hence is not objectively ascertainable, as is reality, but on the contrary is highly subjective, it stands to reason that the fundamental law of evolution according to Comte leads to a result quite different from that which according to Spencer is the necessary effect of evolution.

Under the fundamental law of evolution as formulated by Comte, mankind passes through three successive stages: the theological, the metaphysical, and the positive stage. The characteristics of the first two stages are of no interest in this connection. Important only is the third, the highest stage of social evolution, the necessary result of social evolution and at the same time the ideal state of society. This resembles in many respects Plato's *Republic*.[88] Just as Plato, Comte proceeds from the fundamental dualism of speculative and practical life.[89] The speculative life manifests itself in philosophical or scientific and esthetic or poetical activities, the practical life in industrial activity.[90] Comte assumes as a fundamental law the priority of the more general and simple over the more special and complex [91] and consequently predicts that in the society of the future there will be a preponderance of the speculative over the active life. This preponderance is the characteristic of human progress.[92] Just as in Plato's ideal state the class of the philosophers rules over the working class, in the society of the future, according to Comte's prophecy, the ruling class will be a class of philosophers, that is, of men of science and art. He says that

the future spiritual power will reside in a wholly new class, in no analogy with any now existing, and originally composed of members **issuing, according to their** qualifications, from all orders of existing society. . . . The social power of this class must, like that of Catholicism, precede its political organization. This class will act on the general state of affairs by accomplishing the philosophical labors which will secure its formation long before it can be regularly constituted.[93]

The spiritual power exercised by the new ruling class will be independent of the "temporal power," by which Comte probably means the political government. The task of the spiritual power will be to govern opinions and morals, whereas the function of the temporal power will be to govern the actions, the active life, in conformity with the general ideas elaborated by the spiritual authority. The function of the spiritual authority, he says, will be

that of directing education, while remaining merely consultative in all that relates to action—having, in fact, no other concern with action than that of recalling in each case the appropriate rules of conduct. The temporal authority, on the other hand, is supreme in regard to action, and only consultative in regard to education. Thus the great characteristic office and privilege of the modern spiritual power will be the organization and working of a universal system of positive education, not only intellectual, but also, and more emphatically, moral.[94]

The government, exercising the temporal power, will have only the function of directing the industrial process, that is to say, the economic life. Comte says:

Industrial action is divided into production and transmission of products; the second of which is obviously superior to the first in regard to the abstractness of the work and the generality of the relations. . . . Thus we find the industrial hierarchy formed, the bankers being in the first rank; then the merchants; then the manufacturers; and finally the agriculturists; the labors of the latter being more concrete, and their relations more special, than those of the other three classes. . . . When that time comes the most concrete producers, the laborers, whose collisions with their employers are now the most dangerous feature of our industrial state, will be convinced that the position of the capitalist is owing not to any abuse of strength or wealth, but to the more abstract and general character of his function. The action and responsibility of the operative are less extensive than those of the employer; and the subordination of the one to the other is therefore as little arbitrary and mutable as any other social gradation.[95]

The future society will not be based—as the followers of the natural-law doctrine assert—on the idea of rights, but on the principle of duty:

the constant force of political illusion and quackery will be reformed; and the vague and stormy discussion of rights will be replaced by the calm and precise determination of duties. The one, a critical and metaphysical notion, necessarily prevailed till the negative progression was completed: the other, essentially an organic and positive idea, must rule the final regeneration: for the one is purely individual, and the other directly social. Instead of making individual duty consist politically in respect for universal rights, the rights of each individual will be regarded as resulting from the duties of others towards him.[96]

Consequently there will be no distinction between private and public function; each member of the future society will be a public functionary, an officer of the state; [97] which amounts to a complete socialization or nationalization of human life. As to the economic system, Comte's predictions are rather vague. On the whole it may be characterized as a kind of moderate socialism. Individual property will be, at least in principle, maintained, but it will change essentially its character. It will be rather a duty than a right. Its exercise must never have a merely individual character. The communists are right in rejecting the economic institution of property interpreted according to an individualistic philosophy. According to the new, that is, the positive philosophy, property is or will be "a necessary social function destined for the formation and administration of the capitals, through which each generation prepares the work of the subsequent generation." [98]

The capitalists will consider themselves the depositors of the wealth of society, the use of which will not involve any political responsibility (except in extreme cases), but should lie under a moral supervision, necessarily open to all, from the indisputableness of its principle, and of which the spiritual authority is the natural organ.[99]

Just as in Plato's republic the philosophers, as royal judges, settle the concrete disputes, in Comte's society of the future the speculative authority, in virtue of its higher value and the impartiality of its character, will naturally become the principal arbiter of the various practical conflicts.[100] Also world peace and the establishment of an European or occidental republic [101] are to be expected. All this is the necessary outcome of the social evolution determined by the law detected and formulated by the author of the positive philosophy. Of this law, the fundamental law of evolution, Comte says:

It certainly appears to me that the whole course of human history affords so decisive a verification of my theory of evolution, that no essential law of natural philosophy is more fully demonstrated. From the earliest beginnings of civilization to the present state of the most advanced nations, this theory has explained, consistently and dispassionately, the character of all the great phases of humanity; the participation of each in the perdurable common development, and their precise filiation; so as to introduce perfect unity and rigorous continuity into this vast spectacle which otherwise appears altogether desultory and confused. A law which fulfills such conditions must be regarded as no philosophical pastime, but as the abstract expression of the general reality. Being so, it may be employed with logical security to connect the past with the future, notwithstanding the perpetual variety which characterizes the social succession. . . . Mankind is now at the threshold of the fully positive life, the elements of which are all prepared, and only awaiting their co-ordination to form a new social system, more homogeneous and more stable than mankind has hitherto had any experience of.[102]

The law of progressive evolution is also the main instrument of Herbert Spencer's sociology.

Societies fall firstly into the classes of simple, compound, doubly-compound, trebly-compound; and from the lowest the transition to the highest is through these stages. Otherwise, though less definitely, societies may be grouped as militant and industrial; of which the one type in its developed form is organized on the principle of compulsory co-operation, while the other in its developed form is organized on the principle of voluntary co-operation. The one is characterized not only by a despotic central power, but also by unlimited political control of personal conduct; while the other is characterized not only by a democratic or representative central power, but also by limitation of political control over personal conduct.[103]

This structure [the militant structure of society] . . . is associated with the belief that its members exist for the benefit of the whole and not the whole for the benefit of its members. . . . Absolute subjection to authority is the supreme virtue and resistance to it a crime.[104]

Within a society of the industrial type, however, the opposite ideology prevails:

In place of the doctrine that the duty of obedience to the governing agent is unqualified, there arises the doctrine that the will of the citizens is supreme and the governing agent exists merely to carry out their will. Thus subordinated in position, the regulating power is also restricted in range. Instead of having an authority extending over actions of all kinds, it is shut out from large classes of actions. Its control over ways of living in respect to food, clothing, amusements, is repudiated; it is not allowed to dictate modes of production nor to regulate trade. Nor is this all. It becomes a duty to resist irresponsible government, and also to resist the excesses of responsible government. There arises a tendency in minorities to disobey even the legislature deputed by the majority, when it interferes in certain ways; and their oppositions to laws they condemn as inequitable, from time to time cause abolitions of them.[105]

The industrial structure of society represents the higher, the militant structure the lower type. The transition from the military to the industrial type is the transition from bondage to freedom, from autocracy to democracy, from statism to political and economic liberalism.

The implication is therefore the same as before. All-embracing state functions characterize a low social type; and progress to a higher social type is marked by relinquishment of functions.[106]

The transition from statism to liberalism, which implies the transition from the militant to the industrial type of social organization, is at the same time the evolution from a lower to a higher stage of morality. According to Spencer's evolutionary ethics, "conduct gains ethical sanction in proportion as the activities [are] becoming less and less militant and more and more industrial . . ." [107] A purely industrial form of society is "approaching nearer to the moral idea in its code of conduct than any society not purely industrial." [108]

Spencer seems to assume that human life is an ultimate end and as such a highest value. For he interprets the judgment that a human action is good to mean that the conduct is fitted to achieve as an end the preservation of life. He maintains that "evolution, tending ever towards self-preservation, reaches its limit when individual life is the greatest, both in length and breadth." This evolution takes place in three stages: self-preservation, preservation of offspring, preservation of fellow men.

Evolution becomes the highest possible [value] when the conduct simultaneously achieves the greatest totality of life in self, offspring, and in fellow men; so here we see that the conduct called good rises to the conduct conceived as best, when it fulfills all three classes of ends at the same time.[109]

In this connection Spencer states:

The ultimate question, therefore, is—Has evolution been a mistake; and especially that evolution which improves the adjustment of acts to ends in ascending stages of organization? [110]

Spencer's answer is, of course, that evolution is not a mistake. Nature is always right. Nothing is more characteristic of the evolutionary sociological ethics than this question, whether evolution has been a mistake. It reveals the true nature of this evolution, the highest stage of which—according to Spencer—is possible only within an industrial organization of society. Such a society is not yet completely achieved; but there is an "ingrained" tendency to this kind of organization.[111]

Human life is not the only highest value presupposed in Spencer's moral philosophy. There is another value which also claims the rank of an ultimate end: individual freedom. It seems that it is not the life as such, but the right life, which deserves to be preserved; and there are, Spencer maintains, for every race "laws of right living." [112] "Right living" seems to be living in freedom. For there are "laws of life as carried on in the associated state" [113] and one of these laws of life is the "law of equal freedom," which the author presents in his "formula of justice" as follows: "Every man is free to do that which he wills, provided he infringes not the equal freedom of any other man." [114] Since man, as part of nature, determined by the law of causality, is not free, Spencer's law of equal freedom can refer only to moral-political freedom, that is to say to the norm that man ought to be free from social authority, especially from interference on the part of the state. Thus Spencer, like the natural-law doctrine, deduces from natural and social reality, from laws of nature, moral-political norms. He says:

By inference from the laws of life as carried on under social conditions, and by inference from the dicta of that moral consciousness generated by the continuous discipline of social life, we are led directly to recognize the law of equal freedom as the supreme moral law. And we are indirectly led to such recognition of it by generalizing the experiences of mankind as registered in progressive legislation; since by it we are shown that during civilization there has been a gradual increase in the governmental maintenance of the rights of individuals, and that simultaneously there has been a gradual decrease in governmental trespasses on such rights. And then this agreement is reinforced by the proofs that what is theoretically equitable is economically expedient.[115]

From the equal right of freedom Spencer deduces concrete rights, such as the right of physical integrity, the right of free motion, and especially the right of individual property, which, as Spencer expressly declares, implies that communism is a "violation of justice." [116] He emphasizes that these

rights are but so many separate parts of a man's general freedom. . . . [They] originate from the laws of life as carried on in the associated state. The social arrangements may be such as fully recognize them, or such as ignore them in greater or smaller degrees. The social arrangements cannot create them, but can simply conform to them or not conform to them. Such parts of the social arrangements as make up what we call government, are instrumental to the maintenance of rights, here in great measure and there in small measure; but in whatever measure, they are simply instrumental, and whatever they have in them which may be called right, must be so called only in virtue of their efficiency in maintaining rights.[117]

The function of the state and its positive law is only to maintain the rights established by nature.

Here the natural-law character of this kind of sociology is evident. The law of nature is or implies a social norm. This sociology enables Comte to justify a highly collectivistic political program; and Spencer a radically individualistic political program.

VI

The two most outstanding representatives of the philosophy of history as developed in the nineteenth century are G. W. F. Hegel and Karl Marx. The basic idea of Hegel's philosophy of history is that "Reason" governs the world and, consequently, world history.[118] This Reason implies morality, the laws of which "are the essential Rational." [119] The same idea is expressed by the statement that the history of the world is the "rational necessary course of the World-Spirit." [120] The World-Spirit is but the personification of Reason. This personification is essential. For the history of the world is also the realization of the will of the World-Spirit. The actions of individuals and states, of which history consists, are "the instruments and means of the World-Spirit for attaining its object." [121] And all historical men, in pursuing their own particular aims, execute only, without knowing it, "the will of the World-Spirit." [122] It is hardly possible to distinguish the will of the World-

Spirit from the will of God. To Hegel the idea that Reason directs the world is an application of the "religious truth" that the world is not abandoned to chance but controlled by "Divine Providence," the "Providence of God." This Providence is "Wisdom endowed with an infinite Power which realizes its aim, viz. the absolute rational design of the world." [123] In investigating the course of the World-Spirit in history, Hegel's philosophy constitutes the deliberate attempt of "knowing God" and expressly presents itself as such.[124] Highly significant is the motto of his work: "The history of the world is not intelligible apart from a Government of the World." Hegel's so-called philosophy of history is the myth of the World-Spirit; it is not a philosophy, but a theology of history.

It is an essential element of a theological interpretation of phenomena to assume that God not only is transcendent to but also immanent in the world, which is the manifestation of his will. Since his will is good, is the absolute value, reality must be considered to be perfect and value must be immanent in reality. This view is the core of Hegel's philosophy, according to which world history is the realization of Reason representing the absolute logical as well as ethical value. If this assumption is true, then every historical event must be considered to be the work of the World-Spirit and as such reasonable and good. Indeed, Hegel terminates his work in affirming as its result "that what has happened, and is happening every day, is not only not without God, but is essentially His Work." [125] This is but another, and more sincere formulation of his most quoted thesis: The Real is the Rational and the Rational is the Real.

If God is immanent in the world, if the absolute value is inherent in reality, there is no possibility of judging one actual event or one phase of history as better or worse than another; and if everything by its very nature is necessarily good, value judgments have lost any meaning. However, to distinguish between good and evil is the main task of theology in its capacity as ethics; and it is the specific function of a philosophy of history to differentiate by value judgments one historical event or one phase of history from the other. Without such differentiation a philosophy of history is meaningless. Theology satisfies its need for distinguishing good and evil by introducing—at the cost of consistency—the devil as a countergod into the ethical interpretation of the world. Hegel's philosophy of history accomplishes the same result by the assumption that reality as manifested in world history is, not perfect though on its way to perfection. World history is the progressive realization of Reason. This progress, which is the course of the World-Spirit, is a necessary one, for Reason as the "Sovereign" of the world is endowed with "infinite power." [126]

Since Hegel presents God as Reason, and everyone may understand by Reason what he thinks good and desirable, his theology of history is more flexible than the official Christian theology. Its thoroughly optimistic character, its thesis that the progressive realization of an ideal status of mankind is the necessary result of the historical process, must be welcome to the wishful thinking of any political ideology.

The conflict between the position that God is immanent in the world and, hence, value inherent in reality, on the one hand, and the need to distinguish in reality between good and evil, on the other, presents itself in theology as the problem of theodicy. It is the problem how God, the omnipotent and absolutely good creator of the world, can ordain or permit the evil in nature and society. It is the central problem of theology. Hegel's philosophy proves to be a true theology of history by pretending to offer a solution of this problem. He states: "Our mode of treating the subject [the history of the world] is in this aspect, a Theodicaea—a justification of the ways of God." [127] And at the end of his work, where he formulates the result of his philosophy in the above-quoted statement that all happenings are the will of God, Hegel says of his main thesis that the history of the world is the realization of the World-Spirit: "this is the true Theodicaea, the Justification of God in History." [128]

The essence of the problem of theodicy is the logical contradiction between two propositions, equally important to theology. The one is that God's will is absolutely good; the other is that God's will is omnipotent, that nothing can happen without God's will and that consequently, if there is evil in the world, it must be there by the will of God. As long as the logical law excluding contradiction —which is fundamental to rationalistic science—is considered to be valid, one of the two propositions cannot be true.

In order to reconcile his religious metaphysics, especially his theology of history, with rationalistic science, the right of which to exist he does not deny but to which he assigns in his philosophical system only a subordinate position as compared with that of theology, Hegel has to invent a new logic. It is the synthetic logic of dialectic in contradistinction to the old analytical logic. The most characteristic element of the new logic of dialectic is the elimination of the law of contradiction, according to which two contradictory propositions cannot be true at the same time. Hegel tries to make us believe that in excluding contradiction the old logic commits a fundamental error. For not only is contradiction not a defect of thought, "speculative thought consists only in this, that thought holds fast Contradiction and in Contradiction itself." [129]

In itself it is not, so to speak, a blemish, deficiency, or fault in a thing if a contradiction can be shown in it. On the contrary, every determination, every concrete, every concept is a union of . . . moments which pass over . . . into contradictory moments. . . . Finite things . . . are contradictory in themselves.[130]

In interpreting the relationship of two forces operating in opposite directions as "contradiction," Hegel projects the contradiction from thinking into being. Just as in nature and society two forces determining movements of opposite direction exist at the same time and result in a third movement in a new direction, so two contradictory propositions in thinking do not exclude each other but, as thesis and antithesis, produce, on a higher level, the synthesis, the unity in which the contradiction is resolved, and that means both overcome and preserved. It is contradiction that puts in motion things as well as thoughts. "Motion is existent Contradiction in itself." [131] Contradiction is the principle of self-movement. It is a law of thought and at the same time a law of events.

The assumption that a law of thought can at the same time be a law of events is based, in the last analysis, on the presupposition that the ethical as well as the logical value is inherent in reality, that the Spirit is working in the historical events; that the Real is the Rational. This view—that value is immanent in reality—which in the natural-law doctrine leads to the false conclusion from the "is" to the "ought," is also at the basis of the fundamental fallacy in Hegel's dialectic: the identification of the relationship of opposite forces in external reality with the relationship of contradictory propositions in thinking. The relationship of two opposite forces resulting in a definite movement in nature and society has nothing to do with a logical contradiction. The phenomena concerned can, and must, be described by noncontradictory statements in complete conformity with the principles of the old logic. But with the help of his dialectical logic Hegel obtains the most important results of his philosophy of history—the deification of the state, and the German world empire, as the necessary outcome of historic evolution.

According to Hegel's philosophy,[132] all that exists is rational ("the Real is the Rational"), but the state is "absolutely rational." It is the "realized ethical idea or ethical spirit." It results from the nature of the state "that it has the highest right over the individual whose highest duty in turn is to be a member of the state"; a membership which implies unconditional obedience toward the established authority of the state. The individual, says Hegel, exists only through the state; "he has his truth, real existence and ethical status only as being a member of the state." According to a religious view of the world, nature is a manifestation of God; but according to Hegel, the state is the conscious manifestation of God. Nature is only an unconscious, and, therefore, incomplete manifestation.

The state is the spirit which abides in the world and there realizes itself consciously; while in nature it is realized only as the other of itself or the sleeping spirit. Only when it [the divine spirit] is present in consciousness, knowing itself as an existing object, is it the state.[133]

From a rationalistic point of view, the state exists only in the mind of the individuals who adapt their behavior to the social order we call the state, which is not a real entity as are physical things. According to Hegel, however, the state has even more objective reality than physical nature, for it is a realization of the absolute spirit in the realm of consciousness. Hegel says: "The state is the march of God in the world; its ground or cause is the power of reason realizing itself as will." Every state, whatever it be, participates in the divine essence of the idea, "this actual God." "The state is not a work of art"; only divine reason could produce it. "The nation as a state is the (divine) spirit substantively realized and directly real. Hence it is the absolute power on earth." [134] This means: the state is God on earth.

Another result of Hegel's philosophy of history is that world history, as the unfolding of the World-Spirit's self-consciousness or the progressive realization of Reason, shows four successive stages or epochs. At each stage or epoch a definite nation is dominant; it has an absolute right to govern the world.

In contrast with the absolute right of this nation to be the bearer of the current phase in the development of the World-Spirit, the spirits of other existing nations are void of right, and they, like those whose epochs are gone, count no longer in the history of the world.[135]

The four epochs of world history are represented by four historic world empires. The first was the Oriental, the second was the Greek, the third the Roman, the fourth will be the Germanic world empire.[136] The fourth and last epoch of world history will bring

the unity of the divine and the human. By means of it objective truth is reconciled with freedom, and that, too, inside of self-consciousness and subjectivity. This new basis, infinite and yet positive, it has been charged upon the northern principle of the Germanic nations to bring to completion.[137]

The "northern principle," ascribed to the Germanic nations, will be "the reconciliation and evolution of all contradiction." [138]

Marx's historic materialism, his economic interpretation of history is an unmistakable offspring of Hegel's philosophy of history. For its decisive instrument is Hegel's dialectical logic. It is true that Marx declares:

My dialectic method is not only different from the Hegelian, but is its direct opposite. To Hegel, the life-process of the human brain, i.e., the process of thinking, which, under the name of "the Idea," he even transforms into an independent subject, is the demiurgos of the real world, and the real world is only the external, phenomenal form of "the Idea." With me, on the contrary, the idea is nothing else than the material world reflected by the human mind, and translated into forms of thought. . . . With him [Hegel] it [dialectics] is standing on its head. It must be turned right side up again, if you would discover the rational kernel within the mystical shell.[139]

Hegel is an idealist, Marx a materialist. But Marx, just as Hegel, understands by dialectic: evolution by means of contradiction—a contradiction of which Marx, just as Hegel, maintains that it is inherent in the social reality. The assumption of a "contradictory character" of evolution and especially of capitalistic society is an essential element of the historic or dialectic materialism founded by Marx.[140] Marx, just as Hegel, interprets conflicts in the struggle of life, the antagonism between groups of opposite interests, and especially the incongruity of productive forces and modes of production, as logical contradictions. Marx, just as Hegel, considers value as inherent in reality; but in contradistinction to Hegel, and less consistent than the latter, he does not identify thinking and being. According to Marx, dialectic as a method of thinking "reflects" only the dialectic process in reality. The dialectic method must be used in order to grasp the dialectic of society. But in rejecting Hegel's identification of thinking and being, Marx deprives himself of the only possibility of justifying—so far as this is possible—his fallacious identification of the relationship of opposite forces in nature and society with logical contradiction.

Nothing can show more clearly the futility of the dialectic method than the fact that it enables Hegel to praise the state as a god, and Marx to curse it as a devil. According to the doctrine of Marx and his friend Friedrich Engels, the state is by its very nature a coercive machinery whose function is to maintain the domination of one group—the group of individuals in possession of the means of production, the class of the capitalists—over another group composed of those who do not participate in the ownership of the goods called capital, the class of the exploited proletariat. The state is a coercive organization for the purpose of maintaining the suppression of one class by another. By the revolutionary establishment of socialism, that is by the abolition of private property in, and the socialization of, the means of production, the system of capitalism, and with it the state as a social institution, will disappear.[141] The communistic society of the future will be a stateless society, a society the order of which will be maintained without the employment of force. This will be possible because the social order will naturally be in the interest of everybody, so that nobody will be induced to violate the order. This ideal condition of mankind, although it will not be brought about without a revolution, will nevertheless be the inevitable because the necessary result of the law of historic evolution, the dialectic process of history.

The preceding explanations show that the natural-law doctrine, whether it presents its results as deductions from a law of nature in terms of jurisprudence or as deductions from a law of evolution in terms of sociology or history, operates with a logically erroneous method by which the most contradictory value judgments may be and actually have been justified. From the point of view of science, that is, from the point of view of a quest for truth, such a method is entirely worthless. But from the point of view of politics, as an intellectual instrument in the fight for the realization of interests, the natural-law doctrine might be considered as useful. In his dialogue *The Laws,* Plato distinguishes between lies which are, and those which are not, permissible. Lies are permissible if they are useful to the government: Thus, the government is permitted to make the people believe that only the just man can be happy, even if this be a lie. For, if it is a lie, it is a very useful lie: it guarantees obedience to the law: "No law giver, who was worthy of his salt, could find any more useful lie than this or one more effective in persuading all men to act justly." [142] That the natural-law doctrine, as it pretends, is able to determine in an objective way what is just, is a lie; but those who consider it useful may make use of it as of a useful lie.

A "DYNAMIC" THEORY OF
NATURAL LAW

T HE intellectual situation of our time, resulting from the shaking experiences of the two world wars, is characterized in the field of social philosophy by a revival of the natural-law doctrine, directed against the relativistic positivism which prevailed during the second part of the nineteenth and the first decade of the twentieth century. The essential element of the doctrine,[1] which claims to deduce principles of justice from nature in general and from the nature of man in particular, is its monistic view of the relation between reality and value (facts and norms, the "is" and the "ought"). It maintains that reality and value are not—as dualistic positivism assumes—two separate spheres, but that value is immanent in reality and that consequently it is not—as positivism assumes—a logical fallacy but a legitimate operation to infer from that what *is* that what *ought* to be or to be done. Since value is immanent in reality, value judgments—judgments referring to these immanent values—are as objective, that is, verifiable by experience, as judgments about reality. Positivism, on the other hand, assumes that value judgments are subjective and hence relative only, because they are not a description of facts but, in the last analysis, the expression of wishes and fears.

The natural-law doctrine stands and falls with the assumption that value is immanent in reality. If it is not possible to prove that an objective analysis of reality, that is, an analysis which does not already *presuppose* a definite value or norm, necessarily leads to

From *Louisiana Law Review*, June, 1956.

the assertion of this value or norm, the natural-law doctrine has no foundation.

To secure this foundation and thus to defend the natural-law doctrine against relativistic positivism is the main purpose of a recently published study by John Wild, *Plato's Modern Enemies and the Theory of Natural Law*.[2] By "natural law" Wild understands, in conformity with the traditional doctrine, "a universal pattern of action, applicable to all men everywhere, required by human nature itself for its completion" (p. 64). The theory of natural law is, according to Wild, "a realistic tradition of philosophy, radically empirical in its methodology." It claims "to derive all of its basic concepts from the observation of experienced facts" (p. 73). These facts are "tendencies" inherent in reality or, as Wild puts it, in "existence." "Finite existence is always unfinished. As such, it is essentially characterized by tendencies toward fulfilment and completion" (p. 67). Existence "requires" something for its "completion." It has a "tendential" character. According to the natural-law doctrine as presented by Wild, "the world of nature is in flux toward what is not yet fully possessed." This doctrine holds "that natural entities are in a state of incompletion or potency, and that they are ever tending further towards something they now lack." It is based on a "dynamic view of existence" which is opposed to "logical atomism" which regards existence "as made up exclusively of units which are fully determinate and actual" (p. 65).

The view that reality or existence is "in flux" cannot be rejected, and actually is not rejected by a positivistic philosophy. However, from the point of view of an objective science of nature, the statement that reality is in flux can mean nothing else but that reality is in a state of permanent change. To interpret the change of an entity from one state to another as the realization of a "tendency" is highly problematical. For "tendency" is an ambiguous term. It may mean something like "intention" or "purpose," that is to say, it may imply a teleological or normative view, entirely incompatible with a science whose function is the objective description and explanation of facts. Within such a science, "tendency" can mean only the probable cause of future change in observed phenomena. Wild says: "From observing a kind of action in its measurable effect, the physicist can infer something about the structure of the entity, and from his knowledge of structure he may predict a tendency" (p. 217). If a physicist, on the basis of an objective observation of facts, states the rule that heat has the effect to expand metallic bodies, he may, in a concrete case, predict with a certain degree of probability that a heated metallic body will expand. What he is able to predict is a probable change. The expansion of a heated metallic body is the normal, that is, the regular change which can be expected. The situation is the same in the regular development of the blossoms of a certain tree to an eatable fruit, or of the embryo in the womb of a woman to a human being. If the probable expansion of a heated metallic body, or the development of a blossom to a fruit, or of an embryo to a human being, are called "tendencies" of the metallic body to expand, of the blossom to develop to a fruit, of the embryo to develop to a human being, "tendency" means nothing else but a probable effect or a probable change, and then reality can be described without the use of the ambiguous term "tendency." However, the dynamic theory of natural law cannot dispense with the term "tendency" which is its very cornerstone, and as such means much more than a normal and hence predictable change. The "tendencies," from the alleged observation of which this natural-law doctrine derives its basic concepts, "require" something. "No tendency can be understood without some understanding of what it requires" (p. 219). It requires its realization, which means "completion," and existential completion is "good" (p. 65). "If existence is deprived of what it requires for its completion evil arises" (p. 65). However, a tendency which is nothing but a predictable change of an observed phenomenon does not "require" anything. The predictable expansion of a heated metallic body is not required by the heated body; nor is the development to a fruit required by the blossom, or the development to a human being by the embryo. All these phenomena are nothing but regular and hence predictable changes. The view that a tendency, that is—from the point of view of an objective science of nature—a predictable change of an observed phenomenon, "requires" its realization or completion amounts to the view that a cause requires its effect. This is, in spite of Wild's assertion to the contrary, a typical teleological or normative interpretation of nature. To call a tendency "requiring" its realization an "existential" tendency (p. 68) is not sufficient to prove that such a tendency "exists" in nature or has to be recognized "in accordance with nature" (p. 218). Neither does the nature of a thing require something from this thing, nor does a scientific observer or a supernature require something from nature.

If the view, that there are immanent in nature tendencies which require their realization, is accepted, then each state which is the result of a change must be considered as the realization of a "tendency" requiring this state; all reality or existence must be interpreted as realization of tendencies. For the only reason to assume that a tendency exists is the fact that a change actually has taken place. If a change expected by the observer does not take place, that is to say, if the entity concerned turns to another state than that expected, this state, too, must be considered as the "realization" of a tendency. From the point of view of an objective science of nature, that is, from the point of view of a science which describes and explains that what *is* (without presupposing a norm which prescribes what *ought* to be), there is no reason to evaluate one realization as good and the other as evil. If the blossoms of an apple tree do not develop as the gardener expects, but turn into some uneatable products, the latter are, for a scientific botanist, the necessary effect of certain causes just as the sweetest apple, and hence the realization of a tendency which is as "natural" or "existential" as the one whose realization is the eatable fruit. The fact that the expected change is the normal course of change means only that it is regular, that is, in conformity with a rule describing the actual behavior of existent entities. To identify the normal course of change with goodness, rests on the fallacy of confusing two wholly different meanings of the term "normal": conformity with a rule *des*cribing the actual behavior of entities, and conformity with a rule *pres*cribing a definite behavior of entities, that is, a norm. It is the confusion characteristic of all natural-law doctrines—the confusion of a law of nature and a moral law. That the normal change is good and the abnormal evil are value judgments which cannot be reached within a science describing and explaining reality. They express the relationship of a thing to the requirements which are not immanent in this thing but raised by men, and which, if they refer to the state or the behavior of men, are presented as norms.

II

The differentiation between good and evil, impossible within a description and explanation of reality, is essential to a natural-law doctrine which aims at norms regulating human behavior. If it tries to found these norms on facts, and—as the dynamic doctrine of natural law—on "tendencies" immanent in reality, it must differentiate between good and evil tendencies or qualify the realization of some tendencies as good and their nonrealization as evil. It must project into reality the value which it presupposes. This is just what the dynamic theory of natural law is doing. "The most basic thesis" involved in this theory is that value and existence are closely "intertwined" (p. 64). "There are natural norms embedded in the structure of all material existence" (p. 68). Thereby the fundamental presupposition of the traditional natural-law doctrine is accepted. According to Wild, "those who have responsibly defended this theory have never asserted that value and existence were the same. What has been asserted is that they are distinct, but inseparable." For, "it is by no means obvious and evident that value is totally divorced from fact" (p. 99). If existence or fact cannot be separated from value, how is value connected with existence or fact? Wild says: "If values do not exist in some way, ethical reflection is much ado about nothing." Hence values "exist" in some way; and if there is no other "existence" than that of facts—that something "exists" means, according to the dynamic theory of natural law, the same as that it is a "fact"—values must exist in the same way as facts. Wild says, "it is clear that values and disvalues are facts of *some kind*." If value judgments "are true, they must refer to *some kind* of existent fact" (p. 66). What kind of existence or fact? There is no answer to this question. Even if there are two kinds of "existence" or existent facts, value is one of them, and hence value is—after all—a fact, and even an "existent fact." Therefore the objection that the natural-law doctrine confuses value and fact is not as unjustified as Wild believes. The view that values are existent facts or some kind of existent facts is certainly not more obvious and evident than the opposite view.

The main arguments which Wild sets forth for his thesis that values are facts, are first: that we strive for their "realization" (p.

67). Values may be realized. "Of what real good are the sublimest values if they remain unrealized? This shows that the values really moving us are not separated from existence" (p. 67). The dualistic theory does not deny that values may be "realized." But the statement that a value is "realized" means only that a fact has occurred which in the opinion of the observer is in conformity with a value or a norm presupposed by him as valid. It does not mean that the fact is the value or the norm, or that the value or the norm is a fact of any kind. The second argument is the above-quoted statement that if values do not "exist" in some way ethical reflection is much ado about nothing, or, as it is formulated in another connection: the relativistic dualism of existence and value makes "ethics" and "moral justification" impossible (p. 71); it leads to "moral nihilism" (p. 81); which means: if values are not facts, there are no values in general and no moral values in particular, and hence no moral order is possible. This argument, too, is untenable even if it were true that there can be no moral values or a moral order if values are not facts. From the truth of this statement could not follow that values are facts. The lack of a moral order may be very undesirable, but from the fact that a certain state of affairs is undesirable does not follow that the conditions of the desirable state of affairs exist. However, relativistic and dualistic positivism does not assert that there are no values, or that there is no moral order, but only that the values in which men actually believe are not absolute but relative values, and that there is not *one*, but that there are many different moral orders under whose effective validity men actually live and always have lived; but just because there are so many and so different moral orders their validity—even if very effective—can be considered only as relative. It is inadmissible to identify value with absolute value. Yet only by such identification can the positivistic value theory be accused of moral nihilism.

There is an essential connection between the concept of "value" and that of "norm." A norm constitutes a value. Since, according to the dynamic theory of natural law, values are immanent in reality and reality is not man-made, therefore: "Norms that are not man-made must actually exist in some sense. They must be embedded in the ontological structure of things" (p. 105). The dualistic theory does not deny that norms "exist," just as it does not deny that values exist. But from the statement that a norm "exists" does not follow that it exists like a fact and hence must be embedded in reality. The statement means only that a norm is valid, that it has been created by a human act, and that means that a norm is the specific significance of a human act. This act exists as a fact and can be described by an "is"-statement; but its meaning that something ought to be is not a fact. It can be described only by an "ought"-statement. The view that norms are embedded as facts in reality rests on the confusion of an act with its meaning. This confusion is the basis of the assumption of norms which are not man-made. If they are not made by human beings they must be made by another being endowed with reason and will; solely such a being can issue norms to the effect that men ought to behave in a certain way. If it is not a human being it must be a superhuman being, the same who made reality, God. The view that values are immanent in reality or that norms not made by men are embedded in existence, is based, consciously or unconsciously, on a theological interpretation of the world.

III

After having asserted as a dogma that value and existence are closely intertwined with one another, that value is immanent in reality, Wild is forced to recognize that not only a positive but also a negative value must be considered as some kind of existence, that not only the good but also the evil "exists" somehow like a fact. "Indubitable empirical evidence shows us that evil in some sense really exists, as well as what is good" (p. 65). Then the problem arises how to distinguish good and evil as existent facts. In order to solve this problem Wild introduces the concept of "completion." Existence requires completion or fulfilment; in other terms, there is a tendency toward completion or fulfilment immanent in existence. If this tendency is realized, if existence "fulfils itself," if existence attains what it requires, if it "attains existential completion," it is good; if the tendency toward completion of fulfillment is not realized, if existence does not fulfill itself, if it "is deprived of what it requires for its completion," it is evil—"evil arises" (p. 65). The statement that something, if it is "completed," is good, and if it is not completed, if it is deprived of something, is evil, is tautological, for in the concept of "completion" the value of good and in that of "privation" the disvalue of evil is already implied. The decisive question is: how to recognize by unprejudiced observation of a fact that it is "completed" or "deprived" of something. From the point of view of a mere description and explanation of reality *all* entities are complete as they are, and if the concrete state, in which an entity in the course of its change exists, is interpreted as a state of incompleteness or deprivation, *all* entities are always incomplete or "deprived" of something. A child is incomplete because it is not yet a man, and a man incomplete because not yet old, and an old man incomplete because not yet dead. If the change of a child to a man is interpreted as the realization of a "tendency," then the change of a young man to an old man, and the change of an old man to a dead man must also be interpreted as the realization of a tendency. Then there exists not only a tendency toward life but also a tendency toward death; and if—as the dynamic theory of natural law assumes—the realization of a tendency is good, the realization of the tendency toward death is as good as the realization of the tendency toward life. Then it is impossible to found on tendencies immanent in existence the fundamental norm which, as we shall see later, the dynamic theory of natural law presupposes, namely, that life ought to be preserved and promoted. If value (or disvalue) is immanent in existence, either all existing entities are good or all are evil. Then it is impossible to distinguish *within* existence good and evil, because the one as well as the other coincides with existence. Such a distinction is possible only if a norm is presupposed prescribing what ought to be. Only then it is possible to judge that an entity is complete, which means that it is as it ought to be; or that it is not complete, deprived of something, which means that it is not as it ought to be.

The dynamic theory of natural law is not able to overcome this difficulty. Referring to its fundamental thesis—that natural entities are in a state of incompletion and consequently "are ever tending further towards completion"—Wild asks: "What determines the nature of these existential tendencies?" From the answer to this question we should learn how to recognize, by observing facts, tendencies toward completion and the reason why some tendencies are and some are not realized. But from his answer we learn nothing. He simply refers to the term "nature" in his definition of natural law. "This term signifies a certain determinate structure, or form, which is possessed in common by all individuals of a certain kind or species. Thus, all individual human beings share in common human nature. As in the case of other finite entities this determinate structure or nature, when given existence, produces certain determinate tendencies toward fulfilment" (pp. 65, 66). His answer to the question as to what determines the nature of existential tendencies, that is, tendencies toward completion, is that nature produces tendencies toward fulfillment. That "all individual human beings share in a common human nature" is an empty tautology, since the concept of "individual human being" implies the concept of a common human nature. The statement that an individual is a human being is identical with the statement that it shares human nature. But, what is "human nature"? What are its essential traits? Wild does not answer this question by his statements that "human nature is an ordered set of traits possessed in common by every human individual and essential to his being," and that human reason is capable "to apprehend this common structure and the perfective tendencies characteristic of the human species" (p. 66). Until now the dynamic theory of natural law has nothing else produced but the assertion that there are in human nature, just as in all finite entities, tendencies toward completion, fulfilment, or perfection, that is, the fundamental thesis of its dynamic view of the world, which projects the norms presupposed by it into reality. This projection becomes evident by the fact that Wild, on the basis of nothing else but the unfounded assertion that there are in human nature "perfecting tendencies," arrives at the conclusion: "When so understood and expressed in universal propositions, these tendencies are norms or moral laws" (p. 66).

Later, Wild makes the attempt to justify the view that values or norms are immanent in reality by referring to the fact that "existent entities are certainly judged, sometimes truly judged, to be in a sound or unsound condition" (p. 66). He says: "For any entity whatsoever, to realize its essential tendencies and capacities for action is to be in a sound or healthy state" (p. 73). That probably means: the fact that the essential tendencies of an entity are realized, shows that it is in sound state, or: the fact that we judge the state of an existent entity as sound, shows that an existential tendency is realized. Applying the distinction between sound and unsound states to human nature, Wild says: "Many things happen to a man, either from external influences or from his own free choice, which are not in accordance with his nature and his natural tendencies. If this were not true, we could not distinguish between the healthy or sound state and that which is unhealthy and unsound" (p. 77). It may be assumed that the "essential" tendencies are the "natural" tendencies. If an entity, and especially a human being, is judged to be in a sound or healthy state, essential or natural tendencies are realized. "The realization of these [essential] tendencies is always good; their frustration always evil. Hence, the chasm between fact and value is bridged. . . . The world is dynamic and moving towards completion. There are natural norms embedded in the structure of all material existence" (pp. 67–68).

According to the dynamic theory of natural law, the judgment that an entity is in a sound or unsound state is a statement about an experienced, observable fact and at the same time a value judgment. "In the case of subhuman living things, we refer to incipient tendencies by value terms like requirement or need, and to their fulfillment by others like normal, sound, and healthy. When we analyze the structure in this way, we are recognizing the existential category of goodness—realization of imperfect tendencies. Furthermore, we sometimes argue back from the realization to what it requires of the incipient tendency and speak of a deceased or warped plant in terms of how it should have grown, or of a maimed animal in terms of what it ought to have done to avoid the injury. There is no implication of any conscious teleology in this. We are merely recognizing existential tendencies requiring further acts for their fitting realization in accordance with nature" (p. 218).

The judgment that a living entity is in a sound or healthy state may, indeed, refer to a mere fact, the fact that the vital functions of this entity are not impeded. If this judgment implies the idea that the sound or healthy state is good, it assumes the character of a value judgment, and such value judgment is possible only if the judging subject presupposes a norm requiring that this sound state ought to be. The sound state of a poisonous snake is good for the snake, if we assume that the snake wants to live; but evil for men who destroy the life of these beings in order to save their own life. Men presuppose the norm that human life ought to be preserved, but not—as a rule—that the life of a poisonous snake ought to be preserved. The goodness or badness of a state is not, as its health or sickness is, an experienced, observable fact; it is the conformity or nonconformity with a norm presupposed by the observer. Wild admits that the judgment to the effect that a plant is warped, that it is in an unsound state, implies the idea that it *should* or *ought* to have grown in another way. But this idea does not refer to a fact which can be observed; it refers to a norm presupposed by the observer. We can see that a plant is warped, but we cannot see, we can only require, that it ought not to be warped. An identification of soundness with goodness is especially impossible if goodness means a moral value, and it is a moral value at which a natural-law doctrine is aiming. Moral values apply only to human behavior; and the terms "sound" and "unsound" refer—in the usual language—to biological states rather than to human actions. If applied to human actions we may perhaps say that if a man by his behavior preserves and promotes his own life, his behavior is sound. The soundness of his behavior is an observable fact; it is the effect of his behavior. But the answer to the question of whether such sound behavior is morally good or evil depends on the norms we presuppose. It cannot be found by observing and analyzing the behavior. Such behavior may be judged to be morally indifferent. It may, however, be judged to be under certain circumstances morally evil—if the norm is presupposed that a man ought to sacrifice his life if this is necessary to gain victory over the enemy in war. Suicide which is just the contrary of preserving one's own life is, according to some moral systems, forbidden. It is against human nature and as such evil; according to others, it is under certain circumstances justified in accordance with human nature and as such good. The identification of the fact of soundness with the moral value of goodness is, in spite of Wild's assertion to the contrary, the projection of a subjective value in objective reality.

IV

In order to maintain the view that the distinction between a sound and an unsound state proves that the values of good and evil are immanent in reality, the distinction between essential and not essential or accidental tendencies is introduced. This is not consistent; for in one of its versions the dynamic theory of natural law knows only one type of tendencies: tendencies toward completion.

It asserts that "being has an active or tendential character. Such acts or tendencies are at first imperfect or incomplete. They may be either frustrated with a resulting evil, or completed with a resulting good" (p. 65). "That which exists always contains germinal tendencies towards the right, but these tendencies may become twisted or distorted by chance, by tyrannical manipulations and by mistaken deliberation" (p. 70). Hence: "Many tendencies exist in a privative or unfulfilled state" (p. 217). "That which will complete or activate a tendency is good" (p. 220). From these statements follows that *all* tendencies immanent in reality are directed toward the right, and that their completion or realization is good. The evil which exists—and that it "exists" is expressly admitted (p. 65)—is not interpreted as the realization or completion of a tendency, "completion" meaning realization of the good. There are no "tendencies" toward the wrong. The evil is the result of the fact that a tendency is "twisted" or "distorted" and hence remains in a privative or unfulfilled state. Consequently only part of existence is the realization of tendencies; part of existence is not of this dynamic nature. This, of course, is hardly compatible with a dynamic view of reality whose essence consists in the assumption that there are tendencies immanent in reality. As pointed out, if evil exists it must be interpreted as the realization of a tendency. It is, however, quite understandable why the dynamic theory of natural law does not recognize the existence of tendencies toward the wrong. Such recognition would annihilate its attempt to found the norm of right behavior on existential tendencies, its fundamental thesis that existential, perfective tendencies are "norms or moral laws" (p. 60). Referring to the fact that tendencies may be twisted or distorted, Wild says: "Hence, we cannot infer that what is, is right," (p. 70) which means that we can infer only that right is what is the realization of an untwisted, undistorted tendency. But how can we know that what *is*, is the realization of a tendency which is not twisted or distorted, and as such good, if that what is evil, too, "is," that is to say, is as much existent as that what is good? Wild's answer is: "There is a stable universal standard resting on something firmer than the shifting sand of appetites to which an appeal can be made from the maximal of agreements of a corrupt society. This standard is the law of nature" (p. 70). However, as long as this natural-law doctrine does not answer the question how to distinguish, by an unbiased observation of facts distorted (and as such evil) from undistorted (and as such good) tendencies, it does not furnish this "stable and universal standard."

This standard is not provided by the above-mentioned distinction, which plays a decisive part in the dynamic theory of natural law, the distinction between "essential" or "natural" tendencies which "conform to the nature of man" and tendencies which are not essential or natural, but accidental. Only the former constitute, according to the dynamic theory of natural law, "what is commonly referred to as moral law" (p. 67) and consequently are called "rights" (p. 218). This distinction is hardly compatible with the view that "that which exists always contains germinal tendencies towards the right", although these tendencies may be prevented from reaching their goal by being twisted or distorted (p. 70). For according to this view all tendencies inherent in existence are directed toward the right, and, if this direction is decisive for their being essential, all tendencies must be considered as essential. What is the difference between tendencies which are and those which are not essential or natural? "Some tendencies," Wild says, "are peculiar to the individual entity. But other essential tendencies are shared in common by those possessing a similar nature. Such tendencies, when they are rationally understood, constitute what is commonly referred to as the moral law. The realization of these tendencies is always good, their frustration evil" (pp. 67–68). Only the realization of *essential* tendencies is good and only the frustration of *these* tendencies is evil. The quoted statements seem to imply that essential tendencies are inherent in all existent entities. But if these tendencies constitute moral laws, moral laws would apply not only to human beings, but also to animals, plants, and inanimate things, which of course would be absurd. As a matter of fact, Wild later characterizes "essential," that is, "natural," tendencies in a different way so that they may be considered to be inherent only in human beings. He says that there are two distinguishing features by which a natural or essential tendency is marked: "first, it is shared in common by all members of the species; second, its realization, at least to some degree, is required for the living of human life. Thus the need for food is a natural tendency; the desire to torture other men is not. The first is common to the species, and some degree of realization is required for human life. Hence it is essential. The second lacks this mark . . . . it is unessential or accidental, and also obstructive or evil. The pattern of action which is universally required for the living of human life is essential. This is the standard of natural law" (p. 77). In another connection, Wild asserts: "Human existence is constituted by diverse tendencies, some shared by every human individual and indispensable to human life, others peculiar to certain individuals or groups, and dispensable." Only the former "must be realized to some degree if human life is to be lived at all—for example, the need for food and the need for education. When focused by rational insight they are called rights. They have a right to be realized . . . because they are required by human nature itself and the cosmic causes of human nature" (p. 218).

From the second feature seems to follow that only human beings come into consideration, which is quite understandable from the point of view of a natural-law doctrine which tries to found the norms of the law on tendencies immanent in human nature. Then, the problematical assumption of tendencies in other than human beings seems to be quite superfluous. Tendencies existing in human beings are desires that can hardly be assumed to exist in inanimate things, or in plants, or even in some primitive animals. As a matter of fact, according to the dynamic theory of natural law the tendencies existing in human nature manifest themselves in desires, in "natural desires" which this theory distinguishes from "incidental appetites" (p. 68). The need for food is an essential or natural tendency because it is a natural desire in contradistinction to the desire to torture other men, which is not a natural tendency because—according to the dynamic theory of natural law—it is not shared in common by all members of the species human being. It is true that Wild in another connection (p. 218) characterizes the tendencies "shared by every human individual and indispensable" as "needs" in contradistinction to tendencies "peculiar to certain individuals or groups" which he calls "desires, interests or compulsions." This, however, is incompatible with the distinction presented in the first part of his book. There he says: "The theory of natural law maintains that there is a sharp distinction between raw appetites and deliberate desires elicited with the co-operation of practical reason" (p. 69). This distinction is evidently identical with that between natural desires and incidental appetites. Wild

refers to the "actually felt urges of natural desires." When he proclaims the principle of natural norms grounded in factual tendencies, Wild refers to the "actually felt urges of natural desire"
(p. 68). The "urge" of a natural desire in which a natural tendency
manifests itself is certainly a compulsion. There would be no
"need" for food, if there were no "desire" for it. Only because it
is a desire can it be compared with the "desire" to torture other
men. The need for food is a natural tendency, its realization is—
according to the dynamic theory of natural law—required by human nature, because the desire for food is shared in common by all
human beings. Only the "desire" is a fact. Only as a psychological
or physiological fact is it shared in common by all men. Of course
there may be a "need" for something, that is to say, that something
may be according to our knowledge necessary for the preservation
of human life, without man feeling a desire for it. But this is
something different from an actually felt urge shared in common
by all human beings.

If the norms of natural law are to be grounded on natural desires,
that is, desires shared in common by all human beings, it is hardly
possible to establish a system of natural norms regulating the social life of men. For there is hardly another natural desire shared
in common by all men than that for food. The need for education is certainly not based on a desire actually felt by all men and
is certainly not necessary to preserve the life of man. It is, by the
way, significant, that the dynamic theory of natural law expressly
refers only to these two, of which one does not fulfil the conditions
of an essential or natural tendency, and the other is evidently not
sufficient as basis of a natural social order, even if it were possible
to infer from the fact that all men have a desire for food the norm
that this desire ought to be satisfied. If the desire for food is a
"tendency" then the desire to torture other men, too, is a tendency,
although a tendency which is not shared in common by all men.
This is in open conflict with the view that there are only tendencies
toward the right and that the evil consists in the fact that a tendency—directed to the right—is twisted or distorted. The desire
to torture other men cannot be conceived of as twisted or distorted tendency toward the right. Besides, the tendencies constituting human nature which are desires, are evidently something different from the tendencies immanent in the nature of entities

other than human beings, the tendencies a physicist may predict from the knowledge of the structure of these entities. Then the term "tendency" is used in two totally different meanings. If this is not the case, the tendencies, which the dynamic theory of natural law assumes to exist in that part of nature which is not human, must also be desires or something similar to desires; and then its teleological implication cannot be denied.

V

The "standard of natural law" rests, as Wild asserts, "on the possibility of distinguishing between what is essential to an entity and what is incidental" (p. 77), between "natural" existence and mere existence (p. 76), between "nature" and "existence" (p. 76), so that tendencies which constitute human existence may be considered as unessential and hence as not natural, or as not in accordance with human nature. However, such a distinction is possible only if by "nature" is to be understood existence, not as it actually *is* but as it *ought* to be in conformity with a presupposed norm.

This is, indeed, the meaning of the second feature by which an "essential" tendency inherent in human nature is marked. It is a tendency whose realization is "required for human life." It must be realized "if human life is to be lived at all." The norm presupposed by the dynamic theory of natural law is the norm that human life ought to be lived, or more precisely formulated, that human life ought to be preserved and promoted. It implies that human life, the life of *every* human being, is the highest value.

Wild asserts that the distinction between what is essential and what is accidental consists in "separating out those traits which are necessarily involved in the existence of the thing or relation from those which are merely extrinsic and accidental" (p. 78). However, if a tendency constituting human existence is essential so far as its realization is required, if human life is to be lived, that is to say, so far as it conforms to the presupposed norm that human life ought to be preserved and promoted, then the term "essential" has another meaning than that of a trait necessarily involved in the existence of a thing. If "essential" means necessarily involved in the existence of a thing, then, from the viewpoint of an unbiased de-

scription and explanation of things, there are no traits involved in
the existence of a concrete thing which are not *necessarily* involved.
All its traits are "necessarily" involved because all of them are the
effect of certain causes. To consider them as "necessarily involved"
is the fundamental postulate of an unbiased description and explanation of existence. The statement that a trait involved in the
existence of a thing is not essential but merely accidental does not
refer to the existence of the concrete thing but refers to the relation of this thing to the definition of the concept under which the
concrete thing is subsumed. It does not mean that this trait is not
necessarily involved in the existence of the concrete thing but
only that this trait is not an element of the definition, that it is not
essential but merely accidental as far as the subsumption of the
thing under the definition is concerned. The meaning of a definition is not—as that of a norm—that a thing *ought* to have some
traits, but only that if it has not the traits involved in the definition
it is not the thing defined. Human behavior may be in conflict with
the essential tendency, that is to say, man may violate the norm
that human life ought to be preserved and promoted if, for example, a man commits suicide or murder; but he remains a human
being. If, however, a being lacks one of the traits involved in the
definition of "human being," it is not a human being. Consequently
a tendency constituting human existence is essential or natural only
because its realization is in conformity with the presupposed norm
that human life ought to be preserved and promoted, and not because it is necessarily involved in the existence of a human being.

VI

This norm is evidently, though tacitly, presupposed by Wild's
theory of moral obligation which claims to ground this "existential
category" on "verifiable cognitive judgments that are true or false,"
that is to say, on facts, especially on the fact of tendency (pp. 216,
217). "Obligation" is a fundamental concept of any legal or moral
theory. That an individual is under the obligation or is obligated
to behave in a certain way means that a norm prescribes that he
ought to behave in this way. The obligation is the norm in its relation to the individual whose behavior is prescribed. The statement that a norm or obligation is "binding" upon the individual

means that the individual ought to behave as the norm prescribes. It is important to distinguish as clearly as possible between obligation in this normative sense of the term and the fact that an individual has the idea of a norm or obligation, that this idea has a certain motivating influence on him, and finally leads to a behavior in conformity with the norm. The difference becomes evident when we assume that an individual is under an obligation even if the idea of the norm has no such effect on his behavior, if he actually behaves not in conformity with the norm; even if he has no idea of the norm at all. The latter assumption is usually expressed by the principle that the ignorance of the law is no excuse. If an individual does not behave as he ought to behave in conformity with a norm, we say that he violates his obligation. Only if we assume that he is under an obligation to behave in a certain way even if he does not behave in this way, can we say that he violates his obligation.

The distinction between obligation in the normative sense of this term and the fact that an individual has the idea of an obligation is frequently obscured by an equivocal terminology. It is usual to characterize the binding character of an obligation, as well as the motivating effect which the idea of the norm has in the mind of the individual, as a "necessity." The statement that a norm or obligation "necessitates" the individual to behave in a certain way may mean that if an individual is under an obligation he *ought* to behave in conformity with this obligation. It may, however, also mean that the idea of the norm as motive or cause in the mind of the individual has, as its effect, a behavior in conformity with the obligation. The term "necessitate" is used with two different meanings. The first meaning expresses a normative, the second a causal relation. The same ambiguity prevails in the term "binding." That an obligation is binding upon an individual may not only mean that the individual ought to behave in conformity with the obligation, but also that the idea of the obligation has a motivating effect on him. All attempts at grounding obligation on fact are based on the confusion of obligation in its normative sense with the idea an individual has of an obligation and the motivating effect of this idea.

Wild's theory of obligation is a typical example of this confusion. He is aware of the specific normative meaning of the term obligation, he recognizes that this concept expresses "oughtness," that the "ought" is not identical with the "is" and that the one cannot be inferred from the other. Nevertheless he characterizes obligation as a "human feeling" (p. 66) and asserts that "obligation" "binds or moves us to certain values. This is clearly a factual urge, or tendency, which existentially links us or propels us towards certain values" (p. 67). He says: ". . . we are physically moved or bound by the urge of obligation or oughtness" (p. 68). He expressly defines the "ought," "the basic fact of human nature," as "the actual urge inherent in this nature" (p. 97). That means that he reduces the "ought" to the "is." It is evident that we are "physically moved or bound" only by the idea we have in our mind of an obligation, which may be an "urge," that is, a more or less effective motive and as such a psychological fact, a "feeling" that may "move" us in a certain direction, especially to fulfill the obligation of which we have an idea, and thus to realize a value. But it is certainly not the "oughtness" which physically moves or binds us. For this can be only the effect of an existing fact, and "oughtness" is not a statement about an existing fact. Wild says further: "Obligation seems to be some kind of necessity that obliges and binds" (p. 214). He correctly rejects the theory which interprets obligation as a type of "psychological law," and asserts: "Obligation does not necessitate in *this sense,* for people often do not fulfil their obligations, knowing that they do not" (p. 214). Nevertheless, his own theory of obligation is an (unsuccessful) attempt at grounding moral obligation on natural tendencies immanent in human nature (p. 117), and that means on the psychological fact of natural desires.

According to this theory, moral obligation is the result of the "transformation of raw appetite" (p. 218). There are two steps in this transformation. The first is the "rational recognition of natural needs," that is, needs "required by human nature itself and the cosmic causes of human nature," and their distinction from ephemeral desires. "These needs are felt by the individual as unfinished tendencies in himself and others" (p. 218). "As soon as we recognize a need, we also recognize the universal value that will satisfy the need. The apprehension of such universal values, not relative to the particular interests of this or that individual or group, but tendentially relative to human nature as such is the second step in the complex experience of moral obligation. At this stage, we have the felt urge of existential common tendencies and the rational insight into the nonexistent values required to complete them" (p. 219).

It is not clear whether these two steps of the transformation of raw appetite into moral obligation take place in the theory of obligation or in the soul of the individual. Since Wild speaks of steps in the "experience" of moral obligation, the latter interpretation is not excluded. However, there can be no doubt that the "rational recognition of natural needs and their distinction from ephemeral desires" is a task of the theory of natural law, and that a man may be under a moral obligation without having any idea of this problematical distinction and without recognizing the universal values which satisfy the natural needs. But let us take into consideration only those statements which expressly refer to psychological phenomena in the mind of the individual supposed to be under a moral obligation. The first stage is characterized by the fact that the individual feels a need as unfinished tendency in himself and in others. This is hardly possible. An individual can "feel" only what is going on in himself. He can feel only his own need, he cannot feel the need felt by others. He may know that the need he feels is felt also by others, that it is a need shared in common by all human beings and that its realization is necessary for the preservation and promotion of human life, that it is—in the terminology of the dynamic theory of natural law—a natural or essential tendency. He may, in addition, have the felt urge of this need or tendency and the rational insight into the values required to complete this tendency. If it is assumed, as the dynamic theory seems to assume, that then, and only then, he is under a moral obligation, obligation is identical with a psychological state of the individual which consists of the feeling of an urgent need and some knowledge concerning the nature of this need. Now the question arises as to what is the content of the obligation? It can be only the realization of the value required for the satisfaction of the need. From the fact that a man feels an urgent need of which he knows that it is shared in common by all men and necessary for the preservation and promotion of human life and that he further knows the value that will satisfy the need, follows—according to the dynamic theory of natural law—that he is morally obliged, and that means that he ought, to realize this value. It is a conclusion from that which is to that which ought to be done.

This fallacy could be avoided if the dynamic theory would assert the following basic norm of natural law: men ought to behave in a certain way if they feel an urgent need which they know is shared by all men and that its satisfaction is necessary for the preservation and promotion of human life; and if they know, further, that this behavior constitutes the satisfaction of this need. It is evident that no moral order can be based on such a norm. The fact that a man because of his ignorance does not know or actually does not care that the need he feels is shared by all men, or the fact that he is in error about the value that will properly satisfy this need, cannot free him from the moral obligation concerned. What is still more important is that the need for food is the only need that fulfills the requirements of the dynamic theory. The need for education, the other need indicated by this theory, is—as pointed out—neither shared by all men nor necessary for the preservation of human life. Applied to the need for food—or the "tendency of hunger" as this need in its capacity as "factual foundation" of "moral argument" is also characterized (p. 227)—the dynamic theory leads to the absurd result of a moral obligation to eat and drink. For eating and drinking is the universal value that will satisfy this need.

Eating and drinking may be a natural right, but not an obligation. As a matter of fact, Wild identifies in another connection natural needs or tendencies, such as the need for food, with rights; he emphasizes that these needs or tendencies "have a right to be realized" (pp. 70, 218). There is, however, a fundamental difference between right and obligation, which a legal or moral theory must not ignore. The confusion of these two concepts is a serious defect. There is of course an essential relation between them. The right of one individual to behave in a certain way is conditioned by the obligation of another or all others not to prevent the former from, or to enable him to, exercise his right. A moral theory may assert the obligation not to deprive a man of the means to satisfy his need for food or—as the socialist doctrine does—the obligation to guarantee to everybody a perfect satisfaction of this need. These obligations, however, do not follow from the fact that the need for food is common to all men, but follow exclusively from the assumption that the satisfaction of this need is, as Wild formulates it, "required for the living of human life." This, as pointed out, can mean only: from a norm presupposed by the moral theory asserting these obligations, requiring that human life ought to be preserved and promoted.

VII

This norm cannot be founded on experienced and observable facts. It cannot be proved that a tendency—in the sense of a predictable change or a desire—toward the preservation and promotion of life in general or human life in particular is immanent in nature in general or in human nature in particular.

Life in general and human life in particular is a phenomenon whose existence is restricted to an infinitestimally small part of the universe known to us. It is quite possible that cosmic development will lead to a total destruction of life and especially of human life. Then the assumption of a cosmic tendency directed toward the destruction of life is not excluded. As far as human nature is concerned, there is indeed a fact which could be interpreted to be a tendency toward the preservation and promotion of human life. It is the instinct of self-preservation. However, it is a tendency toward the preservation and promotion of one's own life; and the realization, completion, or fulfillment of this tendency is possible only at the expense of the preservation and promotion of the life of other beings. The need for food, recognized by the dynamic theory of natural law as an essential or natural tendency, dictates the destruction of the life of plants and animals; but as a matter of fact, the instinct of self-preservation is satisfied quite frequently at the expense of the preservation and promotion of the life of other human beings, even if such behavior is not necessary to preserve or promote one's own life. Besides, there are situations in which the life of one human being can be preserved only by the sacrifice of the life of another human being. If the question arises how the majority of men will act in such a situation—and only from their actual behavior a "tendency" immanent in their nature could be inferred—there can be little doubt that the overwhelming majority of men will sacrifice the life of the other in order to save their own life. The realization of the tendency manifested in their behavior is certainly not required "for the living of human life" but for the living of one's own life—and that is a very different requirement. If a natural-law doctrine asserts that preserving or promoting one's own life at the expense of the preservation and promotion of the life of other human beings is against the nature of man, it does not refer to human nature as it actually is, but to human nature as it ought to be in accordance with a norm presupposed. It does not infer a norm from real nature, but it infers an ideal nature from a presupposed norm.

The tendency which manifests itself in the instinct of self-preservation exists not without exceptions, so that a norm of natural law, that is, a norm valid always and everywhere, could not be founded on it, as the statistics of suicide—sometimes even a mass phenomenon—clearly show. This, however, is not the most important objection against an attempt of founding the norms of a social order on the instinct of self-preservation which is the only observable tendency toward the preservation and promotion of human life immanent in human nature. The decisive point is that this tendency is directed toward the preservation and promotion of one's own life, that it is the expression of man's egotism, whereas all moral, and that means social, orders, and especially a moral order which claims to be natural law and hence valid always and everywhere, are directed against man's egotism, his tendency to satisfy his own interests even at the expense of the interests of others. They try to restrict this tendency: they are based on the principle of altruism. The need or desire for food—the main example of a natural tendency on which the dynamic theory of natural law claims to found the norms of this law—is, as such, morally indifferent. What counts is only how this need or desire of one individual is satisfied in relation to the same need or desire of the other individuals; and in this respect this "natural" tendency is no possible basis for natural norms.

If natural norms are "embedded" in existence, as the dynamic theory of natural law asserts (p. 68), these norms must have found expression in positive moral or legal orders, that is social orders which actually exist or have existed in the sense that their norms are or have been effective, that is to say, by and large actually applied and obeyed by men living under these orders. But the fundamental norm presupposed by the dynamic theory of natural law, namely that human life ought to be lived, or, what amounts to the same thing, that the life of every human being ought to be preserved and promoted, has never been recognized by any positive moral or legal system. The norm implies the idea that human life, the life of every human being, is the highest value. This is certainly not the idea of Christian morality, which considers life, that is the life of man in this world, as an evil, and only a transcendental existence in another world as good. The moral or legal systems effectively established among many peoples do not and did not consider the life of all human beings as equally valuable. The legal institution of slavery, implying the right of the owner to dispose of the life of his slave, justified by philosophers as a natural or just institution, is incompatible with the norm requiring the preservation and promotion of human life without any distinction. The moral systems which are at the basis of the positive legal orders of our time recognize war as a legitimate action and, hence, do not presuppose that the life of human beings belonging to the enemy ought to be preserved and promoted. If all these social orders are or have been actually effective, how could they be considered to be against human nature, if human nature is taken as it actually is and manifests itself in the social life of men; and where else could human nature manifest itself if not in the way the overwhelming majority of men actually behave in their mutual relations, and in the way they morally evaluate their behavior. A "realistic" and "empirical" philosophy, such as the dynamic theory of natural law claims to be, certainly is not in a position to deny that social reality is a manifestation of human nature; and social reality is the positive, not an imaginary, natural law.

ABSOLUTISM AND RELATIVISM

IN PHILOSOPHY AND POLITICS

Since philosophy exists, the attempt has been made to bring it in relation with politics. This attempt has succeeded to the degree that today the close connection between political theory and that part of philosophy we call "ethics" has become a truism. But it seems strange to assume—and this essay tries to verify this assumption—that there exists an external parallelism, and perhaps also an inner relationship, between politics and other parts of philosophy such as epistemology (that is, theory of cognition) and theory of values. It is just within these two theories that the antagonism between philosophical absolutism and relativism has its seat; and this antagonism seems to be in many respects analogous to the fundamental opposition between autocracy and democracy as the representatives of political absolutism on the one hand and political relativism on the other.[1]

I

Philosophical absolutism is the metaphysical view that there is an absolute reality, that is, a reality that exists independently of human knowledge. Hence its existence is objective and unlimited in, or beyond, space and time, to which human cognition is restricted. Philosophical relativism, on the other hand, advocates the empirical doctrine that reality exists only within human knowledge, and that, as the object of cognition, reality is relative to the knowing subject. The absolute, the thing in itself, is beyond human ex-

From *American Political Science Review*, Oct., 1948.

perience; it is inaccessible to human knowledge and therefore unknowable.

To the assumption of absolute existence corresponds the possibility of absolute truth and absolute values, denied by philosophical relativism, which recognizes only relative truth and relative values. Only if the judgments about reality refer ultimately to an absolute existence may they aim at absolute truth; that is to say, claim to be true not only in relation to the judging subject but to everybody, always and everywhere. If there is an absolute reality, it must coincide with absolute value. The absolute necessarily implies perfection. Absolute existence is identical with absolute authority as the source of absolute values. The personification of the absolute, its presentation as the omnipotent and absolutely just creator of the universe whose will is the law of nature as well as of society, is the inevitable consequence of philosophical absolutism. Its metaphysics shows an irresistible tendency toward monotheistic religion. It is essentially connected with the view that value is immanent in reality as a creation or emanation of the absolute good, and, consequently, with the tendency to identify truth (that is, conformity with reality) with justice (that is, conformity with an absolute value). Hence a judgment about what is just or unjust can be as objective as a judgment about what is true or false. Value judgments can claim to be valid for everybody, always and everywhere, and not only in relation to the judging subject, if they refer to values inherent in an absolute reality or are established by an absolute authority. Philosophical relativism, on the other hand, as antimetaphysical empiricism, emphasizes the unintelligibility of the absolute as a sphere beyond experience. It insists upon a clear separation of reality and value, and distinguishes between propositions about reality and genuine value judgments which, in the last analysis, are not based on rational cognition of reality but on the emotional forces of human consciousness, on man's wishes and fears. They refer only to relative values. A relativistic philosophy is decidedly rationalistic and consequently has an outspoken inclination to skepticism.

The hypothesis of philosophical absolutism that there is an absolute existence independent of human cognition leads to the assumption that the function of cognition is merely to reflect, like a mirror, the objects existing in themselves; whereas relativistic epistemology, in its most consistent presentation by Kant, interprets the process of cognition as the creation of its object. This view implies that the human subject of cognition is—epistemologically —the creator of his world, a world which is constituted in and by his cognition. Hence, freedom of the knowing subject is a fundamental prerequisite of the relativistic theory of knowledge. This, of course, does not mean that the process of cognition has an arbitrary character. The subject of cognition does not create the object by the process of cognition as God creates the world. There is a correlation between the subject and the object of cognition. The subject is not absolutely free in the process of cognition. There are laws governing this process in which the chaos of sensual perceptions is transformed into a meaningful kosmos. In complying with these laws, rational cognition of reality—in contradistinction to evaluation based on subjective emotions—has an objective character. Since the laws of cognition originate in the human mind, the subject of cognition may be considered as the autonomous lawgiver. His freedom is autonomy.

Philosophical absolutism, on the other hand, if consistent, must conceive of the subject of cognition as completely determined by heteronomous laws immanent in objective reality, and as subjected to the absolute, especially if the absolute is imagined as a personal being and superhuman authority.

The relativistic theory of cognition involves two perils. The one is a paradoxical solipsism; that is, the assumption that the *ego* as the subject of knowledge is the only existent reality, the impossibility of recognizing the simultaneous existence of other *egos,* the egotistic negation of the *tu.*

Such assumption would lead a relativistic epistemology to a self-contradiction. For if the *ego* is the only existent reality, it must be an absolute reality. Uncompromised solipsism is only another type of philosophical absolutism. The other danger is a no less paradoxical pluralism. Since the world exists only in the knowledge of the subject, according to this view, the *ego* is, so to speak, the center of his own world. If, however, the existence of many *egos* must be admitted, the consequence seems to be inevitable that there are as many worlds as there are knowing subjects. Philosophical relativism deliberately avoids solipsism as well as pluralism. Taking into consideration—as true relativism—the mutual relation among the various subjects of knowledge, this theory compensates its inability to secure the objective existence of the one and same world for all subjects by the assumption that the individuals, as subjects of cognition, are equal. This assumption implies that also the various processes of rational cognition in the minds of the subjects are—in contradistinction to their emotional reactions— equal, and thus the further assumption becomes possible that the objects of cognition, as the results of these individual processes, are in conformity with one another, an assumption confirmed by the external behavior of the individuals.

To be sure, there is an undeniable conflict between absolute freedom and equality; but the subject of cognition, as pointed out, is not absolutely free; he is only relatively free—free under the laws of rational cognition. This freedom is not incompatible with the equality of all subjects of cognition. The restriction of freedom by a law under which all subjects are equal is essential to philosophical relativism.

From the point of view of philosophical absolutism, on the other hand, it is not the equality of the subjects; it is, on the contrary, their fundamental inequality in relation to the absolute and supreme being which is essential.

II

In politics, the term "absolutism" designates a form of government where the whole power of the state is concentrated in one single individual, namely, the ruler, whose will is law. All other individuals are subjected to the ruler, without participating in his power, which, for this reason, is unlimited and in this sense absolute. Political absolutism means for the ruled complete lack of individual freedom. It is incompatible with the idea of equality because justifiable only by the assumption of an essential difference between the ruler and the ruled. Political absolutism is synonymous with despotism, dictatorship, autocracy. In the past, the characteristic example is the absolute monarchy as it existed in the seventeenth and eighteenth centuries in Europe, especially in France under Louis XIV, who formulated its idea in the famous phrase: *L'État c'est moi*. In our time, political absolutism is realized in the totalitarian states as established by fascism, national socialism, and bolshevism. Its opposite is democracy based on the principles of freedom and equality. These principles exclude the establishment of a totalitarian, that is, an unlimited, and in this sense, absolute, power of the state, which from a democratic point of view is characterized by the formula *l'État c'est nous.*

The parallelism which exists between philosophical and political absolutism is evident. The relationship between the object of cognition, the absolute, and the subject of cognition, the individual human being, is quite similar to that between an absolute government and its subjects. The unlimited power of this government is beyond any influence on the part of its subjects, who are bound to obey laws without participating in their creation; similarly, the absolute is beyond our experience, and the object of cognition—in the theory of philosophical absolutism—independent of the subject of cognition, totally determined in his cognition by heteronomous laws. Philosophical absolutism may very well be characterized as epistemological totalitarianism. According to this view, the constitution of the universe is certainly not democratic.

There exists not only an external parallelism between political and philosophical absolutism; the former has in fact the unmistakable tendency to use the latter as ideological instrument. To justify his unlimited power and the unconditional submission of all the others, the ruler must present himself, directly or indirectly, as authorized by the only true absolute, the supreme superhuman being, as his descendant or deputy or as inspired by him in a mystical way. Where the political ideology of an autocratic and totalitarian government does not permit recourse to the absolute of a historic religion, as in nazism or bolshevism, it shows an unconcealed disposition to assume itself a dogmatic character by absolutizing its basic value: the idea of the nation or the idea of socialism.

Political absolutism not only uses a metaphysical ideology for its practical purposes, that is, its moral justification; it has also a political theory at its disposal which describes the state as an absolute entity existing independently of its subjects. According to this theory, the state is not merely a group of individuals; it is more than the sum total of its subjects. It is a collective, and that means here a super-individual, body which is even more real than its members, a mystic organism and as such a supreme and superhuman authority, whose visible representative or incarnation is the ruler, whether he be called monarch, Führer, or Generalissimo. It is the concept of sovereignty serving the purpose of this deification of the state which implies the worship of the ruler as a god-like being. In relation to other states, the dogma of sovereignty leads to the negation of international law as a legal order above the states, that is to say, as a set of rules imposing obligations and conferring rights upon the states and thus determining the spheres of their legal existence. Sovereignty, in the sense of absolute supreme authority, can be the quality of one state only. By voluntarily recognizing international law, the sovereign state incorporates these legal rules into its own law and thus extends the validity of its national law, comprising the international law, over all other states or, what amounts to the same, over all other national legal orders. The view that international law is part of one's own national law is advocated by those who insist upon the sovereignty of their own state, and who take it for granted that legal interpretation of facts is identical with interpretation according to their national law, that is, the law of their own state. This juristic imperialism is usually not consistent enough to admit that by this interpretation the own state of the interpreter becomes the sole and absolute legal authority, the god in the world of law.[2]

III

Diametrically opposed to this absolutistic theory of the state is the one which conceives of the state as a specific relation among individuals, established by a legal order—as a community of human beings constituted by this order, the national legal order. In rejecting the sovereignty dogma, this relativistic doctrine considers the state as subject, together with all other states, to the international legal order. In their subjection to international law, all states are equal and members of the international community constituted by international law. According to this view, the state is certainly a legal authority; but not a supreme authority, since it is essentially under the authority of international law. But this law is created, in a thoroughly democratic way, by custom and treaties, that is, by the coöperation of the states subjected to it. As a legal community, the state exists together with all other states within the international community under international law, just as private corporations exist within the state under national law. Thus the state represents only an intermediate stage between the international community and the various legal communities established under the state in accordance with its national law. The relativization of the state is one of the essential objectives of this political theory. It may be characterized as a democratic theory of the state, because it reflects the spirit of democracy. For, just as autocracy is political absolutism—which is paralleled by philosophical absolutism; so democracy is political relativism—which has its counterpart in philosophical relativism.

It might be taken for a more or less superficial analogy between democracy and relativism that the fundamental principles of freedom and equality are characteristic of both; that the individual is politically free so far as he participates in the creation of the social order to which he is subjected, just as the knowing subject—according to relativistic epistemology—is autonomous in the process of cognition; and that the political equality of the individuals corresponds to the equality of the subjects of knowledge, which relativistic epistemology must assume in order to avoid solipsism and pluralism. But a more serious argument for the relationship between democracy and relativism is the fact that almost all outstanding representatives of a relativistic philosophy were politically in favor of democracy, whereas followers of philosophical absolutism, the great metaphysicians, were in favor of political absolutism and against democracy.[3]

IV

The sophists in antiquity were relativists. Their most prominent philosopher, Protagoras, taught that man is the measure of all things; and their representative poet, Euripides, glorified democracy. But Plato, the greatest metaphysician of all times, proclaimed against Protagoras that God is the measure of all things, and, at the same time, rejected democracy as a contemptible form of government. His ideal state is a perfect autocracy.[4] In Aristotle's *Metaphysics*, the absolute appears as "the first mover who is itself unmoved" and stands as a monarch over the universe.[5] Consequently the philosopher presents in his *Politics* the hereditary monarchy as superior to democracy. His teleological interpretation of nature —a result of his metaphysics—is in direct opposition to the mechanistic view of the atomists, who strictly rejected causes which were simultaneously ends and thus became the founders of modern science. It was not by chance that Democritus, who together with Leucippus developed the antimetaphysical theory of atoms, declared: "Poverty in democracy is as preferable to pretended prosperity in monarchy as freedom is to slavery."

In the Middle Ages, the metaphysics of the Christian religion goes hand in hand with the conviction that monarchy, the image of the divine rule of the universe, is the best form of government. Thomas Aquinas's *Summa Theologica* and Dante Alighieri's *De Monarchia* are the classical examples for this coincidence of philosophical and political absolutism. But Nicolaus Cusanus, who in his philosophy declared the absolute as unknowable, in his political theory couched a lance for the freedom and the equality of men. In modern times, Spinoza combined his antimetaphysical pantheism with an outspoken preference for democratic principles in the moral and political fields; but the metaphysician Leibniz defended monarchy. The English founders of antimetaphysical empiricism were decided opponents of political absolutism. Locke affirmed that absolute monarchy was inconsistent with civil society and could be no form of government at all. To be sure, Hume, who much more than Kant deserves to be called the destroyer of metaphysics, did not go as far as Locke; but he wrote in his brilliant essay, *Of the Original Contract,* that the consent of the people is the best and most sacred foundation of government, and in his essay, *Idea of a Perfect Commonwealth,* he sketched the constitution of a democratic republic. Kant, following Hume, showed in his philosophy of nature the futility of any metaphysical speculation, but in his ethics he reintroduced the absolute, which he so systematically excluded from his theoretical philosophy. Likewise, his political attitude was not very consistent. He sympathized with the French Revolution and admired Rousseau; but he lived under the absolute monarchy of the Prussian police state and had to be cautious in his political statements. So in his political theory he did not dare express his true opinion. Hegel, on the other hand, the philosopher of the absolute and objective spirit, was also a protagonist of the absolute monarchy.

V

It was a disciple of Hegel who, in the fight against the democratic movement in Germany during the nineteenth century, formulated the catchword: Authority, not majority! And indeed, if one believes in the existence of the absolute, and consequently in absolute values, in the absolute good—to use Plato's terminology—is it not meaningless to let a majority vote decide what is politically good? To legislate, and that means to determine the contents of a social order, not according to what objectively is the best for the individuals subject to this order, but according to what these individuals, or their majority, rightly or wrongly believe to be their best—this consequence of the democratic principles of freedom and equality is justifiable only if there is no absolute answer to the question as to what is the best, if there is no such a thing as an absolute good. To let a majority of ignorant men decide instead of reserving the decision to the only one who, in virtue of his divine origin, or inspiration, has the exclusive knowledge of the absolute good— this is not the most absurd method if it is believed that such knowledge is impossible and that, consequently, no single individual has the right to enforce his will upon the others. That value judgments have only relative validity, one of the basic principles of philosophical relativism, implies that opposite value judgments are neither logically nor morally impossible. One of the fundamental principles of democracy is that everybody has to respect the political opinion of everybody else, since all are equal and free. Tolerance, minority rights, freedom of speech, and freedom of thought, so characteristic of democracy, have no place within a political system based on the belief in absolute values. This belief irresistibly leads—and has always led—to a situation in which the one who assumes to possess the secret of the absolute good claims to have the right to impose his opinion as well as his will upon the others who are in error. And to be in error is, according to this view, to be wrong, and hence punishable. If, however, it is recognized that only relative values are accessible to human knowledge and human will, then it is justifiable to enforce a social order against reluctant individuals only if this order is in harmony with the greatest possible number of equal individuals, that is to say, with the will of the majority. It may be that the opinion of the minority, and not the opinion of the majority, is correct. Solely because of this possibility, which only philosophical relativism can admit—that what is right today may be wrong tomorrow—the minority must have a chance to express freely their opinion and must have full opportunity of becoming the majority. Only if it is not possible to decide in an absolute way what is right and what is wrong is it advisable to discuss the issue and, after discussion, to submit to a compromise.

This is the true meaning of the political system which we call democracy, and which we may oppose to political absolutism only because it is political relativism.

VI

In the eighteenth chapter of the Gospel of Saint John, the trial of Jesus is described. The simple story in its naïve wording is one of the sublimest pieces of world literature and, without intending it, grows into a tragic symbol of the antagonism between absolutism and relativism.

It was at the time of Passover when Jesus, accused of pretending to be the son of God and king of the Jews, was brought before Pilate, the Roman procurator. And Pilate ironically asked him, who in the eyes of the Roman was but a poor fool, "Then, you are the king of the Jews?" But Jesus took this question very seriously, and, burning with the ardor of his divine mission, answered: "You say so. I am a king. To this end I was born and for this cause came I into the world, that I should bear witness to the truth. Everyone who is on the side of the truth listens to my voice." Then Pilate asked, "What is truth?" And because he, the skeptical relativist, did not know what the truth was, the absolute truth in which this man believed, Pilate—consistently—proceeded in a democratic way by putting the decision of the case to a popular vote. He went out again to the Jews, relates the Gospel, and said to them: "I find in him no fault at all. But you have a custom that I should release to you one at the Passover. Do you wish that I set free to you this king of the Jews?" Then cried they all again, saying: "Not this man, but Barabbas." The Gospel adds: "Now Barabbas was a robber."

For those who believe in the son of God and king of the Jews as witness of the absolute truth, this plebiscite is certainly a strong argument against democracy. And this argument we political scientists must accept. But only under one condition: that we are as sure of our political truth, to be enforced, if necessary, with blood and tears—that we are as sure of our truth as was, of his truth, the son of God.

VALUE JUDGMENTS IN THE
SCIENCE OF LAW

I_N THE theory of law we encounter two kinds of judgments which, both, are usually considered to be value judgments, though there exists an essential difference between them. One refers to the behavior of the subjects of law, and qualifies that behavior as lawful (legal, right) or as unlawful (illegal, wrong). Such concepts as "legal right," "legal duty" and "delict" derive their meaning from judgments of this sort. The judgments of the second kind refer to the law itself or to the activity of the persons who create law. They assert that the legislator's activity or its product, the law, is just or unjust. To be sure, the activity of the judge may also be considered as just or unjust, but only so far as he functions in a law-creating capacity. So far as he merely applies the law, his behavior is qualifiable as lawful or unlawful precisely as is the behavior of those who are subject to the law.

These two kinds of judgments are comparable to judgments which assert that something is good or evil, beautiful or ugly. They imply that a certain object has a certain affirmative or negative value, that it is "valuable" in an affirmative or negative sense. The object of these evaluations may be either a given human behavior, or a legal order, or a legal rule, or a legal institution. The values involved in judgments to the effect that something is lawful or unlawful will here be designated as "values of law," while those involved in judgments to the effect that something is just or unjust, will be called "values of justice."

What is the significance of these judgments? What do they assert?

From *Journal of Science, Philosophy, and Jurisprudence,* July, 1942.

The question can be answered only by an analysis of what those who are concerned with law—legislators, judges, lawyers, parties in law suits, and theoretical jurists—actually mean when making such judgments.

Let us, to begin with, consider the judgments which attribute the quality of "lawful" or "unlawful" to some human behavior— judgments, therefore, which assert a value of law. They may also be called "juristic value judgments," in the proper sense of the term. They are true or false, and their truth or falsehood may be tested. By analyzing the way in which a jurist proves the truth or the falsehood of a judgment such as "the behavior B is lawful," or "the behavior B is unlawful," can the meaning of these judgments be established.

Since law always manifests itself in the form of a definite positive legal order—as French, Swiss, American, or international law—a juristic value judgment is always true or false relative to such a positive legal order. The same behavior may be lawful relative to one order and unlawful relative to another. What then is the method of proving that, relative to a given legal order, theft is unlawful, while the paying of debts is lawful? It is proved by showing that there is a general rule forbidding theft and another such rule prescribing the paying of debts. Our doubt as to whether a certain behavior is lawful or unlawful is resolved when we can point to a legal rule referring, affirmatively or negatively, to the behavior in question.

A rule prescribing or forbidding a certain behavior, we call "norm." The specific meaning of a norm is expressed by the concept of "ought." A norm implies that an individual ought to behave in a certain manner, that an individual ought to do or to avoid doing something. Statements expressing norms are "ought" statements. A behavior is lawful if it "corresponds" to a legal norm; it is unlawful if it "contradicts" a legal norm; it "contradicts" a legal norm if it stands in the relation of polar opposition to that behavior which is lawful. We may also say: an individual behaves lawfully if he behaves as he ought to behave according to the legal order; he behaves unlawfully if he does not behave as he ought to. The juristic value judgment that a behavior is lawful or unlawful, is an assertion of an affirmative or negative relation between the behavior and a norm whose existence is presupposed by the person making the judgment. A juristic value judgment thus presupposes the existence of a norm, of an "ought." The meaning of this value judgment is consequently dependent upon the meaning of the assertion that a norm "exists."

II

According to a widely accepted theory,[1] every value is a function of an interest in the sense of a motor-affective attitude. Desires and volitions are, in particular, instances of interest in this general sense. According to this theory, the judgment that an object is valuable, either affirmatively or negatively, means that somebody is, affirmatively or negatively, interested in the object, that somebody is favorably or unfavorably disposed thereto. A value exists when an interest, that is, a psychic fact, exists; it ceases to exist when this psychic fact vanishes or changes. If the object corresponds to the interest, it has an affirmative value; if it contradicts the interest, its value is negative. An object A contradicts an interest if this interest is an interest in non-A. The interest may be an interest of the person who makes the judgment or of somebody else. On this view the object of a value judgment is, however, always formed by somebody's actual interest. The judgment is not an "ought" but an "is" statement.

A value judgment is, in this interpretation, not itself an act of valuation. A valuation is somebody's emotional reaction to an object, an act of desiring or an act of will. The value judgment asserts that somebody values an object. It refers to an act of valuation but it is not itself such an act. The valuation is a motor-affective act whereas the value judgment is a cognitive act.

If the value of an object is its relation to an interest, it is misleading to speak of "value judgments" as a special sort of judgment. This terminology creates an impression that what these judgments assert does not belong to the realm of reality (actual facts). But the "values" which they assert are, in this interpretation, real (existent) facts. On this theory, value and reality (existence) are not opposed to each other.

They are opposed, however, if the value judgment asserts a relation between the object valued and a norm, an "ought," whose existence is assumed by the person passing the judgment. In this normative theory, the import of the judgment that somebody behaves lawfully or unlawfully, is that he behaves or does not behave as he ought to behave according to the norm, whose existence is presupposed by the judging subject. This value judgment is simultaneously an act of valuation. The value is an "ought" and as such something radically different from all matters of fact.[2] Only if we conceive of the value as a relation between an object and a norm does it make sense to draw a sharp distinction between judgments of value and judgments of fact.

Can it be shown that the judgment asserting the existence of a legal norm is equivalent to a judgment asserting the existence of an interest? If so, the normative theory of value just suggested would be untenable. The "ought" by which we have expressed the meaning of norms, would then be reduced to a natural fact; and the same would also be true of the values of law.

Attempts at such a psychological theory of law have in fact often been made. The legal norm has been described as an expression of a "will"—the "will" of the state or the people or the legislator. On closer examination, however, the fictitious character of this "will" becomes apparent.

The meaning of the statement that a norm exists is determined by the method through which its existence is demonstrated. Suppose we want to find out whether, according to the legal order of a certain state, it is unlawful for a man not to fulfill a promise of marriage. According to some legal orders, such a promise is binding; according to others, it is not. Suppose further that the legal order in which we are interested is of a democratic character. That it is unlawful to break a promise of marriage, is in this case proved by exhibiting a norm rendering such a promise binding. The existence of such a norm is established by the fact that a valid law belonging to the legal order under consideration contains a stipulation to that effect. This law is valid if it has been passed by the parliament of the state in question.

The decision of the parliament is a natural event, a fact of natural reality happening at a certain time and a certain place in the world. It is usually considered as an act of will, an act of "collective will." By a collective will we mean that several individuals have the same will in regard to a given object, that the wills of several individuals are directed toward the same end. In the present case, the common object of the wills of the members of parliament is supposed to be the content of the law that makes a promise of marriage binding. Whether or not this psychological interpretation of a parliamentary decision is correct, may for the moment be left undecided. The parliamentary decision is at any rate a natural event. To describe the process called "parliamentary decision" is to describe a part of reality. If the existence of a legal norm can be proved by showing that a parliament has made such and such a decision, then the "ought" of a legal norm seems to be an "is." And then the statement that one "ought" legally to behave in a certain way would mean that certain individuals have decreed that one has to behave that way. If we suppose that a parliamentary decision is an act of collective will, then the statement in question would mean that certain individuals will it. If the foregoing were correct, then the value judgment that a certain behavior is "lawful" (or "unlawful") would assert that this behavior corresponds (or does not correspond) to the will of certain individuals. The interest theory would thus be applicable also to the juristic value judgments and the values of law. We shall, however, find that such an interpretation of the values of law can not be entertained.

III

The application of the interest theory to the values of law is the result of a fallacious identification of the legal norm and the act by which it is created. The norm and the act creating the norm are two entities which must be clearly kept apart. Failure to make this distinction renders it impossible to arrive at a satisfactory description of the phenomenon of law. This will be shown by the following examples.

A legal norm, owing its existence to a parliamentary decision, obviously first begins to exist at a moment when the decision has already been made and when—supposing the decision to be the expression of a will—no will is any longer there. Having passed the law, the members of parliament turn to other questions and cease to will the contents of the law, if ever they entertained any such will. Since the legal norm first comes into existence upon completion of the legislative procedure, its "existence" can not consist in the will of the individuals belonging to the legislative body. A jurist who wants to establish the "existence" of a legal norm, by no means tries to prove the existence of any psychological phenomena. The "existence" of a legal norm is no psychological phenomenon. A jurist considers a law as "existing" even when those individuals who created it no longer will the content of the law, even in fact when nobody at all any longer wills its content. It is quite possible and often actually the case, that a law "exists" at a time when those who created it are long dead.

Since the law begins to "exist" after the legislative procedure has been completed, the law must be something distinct from this procedure. Juristic terminology therefore designates the "existence" of legal norms by a term which is inapplicable to the existence of the norm-creating act. That a norm "exists," the jurist expresses by saying that it is "valid." The "existence" of a norm is its validity. It is this validity to which the concept of "ought" refers. That a norm possesses validity means that individuals ought to behave as the norm stipulates. A norm-creating act, which is an act of will, can not be said to be "valid." It is there or it is not there; its existence is its "is."

To say that an act "creates" a norm is to use a figure of speech. What may properly be meant is only that a specific relation holds between a certain act that "is," and a legal norm according to which something "ought" to be done. It is the relationship between an act and its meaning. A legal norm is the specific meaning of an act which, because of this meaning, is called a norm-creating act. The existence of a legal norm can be affirmed only if an act has occured the meaning of which is a legal norm. In this the "positiveness" of law consists. The expression "positive" law means that law is a complex of norms "posited" or created by certain acts.

Through its positiveness law differs from so-called natural law. The norms of natural law are not supposed to have been deliberately created by somebody like the norms of positive law. They are assumed to exist in nature independently of the wishes and wills of man, and they can supposedly be found by an examination of nature. The so-called natural law is one of the forms in which the idea of justice appears. But here we are interested solely in positive law. Let us assume that the norm-creating act is an act of will. Then the statement that a valid norm is created by such an act means that men ought to behave in a certain way if certain individuals have expressed a will directed to this behavior. Between the norm-creating act and its meaning (that is, the norm created by this act) a kind of parallelism obtains which is similar to that between physiological processes in the brain and psychological phenomena as, for instance, thoughts and feelings. The norm is not possible without the creating act; but the two are *toto genere* different entities. The creating act is the *conditio sine qua non* of the norm, but it is not its *conditio per quam*.

If the legal norm itself is designated as a will—be it of the state, the people, or the legislator—then the term "will" is used in another sense than when applied to the psychological phenomenon represented by the norm-creating act. To say that it is the "will" of the legal norm that people behave in a certain way, is to give a figurative expression to the idea that people ought to behave in that way. There is in fact a certain similarity between the statement to the effect that somebody *wills* that people behave in a certain way, and the statement that people *ought* to behave that way. The "ought" is, so to speak, a depsychologized will.

A legal norm created by one act may be abolished by a norm created by another act (an *actus contrarius*). Here again the difference between the norm and the creating act is clearly brought out. It is not the preceding act which is abolished by the succeeding act; no act which once has taken place in time and space can be abolished by another act. What is abolished is the norm created by the preceding act. That it is abolished or "annulled" means that it ceases to be valid. It is not the succeeding act which abolishes the norm, it is the norm created by this act which has this effect. This is expressed in the well-known formula *lex posterior derogat priori*. That a norm is derogated or annulled, that it ceases to be valid, means that it is no longer possible to maintain that men ought to behave in conformity with that norm. It is again apparent that the phenomenon of law can not be adequately described without the category of "ought."

A legal norm may cease to "exist," that is, lose its validity, even without the occurrence of any contrary act. Such is the case when, according to its own meaning, the norm is to be valid only for a certain limited time. A statute may, in the very wording of its own text, carry the date of the end of its validity. The moment when the "existence" of the norm is discontinued, is in this example not the moment when the legislator ceases to will the contents of the norm, but a moment determined by the norm itself. A jurist, desirous to find out this moment, does not investigate the state of mind of those who once created the norm, but analyzes the contents of the norm they have created.

IV

Assuming that the norm-creating act is an act of will having the contents of the norm for its object, the interest theory of value seems to find at least an indirect application to the values of law. To be sure, the statement that a behavior is lawful (or unlawful), can not even on this assumption be interpreted to mean that the behavior (or its opposite) is actually desired by certain persons. But, perhaps it might be interpreted to mean that the behavior corresponds to (or contradicts) a norm which was created by an act of will having the content of this norm for its object. However, not even in this modified form can the interest theory be applied to the juristic value judgments. The act by which a legal norm is created is not necessarily an act of will having the content of the norm for its object. An analysis of the legislative procedure in a parliamentary democracy will make this evident.

The parliamentary decision by which, according to the constitution, a law is enacted, is in no way a "collective will," having the contents of the law for its object. It would be so only if a law could not be constitutionally enacted unless every member of parliament actually wanted the provisions of the law, and expressed this will of his in a perceptible manner. But that is not the case. For the enactment of a law the constitution requires merely that a majority of the members should vote for the law. The validity of the law is not affected by the opposing minority whose members do not want the law. If the contents of the law is A, then what the minority members want is non-A. The votes of the minority, however, are an essential part of the legislative process. The act through which a legal norm A is created, is composed of acts of will, of which one part only (the majority) have A for their object, while another part (the minority) have non-A for their object.

We have here provisionally assumed that the members of the

majority will the contents of the law. A closer analysis will show that this assumption is not borne out by the facts. Everybody familiar with parliamentary procedure knows that representatives often vote for a bill without being acquainted with its contents or its essential parts. It is impossible to will something of which one has no knowledge. What a representative actually wills who votes for a bill whose contents he does not know, is another question. Suffice it here to state that it is not the contents of the bill. Nor does the constitution require that all those who vote for a bill should know and will its contents. It is enough that they just vote for it. If a law is extensive and complicated, its contents are usually known only by very few representatives. Most of those who vote for the bill do so, not because they know its provisions and want them, but because they have confidence in those who propose that they should vote for the bill, or because they feel obliged to follow the directives of their party leader. The objection might be raised that, after all, somebody must want the contents of the law. That is true. But those who know and want the contents of the law often do not belong to those whose will is decisive according to the constitution.

Finally, it must be remembered that a law is expressed in words that are often ambiguous and may be interpreted by the law-applying organs in a manner not intended by the legislator. The contention that a norm is always created by an act of will having the contents of the norm for its object, is an obvious fiction. The norm-creating fact does not have to be such an act of will. But in order that we may assert the "existence" of a norm, there must always be some fact that "creates" the norm.

V

That the norm-creating fact is not necessarily an act of will having the contents of the norm for its object, is evident where a legal norm is not created by a special organ, but by custom. A norm of customary law stipulates that people shall behave as they customarily behave. When the members of a social group have followed a certain pattern of behavior for a certain time, the conviction arises within the group that one ought to conform to this pattern. The acts which in this case give rise to a legal norm do not have the contents of this norm for their object. Here there is no legislator to whose will the norm might be attributed. In this case, the

juristic value judgment that a certain behavior is lawful (or unlawful) can not even indirectly be considered as a statement about
a will having this behavior (or its opposite) for its object.

It might, however, seem as if the juristic value judgment were
here identical with another statement about matters of fact. The
statement that somebody behaves in a lawful way in this case might
seem to mean only that he behaves as his fellowmen customarily
behave. This attempt to reduce value judgments to judgments
concerning matters of fact is also due to the fallacy of identifying
the norm and the norm-creating fact. The fact that people customarily behave in a certain way is a condition which underlies the
assertion of the norm that people ought to behave in this way. But
the fact is here not identical with the norm, just as the fact that
the parliament passes a bill is different from the corresponding
norm to which it gives rise. The "is" rule which states that people
actually behave in a certain way, is not the same as the "ought"
norm which stipulates that they ought to behave that way.

Nor can the norm be logically deduced from the "is" rule. From
the fact that something is or happens, it does not logically follow
that it (or something else) ought to be or ought to happen. A natural
fact, in particular an act of will, can be regarded as causing the
"existence" of a norm only if another (higher) norm contains a
stipulation to that effect. Only if we presuppose the norm that one
ought to behave as members of the community regularly do, does
the fact that the debtor ordinarily returns to his creditor the money
plus 5 per cent interest, create a legal norm stipulating 5 per cent
interest. The presupposed norm makes custom into a norm-creating
fact, just as the constitution gives legislative power to the parliament. This norm must be part of the written or unwritten constitution, that is to say, of the complex of norms regulating the creation
of law. It is this norm which is the reason for the validity of all
particular customary legal norms. It is the basis of all juristic value
judgments within a system of customary law.

VI

The reason for the validity of a norm supplies the answer to the
question: why ought one to behave as the norm prescribes? Because the "validity" of a norm is its specific mode of existence, the

reason for the validity of a norm is also the ground for its existence. The reason for the validity of a norm is always another norm, never a fact. The facts which condition the existence of a legal norm—the presence of the norm-creating fact and the absence of the norm-annulling fact—are therefore not the ground for the existence of the norm. They are a *conditio sine qua non* but not a *conditio per quam*. A fact entails the existence of a certain legal norm, only if there is a higher norm which makes the existence of the norm dependent upon this fact. The lower legal norm possesses validity because it was created in accordance with the provisions of the higher norm. If we ask why a certain legal norm is valid, the answer is always in terms of another (higher) norm which regulates the creation of the former (lower) norm, that means, which determines the facts that condition the existence of the former (lower) norm.

If we continue our search for reasons why the legal norms are valid, we shall ultimately arrive at a last norm, whose creation has not been determined by any higher norm. The series of reasons for the validity of a norm is not infinite like the series of the causes of an effect. There must exist one ultimate reason, one basic norm, which is the source of the validity of all norms belonging to a certain legal order. Though the existence of every norm is conditioned by a certain fact, it is not a fact but a norm that is the reason why all norms of the system exist—and that means, are valid. This clearly shows that a norm is not identical with its conditioning fact.

VII

The same conclusion is forced upon us when we apply the analysis of juristic value judgments to that domain of law where the norms owe their existence not to custom, but to legislative acts. Suppose that some racketeers decide that all owners of night clubs in a certain city have to pay them a certain "tax." Even if, by the use of threats, they should be able to enforce their decision, the decision would still not constitute any legal norm and consequently could not be the basis of a juristic value judgment. Juristic value judgments presuppose a legal norm as standard, and a legal norm can be created only by persons who are considered legal authorities.

That is what makes the difference between the members of a legislative body and the members of a criminal gang. The former possess the quality of legal authorities; they have the capacity of
creating legal norms because a legal norm, namely the constitution, has accorded to them this quality. Statutes passed by parliament are valid because they have been created in the manner the
constitution prescribes. This norm of the constitution is the reason
why statutes are valid norms. And, in this sense, the constitution is
a norm or a set of norms of a higher level than the norms which the
statutes represent. Statutory and customary law are based upon
the constitution just as the decisions of the courts, that is, the
individual norms the courts establish, are based upon the statutes.
That one legal norm is "based" upon another, means that the
latter is the reason why the former is valid ("exists").

The legislative function of parliament is based upon the constitution; the decision of the criminal gang is not. Therefore when
parliament passes a tax bill it is a legal act, whereas the analogous
decision of the criminal gang is an illegal act. The legal norm created by the legislator presupposes the norms of the constitution,
and in the same way, the value judgment that a behavior is lawful
or unlawful—because it conforms or does not conform with a
statute—presupposes a value judgment to the effect that the function of the legislator is a legal function.

This latter value judgment is a statement about the relation between the legislative function and the constitution. The constitution, like a statute or a norm of customary law, is the work of
human beings. It originates either in custom or in a deliberate
act of certain individuals, "the fathers of the constitution." The
relation between the norm of the constitution and the fact creating
it, is the same as that between a norm established on the basis of
the constitution and the facts creating this norm. The act creating
the constitution must likewise be qualified by a higher norm as a
norm-creating act. The statutes are valid because they have been
created by persons authorized by the constitution. The constitution is, as we have seen, the reason why the statutes possess validity
or normative existence. Why does the constitution possess validity?
Why do we consider as binding the norms which the "fathers of
the constitution" decided upon? From what source does the constitution derive its validity, its normative existence? The existence

or validity of the constitution itself has to be based upon a norm. A norm can not receive its validity from anything but another norm. An "ought" must always be deduced from another "ought"; it never follows from a mere "is."

The norm which confers validity upon a constitution may be a previous constitution in accordance with the provisions of which the new constitution was established. In such a series of constitutions one must historically be the first. And the norm giving the "fathers" of this first constitution their authority, that is, a norm according to which one ought to behave in conformity with their decisions, cannot itself be a positive legal norm created by any legislative act. It is a norm presupposed by those who consider the establishment of the first constitution and the acts performed in conformity with it as law-creating acts. The science of law reveals this presupposition by an analysis of juristic thinking. The result of this analysis is the statement: If the historically first constitution, and the norms issued on this basis, are to be considered as legally binding norms, then a norm must be presupposed to the effect that one ought to behave in conformity with the historically first constitution. This norm is the basic norm of a national legal order. Since we can speak of a legally binding order only if we presuppose this norm (which is not a norm of positive law), it may be called a hypothetical norm. This basic norm is the foundation of all juristic value judgments possible within the frame of the legal order of a given state.

VIII

The legal order of a state is thus a hierarchical system of legal norms. In a grossly simplified form, the following picture presents itself: The lowest level consists of the individual norms created by the law-applying organs, especially the courts. These individual norms are dependent upon the statutes which are the general norms created by the legislator, and the rules of customary law which form the next higher level of the legal order. These statutes and rules of customary law in turn depend upon the constitution which forms the highest level of the legal order considered as a system of positive norms. "Positive" norms are norms created by acts of human beings. The norms belonging to a lower level derive their validity from the norms belonging to the next higher level. If we do not take into consideration international law as a legal order superior to national law, the constitution of a state represents the highest level within a national legal order. Then, the norms of the constitution do not receive their validity from any positive legal norm but from a norm presupposed by juristic thinking, the hypothetical basic norm.

The juristic value judgments show a stratification corresponding to that of the legal norms. Since every juristic value judgment asserts a relation between a human behavior and a legal norm, these judgments form a system exhibiting the same structure as the system of legal norms. The juristic value judgments may refer either to the behavior of the subjects of the legal order or to the behavior of the norm-creating and norm-applying organs. The behavior of the subjects can be judged either according to the individual norms established by the courts (and other law-applying organs), or directly according to the general norms embodied in the laws on the basis of which the courts (and other law-applying organs) make their decisions. Accordingly, the statement that a subject's behavior is lawful (or unlawful), may mean that this behavior corresponds to (or contradicts) the decision of a court, or that it corresponds to (or contradicts) a statute or a rule of customary law, on the basis of which the judicial decision is made.

The value judgment that a judicial decision is lawful or unlawful concerns the relation of the judicial decision to a statute or a rule of customary law. It asserts that the judicial decision is (or is not) in conformity with the statute or the rule of customary law. As already mentioned, a value judgment asserting the lawfulness of a subject's behavior may have this significance, too. The value judgment that a legislative act or a custom is lawful (legal), means that it is in conformity with the constitution conferring upon the legislative organ or the custom the power of creating law. Finally, the question arises as to whether the constitution, or, more exactly, the act by which the constitution is established, is legal and consequently whether the constitution is a legally binding norm (or a set of legally binding norms). It is evident that a value judgment to this effect is possible if the constitution is not the historically first constitution of the state concerned. Then the judgment means that the establishment of the constitution is or is not in conformity with the provisions of the previous constitution concerning its amendment. However, is such a value judgment possible with respect to the establishment of the historically first constitution? It is obvious that if we did not assume that the creation of the first constitution was legal, we would not be able to maintain that the legislative function of parliament or the creation of law by custom was legal. Nor could we distinguish between lawful or unlawful decisions of the courts. Finally we would also lack any standard on which to judge the subject's behavior as lawful or unlawful. The value judgment that the creation of the first constitution is legal, is the necessary foundation for all other juristic value judgments.

IX

The value judgment that the creation of the first constitution is legal means that the individuals who created it were authorized to do so by a certain norm. If we do not go beyond the boundaries of national law [3] we are unable to find any positive legal norm fulfilling such a function. It is, as we have seen, not a norm created by an act of will, but a norm presupposed in juristic thinking. We have to postulate such a norm in order to be able to maintain the "existence" of any positive legal norms and to be able to make any juristic value judgments. This conclusion cannot be avoided, for example, by tracing the authority of the "fathers of the constitution" to the will of God, as is sometimes done. To do so means to predicate the validity of the constitution on the supposed fact that God gave the originators of the constitution their authority. This command of God is again a norm, a transcendental norm since it falls outside the scope of human experience, but "positive" since—according to religious belief—it was created by the act of a superhuman will. This "positive" norm can be recognized as valid only if we presuppose the norm that one shall obey the commands of God. That, however, is a norm that has not been created by any act, be it human or superhuman, but is only postulated by the human mind. If one refuses to accept a metaphysical explanation of the authority of the originators of the constitution, one is forced to stop at the norm which has here been presented as the hypothetical basic norm.

X

To be true, this basic norm is not created by any organ of the legal community in accordance with the provisions of a higher norm. It is an assumption made in juristic thinking, but by no means arbitrary. An analysis of juristic thinking shows that jurists consider a constitution as valid only when the legal order based on it is effective. This is the principle of effectiveness. That a legal order is "effective" means that the organs and subjects of this order by and large behave in accordance with the norms of the order. An order can be effective as a whole even if one norm or other is not applied or not obeyed in certain cases where, according to its own meaning, it ought to be applied or obeyed. This principle is assumed by jurists, when they interpret the act by which the first constitution was established as a norm-creating act, and the constitution as a legal norm. In consequence of this principle, a constitution originates in a legitimate authority, provided that the legal order, created on the basis of the constitution, is effective as a whole. The principle of effectiveness is the general basic norm that juristic thinking assumes whenever it acknowledges a set of norms as the valid constitution of a particular state. This norm may be formulated as follows: men ought to behave in conformity with a legal order only if this legal order as a whole is effective. In its application to a concrete legal order, the national law of a definite state, it is the basic norm of this normative system. The value judgment that a given constitution is valid, that the creation of the constitution is a legal act, means that it conforms with this general basic norm.

That the principle of effectiveness is really presupposed by jurists is perhaps most evident in the juristic interpretation of a revolution. Revolution consists in the fact that one constitution is replaced by another, not in accordance with its own provisions, but by force. In the view of jurists, what deprives the old constitution of its validity, its legal existence, is precisely the fact that it has lost its effectiveness, that is to say, that it has ceased to correspond to the general basic norm which establishes the principle of effectiveness. And the new constitution is considered as valid only when it becomes effective, that is, when it corresponds to this principle. The government that is brought to power through the revolution and that issues the new constitution, is a legitimate authority only when it is able to render the new order effective.

XI

The principle of effectiveness refers, in the main, to the legal order as a whole, not to the isolated legal norm. An isolated legal norm may be "valid" even if it does not prove effective in every single case. The legal norm that the judge shall punish a thief is effective if the judge actually punishes the thief. The value judgment that a judge who fails to punish a thief behaves unlawfully, is possible only where the legal norm is ineffective. The effectiveness of the isolated legal norm can not be a condition for its validity, because otherwise negative juristic value judgments—judgments to the effect that a behavior is unlawful—would never be possible. However, if a particular legal norm remains permanently ineffective, the norm is deprived of validity by *desuetudo,* which is, so to speak, a negative custom.

On the other hand, the isolated legal norm can be valid only if the constitution is valid; it is upon the constitution that the validity of every legal norm is based. And the constitution is valid only if the total legal order, according to the general basic norm, is effective. The effectiveness of the legal order as a whole is thus a condition for the validity of each separate norm belonging to the order.

The existence of a positive legal norm accordingly presupposes: (1) the effectiveness of the total legal order to which the norm belongs; (2) the presence of a fact "creating" the norm; and (3) the absence of any norm "annulling" it.

A juristic value judgment asserting the conformity or nonconformity of a certain act with a certain legal norm implies the assertion of the existence of this norm. The existence of a norm, its validity, as pointed out, is different from the existence of a fact, and this difference should always be kept in mind. But, since the existence of a legal norm is conditioned by definite facts, it can—indirectly—be verified in an objective way by demonstrating the existence of these facts: the effectiveness of the total legal order to which the norm belongs and the presence of the fact "creating" the norm. As far as the value judgment is concerned that asserts the legality or, what amounts to the same, the validity of the historically first constitution by asserting its conformity with the presupposed basic norm, that is, the principle of effectiveness, this judgment cannot be verified by demonstrating the presence of an act creating this norm; but it can be verified by demonstrating the effectiveness of the legal order, established in conformity with the constitution. For this effectiveness is an objectively verifiable fact. In so far as such objective verification of juristic value judgments is possible, the value of law is an objective value.

XII

The value of law, as conceived by the normative theory, is objective also in another sense. According to this theory, a valuable object is valuable for everybody. According to the interest theory, on the other hand, an object is valuable only for a person who has an interest in the object, who wishes or wills this object (or its opposite). If—as the normative theory maintains—the values of law, the qualities "lawful" and "unlawful," "legal" and "illegal," lie in the relations of a behavior to a legal norm, then a behavior is valuable not only for a certain individual—for example, not only for the individual subject of that behavior—or only for the individual who by an act of his will creates the legal norm (if a norm is ever created in that way); a behavior is lawful or unlawful "for everybody," just as a thing is heavier or lighter than air "for everybody." [4]

This objectivity of the values of law is limited only so far as its existence implies the existence (that is, the validity, the "ought") of a legal norm, and this in turn is dependent upon the presupposition of the basic norm. This presupposition is, it is true, made only on the condition that a certain objectively verifiable fact is there. Taking the basic norm for granted, we may submit the juristic value judgments based on the presupposed basic norm to an objective test. But there is no necessity to presuppose the basic norm. One may abstain from interpreting human behavior according to legal norms, that is according to the meaning implicit in certain human acts. The system of norms that we call "legal order" is a possible but not a necessary scheme of interpretation. An anarchist will decline to speak of "lawful" and "unlawful" behavior, of "legal duties" and "legal rights," or "delicts." He will understand social behavior merely as a process whereby one forces the other to behave in conformity with his wishes or interests. The anarchist will reject the normative theory of value and accept only the interest theory. He will, in short, refuse to presuppose the basic norm which prescribes that one ought to behave in accordance with the meaning implicit in certain human acts.

XIII

This is the reason why it is possible to maintain that the idea of a norm, an "ought," is merely ideological. An ideological concept is a concept which fulfils another function than that of describing and explaining reality. If we conceive of the law as a complex of norms and therefore as an ideology, this ideology differs from other, especially from metaphysical, ideologies so far as the former corresponds to certain facts of reality. Though a legal norm is not identical with any natural fact, the existence of a legal norm is dependent upon certain objectively verifiable facts. If the system of legal norms is an ideology, it is an ideology that is parallel to a definite reality.[5] This reality consists in the effectiveness of the system as a whole, and in the facts which constitute the creation or the annulment of particular norms. It may be called a social reality, if one bears in mind that the designation "social" presupposes that this reality is interpreted in the light of a normative ideology. This social reality is often opposed to law as "power" is opposed to norm. In this sense the law may be considered as the specific ideology of a certain historically given power. This power is usually identified with the state. The state is said to be the power "behind" the law. This dualism of law and state is often an expression of the dualism of a social reality and an ideology conditioned and determined by this reality.

XIV

The value of justice is not of the same nature as the value of law. When we evaluate a legal order or a particular legal institution as just or unjust, we intend to say something more than when we call a dish of food "good" or "bad," meaning that we find or do not find it tasty. The statement that a legal institution, for instance slavery or private property, is just or unjust, does not mean that somebody has an interest in this institution or in its opposite. The interest theory does not give a correct analysis of what a statement of this sort intends to express. Such a statement means that the institution in question corresponds or does not correspond to a norm whose validity is presupposed by the person making the statement. A judgment which states that something is just or unjust claims to affirm an objective value.

The norms which are actually used as standards of justice vary from individual to individual and are often mutually irreconcilable.[6] For example, whereas the liberal regards freedom as the ideal of justice (that is, believes in the norm that everybody ought to enjoy freedom), the socialist sees the ideal in equality (that is, believes in the norm that everybody ought to enjoy the same economic welfare). When these two ideals are found to be incapable of simultaneous realization, the liberal prefers to have freedom at the cost of equality, while the socialist prefers equality at the cost of freedom. A social order that is just from the liberal's point of view is unjust from the socialist's point of view. Something is just or unjust only for an individual for whom the appropriate norm of justice exists, and this norm exists only for those who, for some reason or other, wish what the norm prescribes.

Liberalism and socialism are by no means the only ideals of justice. The norm of justice has a different meaning for a pacifist and an imperialist, for a nationalist and an internationalist, for a religious believer and an atheist. Primitive man has another conception of justice than civilized man. It is impossible to determine the norm of justice in a unique way. It is ultimately an expression of the interest of the individual who pronounces a social institution to be just or unjust. But that is something of which he is unconscious. His judgment claims to assert the existence of a justice independent of human will. This claim to objectivity is particularly evident when the idea of justice appears under the form of "natural law."[7] According to the doctrine of natural law, the norm of justice is immanent in nature—the nature of men or the nature of things—and man can only apprehend but not create or influence this norm. The doctrine is a typical illusion, due to an objectivation of subjective interests.

In this sense, the interest theory may indeed be applied to the values of justice. These values do not, it is true, consist in a relation to an interest but in a relation to a norm. This norm, however, contrary to the opinion entertained by the judging person, is not objective, but dependent upon a subjective interest of this person. Hence, there is not one unique standard of justice; what we actually do find are many different and often conflicting ideals.

There is, however, only one positive law. Or—if we wish to account for the existence of the various national legal orders [8]— there is for each territory only one positive law. Its contents can be unambiguously ascertained by an objective method. The existence of the values of law is conditioned by objectively verifiable facts. To the norms of positive law there corresponds a certain social reality, but not so to the norms of justice. In this sense, the value of law is objective, while the value of justice is subjective. And this holds true even though sometimes a great number of people have the same ideal of justice. Juristic value judgments are judgments that can be tested objectively by facts. Therefore they are admissible within a science of law. But it should be noted that the question as to whether in a concrete case a definite behavior is legal or illegal, is to be decided by the competent legal authority, not by the science of law. Judgments of justice can not be tested objectively. Therefore a science of law has no room for them. Judgments of justice are moral or political value judgments, in contradistinction to juristic value judgments. They intend to express an objective value. According to their meaning, the object to which they refer is valuable for everybody. They presuppose a norm which claims to be objectively valid. But the existence and contents of this norm can not be verified by facts. It is determined only by a wish of the subject making the judgment.

This investigation of the value judgments appearing within the science of law seems to establish the following results, important to a general theory of value: (1) Value is not necessarily a relation to an interest. Value can also consist in a relation to a norm; (2) the concept of a norm (an "ought") is indispensable for the description of certain phenomena. It has no metaphysical implication. It is a category of juristic and any kindred "normative" thinking; (3) if the statement that an object has value asserts a relation between the object and an interest, it is a statement about reality. There is no reason to distinguish this statement terminologically as "value judgment" from other statements. A "value judgment" in the sense of a statement essentially different from any statement about reality asserts a relation between an object and a norm whose existence is presupposed by the person making this statement. The meaning of a norm is understood as an "ought" in contradistinction to an "is." The value judgment is then simultaneously an act of valuation; (4) a value is subjective if its object is valuable only for those who are interested in this object. Such is the case when the norm, which is the standard of the value, in its existence and content is determined only by an interest of the person who presupposes the norm. A value is objective if its object is valuable for everybody. That is the case if the norm, which is the standard of the value, is in its existence and content determined by objectively verifiable facts.

THE LAW AS A SPECIFIC
SOCIAL TECHNIQUE

THE ESSENCE OF LEGAL TECHNIQUE

SOCIAL TECHNIQUE OF DIRECT AND INDIRECT MOTIVATION

THE living together of human beings is characterized by the fact that their mutual behavior is regulated. The living together of individuals, in itself a biological phenomenon, becomes a social phenomenon by the very fact of being regulated. Society is ordered living together, or, more accurately put, society is the ordering of the living together of individuals.

The function of every social order is to bring about a certain mutual behavior of individuals—to induce them to certain positive or negative behavior, to certain action or abstention from action. To the individual the order appears as a complex of rules that determine how the individual ought to behave in relation to other individuals. Such rules are called norms.

According to the manner in which the socially desired behavior is brought about, various types of social orders can be distinguished. These types—it is ideal types that are to be presented here—are characterized by the specific motivation resorted to by the order to induce individuals to behave as desired. The motivation may be indirect or direct. The order may attach certain advantages to its observance and certain disadvantages to its nonobservance, and hence make desire for the promised advantage or fear of the threatened disadvantage a motive for behavior. Behavior conforming to the order is achieved by a sanction provided by the order itself. The principle of reward and punishment—the principle of retribution—fundamental for social living, consists in associating conduct in accordance with the order and conduct contrary to the

From *The University of Chicago Law Review*, Dec., 1941.

order with a promised advantage or a threatened disadvantage respectively, as sanctions.

The order can, however, even without promise of a reward for obedience and without threat of a disadvantage for disobedience, that is, without decreeing sanctions, require conduct that appeals directly to the individuals as advantageous; so that the mere idea of a norm decreeing this behavior suffices as a motive for conduct conforming to the norm. In social reality this type of direct motivation is seldom found in pure form.

In the first place, there are hardly any norms whose purport appeals directly to the individuals whose conduct they regulate so that the mere idea of them suffices for motivation. Moreover, the social behavior of individuals is always accompanied by a judgment of value, namely, the idea that conduct in accordance with the order is "good" whereas that contrary to the order is "bad." Hence obedience to the order is usually connected with the approval of one's fellow men; disobedience, with their disapproval. The effect of this reaction of the group to conduct of the individuals in accordance with or at variance to the order, is that of a sanction of the order. From a realistic point of view the decisive difference is not between social orders whose efficacy rests on sanctions and those whose efficacy does not. Every social order is somehow "sanctioned" by the specific reaction of the community to conduct of its members corresponding to or at variance with the order. This is also true of highly developed moral systems which most closely approach the type of direct motivation by sanctionless norms. The only difference is that certain social orders themselves provide definite sanctions, whereas in others the sanctions consist in the automatic reaction of the community not expressly provided by the order.

The sanctions provided by the social order itself may have a transcendental, that is a religious, or a social-immanent character.

In the first case, the sanctions provided by the order consist in advantages or disadvantages that are to be applied to the individuals by a superhuman authority, a being characterized more or less as God-like. According to the idea that individuals have of superhuman beings in the beginnings of religious development, they exist not in a Hereafter different from the Here, but closely connected with men in the nature surrounding them. The dualism of the Here and the Hereafter is still unknown to primitive man. His first gods are probably the souls of the dead, especially dead ancestors, that live in trees, rivers, rocks, and especially in animals. It is they that guarantee the maintenance of the primitive social order by punishing its violation with death, sickness, bad luck in the chase, and in similar ways and by rewarding its observance with long life, health, and luck in hunting. Retribution does indeed emanate from divinity, but it is realized in the Here. For nature is explained by primitive man according to the principle of retribution. We may conjecture that the earliest social order has a religious character. Originally it knows only religious sanctions, that is, those emanating from a superhuman authority. Only later do there appear, at least within the narrower group itself, side by side with the transcendental sanctions, sanctions that are socially immanent, that is to say, socially organized, to be fulfilled by the individuals according to the provisions of the social order. In relations among the groups, blood revenge appears very early as a reaction against an injury considered unjustified and due to a member of a foreign group.

The group from which this reaction issues is a community based on blood relationship. The reaction is induced by fear of the soul of the murdered person. The soul of the dead cannot revenge himself upon the murderer if the latter belongs to a foreign group. Hence the soul of the dead compels his relatives to carry out the revenge. The sanction so socially organized is itself guaranteed by a transcendental sanction. Those who fail to revenge the death of their relative upon the foreign murderer and his group are threatened by the murdered man with sickness and death. It seems that blood revenge is the earliest socially organized sanction. It is worthy of note that originally it had an intertribal character. Only when the social community comprised several groups based on blood relationship did blood revenge become an intratribal institution.

In the further course of religious development, the divinity is conceived of as pertaining to a realm very different from the Here, and far removed from it, and the realization of divine retribution is put off to the Hereafter. Very often this Hereafter is divided— corresponding to the two-fold character of retribution—into a heaven and a hell. In this stage, the social order has lost its purely religious character. The religious order functions only as a supplement and support to the social order. The sanctions of the latter are exclusively acts of human individuals regulated by the social order itself.

Of the two sanctions here presented as typical—the disadvantage threatened in case of disobedience (punishment, in the broadest sense of the term), and the advantage promised in case of obedience (the reward)—the first plays a far more important role than the second in social reality. That the technique of punishment is preferred to that of reward is especially clearly seen where the social order still has a distinctly religious character, that is, is guaranteed by transcendental sanction. Behavior of primitive peoples conforming to the social order—especially the observance of the numerous prohibitions called "taboos"—is determined principally by the fear that dominates the life of such peoples. It is fear of the grievous evil with which the superhuman authority reacts against every violation of traditional customs. If violations of the social norms are much less frequent in primitive societies than in civilized societies, as ethnologists report, it is principally this fear of the revenge of the spirits—fear of a punishment that is of divine origin but which takes place Here—which is responsible for this effect of preserving social order. The hope of reward has only a secondary significance. And even in more highly developed religions, where divine retribution is no longer or not only realized in this world, but in the Hereafter, the idea of a punishment to be expected after death holds first place. In the actual beliefs of mankind, fear of hell is much more lively and the picture of a place of punishment is much more concrete than the usually only very vague hope of reward in heaven and the utterly colorless idea of a future paradise. Even when the wish-fulfilling fantasy of individuals is not limited by any restrictions, it imagines a transcendental order whose technique is not entirely different from the technique of empirical society.

This may be referable to the fact that religious ideology always mirrors, more or less accurately, social reality. And in this, as far as the organization of the group is concerned, essentially only one method of bringing about socially desired behavior is taken into account: the threat and the application of an evil for contrary behavior—the technique of punishment. The technique of reward plays a significant role only in the private relations of individuals.

The evil applied to the violator of the order when the sanction is socially organized, consists in a deprivation of possessions—life, health, freedom, or property. As the possessions are taken from him against his will, this sanction has the character of a measure of coercion. This does not mean that in carrying out the sanction physical force must be applied. This is necessary only if resistance is encountered. But resistance is rare where the authority applying the sanction possesses adequate power. A social order that seeks to bring about the desired behavior of individuals by the enactment of such measures of coercion is called "coercive order." As such it presents a contrast to all other possible social orders—those that provide reward rather than punishment as sanctions, and especially those that enact no sanctions at all, relying on the technique of direct motivation. In contrast to the orders that enact coercive measures as sanctions, the efficacy of the others rests not on coercion but on voluntary obedience.

Yet this contrast is not as distinct as it might at first sight appear. This is apparent from the fact that the reward, as a technique of indirect motivation, has its place between indirect motivation through punishment—as a technique of coercion; and direct motivation—the technique of voluntary obedience. Voluntary obedience is itself a form of motivation, that is of coercion, and hence is not freedom, but it is coercion in the psychological sense. The element of psychic coercion cannot serve as the criterion for distinguishing among different types of social orders. For the efficacy of every social order rests on psychic coercion, because it rests upon motivation. If coercive orders are contrasted with those that have no coercive character but rest on voluntary obedience, this is possible only in the sense that one enacts measures of coercion as sanctions whereas the other does not. And these sanctions are only coercive measures in the sense that certain possessions are taken from the individuals in question against their will.

In this sense the law is a coercive order.

LAW AS COERCIVE ORDER MONOPOLIZING THE USE OF FORCE

If the social orders—so extraordinarily different in their tenors, and in force at different times and among the most different peoples —are called "legal orders," it might be supposed that this term is almost devoid of meaning. What could the so-called law of ancient Babylonians have in common with the law—likewise so called—that prevails today in the United States? What could the social order of a Negro tribe under the leadership of a despotic chieftain have in common with the constitution of the Swiss republic? Yet there is a common element which justifies this terminology, that enables the word "law" to appear as the expression of a concept with a socially highly significant meaning. For the word refers to that specific social technique of a coercive order, which, despite the vast differences between the law of ancient Babylon and that of the United States of today, between the law of the Ashantis in West Africa and that of the Swiss in Europe, is yet essentially the same for all these peoples differing so vastly in time, place, and culture—the social technique which consists in bringing about the desired social conduct of men through threat of coercion for contrary conduct.

While recognizing law as the specific social technique of the coercive order, we can contrast it with other social orders which pursue in part the same purposes as the law, but by different means. Law is a specific social means, not an end. Law, morality, and religion—all three forbid murder. But the law does this by providing: if a man commits murder, then another man, designated by the legal order, shall apply against the murderer a certain measure of coercion, prescribed by the legal order. Morality limits itself to requiring: thou shalt not kill. And if a murderer is morally ostracized by his fellow men—and many a person refrains from murder not so much because he wants to avoid the punishment of the law, as to avoid the moral disapprobation of his fellow men—the great distinction still remains, that the reaction of the law consists in a measure of coercion enacted by the order, and socially organized; whereas the moral reaction against immoral conduct is neither provided by the moral order, nor, if provided, socially organized. In this respect religious norms are nearer to legal norms than moral norms are. For religious norms threaten the murderer with punishment by a superhuman authority. But the sanctions which the religious norms lay down have a transcendental character; they are not socially organized sanctions, even though provided by the religious order. They are probably more effective than the legal sanctions. Their efficacy, however, presupposes belief in the existence and power of a superhuman authority. It is not the effectiveness of the sanctions that is here in question, however, but only whether and how they are provided by the social order. The socially organized sanction is an act of coercion which a person determined by the order directs, in a manner determined by the order, against the person responsible for conduct contrary to the order. The sanction is the reaction of the order—or the reaction of the community constituted by the order—to evildoers. The individual who carries out the sanction acts as an agent of the social community. The legal sanction is thus interpreted as an act of the legal community; the transcendental sanction—the sickness or death of the sinner—is an act of the superhuman authority of the deceased ancestors, of God.

Among the paradoxes of the social technique here characterized as a coercive order is the fact that its specific instrument, the coercive act, is of exactly the same sort as the act which it seeks to prevent in the relations of individuals; that the sanction against socially injurious behavior is itself such behavior. For that which is to be accomplished by the threat of forcible deprivation of life, health, freedom, or property is precisely that men in their mutual conduct shall refrain from forcibly depriving one another of life, health, freedom, or property. Force is employed to prevent the employment of force.

This contradiction is only apparent, however. The law, to be sure, is an ordering for the promotion of peace, in that it forbids the use of force in relations among the members of the community. Yet it does not absolutely preclude the use of force. Law and force must not be understood as absolutely at variance with each other. Law is an organization of force. For the law attaches certain conditions to the use of force in relations among men, authorizing the employment of force only by certain individuals and only under certain circumstances. The law allows conduct which, under all other circumstances, is to be considered as forbidden. To be forbidden means to be the very condition for such a coercive act as a sanction. The individual who, authorized by the legal order, applies the coercive measure (the sanction), acts as an organ of this order or of the community constituted thereby. Hence one may say that law makes the use of force a monopoly of the community. And precisely by so doing, law pacifies the community.

Peace is a condition in which force is not used. In this sense of the word, law provides only relative, not absolute peace—it deprives the individual of the right to employ force but reserves it for the community. The peace of the law is not a condition of absolute absence of force, a state of anarchy; it is a condition of a force monopoly of the community.

A community, in the long run, is possible only if each individual respects certain interests—life, health, freedom, and property of everyone else—that is to say, if each refrains from forcibly interfering in these spheres of interest of the other. The social technique that we call "law" consists in inducing the individual, by a specific means, to refrain from forcible interference in the spheres of interests of others: in case of such interference, the legal community itself reacts with a like interference in the spheres of interests of the individual responsible for the previous interference. Forcible interference in the spheres of interests of another, the measure of coercion, functions as delict and also as sanction. Law is an order according to which the use of force is forbidden only as a delict, that is, as a condition, but is allowed as a sanction, that is, as a consequence.

Inasmuch as forcible interference in the spheres of interest of the individual is permitted only as a reaction of the community against prohibited conduct of that individual, inasmuch as forcible interference in the spheres of interest of the individual is made a monopoly of the community, definite spheres of interest of the individual are protected. As long as there exists no monopoly of the community in forcible interference in the spheres of interest of the individual, that is to say, as long as the social order does not stipulate that forcible interference in the spheres of interest of the individual may only be resorted to under definite conditions— namely, as a reaction against socially harmful interference in the spheres of interest of the individuals, and then only by stipulated individuals—so long are there no spheres of interest of the individual protected by the social order. In other words, there is no state of law, which, in the sense developed here, is essentially a state of peace.

THE IDEA OF A COMMUNITY WITHOUT FORCE

Our investigation thus far results in the formulation that the specific social technique that we call "law" consists in the establishment of a coercive order by means of which a community monopoly is constituted for applying the measures of coercion decreed by the order. Now the question arises whether this social technique, the law as a social technique, is unavoidable. Perhaps it is only the peculiar content of a social order which makes it necessary to establish this order as coercive. Perhaps it is possible to give the social order such a content, to prescribe such conduct for the individuals, that it will no longer be necessary to prescribe coercive measures as sanctions for contrary conduct, because nobody would have an inducement to such contrary behavior. Perhaps there is a social order which would make possible a substitution of direct motivation, of voluntary obedience, for the specific technique of the law. The question of the necessity of the law is identical with the question of the necessity of the state. For the state is a coercive order, a relatively centralized, relatively sovereign, legal order—a community constituted by such a legal order. If the state is defined as a political organization, it means it is a coercive order. The specifically "political" element consists in nothing but the element of coercion.

History presents no social condition in which large communities were constituted other than by coercive orders. Even the social communities of the most primitive peoples rest on religious coercive orders gradually becoming secularized. They are legal communities. The only reason we do not call them states is because the necessary degree of centralization is still lacking. History confirms the saying: *ubi societas, ibi jus.*[1] Yet man has never been satisfied with this historic fact. He has always desired a condition in which force—even used as sanction—would no longer be exercised by man against man. Therefore there have always been optimists who deem such a condition possible, and political dreamers who believe in a development leading to a "free" society, that is, a society free from all coercion, one in which there will no longer be any law, or any state.

This is the doctrine of theoretical anarchism. It presupposes a social order immanent in nature, a kind of natural law, which differs from positive law by the fact that it requires no socially organized sanctions and therefore is no law in the sense we call "law" the coercive orders to be found in historical reality. He who believes in the existence of such a natural social order believes in the existence of an order whose binding character results directly from its content; because this order regulates human behavior in a way that corresponds to the nature of men and to the nature of their relationships and is, therefore, a way satisfactory to all individuals whose conduct is regulated. For this very reason no measures of coercion are required as sanctions for behavior which is at variance with the natural order. Such a possibility is excluded. The natural order is just, that is, it makes all men happy. There is no need to compel people to their own happiness. Hence one needs no state, or, what amounts to the same thing, no positive law. The efficacy of the natural order rests on voluntary obedience. The idea of a natural social order, in the last analysis, is the anarchistic idea of the Golden Age that Ovid portrays in his classic verses:

> Aurea prima sata est aetas, quae vindice nullo,
> sponte sua, sine lege fidem rectumque colebat.
> poena metusque aberant, nec verba minantia fixo
> aere legebantur, nec supplex turba timebat
> iudicis ora sui, sed erant sine judice tuti.[2]

For social pessimism, the Golden Age is the eternally lost paradise of the past. Social optimism places it in the future. It is in either case an illusion, the product of wishful thinking.

If it were possible for the human mind to establish the content of a social order that could count on the voluntary obedience of all subjects—because it corresponded to the nature of man and his mutual relations requiring of human beings only what they themselves wished—an order that would make everyone happy and was therefore a just order, then it would be hard to understand why such an order had not yet been realized. For ever since mankind has thought at all, the most illustrious minds have striven to think up such an order, to answer the question of justice. Yet this question is as far from being answered today as it ever was. None of the numerous attempts to solve the problem of social technique can be said to be nearly as satisfactory—that is, coming as near general satisfaction—as the solution of any one of the innumerable problems of the technique of natural science. This in itself proves that the much-sought-after natural or just order, if it is discoverable at all, cannot be so constituted that everyone will immediately recognize it as just, and therefore be ready to obey it. On the basis of our knowledge of human nature it must be considered very unlikely that any social order, even one which, in the opinion of its creators, assures to individuals every desired advantage, can escape the risk of being violated, and hence need take no precautions against actual or potential violators by coercive measures. It would have to be an order that permitted everyone to do or refrain from doing whatever he wanted. But such an order is in reality the suspension of all social order; it is the reëstablishment of a state of nature, which means a state of anarchy.

And this is perhaps the deepest meaning of this self-contradictory idea of a natural social order: the negation of society. The illusion that it is possible to go "back to nature" is based on the belief that man is "by nature" good. It ignores the innate urge to aggression in man. It ignores the fact that the happiness of one man is often incompatible with the happiness of another, and that therefore a natural just order that guarantees happiness to all, and so does not have to react against disturbances with measures of coercion, is not compatible with the "nature" of men as far as our knowledge of it goes. The "nature" of a natural social order is not the same as the nature of our scientific experience, it is a moral postulate. To count on a human nature different from that known to us is Utopia. This is not to say that human nature is unchangeable, but only that we cannot foresee how it will change under changing circumstances.

The Utopian character of the idea of a social condition not regulated by any coercive order—a society of the future without law or state—appears clearly in the doctrine which has, up to now, most successfully represented this idea politically—the doctrine of Marxian socialism.[3] This doctrine explains the necessity of the state and of what it terms "bourgeois" law, by the fact that society is divided into classes—one possessing and the other without possessions, exploited by the first. According to it the only function of the coercive apparatus represented by the state and its law is to maintain this condition. As soon as the conflict of classes ceases by the abolition of private property and the socialization of the means of production, as well as by planned control of the processes of production; and as soon as a classless society has been attained, the apparatus of coercion will become superfluous. In such a social condition, the state "dies"; with it, law disappears. "The place of government of persons is taken by the administration of things, and the conduct of the processes of production."[4] The establishment of this condition marks "the leap of mankind out of the reign of necessity into that of freedom." [5] On the road to this anarchical society, the dictatorship of the proletariat—the proletarian class state—is only a necessary transition. The political theory of Marxian socialism is pure anarchism. It is distinguishable from the doctrine directly called "anarchism," as for instance that of Bakunin, not by its aim. The aim of both doctrines, a community constituted without coercion, resting on voluntary obedience of the individuals, a classless and therefore stateless community. The so-called "anarchists" believe that one can do away with the state at once, whereas Marxists teach that, after the place of the capitalist state has been taken by that of the socialist state—the so-called dicatorship of the proletariat—the state will gradually disappear of itself.

He who thinks that such a stateless society is possible is closing his eyes to the fact that an economic organization such as that which socialism is aiming for, must necessarily have an authoritative character. A planned economy of such immense scope—embracing if possible the whole earth—can only be managed by a gigantic hierarchically organized administrative body, within which each individual, as an organ of the community, will have a definite function to perform, precisely regulated by a normative order. Upon the conscientious observance of these norms depends the productivity of the whole system, and it is just the higher degree of productivity which is to give the planned economy, according to its adherents, the advantage over capitalistic production. If one calls the latter "anarchy" of production, it is because one contrasts it with the socialistic economy which is the opposite of anarchy. The norms of the socialistic ordering of the economic life can appear only in the form of commands directed by individuals to individuals, a "government over individuals." Never can "direction of the processes of production" take the place of "government over individuals," as the Marxian theory formulates it. For the processes of production are aggregates of human transactions that proceed according to the scheme of commanding and obeying. A social order that completely regulates the system of economic production and the distribution of the products and is carried out by organs of the community must of necessity extend its competence to fields other than economic. Such a social order, more than any other, has a tendency to become totalitarian, regulating all cultural realms and, not least, the sexual relations of the individuals. Such an order, more than any other, will need ideological justification, and hence will not leave metaphysical-religious spheres untouched. It must necessarily limit the freedom of the individual much more severely than any state ever has. For this reason alone such a state must count on disturbances on the part of its citizens no less than must the legal orders of bourgeois society.

Let us leave out of consideration here the fact that laziness and stupidity will not quite disappear even in the socialistic community and must here be much more dangerous for the continuance of the order than in a capitalistic state; let us assume that violations of the legal order of this latter state occur for the most part on economic grounds, and that in the socialistic state such grounds are completely lacking. Still one must assume that here other causes for behavior not corresponding to the order will play so much the greater role. If it is not the incompletely satisfied economic needs of the individual that may lead to a disturbance of the order, it must be other needs—needs arising from his desire for prestige, his libido, and last but not least, from his religious emotions. There may be a difference of opinion about the justification for such needs and the permissible extent of their satisfaction, but their existence cannot be denied. And furthermore one cannot deny that these needs must make themselves felt the more strongly the more the economic needs are satisfied, and that no solution of the problems arising in this connection is to be expected from the idea of economic socialism. Desire for prestige, libido, and religious emotion are no less revolutionary factors than hunger and thirst. Only a view that identifies society with economy can fail to see the great dangers that threaten a social order from this direction.

If one must admit that a socialistic order cannot count in all directions upon the voluntary obedience of its subjects, that it must, like a bourgeois society, anticipate a conduct of persons not in conformity with the order, then one must also admit that even this order cannot refrain from proceeding against these persons with measures of coercion, that is, with measures which, if necessary, must be applied against the will of the persons acting in a socially harmful manner.

In a socialistic community, measures to prevent crimes may be used to a greater extent than is possible in the legal community of the capitalistic state. On the basis of our knowledge of such methods in the past, however, we cannot expect that preventive measures can be so effective as to render repressive measures wholly superfluous. As long as we remain in the domain of experience, we must assume that even a socialistic order must be a coercive order, and that the state will not die off, but that its order will acquire a different content. Even socialism cannot get along without the social technique called "law." Even in a socialistic society it is true that *ubi societas, ibi jus.*

The Evolution of Legal Technique

DIFFERENTIATION OF THE DYNAMIC RELATION BETWEEN CREATION AND APPLICATION OF LAW

If coercion is an essential element of law in the sense presented here, then every legal order, regarded from a technical point of view, must be presented as a complex of norms in which coercive measures are decreed as sanctions. All other facts to which the legal order applies come into consideration only as conditions of the sanction. The specific technique of the law—the technique of indirect motivation—consists in the very fact that it attaches certain coercive measures as consequences to certain conditions. Morality, whose technique is direct motivation, says thou shalt not steal. The law says, if one steals, he shall be punished. The moral norm regulates the behavior of one individual; the legal norm, always that of at least two individuals, the one whose behavior furnishes the condition of the sanction (the subject) and the one whose function it is to apply the sanction (the organ). The decisive, though not the only, condition of the sanction is that conduct of the subject which, according to the intent of the legal order, should be avoided—the delict. The legal order, by attaching a sanction to this conduct, and thus characterizing it as delict, seeks to induce the opposite conduct—that which will not invoke the sanction. To say that a person has a legal duty to behave in a certain way means that he is threatened with a sanction for contrary behavior, that is, for a delict. The relation established by the legal norm between delict and sanction is the fundamental relation of the law, so far as it is regarded in a state of rest. It is the fundamental relation of the statics of the law.

If we now look at the law in its specific movement, if we regard the process of the creation of the law, we observe a specially significant fact for the technique of the law, namely that it regulates its own creation. A norm belongs to a certain legal order only if it has come into being in a certain way—a way stipulated by a norm of that order itself. This is the essence of positive law.

There are two methods of creating law: custom, the repeated similar conduct of the subject; and legislation (in the broadest sense of the word), the conscious act of a special organ set up for the purpose of creating law. All law is—according to the provisions of the legal order—created by custom or legislation. In this it is distinguishable from natural law, which need not be created by the act of man, since it issues directly from the nature of men or the nature of the relations of men, and as such need only be recognized by man.

Positive law not only has to be created, but must be applied. In the progression from creation of the law to its application lie the typical dynamics of the law. It is also characteristic of the technique of the law that these dynamics unfold in at least two stages. The law is first created as a general norm. The application of the general norm to a concrete case consists in determining whether the condition established by the norm in an abstract manner is present, so that a concrete sanction, determined by the norm only in an abstract fashion, can be decreed or applied. If the application of the concrete sanction is preceded by the decreeing of this sanction, then there are three stages of the dynamic legal process: the creation of the general norm, the creation of the individual norm decreeing the sanction, and the execution of the individual norm. The process of the creation of the general norm may, however, itself be split into several stages. An example is the relationship between a constitution and the statutes enacted by the lawmaking body on the basis of that constitution. The executive organs issue ordinances or regulations on the basis of these statutes. The ordinances or regulations are then applied to the concrete case by the judicial or administrative organs. Every legal order forms a hierarchy of general and individual norms, the lowest step of which is the execution of a concrete measure.

The steps of these legal dynamics tend to increase. The dynamics of the primitive legal order has only two stages: the development of the general norm through custom, and its application by the subject whose interests, protected by this norm, have been violated. This subject is authorized by the legal order to react against the violator of the law with the sanction provided by it. Primitive law is characterized by the technique of self-help. Blood revenge is a typical example: the subject himself whose interests have been violated, and not a special organ, must determine whether or not a delict has been committed. The subject himself must fulfill the sanction; it is not decreed by an individual norm, enacted and executed by an organ different from the injured. The primitive law of self-help is characterized by the fact that the general norm is applied directly to the concrete instance without an individual norm. Only after courts have developed does an individual norm insert itself between the general norm and its application to a concrete case, the execution of the sanction. This individual norm is the decree of the sanction by court decision. On the other hand, the process of creation of the general norms also changes in the course of development, so that the dynamic legal process finally is spent in a complicated series of numerous stages.

DIFFERENTIATION OF THE STATIC RELATION BETWEEN DELICT AND SANCTION

Differentiation of the sanction: criminal law and civil law.—Not only the dynamic relation between the creation of law and its application, but also the static relation between delict and sanction is subject to a typical change. Originally there was only one sort of coercive measure—punishment, in the narrower sense of the word, involving life, health, freedom, or property. The oldest law was only penal law. Later a differentiation in the sanction came about. In addition to punishment, there appeared civil execution, the coercive deprivation of property to compensate for illegally caused damage. That is to say that civil law developed alongside of penal law. But the civil law, regulating the economic relations of individuals, guarantees the behavior desired in this field in a manner not essentially different from that in which penal law does the same thing in its field. Namely, it establishes in the last analysis, sometimes indirectly, a measure of coercion for contrary conduct—its own specific measure of coercion, civil execution. Penal law is distinguishable from civil law principally through the fact that its sanction has a different character. The difference lies not so much in the outward circumstance of the sanction. The sanction is in both instances a coercive measure, by which an individual is divested of possessions. Civil execution involves only property. But this is true also of fines. The difference between penal and civil sanction lies rather in its purpose. Civil sanction is to make reparation of the damage caused by the socially harmful conduct; penal sanction is retribution, or—according to the modern view—prevention. But this difference is only relative. For one can hardly deny that the civil sanction also has a preventive function, even if only secondarily.

The relative difference between criminal and civil sanction is expressed in the content of the legal order. This legal order contains specific provisions for the use of the property forcibly taken. In case of a civil sanction this property is to be turned over to the illegally wronged subject; in case of a criminal sanction it falls to the legal community.

A further difference lies in the procedure that leads to the two sanctions as it developed in the different legal orders. The judicial process aimed at civil execution is initiated only upon demand of a specific subject interested in the execution; the judicial process aimed at the application of punishment is initiated *ex officio,* upon demand of an organ of the community. A civil process has the form of a dispute between two parties, the plaintiff and the defendant; a civil delict is the violation of a right. He who, by his suit, can set in motion the procedure which leads to civil sanction, is the subject of a right.

The according of such rights to the subject and the possibility of pursuing them in a contentious procedure characterize the technique of a legal order that regulates economic life according to the principle of private property. The available economic goods are at the exclusive disposition of private persons, and this enjoyment of private property is achieved, essentially, by free contract among individuals. The "right" which the subject has to a thing consists in the power accorded the subject by the legal order to prevent any other subject from interfering with his enjoyment thereof. The specific method of preventing such interference is the possibility accorded by the legal order of setting in motion the coercive process against anyone who disturbs or interferes with the object in that enjoyment.

This power of the subject is a political power, a public function *par excellence*. But in this system it is ideologically called a specific sphere of "private" interest; the norms granting this power are called "private" law; the power itself, a "private" right. A consequence of this technique of "private" right is that the process by which the general legal norm is applied to the concrete case, the civil sanction decreed and executed against the delinquent, has the character of a contentious procedure. Only in imitation of the civil procedure does the penal procedure in which the criminal sanction is decreed and applied still have the outward character of a dispute, although here no subjective rights usually exist any longer. When, instead of the subject whose interests have been injured by the criminal delict, an organ of the community appears as plaintiff, one can speak only in a very figurative sense of a "right" of the community to cessation of the delict. But even aside from the fact that the application of the legal norm in both civil and criminal law takes place in the form of a contentious procedure, the social technique is in both cases essentially the same: reaction against the delict in the form of an act of coercion as a sanction.

Differentiation of the sanction: collective responsibility and individual responsibility.—The delict is a condition of the sanction. It has been demonstrated that one is legally obligated to certain behavior when contrary behavior is threatened with a sanction. The specific sanction of the law is an act of coercion—depriving one forcibly of life, health, freedom, or property. Against whom is this sanction directed? Whose life, health, freedom, or property is to be forcibly taken away? In accordance with the answer to this question, the technically primitive legal order is distinguished from the technically developed legal order. It corresponds to a more refined sense of justice which will direct the sanction only against those whose behavior constitutes the legal duty, and whose undutiful behavior, therefore, constitutes the delict as the condition of the sanction. If a legal order forbids murder, that is to say, if it provides a punishment for committing murder, then the punishment is to be directed against the murderer and only the murderer; in other words, against the individual, who, under obligation to abstain from murdering, has, in violation of his duty, committed murder. If we call the individual against whom the sanction is directed the one who is responsible for the delict, then the requirement of the more refined legal technique runs as follows: Only he who commits the delict, only the delinquent, is to be responsible for the delict. This is the principle of individual responsibility.

Primitive legal orders, however, do not meet this requirement. It is not contrary to a primitive sense of justice to direct the sanction not only against the murderer himself, but against his relatives, against all those belonging to his family or his tribe, in other words, against the members of the circumscribed group to which he belongs. Not only he who actually committed the delict is responsible, but others as well. Even in the Bible it is taken as a matter of course that for the sins of the father, the children and the children's children shall be punished.[6] The circle of those responsible is defined by the fact that they belong to a definite social group, to the same legal community. This is the principle of collective responsibility.

This principle may hark back to the fact that according to primitive conception a very close bond exists between an individual and the other members of his group. Primitive man identifies the individual with his group—with all other members of it. Primitive man does not regard himself as a self-sufficient individual, different from and independent of his group, but as an integral element of it. For him it is a matter of course that each member of the group is responsible for every other member. Just as a heroic deed of one member of the group calls forth satisfaction and pride from all others, so it is also deemed just that a delict of one member of the group should be avenged on all its members. Collective responsibility is a typical element of the state of justice in which the principle of self-help still subsists. Blood revenge, that typical form of self-help, is by no means directed against only the person who has committed the deed to be avenged, but against his whole family. It is the reaction of one group against another group.

The technical development of the law is characterized by the progress from collective toward individual responsibility.

Differentiation of the delict: absolute liability and culpability. —Closely connected with the difference between individual and collective responsibility is another distinction, which also concerns the solution of the problem of responsibility. To be responsible for a socially harmful or socially useful result, it does not suffice, according to modern, ethical views, for the result to have been brought about by one's own conduct. The result must have been brought about in a definite manner.

If a person commits an act harmful to society—a delict—a specific mental connection called "intent" or "negligence" must exist between conduct and result; certain mental elements called "culpa" must be present. For example, in felling a tree somebody kills a man. If the man felling the tree is made responsible for the death of the person without regard to whether he acted with intent or negligence, then it is a case of absolute liability. If, however, the feller of the tree is punished only if he intended by his actions to bring about the death of the man, or if he negligently failed to give warning of the existing danger, then it is a case of culpability. This principle is unknown to primitive legal orders; there the principle of absolute liability prevails. Whoever brings about, no matter how, a result designated by the legal order as socially injurious is punishable. Where the principle of collective responsibility exists, absolute liability is almost unavoidable, for there the sanction is directed to include persons who have not themselves brought about the result but who merely belong to the same social community as the perpetrator. If the principle of collective responsibility is supplanted by that of individual responsibility, the way is also made free for the substitution of the principle of culpability for that of absolute liability.

The technical development of the law is characterized by progress not only from collective to individual responsibility, but also from absolute liability to culpability. But it should be noted that this is only the formulation of a general rule which exhibits important exceptions. Even in modern legal orders the principle of collective responsibility and that of absolute liability have by no means been given up. Thus the first principle is exhibited in the law of so-called juristic persons; the second, in many spheres of civil law. The form of culpability called "negligence" is not far removed from absolute liability. Especially in international law, both principles are still to be regarded as controlling.

Centralization

For the technical development of the law the process of centralization is important. Primitive law is decentralized. It knows as yet no organ functioning according to the principle of the division of labor. All functions of creation as well as application of the legal norms are performed by all subjects. Special organs for the different functions develop only gradually. In the field of law the same process takes place as in economic production, which becomes more centralized as it develops.

In the field of law this process is characterized by the surprising fact that the centralization of the law-applying function precedes the centralization of the law-creating function. Long before special legislative organs come into existence, courts are established to apply the law to concrete cases. The law, thus applied, is customary law—law created by a specific method. The peculiarity of this method is that the general legal norms are created by collaboration of all individuals subject to the legal order. It is a decentralized means of creating law. During thousands of years it was the only way of creating general legal norms. The application of the law, however, long ago became the exclusive function of special organs; it was centralized. No longer is each individual authorized to decide whether or not his rights have been violated, whether or not he will react by a sanction against another individual, responsible for the violation of law. Such decisions have long been entrusted to judges, special organs different from and independent of the parties in conflict. The general norms, however, in accordance with which judges decide such conflicts, are not always created by a central organ; they still have the character of customary law. Customary law forms an important part of the legal order even in technically highly developed legal communities.

The procedure of applying general legal norms to concrete cases involves—as we have seen—three phases: first, the conditioning facts must be established, especially the delict; second, the sanction provided by the general legal norm must be ordered to be applied to the concrete case; and third, this sanction must be executed against the person responsible for the delict. The three stages of this procedure do not necessarily become centralized at the same time. Historically, the centralization of the first two stages has probably preceded the centralization of the third. Probably only the establishment of the fact of a concrete law violation was at first given over to an objective authority, a court.

This step is important. For upon the decision of the question whether or not in a concrete case a delict has been committed depends the possibility of applying to this concrete case the general norm that attaches a sanction to this delict. If a legal order attaches to a certain fact as condition a certain consequence, then it must determine in what manner, and especially by whom, the existence of the conditioning fact is to be established. It is a fundamental, though often overlooked, principle of legal technique that there are no absolute, directly evident facts in the province of law, no "facts in themselves," but only facts established by the competent authority in a procedure prescribed by the legal order. It is not theft as a fact in itself to which the legal order attaches a certain punishment. Only a layman formulates the rule of law in that way. The jurist knows that the legal order attaches a certain punishment only to a theft established by the competent authority following a prescribed procedure. To say that A has committed a theft can only express a subjective opinion. In the province of law only the authentic opinion, that is, the opinion of the authority instituted by the legal order to establish the fact, is decisive. Any other opinion as to the existence of a fact as determined by the legal order is irrelevant from a juristic point of view.

If the legal order establishes no special organs for determining the conditioning facts, especially the delict, then it is the interested parties themselves that are called upon by the legal order to establish the existence of these facts in the concrete case. Such is the condition of a primitive decentralized legal order. If under such circumstances one subject claims to have been injured by the behavior of another subject and the latter denies it, the essential issue remains undetermined. It can be determined in a primitive decentralized legal order only by agreement of the parties to the dispute. It is obvious that such agreement can seldom be reached. If a subject proceeds without such agreement to an act of coercion against another subject, it is uncertain whether his act constitutes a sanction or a delict in the sense of the legal order, that is, whether in this case the legal order was being applied or violated. Hence, for the technical development of the law, no other step was of such importance as the establishment of courts. Only by the centralization of this phase of the application of the law was application of the law in all cases possible.

The centralization of the other two phases of the application of the law (the decreeing and the executing of the sanction) is of lesser importance. It seems to be the last step. With it the legal status of self-help is supplanted. In its place appears execution of the sanction by a special organ of the community.

It seems, however, that the state of self-help was only gradually eliminated. In the early days, the courts were hardly more than tribunals of arbitration. They had to decide whether or not the delict had actually been committed, as claimed by one party, and whether or not that party was authorized to execute a sanction against the other, if the conflict could not be settled by peaceful agreement between them. To bring about such a peaceful agreement, enabling the vendetta to be replaced by wergild, was probably the first task of the tribunal. Only at a later stage does it become possible completely to abolish the procedure of self-help. The execution of the sanction by a central organ of the legal community, authorized to punish the guilty individual, presupposes a concentration of the means of power and the existence of a central organ with all these means of power at its disposal. To centralize the execution of the sanctions provided by the legal order the legal community needs not only courts but also a powerful administration.

A legal community which has an administration and courts is a state. The state, as we have pointed out, is a centralized legal order —a community constituted by a centralized legal order. From a technical point of view it is characteristic that a legislative organ is not an essential requisite of a state. It is the centralization of the judicial and administrative, not the lawmaking function, which makes a primitive community a state. The jurisdiction of state courts is older than state legislation.

Although the court preceded the legislative organ, it was not the first central organ. The first central organ was probably the chieftain, in his position as military leader of his group in war against another group. Just as the first socially organized sanction, blood revenge, appears in the relation of one group to another, so also centralization was first applied to intertribal relations. In the beginning, however, the position of the chieftain is of no importance for the formation of intratribal law. As soon as his position becomes a permanent institution and is concerned with intratribal legal matters, the chief appears as judge, not as legislator.

Apart from war and the other relations with foreign states, which are regulated by international law, in the beginning of the development the judicial and legislative functions stand in the foreground, the administrative functions in the background. In recent times this relationship has changed in favor of the administrative function—the judicial state has become an administrative state. This is so, chiefly in the sense that no longer are the courts only called upon to apply the laws but, to an increasing extent, the administrative authorities as well; that side by side with civil and penal laws administrative laws appear in increasing numbers. The latter can achieve the aims of the administration by seeking to bring about by threat of a sanction conduct of the citizen considered desirable by the administration. For example, by a law the citizens are obliged to lay out a public road, or to build a school, install instructors, and have their children taught. If they fail to do this, they are punished by special administrative authorities. In such a case the technique of the national administration is the same as that of the national judiciary. This is the type of indirect administration. The type of direct administration of the state is presented by the cases where the public road is laid out, the school is built, and instruction is furnished not by private persons but by public organs. This activity, termed direct administration, is quite different from the judicial. It appears not among the duties of private subjects, but among the duties of public organs. They are individuals who are characterized in a specific way determined by the legal order. Since the purpose of the administration, even in direct administration, is achieved by individuals being legally obligated to this activity, that is to say that the re-action to contrary conduct is a measure of coercion, even direct administration remains within the framework of the specific technique of the law—indirect motivation.

The development of the state is clearly proceeding in the direction of an accelerated increase in direct administration. The legal technique of direct administration is the technique of the socialistic state in distinction to that of the liberal-capitalistic state, which, so far as it develops administrative activity, prefers the technique of indirect administration. The path from indirect to direct administration of the state is also the path of increasing centralization.

The distinction between centralization and decentralization is, finally, also decisive for the relations among states. International law is a radically decentralized legal order. Its technique reveals all typical characteristics of a primitive law; the creation by custom of the norms valid for the whole realm of the legal community; no special organs for the application of the general legal norms to the concrete case, but, instead, self-help on the part of the subject whose rights have been injured; collective responsibility, absolute liability. A particular peculiarity of the technique of international law is that its subjects are juristic persons—states. A juristic person is the personification of a legal order, in whole or in part. To say that a legal order obligates and authorizes a juristic person is not to say that it does not obligate and authorize individuals. It means only that the legal order obligates them not directly but indirectly, through the medium of another legal order, the one whose personification is regarded as the subject of the obligating, authorizing legal order. To say that international law obligates and authorizes states means that international law obligates and authorizes individuals in their capacity as organs of the states, individuals who are designated by a national legal order to be organs of this order or of the community constituted by it. That means that the norms of the international legal order are not complete norms; in order to be applied at all they must be supplemented by the norms of the national legal orders. This supplementation consists in the designation of the individuals who, in their capacity as organs of the states, have to fulfil the international duties and to exercise the international rights of the states. This is the rule. As an exception there are also norms of international law determining directly the individuals whose conduct forms the substance of the international duties and rights of the states.

One may assume that the technical development of international law is progressing on the same path as that already taken by the development of the legal orders of the states. Very suggestive is the fact that in international law the centralization has begun with the establishment of courts. They are the first relatively centralized organs of international law. To the extent that the direct obligating and authorizing of individuals and centralization increases in international law, the boundary between national and international law tends to disappear, and the legal organization of mankind approaches the idea of a world state.

WHY SHOULD THE LAW
BE OBEYED?

W<small>HAT</small> is the reason for the validity of the law? To assess the various answers to this question certain terms must be clarified. By "law," positive law—either national or international—is understood. By "validity," the binding force of the law—the idea that it ought to be obeyed by the people whose behavior it regulates—is understood. The question is why these people ought to obey the law.

We do not ask whether positive law is valid—that it is so is presupposed by a theory of positive law; it is an essential characteristic of positive law. The subjective meaning of the acts by which the norms (i.e., prescriptions, commands) of positive law are created is, necessarily, that these prescriptions ought to be obeyed. But, again, why is their *subjective* meaning considered to be their *objective* meaning as well? Not every act whose subjective meaning is a norm is objectively one also. For example, a robber's command to hand over your purse is not interpreted as a binding or valid norm. Reformulated, our question then is: Why do we interpret the acts by which positive law is created as having not only the subjective but also the objective meaning of binding norms?

II

A frequently accepted answer is that men ought to obey positive law because and to the extent that it conforms with the principles of morals. The moral principles which refer to the law-making and law-applying activities of men constitute the ideal of justice; ac-

257

cording to this view, then, the reason for the validity of law is its justice. To the question, how these moral principles are to be ascertained, the typical answer is that they are, so to speak, immanent in nature: by exploring nature we can find these principles, which form the natural law; they are superior to positive, man-made law.

The foregoing views constitute the natural-law doctrine, which conceives of nature as a law-making authority. According to this doctrine positive law derives its validity from natural law. Men ought to obey positive law because and to the extent that nature commands it; and nature commands it only to the extent that positive law conforms to natural law.

Even if it is accepted that norms regulating human behavior can be deduced from nature, the question arises why men ought to obey these norms. To this further question the natural-law doctrine has no answer. The doctrine simply presupposes—perhaps as self-evident—that men ought to obey the commands of nature. This is the fundamental hypothesis of that doctrine, its basic norm, its reason for the validity of law.

However, this fundamental hypothesis cannot be accepted by a theory of positive law, for the reason that it is impossible to deduce from nature norms regulating human behavior. Norms are the expression of a will, and nature has no will. Nature is a system of facts connected by the principle of causality. To conceive of nature as a normative authority, that is, as a superhuman being endowed with a norm-creating will, is an animistic superstition, or the result of a theological interpretation of nature as a manifestation of God's will.

There is another reason. The natural-law doctrine that positive law is valid because it conforms with justice leads to one or the other of the following two results—both unacceptable to a theory of positive law:

(a) If every positive law is considered valid, then every positive law—according to the natural-law doctrine—must be considered as just, as conforming to natural law. In this way, every man-made law can be justified by endowing it with superhuman authority— a conscious or unconscious endeavor of many natural-law theorists. If, however, every positive law is just, then law and justice are identical; and, then, to say that law is valid because it is just

WHY SHOULD THE LAW BE OBEYED?

amounts to saying: the reason for the validity of law is law; law ought to be obeyed because law ought to be obeyed.

(b) If law is identified with justice, positive law with natural law, then the concepts of justice or natural law becomes meaningless. They are meaningful only if a possible antagonism exists between justice or natural law on the one hand, and positive law on the other. And such an antagonism is inevitable as soon as the content of the principles of justice or natural law is to be identified. As a matter of fact, outstanding representatives of the natural-law doctrine have proclaimed, in the name of justice or natural law, principles which not only contradict one another but are in direct opposition to many positive legal orders. There is no positive law that is not in conflict with one or the other of these principles; and it is not possible to ascertain which of them has a better claim to be recognized than any other. All these principles represent the highly subjective value judgments of their various authors about what they consider to be just or natural. If a positive law is valid only if conforming, and nonvalid if not conforming, with justice or natural law, then every positive law could be considered as nonvalid when compared with one of these principles. For example, if individual property is a natural right, as some authors declare, then the legal order of a communist state is not valid and merely the organization of a band of gangsters. But if individual property is against nature, as other authors assert, the legal order of a capitalist state has no chance of being recognized as a valid law which its citizens ought to obey. If, as Locke taught, democracy is the only natural and just form of government, then obedience to the so-called law established by an autocratic government cannot be justified. And if Filmer's natural-law doctrine is accepted according to which democracy is the most unjust form of government because in conflict with the will of God, who does not govern the world in a democratic way, then there is no reason for the validity of a democratic law, and law-making is the exclusive right of an absolute monarch. There can be no doubt that this second result of the natural-law doctrine is as unacceptable to a science of positive law and especially to comparative jurisprudence as the first one.

To say, therefore, that positive law is valid, because it is just, is no answer to our question. If positive law derives its validity from natural law, then positive law has no validity in itself. It is solely the norms of natural law which men ought to obey. The natural-law doctrine does not answer the question why positive law is valid, but the totally different question why natural law is valid. And the answer to this question is a hypothesis. It is the presupposed norm that men ought to obey the commands of nature. It is its basic norm.

III

There is another doctrine—Christian theology—which offers an answer to our question. St. Paul says: "Let every person be subject to the governing authorities. For there is no authority except from God, and those that exist have been instituted by God. Therefore he who resists the authorities resists what God has appointed, and those who resist will incur judgment. For rulers are not a terror to good conduct but to bad. Would you have no fear of him who is in authority? Then do what is good and you will receive his approval, for he is God's servant for your good." (Rom. XIII:1 ff.) This is a justification of any positive legal order issued by an established authority. Men ought to obey any positive law because their obedience is commanded by God whose representatives the law-making authorities are. They are authorized by God to make law; and, consequently, this law must be considered not merely as a man-made law but as a law which originates in the will of God. In the last analysis, man's obedience is due to God and not to positive law as such.

However, the statement, men ought to obey positive law because God commands it is not a final answer to the question why positive law is valid. For even if the fact is taken for granted that God issued this command, the question arises why men ought to obey the commands of God. Since the validity of a norm can be derived only from another higher norm, the true meaning of Paul's answer to our question is: men ought to obey positive law because men ought to obey the commands of God, who commanded obedience to positive law. That men ought to obey God's commands is a norm which cannot be presented as issued by God. For if an authority issues a norm prescribing that an individual ought to obey the command of another individual, this norm implies the authorization of the other individual to issue the command,

and the individual authorized by this norm is subjected to it just as the individual obliged to obey. Hence an authority issuing such a norm would have to be considered superior to both. God cannot issue a norm authorizing God to give commands, because God is himself the supreme authority. Consequently, the norm that men ought to obey the commands of God, cannot be a norm issued by an authority; it can only be a norm presupposed by theology, its metaphysical hypothesis, its basic norm. It is—according to this theological doctrine—the reason for the validity of law.

Such a metaphysical hypothesis is acceptable only from the point of view of a religion; and the fact that God commanded men to obey positive law can be taken for granted only from the point of view of the Christian religion as established by St. Paul; and even from this viewpoint it is contestable because hardly compatible with the original teaching of Christ. The hypothesis as well as the fact can certainly not be accepted from the point of view of science in general, and of a science of law in particular. Science does not and cannot operate on the basis of metaphysical assumptions—assumptions of an entity or a fact beyond any possible human experience and especially beyond human reason.

The answer which Christian theology gives to our question, just as the answer of the natural-law doctrine, finds the reason for the validity of law in a higher order, placed above positive law—in a divine or a natural order. According to both doctrines positive law has in itself no validity. It is the validity of the divine or the natural order which is the concern of the two doctrines; and the reason for this validity is a basic norm that is not issued by the authority of the divine or natural order, but presupposed as a hypothesis by each doctrine.

IV

This analysis of the two doctrines shows, first, that their hypotheses are not acceptable by a science of positive law. Second, if the validity of this law, its own immanent validity, is in question, the reason for it must not be sought in another, higher order; positive law must be supposed to be a supreme, a sovereign order.

This order is characterized by a hierarchical structure. Its basis is the written or unwritten constitution; on it rest the statutes enacted by the legislators; the courts and administrative organs then apply the statutes by creating individual norms. We ought to obey the decisions of a judge or administrator, ultimately, because we ought to obey the constitution. If we ask why we ought to obey the norms of the existing constitution, we may be referred to an older constitution that has been replaced in a constitutional way by the existing constitution; and in this way we arrive finally at the historically first constitution. To the question why we ought to obey its provisions a science of positive law can only answer: the norm that we ought to obey the provisions of the historically first constitution must be presupposed as a hypothesis if the coercive order established on its basis and actually obeyed and applied by those whose behavior it regulates is to be considered as a valid order binding upon these individuals; if the relations among these individuals are to be interpreted as legal duties, legal rights, and legal responsibilities, and not as mere power relations; and if it shall be possible to distinguish between what is legally right and legally wrong and especially between legitimate and illegitimate use of force. This is the basic norm of a positive legal order, the ultimate reason for its validity, seen from the point of view of a science of positive law. It is the ultimate reason for the validity of positive law, because, from this point of view, it is impossible to assume that nature or God command obedience to the provisions of the historically first constitution, that the fathers of the constitution were authorized by nature or God to establish it. The basic norm that we ought to obey the provisions of the historically first constitution is not created by the legal authority, that is to say, it is not a positive norm created in conformity with the constitution; it is a norm which—as the science of positive law tells us— we presuppose as a hypothesis if we consider the coercive order regulating effectively human behavior within the territory of a state as a normative order binding upon its inhabitants. This presupposition is not a product of free imagination; for it refers to objectively ascertainable facts: the establishment of a constitution and the acts which on the basis of this constitution create and apply the general and individual norms of a coercive order. It legitimatizes the subjective meaning of these acts as their objective significance. It is the application of the general principle of effectiveness, which, as a normative principle, plays an important part in the realm of law.

Thus, legal positivism answers the question why law is valid by referring to a hypothesis that may or may not be accepted—in other words by justifying obedience to law only conditionally. It has, therefore, often been declared that this answer is not a satisfactory solution of the problem and that, therefore, the solution of the natural-law doctrine or of theology is preferable. However, in this respect there is no difference between legal positivism on the one hand and the natural-law doctrine or theology on the other. The reason for the validity of law is according to all three of them a hypothetical basic norm. Just as the basic norm of legal positivism is not issued by the legal authority but is presupposed in juristic thinking, the basic norms of the natural-law doctrine and of Christian theology are not issued by nature or by God but are presupposed as hypotheses by these doctrines. Consequently, these doctrines, too, can justify obedience to law only conditionally. The only difference is that the validity for which the basic norm of legal positivism furnishes the reason is the inherent validity of the positive law, whereas the validity for which the basic norm of the natural-law doctrine or that of Christian theology furnishes the reason, is the validity of a natural or a divine order.

V

The question for the reason of the validity of law was restricted in the foregoing considerations to national law. Now, if we consider international law as valid only if recognized on the basis of the constitution by the legal authority of national law, or, expressed in the usual terminology, if recognized by the government of a sovereign state, our answer, as applied to international law, is the same: a presupposed basic norm. For, then, the reason for the validity of national law implies the reason for the validity of international law which is only part of national law. However, if we consider international law as a legal order superior to national legal orders, the situation changes. For the principle of effectiveness applied in the basic norm of national law is a norm of positive international law. According to this law an independent govern-

ment in effective control of the population of a definite territory
—even if this government is not established in conformity with
the constitution but by revolution—is the legitimate government;
the community under such a government is a "state" in the sense
of international law; the coercive order through which the effective
control is exercised is the valid law of this state; and the acts by
which the norms of this order are created and applied are legal
acts. St. Paul taught that every established government is instituted
by God. Likewise, legal positivism teaches that every established
government is instituted by international law. According to the
principle of effectiveness, a norm of international law, the constitution of a state is valid if the coercive order derived from it is
by and large effective. This positive norm of international law,
conceived of as superior to national law, has the same function as
the hypothetical, that is, presupposed basic norm of a national legal
order, conceived of as a sovereign order or—as usually formulated
—as the law of a sovereign state. It is the reason for the validity of
national law. Precisely because the reason for the validity of national law is a norm of international law, the latter may be
considered as superior to the former. But this norm of international law is not the ultimate reason for the validity of national
law. For, now, the question arises: Why is this norm of international law valid? And, finally: Why is international law as a whole
valid? We can find the answer to the last question in the same way
as the answer to the question on national law, because international law and not national law is now conceived of as a sovereign
order. If national law ("the state") is still characterized as sovereign,
this "sovereignty" can only mean that the state, or, what amounts
to the same thing, the national legal order constituting the state,
is subordinated not to another national legal order but only to the
international legal order—that the state is "independent." If we
now ask why international law is a valid normative order, we may
start from the question why a certain act performed by state A in
relation to state B is legal or illegal. The answer may be: Because it
is in conformity or not in conformity with a treaty concluded between A and B, and because according to a norm of international
law the states ought to respect the treaties they have concluded.
This is the norm *pacta sunt servanda*. It is a norm of customary
international law. The norm of international law which repre-

sents the reason for the validity of national law is, likewise, a norm
of customary law; and international law is composed of norms of
customary law and of conventional law—the latter being law created by treaties, on the basis of customary law. Hence the reason
for the validity of international law, its basic norm, is a norm
which institutes custom as a law-creating fact—the norm that
states ought to behave as states customarily behave in their mutual
relations.

This norm, however, cannot itself be created by custom. A statement to the contrary would be the same logical fallacy as the
statement that nature authorizes nature, or God authorizes God to
issue commands. The norm authorizing state custom to create law
binding upon the states can only be a norm presupposed by those
who interpret the mutual relations of states not as mere power relations but as legal relations, as obligations, rights, and responsibilities; by those, again, who consider the acts of the states as
legal or illegal, that is to say, as relations regulated by a valid legal
order. It is a hypothesis—the condition—under which such an
interpretation is possible. This hypothesis, the basic norm of international law, is, in the last analysis, also the reason for the validity
of the national legal orders.

THE PURE THEORY OF LAW

AND ANALYTICAL

JURISPRUDENCE

THEORY OF LAW AND PHILOSOPHY OF JUSTICE

THE Pure Theory of Law [1] is a theory of positive law—a general theory of law, not a presentation or interpretation of a special legal order. From a comparison of all phenomena which go under the name of law, it seeks to discover the nature of law itself, to determine its structure and its typical forms, independent of the changing content which it exhibits at different times and among different peoples. In this manner it derives the fundamental principles by means of which any legal order can be comprehended. As a theory, its sole purpose is to know its subject. It answers the question of what the law is, not what it ought to be. The latter question is one of politics, while the pure theory of law is science.

It is called "pure" because it seeks to preclude from the cognition of positive law all elements foreign thereto. The limits of this subject and its cognition must be clearly fixed in two directions: the specific science of law, the discipline usually called jurisprudence, must be distinguished from the philosophy of justice, on the one hand, and from sociology, or cognition of social reality, on the other.

To free the concept of law from the idea of justice is difficult, because they are constantly confused both in political thought and in general speech, and because this confusion corresponds to the tendency to let positive law appear as just. In view of this tendency, the effort to deal with law and justice as two different problems falls under the suspicion of dismissing the requirement that positive law should be just. But the Pure Theory of Law simply de-

From *Harvard Law Review*, Nov., 1941.

clares itself incompetent to answer either the question whether a given law is just or not, or the more fundamental question of what constitutes justice. The Pure Theory of Law—a science—cannot answer these questions because they cannot be answered scientifically at all.[2]

NORMATIVE AND SOCIOLOGICAL JURISPRUDENCE

Positive law, which is the object of the Pure Theory of Law, is an order by which human conduct is regulated in a specific way. The regulation is accomplished by provisions which set forth how men ought to behave. Such provisions are called norms, and either arise through custom, as do the norms of the common law, or are enacted by conscious acts of certain organs aiming to create law, as a legislature acting in its law-making capacity.

Legal norms may be general or individual in character. They may regulate beforehand, in an abstract way, an undetermined number of cases, as does the norm that if anyone steals he is to be punished by a court; or they may relate to a single case, as does a judicial decision which decrees that A is to suffer imprisonment for six months because he stole a horse from B. Jurisprudence sees the law as a system of general and individual norms. Facts are considered in this jurisprudence only to the extent that they form the content of legal norms. For example: jurisprudence takes cognizance of the procedure by which legal norms are created, for this procedure is prescribed by the norms of the constitution; of the delict, because it is defined by a norm as a condition of the sanction; of the sanction, which is ordered by a legal norm as a consequence of a delict. Only norms—provisions as to how individuals ought to behave—are objects of jurisprudence, never the actual behavior of individuals.

If we say that a norm "exists" we mean that a norm is valid. Norms are valid for those whose conduct they regulate. To say that a norm is valid for an individual means that the individual ought to conduct himself as the norm prescribes; it does not mean that the individual necessarily behaves so that his conduct actually corresponds to the norm. The latter relationship is expressed by saying that the norm is efficacious. Validity and efficacy are two distinct qualities; and yet there is a certain connection between the two. Jurisprudence regards a legal norm as valid only if it belongs to a legal order that is by and large efficacious; that is, if the individuals whose conduct is regulated by the legal order in the main actually do conduct themselves as they should according to the legal order. If a legal order loses its efficacy for any reason, then jurisprudence regards its norms as no longer valid. Still, the distinction between validity and efficacy is a necessary one, for it is possible that in a legal order which is on the whole efficacious, and hence regarded as valid, a single legal norm may be valid but not efficacious in a concrete instance, because, as a matter of fact, it was not obeyed or applied although it ought to have been. Jurisprudence regards law as a system of valid norms. It cannot dispense with the concept of validity as a different concept from that of efficacy if it wishes to present the specific sense of "ought" in which the norms of the law apply to the individuals whose conduct they regulate. It is this "ought" which is expressed in the concept of validity as distinguished from efficacy.

If jurisprudence is to present law as a system of valid norms, the propositions by which it describes its object must be "ought" propositions, statements in which an "ought," not an "is," is expressed. But the propositions of jurisprudence are not themselves norms. They establish neither duties nor rights. Norms by which individuals are obligated and empowered issue only from the law-creating authority. The jurist, as the theoretical exponent of the law, presents these norms in propositions that have a purely descriptive sense, statements which only describe the "ought" of the legal norm. It is of the greatest importance to distinguish clearly between legal norms which comprise the object of jurisprudence and the statements of jurisprudence describing that object. These statements may be called "rules of law" in contradistinction to the "legal norms" issued by the legal authority.

The rule of law, using the term in a descriptive sense, is, like the law of nature, a hypothetical judgment that attaches a specific consequence to a specific condition. But between the law of nature and the rule of law there exists only an analogy. The difference lies in the sense in which condition and consequence are connected. The law of nature affirms that when an occurrence (the cause) takes place, another occurrence (the effect) follows. The rule of law, using the term in a descriptive sense, says that if one individual behaves in a certain manner, another individual ought to behave in a given way. The difference between natural science and jurisprudence lies not in the logical structure of the propositions describing the object, but rather in the object itself, and hence in the meaning of the description. Natural science describes its object—nature—in *is*-propositions; jurisprudence describes its object—law—in *ought*-propositions. In view of the specific sense of the propositions in which jurisprudence describes its object, it can be called a normative theory of the law. This is what is meant by a specifically "juristic" view of the law.

This sort of jurisprudence must be clearly distinguished from another which can be called sociological.[3] The latter attempts to describe the phenomena of law not in propositions that state how men ought to behave under certain circumstances, but in propositions that tell how they actually do behave; just as physics describes how certain natural objects behave. Thus the object of sociological jurisprudence is not legal norms in their specific meaning of "ought-statements," but the legal (or illegal) behavior of men. It is supposed possible by observation of actual social happenings to achieve a system of rules by means of which this behavior, characterized as "law," can be described. These rules are supposed to be of the same sort as the laws of nature, and hence, like them, to afford the means for predicting future happenings within the legal community, future conduct to be characterized as law.

The Pure Theory of Law by no means denies the validity of such sociological jurisprudence but it declines to see in it, as many of its exponents do, the only science of law. Sociological jurisprudence stands side by side with normative jurisprudence; neither is able to replace the other because each deals with different problems. It is on just this account that the Pure Theory of Law insists upon clearly distinguishing them from each other, in order to avoid that syncretism of method which is the cause of numerous errors. What must be avoided is the confounding—as frequent as it is misleading—of cognition directed toward a legal "ought," with cognition directed toward an actual "is."

Normative jurisprudence deals with the validity of the law; sociological jurisprudence with its efficacy; but just as validity and efficacy are two different aspects of the law that must be kept clearly apart, yet which stand in a definite relation to each other, so there exists between normative and sociological jurisprudence, despite the difference in the direction of their cognitions, a considerable connection. The sociology of law cannot draw a line between its subject—law—and the other social phenomena; it cannot define its special object as distinct from the object of general sociology—society—without in so doing presupposing the concept of law as defined by normative jurisprudence. The question of what human behavior, as law, can form the object of sociology, of how the actual behavior of men to be characterized as law is distinguishable from other conduct, can probably be answered only as follows: "law" in the sociological sense is actual behavior that is stipulated in a legal norm—in the sense of normative jurisprudence—as condition or consequence. The sociologist regards this behavior not—as does the jurist—as the content of a norm, but as a phenomenon existing in natural reality, that is, in a causal nexus. The sociologist seeks its causes and effects. The legal norm, as the expression of an "ought," is not for him, as for the jurist, the object of his cognition; for the sociologist it is a principle of selection. The function of the legal norm for the sociology of law is to designate its own particular object, and lift it out of the whole of social events. To this extent, sociological jurisprudence presupposes normative jurisprudence. It is a complement of normative jurisprudence.

To the extent that sociology of law attempts to describe and as far as possible to predict the activity of the law-creating and law-applying organs, especially of the courts—a task that its American representatives place foremost—its results cannot be very different from those of normative jurisprudence. To be sure, the meaning of the propositions of sociological jurisprudence is, as we have seen, completely different from that of the propositions of normative jurisprudence. The latter determines how the courts should decide in accordance with the legal norms in force; the former how they do and presumably will decide. But since normative jurisprudence regards legal norms as valid only if they belong to a legal order that is generally efficacious, that is, actually obeyed and applied, no great difference can exist between the actual and the lawful conduct of law-applying organs. As long as the legal order is on the whole efficacious there is the greatest probability that the courts will actually decide as—in the view of normative jurisprudence—they should decide. The activities of the law-creating organs, however, especially of the legislative organs, that are not bound by legal norms in force or are bound only to a very slight extent, cannot be predicted with any degree of probability. The predictability of legal functioning by sociological jurisprudence is directly proportional to the extent to which that functioning has been described by normative jurisprudence.

Whether the prediction of future occurrences is an essential task of natural science, and hence by analogy one of sociology, is doubtful. The sociology of law at any rate has other more promising problems. It not only has to describe and if possible to predict the actual conduct of the individuals who create, apply, and obey the law; it must also explain it causally. In order to fulfill this task, it must investigate the ideologies by which men are influenced in their law-creating and law-applying activities. Among these ideologies the idea of justice plays a decisive role. The ideologico-critical analysis of this idea is one of the most important and promising tasks of a sociology of law.

THE CONCEPT OF THE NORM

Since the Pure Theory of Law limits itself to cognition of positive law, and excludes from this cognition the philosophy of justice as well as the sociology of law, its orientation is much the same as that of so-called analytical jurisprudence, which found its classical Anglo-American presentation in the work of John Austin. Each seeks to attain its results exclusively by analysis of positive law. While the Pure Theory of Law arose independently of Austin's famous *Lectures on General Jurisprudence*,[4] it corresponds in important points with Austin's doctrine. It is submitted that where they differ the Pure Theory of Law has carried out the method of analytical jurisprudence more consistently than Austin and his followers have succeeded in doing.

This is true especially as to the central concept of jurisprudence, the norm. Austin does not employ this concept, and pays no attention to the distinction between "is" and "ought" that is the basis of the concept of the norm. He defines law as "rule," and "rule" as "command." He says, "Every *law* or *rule* . . . is a *command*. Or, rather, laws or rules, properly so called, are a *species* of commands." [5]

A command is the expression of the will of an individual directed to the conduct of another individual. If it is my will that someone behave in a certain manner, and if I express my will as regards this other individual in a certain way, my expression is a command. Thus a command consists of two elements: a wish directed toward someone else's behavior, and its expression in one way or another. There is a command only so long as both the will and its expression are present. If someone issues a command to me, and before its execution I have adequate reason to assume that it is no longer his will, then neither is it any longer a command, even though the expression of his will should remain. But a so-called "binding" command is said to persist even if the will, the psychic phenomenon, has lapsed. More accurately, however, that which persists is not really the command, but rather my obligation. A command, on the other hand, is essentially a willing and its expression.

Hence legal rules, which according to Austin constitute the law, are not actually commands. They exist, that is to say, they are valid and obligate individuals, even if the will by which they were created has long ceased to be. It may even be said to be doubtful whether some instances in which legal obligations exist as to certain behavior ever represented the real will of anyone. An example will illustrate this.

If one calls a statute constitutionally enacted by a legislature a command, or, what amounts to the same thing, the "will" of the legislators, this expression has almost nothing to do with the true concept of "command." The statute is valid, that is, binding, even after all the members of the legislature that enacted it have died; then, therefore, the content of the statute is no longer the "will" of anyone, at least not of anyone competent to will it. Thus a binding law cannot be the psychological will of the lawmakers even though a real act of will is necessary to make the law. And an analysis of the constitutional process by which a statute comes into being shows that even the act creating a binding law need by no means represent any will to the behavior required by the statute. The statute is enacted when a majority of the legislators have voted for a bill submitted to them. The content of the statute is not the "will" of the legislators who vote against the bill; their will is expressly contrary. Yet their expressions of will are just as essential to the existence of the statute as are the expressions of will of the members who voted for it. The statute is an enactment of the whole legislature, including the minority, but this obviously does not mean that its content is the will—in the psychological sense—of all the members of the legislature. Even if one takes into consideration only the majority that voted for the bill, the assertion that the statute was the will of the majority is patent fiction. Voting for a bill by no means implies actually "willing" the content of the statute. Psychologically one can "will" only something of which one has an idea; one cannot "will" something of which one knows nothing. And it is indubitable that in very many if not all cases, a large proportion of the members of a legislature who vote for a bill either do not know its content or know it very superficially. That a legislator raises his hand or says "Aye" when the vote is being taken does not mean that he has made the content of the bill the content of his own will, in the way in which a man who "commands" another to act in a certain way "wills" this conduct.

Clearly, therefore, if a particular law is called a command, or, what amounts to the same thing, the "will" of the lawmaker, or if law in general is called the "command" or "will" of the "state," this can be taken as only a figurative expression. Usually an analogy lies at its root. When definite human behavior is "enacted," "provided," "prescribed," in a rule of law, the enactment is quite similar to a true command. But there is an important difference. The statement that a command exists means that a psychic phenomenon—a will—is directed toward certain human behavior. Human behavior is enacted, provided, or prescribed by a rule of law without any psychic act of will. Law might be termed a "depsychologized" command. This appears in the statement that man "ought" to conduct himself according to the law. Herein lies the importance of the concept of "ought," here is revealed the necessity for the concept of the norm. A norm is a rule stating that an individual ought to behave in a certain way, but not asserting that such behavior is the actual will of anyone.

A comparison of the "ought" of the norm with a command is apt only to a very slight extent. The law enacted by the legislator is a "command" only if it is assumed that this command has binding force. A command which has binding force is, indeed, a norm. But without the concept of the norm, the law can be described only with the help of a fiction, and Austin's assertion that legal rules are "commands" is a superfluous and dangerous fiction of the "will" of the legislator or the state.

THE ELEMENT OF COERCION

In accordance with the assertions of analytical jurisprudence, the Pure Theory of Law regards the element of coercion as an essential characteristic of the law. Austin [6] and his followers characterize law as "enforcible" or as a rule "enforced" by a given authority. By this they mean that the legal order "commands" the individual to act in a certain fashion, and "forces" men in a specific way to obey the commands of the legal order. The specific means by which the law "enforces" the obedience of individuals consists in inflicting an evil called a sanction in case of disobedience. The "coercion" which according to this view is characteristic of the law is a psychic one; obedience to the commands of the law is achieved through fear of the sanction.

From the standpoint of a strictly analytical method, this formulation is not correct. It has reference to the behavior of the citizen and the organs applying the law, but it may well be doubted whether the lawful behavior of individuals is brought about by fear of the threatened sanction. So far as we know anything about the motives for the behavior of individuals, we may surmise that moral or religious motives, for instance, are important, and even perhaps more effective than fear of the sanction of the law. And psychic coercion is not a specific element of the law. Moral and religious norms as well are coercive in this psychological sense. For the rest, this question as to the motives for lawful behavior is beside the purpose of cognition directed only to the content of the legal order.

We are here in the presence of a problem of sociological, not analytical or normative, jurisprudence. The latter can only affirm that the law sets up coercive measures as sanctions that are to be directed under definite conditions against definite individuals. From this standpoint, it is not the psychic coercion that proceeds from the idea men have of the law, but the outward sanctions which it provides that are of the law's essence.

Among the conditions to which the law attaches the sanction as a consequence, the delict is decisively important. The delict—with a limitation mentioned later—is such conduct of the individual against whom this sanction is directed, which is the opposite of the conduct that the law prescribes. Hence the sanction is provided for the very case where the law fails in a concrete instance to achieve its purpose, for the case in which obedience to the law does not receive the enforcement that Austin maintains is essential to law. Hence the law is not, as Austin formulates it, a rule "enforced" by a specified authority, but rather a norm which provides a specific measure of coercion as sanction. The nature of the law will not be grasped if one characterizes it as does Austin, as a command to conduct oneself lawfully. The law is a decree of a measure of coercion, a sanction, for that conduct called "illegal," a delict; and this conduct has the character of "delict" because and only because it is a condition of the sanction.

The legal norm refers to the conduct of two entities: the citizen, against whose delict the coercive measure of the sanction is directed; and the organ that is to apply the coercive measure to the delict. The function of the legal norm consists in attaching the sanction as a consequence to certain conditions among which the delict plays a leading part. Looked at from a sociological point of view, the essential characteristic of law, by which it is distinguished from all other social mechanisms, is the fact that it seeks to bring about socially desired conduct by acting against contrary socially undesired conduct—the delict—with a sanction which the individual involved will deem an evil. Analytical jurisprudence takes into consideration only the content of the legal order, and hence only the connection between delict and sanction.

Although Austin recognizes the essential significance of the sanction for the concept of law, he fails to describe the legal norm in a manner corresponding to this understanding. The Pure Theory of Law is only drawing an obvious conclusion when it formulates the rule of law (using the term in a descriptive sense) as a hypothetical judgment, in which the delict appears as an essential condition, the sanction as the consequence. The sense in which condition and consequence are connected in the legal norm is that of "ought." If one steals, he ought to be punished; if one does not make good tortious damage, civil execution ought to issue against him. In this way the science of law describes the relations which the legal norm, issued by the legal authority, establishes between delict and sanction. It is precisely by establishing this relation that the legal norm imposes duties and confers rights upon the individuals subjected to law.

THE LEGAL DUTY

The Pure Theory of Law stresses the primary character of the concept of duty in relation to that of right, just as Austin does. "Duty is the basis of Right." [7] To say that an individual is legally obligated to observe certain conduct, means that a legal norm provides a sanction for contrary behavior, a delict. Normally the sanction is directed against the individual who has committed the delict. It can happen, however—and in primitive legal orders this is the rule—that the sanction is directed not alone against the delinquent but against other individuals: those who stand in a specific relation to the delinquent. They are individuals who belong to the same legal group as the delinquent—to the same family, tribe, or state. If the sanction is directed only against the delinquent himself, then it is a case of individual responsibility. If the sanction is directed against the fellow members of the group, it is a case of collective responsibility. Such is the blood revenge or vendetta of the primitive law. Such is the operation even today of international law, whose sanctions (reprisal and war) are directed against the state as an entity—in effect, therefore, against the citizens of the state whose organ has violated the law. The fact that the sanction can be directed against individuals other than the delinquent makes it necessary to distinguish between the idea of duty and that of liability or responsibility. The liability rests upon the individual against whom the sanction is directed. The duty rests upon the potential delinquent who may by his behavior commit the delict. Normally, in modern law the subjects of the duty and liability are one and the same. But as an exception collective responsibility is still possible—is, indeed, the rule of international law today.

In the theory of Austin, this clear separation between the concept of duty and responsibility is not made. Austin proceeds from the supposition that the sanction is always directed against the individual who commits the delict, and takes no account of the cases in which the sanction is not directed against the delinquent but against someone who stands in a specific relation to him. Hence he fails to see the difference that exists between "to be obliged to maintain a certain behavior," and "to be responsible for a certain behavior." He defines legal duty: " 'To be obliged to do or forbear,' or 'to lie under a *duty* or *obligation* to do or forbear,' is to be liable or obnoxious to a sanction, in the event of disobeying a command." [8] But how is it when it is not the delinquent individual, but another who is exposed to the sanction? Then, according to Austin, the legal norm would not have set up any duty at all. But, also according to Austin, it is the nature of a legal norm to set up a legal duty. It is the "command," which, says Austin, obliges the individual.

It is this concept of the command which prevents Austin from distinguishing between duty and liability. According to Austin, a legal norm is a command to legal behavior. The decreeing of the sanction does not appear in the norm which obligates the individuals. Only if one characterizes the legal norm, as does the Pure Theory of Law, as a norm by which a sanction is decreed for illegal conduct, can one distinguish the case in which the sanction is directed against the individual who acts contrary to the "command" of the law, from the case in which the sanction is directed against someone who is made responsible for the delict committed by another.

THE LEGAL RIGHT

The word "right" has many meanings. It is used both in the sense of a right to conduct oneself in a certain way, and in the sense of a right that someone else should conduct himself in a certain way. To say that someone has a right to behave so, may only mean that he has no duty to behave otherwise; he is free. For instance, I have a right to breathe, think, walk in the park. This freedom is only the negation of a duty. But the phrase may also have the positive meaning that someone else is obliged to behave correspondingly. For example, that I have a right to use an object in my possession implies a duty on every other person not to disturb me in its use; or that I have the right to express my opinion means that it is the duty of the state—more correctly, of the organs representing the state—not to hinder my expression. That the right of one presupposes the duty of another is specially clear when the right is to certain conduct by someone else. That I have a right to have a certain man pay me a sum of money necessarily implies that it is his duty to pay. Every true right that is not mere negative freedom from a duty consists of a duty of another, or many others. "Right" in this sense is a "relative" duty. Austin's statement is apposite: ". . . the term 'right' and the term '*relative* duty' signify the same notion considered from different aspects." [9]

But Austin's theory contains no concept of right different from that of duty. Such a right exists when the legal order accords a person the opportunity to make the duty of another effective by bringing a suit and thus setting in motion the sanction provided for violation. Only in this case does the right of A to conduct on the part of B fail to coincide with the duty of B toward A. Only in this case is the legal situation incompletely described by stating that B is under an obligation to A to act in a certain way. Hence the Pure Theory of Law restricts the concept of a right to this situation. Only here is there a separately existing right in the narrow sense of the word.

THE STATIC AND DYNAMIC THEORY OF LAW:
THE HIERARCHY OF NORMS

Analytical jurisprudence, as presented by Austin, regards law as a system of rules complete and ready for application, without regard to the process of their creation. It is a static theory of the law. The Pure Theory of Law recognizes that a study of the statics of law must be supplemented by a study of its dynamics, the process of its creation. This necessity exists because the law, un-like any other system of norms, regulates its own creation. An analysis of positive law shows that the process by which a legal norm is created is regulated by another legal norm. Indeed, usually other norms determine not only the process of creation,. but also, to a greater or lesser extent, the content of the norm to be created. Thus a constitution both regulates the procedure by which statutes are created, and contains provisions, mostly nega-tive, concerning their content. For example, freedom of speech, press, and religion must not be limited by statute, or only in a certain way. Similarly, while laws concerning civil and criminal procedure regulate the way in which the individual norms of judicial decisions are made, a civil or a penal code determines by its general norms the content of these individual norms. In the same way, in a system of customary law such as the common law, the content of judicial decisions is defined by preëxisting general norms to a much greater degree than is the content of statutes by the constitution. The difference between legal norms that deter-mine the mode of creation of other legal norms and those that de-termine their content is expressed in Anglo-American terminology by a distinction between "adjective" and "substantive" law.

The relation existing between a norm which governs the crea-tion or the content of another norm and the norm which is created can be presented in a spatial figure. The first is the "su-perior" norm; the second the "inferior." If one views the legal order from this dynamic point of view, it does not appear, as it does from the static point of view, as a system of norms of equal rank, standing one beside the other, but rather as a hierarchy in which the norms of the constitution form the topmost stratum. In this functional sense, "constitution" means those norms that determine the creation, and occasionally to some extent the con-tent, of the general legal norms which in turn govern such indi-vidual norms as judicial decisions. It is a complex of norms which regulates primarily the organs and the procedure of legislation, and which includes also the norm by which custom is recognized as a creator of law. To be included within this complex, a norm need not be found in a written constitution—it may be a part of the unwritten constitution created by custom.

The relation between a norm of a higher level and one of a

lower, for instance, that between a constitution and a statute enacted in accordance with it, means also that in the higher norm is found the reason for the validity of the lower; a legal norm is valid because it has come into being in the way prescribed by another norm. This is the principle of validity peculiar to positive law. It is a thoroughly dynamic principle. The unity of the legal order is achieved by this connection. If one asks the reason for the validity of a judicial decision, the answer runs: the decision containing the individual norm, by which, for example, A is obligated to pay B $1000, is valid because the decision came into being by the application of general norms of statutory or customary law that empower the court to decide a concrete case in a certain manner. The general norms so applied are valid because they were created in accordance with the constitution. What is the reason for the validity of the constitution? The norm from which the constitution derives its validity is the basic norm of the legal order. This basic norm is responsible for the unity of the legal order. The question of which is the basic norm responsible for the unity of a national legal order can be answered only in connection with the relation in which national law stands to international. And this question presupposes a clear insight into the relation of law and state.

THE LAW AND THE STATE

One characteristic of Austin's doctrine is its lack of a legal concept of the state. The concept of an "independent political society" plays a certain role in his teachings, but it is not a legal concept, and Austin himself does not call this "independent political society" a state. By it he means a society consisting of a sovereign and subjects.[10] The sovereign may be an individual or a group, but never all persons comprising the political society. Austin says "all judge-made law is the creature of the sovereign or state," [11] but "state" here obviously means not a political society, but rather the bearer of the sovereignty within the society. For the rest, Austin seldom uses the word "state" and reveals a disinclination for the concept. When he says that law is created by the "state," he means: "Every positive law . . . is set by a sovereign person, or a sovereign body of persons," [12] that is to say, by that part of the political society in which the sovereignty resides.

As all law emanates from the sovereign, the sovereign himself is not subject to the law. One of the main principles of Austin's theory is that sovereign power is incapable of *legal* limitation.[13] The essence of sovereignty consists, according to Austin, in the fact that the individual or group designated as sovereign will "not be habitually obedient to a determinate human superior." [14] This concept of the sovereign is sociological or political, but not juristic—yet it is an essential element of Austin's jurisprudence, which teaches that law is to be understood only as the command of the sovereign. This is difficult to reconcile with the theoretic method of analytical jurisprudence, which derives its concepts only from an analysis of positive law. In the norms of positive law no such thing as a "sovereign," a person or group "incapable of legal limitation," can be found. The central difficulty is that the jurisprudence of Austin, while it deals with the concept of a sovereign which is not the state but only an organ of the state, does not concern itself at all with the problem of the state itself.

On this point there is a great difference between Austin's analytical jurisprudence and the Pure Theory of Law. The latter does not deny the traditional view that the state is a political society; but it shows that a number of individuals can form a social unit, a "society" or, better, "community," only on the basis of an order, or, in other words, that the element constituting the political community is an order. The state is not its individuals; it is the specific union of individuals, and this union is the function of the order which regulates their mutual behavior. Only in this order does the social community exist at all. It is a political community, because and to the extent that the specific means by which this regulatory order seeks to attain its end is the decreeing of measures of coercion. The legal order is such a coercive order, as we have seen. One of the distinctive results of the Pure Theory of Law is its recognition that the coercive order which constitutes the political community we call "state," is a legal order. What is usually called "the legal order of the state," or "the legal order set up by the state," is the state itself.

Law and state are usually held to be two distinct entities. But if it be recognized that the state is by its very nature an ordering of human behavior, that the essential characteristic of this order, coercion, is at the same time the essential element of the law, this traditional dualism can no longer be maintained. By subsuming the concept of the state under the concept of a coercive order which can only be the legal order, by giving up a concept of the state distinct in principle from the concept of law, the Pure Theory of Law realizes a tendency inherent in the doctrine of Austin. Austin rightly felt that a *political* concept of the state had no place in a juristic theory. Hence he seeks to dispense with it. But he substitutes for it another political concept, that of the "sovereign," instead of establishing a *legal* concept of the state.

The state which "possesses" a legal order is imagined as a person. This "person" is only a personification of the unity of the legal order. The dualism of state and law arises from hypostatizing the personification, asserting this figurative expression to be a real being, and so opposing it to the law. If, however, juristic thinking is freed from this fiction, then all problems concerning the relation of state and law are revealed as illusory. Thus the much-mooted question whether the state creates the law is answered by saying that men create the law, on the basis of its own definite norms. The individuals who create the law are organs of the legal order, or, what amounts to the same thing, organs of the state. They are organs because and to the extent that they fulfill their functions according to the provisions of the legal order which constitutes the legal community. For an individual to be an organ of the state means only that certain acts performed by him are attributed to the state, that is, are referred to the unity of the legal order. If it be asked why a certain act of an individual is imputed to the state, there is no other answer than that this conduct is determined by the legal order. The criterion of this imputation of a human act to the state is purely juristic in character. If a norm of the legal order is created in accordance with the stipulations of another norm of this legal order, then the individual who creates the law is an organ of the legal order, an organ of the state. In this sense it can be said that the state creates the law, but this means only that the law regulates its own creation.

If one resolves the dualism of law and the state, if one recognizes the state as a legal order, then the so-called elements of the state—territory and population—appear as the territorial and personal spheres of validity of the national legal order. What Austin calls the "sovereign" appears as the order's highest organ, and sovereignty is then not a characteristic of the individual or group of individuals comprising this organ, but a characteristic of the state itself. For sovereignty to be a characteristic of the *national* legal order, however, can mean only that above this order no higher order is assumed.

INTERNATIONAL AND NATIONAL LAW

If there is a legal order superior to the national legal orders, it must be international law. Whether it is really law in the same sense as national law, and whether, as a legal order, it stands above the national legal orders, are the two decisive questions. Austin answers both negatively, admitting the validity of international law only as "positive international morality." [15] Therefore the theory of international law, like the theory of the state, is eliminated from the province of Austin's jurisprudence. The Pure Theory of Law, on the other hand, shows that it is quite possible to consider international law as real law, since it contains all essential elements of a legal order. It is a coercive order in the same sense as national law: it obligates states to definite mutual behavior, in that it provides sanctions against contrary conduct. The sanctions provided by international law are reprisals and war. The Pure Theory of Law attempts to prove that according to international law not only reprisals but war, as well, is permissible only as a reaction against a wrong that has been suffered. The Pure Theory of Law shows that the principle of *bellum justum* is a principle of positive international law. International law is real law, but it is primitive law. This is so especially because the reaction against the delict, the execution of the sanction, is left to the state itself, the very subject whose rights are infringed, instead of being delegated to a central organ as in the national legal order. Thus the international legal order is radically decentralized, and for this reason the international community constituted by international law is not a state, but only a union of states. A certain degree of centralization is essential to the state. Similarly the completely decentralized community of a primitive tribe is not a state, although there is no doubt that the order constituting it is a legal order.

There are today two opposing views in regard to the relation between national and international law, the one dualistic and the other monistic. The former maintains that national law and international law are two completely distinct and mutually independent systems of norms, like positive law and morality, for instance. The Pure Theory of Law shows that such a dualistic concept of the relation between national and international law is logically impossible, and that none of the followers of the dualistic theory is able to maintain his point of view consistently. If one assumes that two systems of norms are considered as valid simultaneously from the same point of view, one must also assume a normative relation between them; one must assume the existence of a norm or order that regulates their mutual relations. Otherwise insoluble contradictions between the norms of each system are unavoidable, and the logical principle that excludes contradictions holds for the cognition of norms as much as for the cognition of natural reality. When positive law and morality are asserted to be two distinct mutually independent systems of norms, this means only that the jurist, in determining what is legal, does not take into consideration morality, and the moralist, in determining what is moral, pays no heed to the prescriptions of positive law. Positive law and morality can be regarded as two distinct and mutually independent systems of norms, because and to the extent that they are not conceived to be simultaneously valid from the same point of view. But once it is conceded that national and international law are both positive law, it is obvious that both must be considered as valid simultaneously from the same juristic point of view. For this reason, they must belong to the same system of norms, they must in some way supplement each other.

The monistic theory meets this logical requirement. It regards national and international law as one system of norms, as a unity. Opinions differ, however, as to how this whole is constructed. Some assert international law to be a part of national law—those norms of national law that regulate the relation of the state to other states. The rules admitted to be international law can bind the individual state only when the latter recognizes them and thereby takes them over into its own legal order. This is the theory of the primacy of national law, obviously proceeding from the idea that the state is sovereign, that is, that the national legal order is an order of the highest rank, above which no other order can be deemed valid. As this is true for each of the many national legal orders, there is, according to this theory, not one international law, but as many as there are national legal orders. In truth, there is no international law at all as such, but only national law. The relationship between the different national legal orders can be established only from the point of view of one given order, whose norms alone determine its relations to the other orders. From such a point of view, that is, from the standpoint of a definite national legal order, all other orders appear not as sovereign, but rather as delegated orders. They are systems of valid norms only to the extent that they are recognized as such by the state whose legal order constitutes the point of departure.

The Pure Theory of Law shows that this monistic theory is indeed logically possible, but that it is not consonant with the idea, that all states or national legal orders are of the same rank. The primacy of national law means the primacy of one national legal order not only in regard to international law, but in regard to all other national legal orders. The idea quite generally held, that all states form a community in which they stand side by side on a footing of equality, is possible only on the assumption that above the states, or above the national legal orders, there is a legal order that makes them equal by defining their mutual spheres of validity. This order can be only international law. The Pure Theory of Law shows by an analysis of positive international law that it actually does perform the function just mentioned, and hence can be regarded—if one forgoes the assumption of the sovereignty of the individual state—as a system of norms standing above the national legal orders, according them equal rank, and binding them together into a universal legal order. This is the theory of the primacy of international law. Its theoretic basis was revealed for the first time by the Pure Theory of Law.

There is nothing to prevent this interpretation of the legal material except the idea of the sovereignty of the state. One of the most important results of the Pure Theory of Law is that sovereignty, in the specific sense which this idea has in a theory of law, is not a real characteristic of a real thing. Sovereignty is a judgment of value, and as such it is an assumption. The individualistic philosophy of the eighteenth and nineteenth centuries proceeded from the idea that the human individual was sovereign, that is, of the highest value. From this it was concluded that a social order can be binding on the individual only when it is recognized by the individual as binding. From this came the doctrine of the social contract, which still has its exponents; but today the inclination is rather to a universalistic philosophy of values according to which the community is superior to the individual.

In the sphere of international relations the view that the state is essentially sovereign is an individualistic philosophy, based on the individuality of the state. The dogma of sovereignty is not the result of scientific analysis of the phenomenon of the state, but the assumption of a philosophy of values. Consequently it cannot be contradicted scientifically. One can only show that an interpretation which proceeds from another assumption—namely, from that of the sovereignty of the international legal community—is just as possible, and that positive international law itself, so far as its validity is admitted, requires this interpretation.

The analysis of positive international law made by the Pure Theory of Law shows that its norms are incomplete and need supplementing by the norms of the national legal orders. The generally accepted proposition that international law obligates only states means not that international law does not obligate individuals, but rather that while, like every law, it obligates individuals, it does so indirectly, through the medium of national legal orders. To say that international law obligates a state to certain conduct means that international law obligates an individual as an organ of this state to such conduct, but that international law determines directly only the conduct, leaving the national legal order to determine the individual whose conduct forms the content of the international obligation. Thus international law presupposes the simultaneous validity of national legal orders within one and the same system of legal norms that embraces international law as well.

A generally recognized principle of international law, formulated in the usual manner, reads as follows: If a power is established anywhere, in any manner, which is able to ensure permanent obedience to its coercive order among the individuals whose behavior this order regulates, then the community constituted by this coercive order is a state in the sense of international law. The sphere in which this coercive order is permanently effective is the territory of the state; the individuals who live in the territory are the people of the state in the sense of positive international law. This is the principle of effectiveness, so important throughout international law. By this legal principle, international law defines the territorial and personal spheres of validity of the national legal orders, spheres which each state is bound to respect. By it also is determined the validity of the national orders. These are valid, in the sense of international law, because and to the extent that they satisfy the requirement of effectiveness. If jurisprudence, as we have shown, considers a legal norm as valid only when it belongs to a legal order which is in the main effective, it is using a principle of positive law itself, a principle of international law.

Since the national legal orders find the reason for their validity in the international legal order, which at the same time defines their spheres of validity, the international legal order must be superior to each national order. Thus it forms, together with them, one uniform universal legal system.

As it is the task of natural science to describe its object—reality —in one system of laws of nature, so it is the task of jurisprudence to comprehend all human law in one system of rules of law. This task Austin's jurisprudence did not see; the Pure Theory of Law, imperfect and inaccurate though it may be in detail, has gone a measurable distance toward this accomplishment.

LAW, STATE, AND JUSTICE IN
THE PURE THEORY OF LAW

I<small>T IS</small> a characteristic element of that primitive interpretation of nature we call animism to imagine a soul, spirit, or deity within or behind the phenomena, in order to explain their existence or function, and thus to substitute for a real explanation a reduplication of the world. Why is it that a tree grows and a river flows? Because there is an invisible dryad in the visible tree, a nymph in the river, answered the primitive Greeks, who created the god Helios behind the sun and the goddess Selene behind the moon, thus personifying these things. The tendency to personify has its origin in animism. The progress of natural science consists to a great extent in its emancipation from animism; and if the development of social sciences still lags far behind that of natural science it is due, among other things, to the fact that in this field animistic and hence personifying thinking is not completely exterminated. The Pure Theory of Law considers it as one of its main tasks to free the science of law from the relics of animism, which play a particularly dangerous role whenever jurists operate with the concept of juristic person. If we speak in terms of "person," if we say, a juristic person acts or a juristic person has a legal right or a legal duty, we must always ask what is personified, and try to describe the legal phenomena concerned in terms of legal relations among individual human beings, that is to say in terms of human relations determined by the law.

A typical example of animistic reduplication of the object of

From *The Yale Law Journal*, Jan. 1948. This essay is a reply to G. Merle Bergman, "The Communal Concept of Law," *The Yale Law Journal*, LVII (Nov., 1947), 55 ff.

knowledge is the dualism of law and state still maintained by traditional jurisprudence and political theory. It can hardly be denied that the law is a social order, that is to say an order regulating the mutual behavior of human beings. An order is a set of rules prescribing a certain human behavior, and that means a system of norms. The saying that the purpose of the law is to establish order, creates the illusion that there are two things, the law on the one hand and order on the other hand. But the law is itself the order which those who speak of "law and order" have in mind.

Like any science, the science of law must first of all define its object by differentiating it from other similar objects, in answering the question: what is the law as object of a particular science? Like any science, the science of law must, in defining its object, proceed from a certain usage of language, from the usual meaning of the word by which its object is designated. One must see whether the social phenomena termed "law" present a characteristic in common distinguishing them from other social phenomena —a characteristic sufficiently significant to constitute a general concept for the rational understanding of social life. If the Pure Theory of Law assumes that coercion is an essential element of law, it does so because a careful examination of the social orders termed "law" in the history of mankind shows that these social orders, in spite of their great differences, present one common element, an element of great importance in social life: they all prescribe coercive acts as sanctions. In defining the concept of law as a coercive order, that is to say as an order prescribing coercive acts as sanctions, the Pure Theory of Law simply accepts the meaning that the term "law" has assumed in the history of mankind.[1] In defining the law as a coercive order the Pure Theory of Law conceives of the law as a specific social technique. This technique is characterized by the fact that the social order, termed "law," tries to bring about a certain behavior of men, considered by the lawmaker as desirable, by providing coercive acts as sanctions in case of opposite behavior.[2]

The definition of the concept of law as a coercive order refers to the contents of the norms of law; it means that these rules provide for coercive acts as sanctions. It does not mean that the idea men have of the law exercises psychic coercion upon them, coerces them to conform their behavior to the law. But it cannot be denied that a legal order is considered to be valid only if the human behavior to which this order refers is, by and large, in conformity with the order. If this conformity—in whatever way it may be brought about—is termed "effectiveness," then effectiveness is a condition of the validity of the law. But it is no specific element of the concept of law. No social order, not even the one we call "morality" or "justice," is considered to be valid if it is not to a certain extent effective, that is to say if the human behavior regulated by the order does not at all conform to it. It is the effectiveness of a social order that, in the usual language, is called the power or might behind the order. Why a given legal order is actually effective, why men behave lawfully, is difficult to say, because we have no adequate method of ascertaining the motives of lawful behavior. Fear of the sanctions provided by the law, especially if the execution of the sanctions is centralized, may play a decisive role; but it is not impossible that a legal order, or parts of it, are effective for other reasons. Hence, effectiveness as a condition of the validity of the law must not be confused with coercion as an essential element of the concept of law.[3]

II

As to the relationship between law and state, it is usual to say that the state is a political community which creates or enforces the social order called "law." This statement presupposes that state and law are two different things, the one a community, a body of individuals, the other an order, a system of norms. But what is a community? When do several human beings form a community, when are they members of a community presented as a body? A science of law, I think, is not supposed to take these figures of speech literally. What, then, is their real meaning? The term "community" seems to indicate that individuals forming a community have something in common. It is evident that not everything individuals have in common constitutes a community. Not all men who have dark hair in common form a community, at least not in the sense that the state is a community. Sometimes one assumes that a community is a community of interests, that is to say that individuals who have interests in common form a community.[4] This is certainly not true. Common interests may be the reason for establishing a community; but not all individuals who have interests in common form a community; and there are communities of individuals that are not at all based on a common interest of these individuals, communities which comprise individuals of quite opposite interests. But to present them as communities of interests is to the ideological advantage of those in whose preponderant interest the communities are established. Those may be a majority or a minority of the individuals who form the community. To identify the concept of community with that of a community of interests means to countenance this ideological interest. A typical example is the definition of the state as a community based on the common interest of its subjects, or as a community established for the purpose of realizing the common interest of its subjects. This definition evidently ignores the fact that the people of a state are, with respect to the real interests of the individuals, not necessarily a homogeneous body, that the people are almost always divided into antagonistic groups of interest, that there is not, and there never was, a state within which there is not a greater or smaller number of individuals whose interests—as they rightly or wrongly understand them—are in direct opposition to those on which this community is established or which this community is realizing. The assertion that the community called "state" is based on the common interests of its subjects amounts to the doctrine that this community is based on the consent of all its members. It is the old fiction of the social contract. It can be maintained only by the aid of the other fiction that he who remains within the community consents to its order and thus shows that it is in his interest. *Qui tacet consentire videtur.* This is one of the worst legal fictions invented by the Roman jurists. The statement that the state is a community based on or working for the common interests of all its subjects, is of the same nature as the statement that Plato advocates in his Dialogue *Laws:* that only the just man is happy, the unjust man unhappy. Of this statement he says that if it is a lie it is a useful lie, for it induces the citizens to obey the law, and that means according to Plato, to be just. Hence the government is justified in making the citizens believe it.[5]

The fact that several individuals have an interest in common does not constitute a community any more than the fact that they have dark hair in common. Individuals form a community only if there exist specific relationships among them; and a legal community exists if these relationships are determined by the law. In an extensive study of this problem I have shown that the inter-individual relations, which constitute the community we call "state," are legal relations, that it is impossible to determine the unity in the plurality of individuals we call "state" by a criterion independent of the social order we call "the law of the state," to define the state as a metajuristic entity.[6] As far as I can see, the arguments advanced in that study have never been refuted. The legal character of the community called "state" is particularly manifest when the state is considered in the relations which usually are assumed to exist between this community as a political body and the law. If we say that the state creates or enforces the law, the state is presented as an acting person. But the state can act only through individual human beings. When may an act, performed by a human being, be interpreted as an act of the state? What is the criterion for this imputation of the act of a visible being to the invisible person of the state? The problem of the state is essentially the problem of this imputation. The only possible answer is that an act performed by a human being may be imputed to the state if this act is determined by the legal order in a specific way. As long as no other satisfactory answer to the question as to the criterion for this imputation is available, my thesis that the state as an acting person and as subject of duties and rights is nothing but a juristic construction stands unshaken. That the state creates the law means that human beings in their capacity as organs of the state create the law; and that means that they create the law in conformity with legal norms regulating the creation of the law.[7] That the state enforces the law means that a human being acting as an organ of the state executes a sanction provided for by the law. Human beings performing acts of state are acting as "organs of the state." That is a figure of speech meaning that their acts are imputable to the state, and that necessarily means that these acts are legal acts.

The human relations which, in their sum total, are called "a community" are always determined by an order regulating the mutual behavior of the individuals concerned. This social order constitutes the community. It is this order that the individuals who belong to the community have in common. The social order and the community constituted by it are not two different things. An individual, together with other individuals, belongs to a community only in so far as his behavior in relation to the other individuals is regulated by the order. To be a member of the community means nothing else but to be subjected to this order. To avoid the misleading appearance of a dualism of social order and community it would be more correct to say the social order is the community, not the social order constitutes the community.

If the state is a community, it is a legal community. As a community it is the legal order of which we say in a not perfectly correct way that it constitutes the community. Who could deny that the state is a social order? And if this statement is accepted, what other order than a legal order could the state be if—expressed in the usual language—it is essential to the state to have or to establish or to enforce a legal order?

However, to say that the state as a social order is identical with the law is not correct.[8] Not every legal order is a state. Only a relatively centralized legal order is termed a state. The personification of this legal order is the state as an acting person. To take this figure of speech literally, to hypostatize the personification, and then to speak of the state as a thing different from "its" legal order, to imagine the state as the authority, community, or power behind the law—just as Helios was imagined behind the sun, Selene behind the moon—and to make the state the god of the law: this is the relic of animism in jurisprudence and political theory, which the Pure Theory of Law tries to eliminate, because it leads to sham problems and empty tautologies.[9] It seems to be a fruitless endeavor. For, the political interest in making the people believe in a god of the law is stronger than the interest in a scientific analysis and correct description of the phenomena concerned.

III

The Pure Theory of Law restricts itself to a structural analysis of positive law based on a comparative study of the social orders which actually exist and existed in history under the name of law.

Hence the problem of the origin of the law—the law in general or a particular legal order—meaning the causes of the coming into existence of the law in general or of a particular legal order with its specific content, are beyond the scope of this theory. They are problems of sociology and history and as such require methods totally different from that of a structural analysis of given legal orders. The methodological difference between a structural analysis of law on the one hand, and sociology and history of law on the other hand, is similar to that between theology and sociology or history of religion. The object of theology is God, presumed to be existing; the object of sociology and history of religion is men's belief in God or in gods, whether the object of this belief does or does not exist. The Pure Theory of Law deals with the law as a system of valid norms created by acts of human beings. It is a juristic approach to the problem of law. Sociology and history of law try to describe and explain the fact that men have an idea of law, different at different times and in different places, and the fact that men do or do not conform their behavior to these ideas. It is evident that juristic thinking differs from sociological and historical thinking. The "purity" of a theory of law which aims at a structural analysis of positive legal orders consists in nothing else but in eliminating from its sphere problems that require a method different from that appropriate to its own specific problem. The postulate of purity is the indispensable requirement of avoiding syncretism of methods, a postulate which traditional jurisprudence does not, or does not sufficiently, respect. Elimination of a problem from the sphere of the Pure Theory of Law, of course, does not imply the denial of the legitimacy of this problem or of the science dealing with it. The law may be the object of different sciences; the Pure Theory of Law has never claimed to be the only possible or legitimate science of law. Sociology of law and history of law are others. They, together with the structural analysis of law, are necessary for a complete understanding of the complex phenomenon of law. To say that there cannot be a pure theory of law because a structural analysis of the law, restricting itself to its specific problem, is not sufficient for a complete understanding of the law amounts to saying that there can be no science of logic because a complete understanding of the psychic phenomenon of thinking is not possible without psychology.[10]

Like the question of the origin of the law, the question of whether a given legal order is just or unjust cannot be answered within the framework and by the specific methods of a science directed at a structural analysis of positive law. This does not necessarily imply that the question of what is justice cannot be answered in a scientific, and that is to say in an objective, way at all. But even if it were possible to decide objectively what is just and what unjust, as it is possible to determine what is an acid and what a base, justice and law must be considered as two different concepts. If the idea of justice has any function at all, it is to be a model for making good law and a criterion for distinguishing good from bad law.

There is, however, in traditional jurisprudence a terminological tendency to identify law and justice, to use the term law in the sense of just law, and to declare that a coercive order which on the whole is effective and therefore a valid positive law, or a single norm of such a social order, is no "real" or "true" law if it is not just. This use of the term "law" has the effect that any positive law, or single norm of a positive law is to be considered at first sight as just, since it presents itself as law and is generally called "law." It may be doubtful whether it deserves to be termed law, but it has the benefit of the doubt. He who denies the justice of such "law" and asserts that the so-called law is no "true" law, has to prove it; and this proof is practically impossible since there is no objective criterion of justice. Hence the real effect of the terminological identification of law and justice is an illicit justification of any positive law.

There is not, and cannot be, an objective criterion of justice because the statement: something is just or unjust, is a judgment of value referring to an ultimate end, and these value judgments are by their very nature subjective in character, because based on emotional elements of our mind, on our feelings and wishes. They cannot be verified by facts, as can statements about reality. Ultimate value judgments are mostly acts of preference; they indicate what is better rather than what is good; they imply the choice between two conflicting values, as for instance the choice between freedom and security. Whether a social system that guarantees individual freedom but no economic security is preferable to a social system that guarantees economic security but no individual freedom, depends on the decision whether freedom or security is the higher value. It is hardly possible to deny that there exists a definite difference between the statement that freedom is a higher value than security, or vice versa, and the statement that water is heavier than wood. There are individuals who prefer freedom to security because they feel happy only if they are free, and hence prefer a social system and consider it just only if it guarantees individual freedom. But others prefer security because they feel happy only if they are economically secure, and hence consider a social system just only if it guarantees economic security. Their judgments about the value of freedom and security and hence their idea of justice are ultimately based on nothing but their feelings. No objective verification of their respective value judgments is possible. And since men differ very much in their feelings, their ideas of justice are very different. This is the reason why in spite of the attempts made by the most illustrious thinkers of mankind to solve the problem of justice, there is not only no agreement but the most passionate antagonism in answering the question of what is just. Quite different is the situation with respect to statements about reality. The statement that water is heavier than wood can be verified by experiment, showing that the statement conforms to facts. Statements about facts are based, it is true, on the perception of our senses controlled by our reason, and hence are in a certain sense subjective too. But the perceptions of our senses are in a much higher degree under the control of our reason than are our feelings, and as a matter of fact nobody doubts that water is heavier than wood. Even if we accept a philosophy of radical subjectivism and admit that the universe exists only in the mind of man, we must nevertheless maintain the difference which exists between value judgments and statements about reality. The difference may be relative only as a difference between degrees of subjectivity ("objective" meaning the lowest possible degree of subjectivity). But the relative difference is considerable enough to justify the differentiation between a judgment about what is just and a statement about what is the law, the positive law. "Positive" law means that a law is created by acts of human beings which take place in time and space, in contradistinction to natural law, which is supposed to originate in another way. Consequently, the question of what is the positive law, the law of a certain country or the law in a concrete case, is the question of a law creating act which has taken place at a certain time and within a certain space. The answer to this question does not depend on the feelings of the answering subjects; it can be verified by objectively ascertainable facts, whereas the question of whether a law of a certain country or the decision of a certain court is just, depends on the idea of justice presupposed by the answering subject, and this idea is based on the emotional function of his mind.[11]

The terminological identification of law and justice is one of the characteristic elements of the natural-law doctrine, which presents justice under the name of "natural" law. Positive law is "law," too; and as long as it is not proved to be at variance with natural law is to be considered as true law. Almost all followers of the natural-law doctrine assume, expressly or tacitly, that there exists a presumption in favor of the conformity of positive with natural law. The historical function of the natural-law doctrine was to preserve the authority of the positive law. The doctrine had, and still has, by and large, a conservative character. It is true that revolutionary movements also used this doctrine to justify their demands. But the classic exponents of the natural-law doctrine were by no means revolutionaries.[12]

The presumption in favor of the positive law is sustained by an important consequence of the dualism of natural and positive law. The acts of human beings by which, from the point of view of legal positivism, the law is created, such as custom, legislation, judicial decision, consequently have a constitutive character; but they must be interpreted by natural-law doctrine as merely declaratory. From the point of view of that doctrine the organs of the community do not produce the law, they only re-produce a pre-existing law created by God, nature, human reason, or in some other mysterious way. The organs of the community may, it is true, fail to fulfill their task of finding the law and formulating it in an adequate way, but it must be assumed that, on the whole, they succeed; otherwise there would be no law realized in the world. Besides, who could be more competent to decide what natural law prescribes and whether the positive law conforms to the natural law, the true law, than the organs of the community whose task it is to find this law? To confer this competence not on the organs of the community but exclusively on the subjects supposed to obey the law, would amount to establishing anarchy. As paradoxical as it seems, it is nevertheless a fact that the doctrine which denies that the positive-law makers really are what they pretend to be—the creators of the law—has the effect, if not the purpose, of strengthening their authority.

Hence the doctrine of a dual law, the true law (created by a mysterious authority) and the positive law (a mere reproduction of the former) appears in many disguises. It is, for instance, the basis of Rousseau's distinction between the "general will" (*volonté générale*) and the "will of all" (*volonté de tous*). The "general will" is always right, and that means just, because it is always directed at the common interest of the members of the community. The organs of the community, in making law, have only to express the general will. They may or may not succeed; even a decision adopted unanimously or by the majority of the people may fail to express the general will and hence be not binding upon the subjects.[13] But how does the general will come into existence if not by a unanimous or a majority vote of the people? Who is competent to decide whether in a concrete case the "will of all," especially the will of the majority, is or is not in conformity with the "general will"? There is no answer to this question in Rousseau's classic work, although it is just upon the answer to this question that the applicability of his doctrine depends.

When Rousseau discusses the voting procedure, however, he states that "the vote of the majority always binds all the rest," that "the general will is found by counting votes," that voting for or against a bill only means deciding whether the suggested bill is or is not "in conformity with the general will, each man, in giving his vote, stating his opinion on that point." To be in the minority "proves" one to be mistaken about what the general will is.[14] Thus the majority is always right; the introduction of the mysterious entity "general will" and the dualism of the "general will" and the "will of all" amount to a highly problematical justification of a definitive form of government, to the identification of justice with democracy.

Another form of the doctrine of dual law was presented by the German historical school, allegedly opposed to the natural-law doctrine. The followers of this school started from the basic assumption that the law, like language and religion, is essentially connected with the specific character of a people; an assumption which is highly paradoxical in view of the fact that the German people was forced to give up their own law and their own religion and to adopt the Roman law and the Christian religion, both of which originated with totally different peoples and in documents written in foreign languages. In spite of these historical facts, the German school maintains that the law originates in the spirit of the people (*Volksgeist*), which is the real creator of the law. Hence even customary law is not created by custom. Custom is not a law-creating fact; it is only evidence [15] of preëxisting law created by the mysterious spirit. But custom is considered by the German school as absolute reliable evidence; thus customary law is true law and as such preferred to statutory law. As to statutory law, the most prominent representative of this school, Savigny, declared that legislation is a rather problematical function of the state and better omitted. He seriously tried to prove that at his time "the making of a good code was not possible." [16] This was the time when the Code Napoléon, that splendid product of the French Revolution, was issued. But it was against just this Code, against the French Revolution and its successful attempt to replace old by new law, clearly created by legislative acts, that Savigny's theory was directed. Its political tendencies are unmistakable; they explain the hypothesis of an invisible and intangible lawmaker, called the "spirit of the people." The people, Savigny says, respect much more "what has not a visible and tangible origin" than "what has been made before our eyes by men of our own kind." [17] Savigny tried to prove that the Roman law was customary law. In maintaining that customary law is created by the spirit of the people and preferable to statutory law, he tried to sustain the authority of the Roman law, which at his time was positive law in Germany.

A similar doctrine is the doctrine of "social solidarity" (*solidarité sociale*) as the creator of true law, the "objective law" (*droit objectif*) presented at the beginning of the twentieth century by the French sociological school, whose most prominent jurist was

Leon Duguit. According to his doctrine the legislative and judiciary organs of the state do not create the law, but only ascertain (*constatent*) and enforce a preëxisting law originating in the "social solidarity." The positive law is binding only if it conforms to the "objective" law. The authority called "social solidarity" is no less mysterious than the "general will" of Rousseau and the "spirit of the people" of the German historical school. The doctrine that positive law, in order to be binding, must conform to the "objective law" created by the "social solidarity," is applicable only if this doctrine furnishes an answer to the question, who is competent to decide whether in a concrete case positive law is or is not in conformity with the "objective law," the true and just law. This is obviously the decisive question. And it is highly characteristic that Duguit does not even discuss it. He says of the objective law originating in social solidarity that "it is the law of man as a social being . . . man feels it or conceives of it, the scholar formulates it, the positive legislator ascertains it [*constate*] and secures respect for it." [18] But what is the "objective law," if one man's feeling or concept of this law differs from that of others, if one scholar formulates it in a different way from another, if the positive legislator ascertains as "objective law" rules which, according to the feelings or ideas of one who is supposed to obey the positive law, are not "objective law"? It is hardly possible that an individualist and a socialist can agree about what "social solidarity" requires, or what the "objective law," the true or just law, is. Duguit ignores this problem because he simply takes for granted that what he, from his rather individualistic point of view, considers to be objective law is the objective law *par excellence*.

As for the question who is competent to decide whether a positive law is or is not in conformity with the "objective law," only two answers are possible. The one is that it is within the exclusive competence of the positive-law maker, the legislator and the judge, to decide this question if it is disputed. If so, the positive law will always be declared to be in conformity with the "objective law," and the dualism of the two laws has the effect of a justification of the positive law by a fictitious "objective law." The other possibility is that any individual is competent to decide the crucial question. Then the individuals who are the law-making organs of the community have the same right to decide the question as the individuals who are subjected to the positive law. Duguit says that the positive law is imperative only if it is the expression of the "objective law." In itself, the positive law is not imperative, because those who issue it are human beings just as those at whom the positive law is directed; and since human beings are equal, no individual has any right to command others.[19] If so, the opinion of an individual acting as legislator or judge is as good as the opinion of an individual to whose behavior the statute or judicial decision refers. If the legislator or judge is of the opinion that the statute or the judicial decision issued by them is in conformity with the "objective law"—and if they were not of this opinion they would not have issued the statute or the judicial decision—this opinion must have the same weight as the opinion of an individual who refuses to comply with the statute or the judicial decision, because he thinks that they are not in conformity with the "objective law." The possibility that a positive law *is* objectively in conflict with the "objective law" is practically excluded if there is no objective authority to decide the dispute about the issue. What in reality exists are only contradictory opinions on what the "objective law" is. But the opinion of the governing individuals differs from the opinion of the governed individuals because the former have the power to enforce their opinion; and their competence to enforce a law which they think is in conformity with the "objective law" cannot be abolished by the contrary opinion of the governed subjects, since the opinion of the governed individuals carries at least no greater authority than the opinion of the governing individuals. Hence, the situation which exists when not only the government but also those subject to the government are competent to judge whether positive law is in conformity with "objective law," is practically not very different from the situation which exists when this judgment is reserved to the government. In both cases the dualism of positive and "objective law" has, just as the dualism of positive and natural law, the effect—if not the purpose—of justifying the one by the other.[20]

These examples perhaps suffice to explain why the Pure Theory of Law insists upon a clear separation of the concept of law from that of justice, be it called natural, true, or objective law, and why the Pure Theory of Law renounces any justification of positive law by a kind of superlaw, leaving that problematical task to religion or social metaphysics.

CAUSALITY AND RETRIBUTION

If we are to accept the results of modern physics and the significance ascribed to them by eminent exponents of this most exact of all natural sciences, we are in the midst of an important transformation of our conception of the universe. The notion that the law of causality absolutely determines all events has been shaken, and if this law is not to be entirely eliminated from scientific thinking, its interpretation must at least be essentially modified. In the course of this controversy the question arises as to the source of the belief that events are determined by an absolute law, that is, the origin of the assumption, which we take for granted, that each event must be the necessary effect of a cause according to an inviolable law. We must try to show how the belief in causality has arisen in the evolution of human thought.

We are here assuming that causality is not a form of thought with which human consciousness is endowed by natural necessity —what Kant calls an "innate notion"—but that there were periods in the history of human thought when men did not think causally. We are also assuming that the law of causality as a principle of scientific thought first appears at a relatively high level of mental development. Indeed, the conception of causality is thoroughly foreign to the thinking of primitive peoples who interpret nature according to social categories rather than causality.[1] For primitive man there is no such thing as "nature" in the sense of a connection of elements determined by causal laws and distinct from society. What civilized man understands by nature is for primitive man,

From *Philosophy of Science*, Oct., 1941.

with his animistic, or more exactly with his personalistic way of thinking, only a part of society and is therefore governed by the same laws. The so-called natural man, who is really a social man in every respect, believes that the legal order of his community also governs nature. Therefore he interprets nature by the same principles which determine his relationship to other members of his group. The fundamental rule of the primitive social order, however, is the principle of retribution, which completely dominates the thoroughly social consciousness of primitive man. It is the principle according to which a man returns good for good, and evil for evil, and expects therefore to be punished for a wrong he or a member of his group commits, to be rewarded for his or his fellow's merit.[2] He expects to be punished or rewarded not only for his bad or good behavior toward men but also for his behavior toward nature. For, in the opinion of primitive man, nature reacts to the behavior of men in the same way as men react to one another. The interpretation of nature according to the principle of retribution is expressed in the actual attitude of primitive man toward animals, plants and lifeless objects, and especially in his religion and his myths.

We are assuming that the condition of contemporary primitive man is similar to the previous state of civilized man and that in his development civilized man has passed through a primitive stage whose traces still subsist in certain customs, tales, religious ideas, and so forth. If this assumption is granted, we may suppose that scientific and especially causal thinking grows, like all civilization, out of primitive beginnings which can be reconstructed from given ethnographical materials. We are fortunately in a position to ascertain when and where the modern notion of causality took shape in the consciousness of man. This was in the natural philosophy of the ancient Greeks. This philosophy, however, had its origin in mythical and religious conceptions which fully correspond to what we know of the mentality of primitive man. In these conceptions the idea of retribution plays a decisive part.

I

Greek natural philosophy, the first great attempt at scientific comprehension of reality, was still affected by the conception of values derived from the social sphere. The social categories were accepted without question and were considered to be such an incontestable part of human knowledge that they were taken as a starting point for the first attempt to grasp reality. In early Greek philosophy as in the mythical thinking of primitive man, nature is explained by analogy to society. The authoritarian community, the state, furnished the pattern of the order according to which an attempt was made to comprehend the universe. It was the state which furnished the original pattern for this first natural science, since men had become accustomed to regard the state as order itself, and, due to much older theological speculation, as an absolute value.

But the analogy of nature and society constantly weakens as a result of progressive observations. The idea of a universal law of nature, at first only a projection of the law of the state into the cosmos, is visibly freed from its prototype and given a fully independent meaning. The law of the state, the norm, on one hand, and the law of nature, the law of causality, on the other, become two totally different principles.

If Thales of Miletus, with whom Greek philosophy begins, and Anaximander and Anaximenes seek a fundamental principle, ἀρχή, by which the universe may be explained in terms of unity, they are thinking of something which governs it monarchically. The law of the ἀρχή here establishes a μοναρχία, and ἀρχή means not only "beginning" but also "government" or "rule." It is surely no accident that the philosophy of nature flourished at a time when the influence of oriental despotism was gaining strength in Greece.[3] Anaximander, as is well known, designates the ἄπειρον, the unlimited, the fundamental principle of the world, as ἀρχή, and expressly says that this ἄπειρον embraces everything and directs everything.[4] Anaximenes considers the basic substance to be air. But he conceives this air as a being endowed with reason and will which rules the world like a god. The air of Anaximenes is the "soul" of the world [5] and, as such, the first reason, the cause of events and of motion. For Thales, too, the soul seems to have been something moving, for he is said to have maintained that the magnet must have a soul since it moves iron, that is, attracts it. The cause, as the mover, is thought of in an animistic or rather personalistic way; it intentionally sets something in motion; it governs something; it attracts something as a magnet attracts iron.[6]

This way of looking at things is not entirely foreign to the popular idea of causality today. We can understand the idea that the soul is the cause of motion, and thus the cause itself, only if we do not forget that the idea of the soul as something which exists in the living and continues the personality of its host after death, grew from the conception of the soul as something which begins its existence only after death. The original function of this soul of the dead, its first "effect," so to speak, was revenge.

This idea of causation reminds one in other respects, too, of the primitive conception of retribution. The cause attracts the effect, just as the wrong, or more exactly, the man by his wrongful act, attracts punishment. The fact that the idea of retribution plays a decisive role in the notion of the ἀρχή, the fundamental principle, is shown chiefly in the doctrine that since things affect one another, they must originate from the same source. For only when they originate from the same source do they have the same nature, and only like things can react on one another, that is, only things alike in a specific sense can help or injure one another. The thesis that only like things can affect like things, that the cause must be equal to its effect, in which form this idea still subsisted in nineteenth-century physics, clearly had its origin in the principle of retribution. Here it has its proper sense; namely, that between punishment and wrong, between reward and merit, exists a sort of equality. This equality is primarily a qualitative one, since bad begets bad and good begets good. In the play *Agamemnon*, Aeschylus [7] expresses the thought that the traditional belief, too much luck brings bad luck, is erroneous. It is rather sin which engenders bad luck. The bad luck consists in the commission of another sin, for one ill deed creates another, as parents produce children similar to themselves.

But the likeness of wrong and punishment, merit and reward, is not only qualitative; it is quantitative too, since the greater the wrong the greater must be the punishment, the greater the merit the greater the reward. A fragment of Herakleitos runs: "Greater deaths receive greater rewards." [8] If the things are to bear a relationship of cause and effect, they must be "equal" in nature, as are wrong and punishment, merit and reward. For this reason they must originate from the same primary element, water or air.

In another aspect, the idea of likeness contained in the notion of ἀρχή appears as the idea of equilibrium, which, so far as it means justice, is the specific function of retribution, which weighs punishment against wrong, reward against merit, as on scales, and balances them. Thales taught that water was the primary element. Since the transformation of this substance into things other than water is not easily explainable, Anaximander begins with the ἄπειρον, that is with the infinite, an eternal, imperishable substance, out of which come the opposites, wet and dry, cold and hot. Finite things always conflict with one another, for example hot fire with cold air, dry earth with the wet sea. Preponderance of one over the other is unjust, their equilibrium just. Heat creates injustice in summer; cold, in winter. In order to attain equilibrium, they must be returned to their common cause—to their ἀρχή.[9] If fire gradually dries up water, it is an injustice which must ultimately lead to the destruction of the world. Fire mixed with water, however, loses its special nature and becomes the primary substance. Its function is, however, to be represented as equilibrium in the sense of retributive justice. Only in this sense of universal justification is it an universal explanation of the world. If one assumes that this is the fundamental idea of Anaximander, one can understand the following fragment: "Into that from which things take their rise they pass away once more, according to necessity. For they make reparation and satisfaction to one another for their injustice according to the order of time." [10] Here for the first time in the thinking of mankind the notion of an immanent law which governs the whole of the universe, is comprehended.[11] It is the earliest statement of the law of causality. But, though generalized, it is still essentially the law of retribution.[12] Chronologically the cause, as the wrong, must precede the effect, as the punishment. Just as necessity (τὸ χρεών) is the compulsion of the legal rule of retribution, so is the chronological order, the earlier and the later, the sequence of wrong and punishment. In this dynamism of retribution, scientific thought for the first time realizes the time category. The reason that modern science still characterizes the relationship of cause and effect as asymmetrical and still maintains that the cause must precede the effect in time, is that the cause was originally the wrong, and the effect was the punishment.

Like Anaximander, Herakleitos also sees a tension of opposites in nature, and, like him, interprets it by means of a purely social category, that of war. His saying, "War is the father of all and the

king of all," [13] is well known and often cited. But while Anaximander saw injustice in the strife of things, Herakleitos taught
"We must know that war is common to all and strife is justice
(δίκη) and that all things come into being and pass away through
strife." [14] In this war which the elements wage with one another,
he recognizes a universal law of life; and this law, the "central
idea of his whole philosophy," is "the idea of the logos which is
eternal, transcendental, universal reason ruling over all things." [15]
"Men are as unable to understand it when they hear it for the first
time, as before they have heard it at all. For, though all things
come to pass in accordance with this Word [law], men seem as if
they had no experience of them." [16] It is obviously the law of causality that is meant by the logos, according to which all things come
to pass. Thus the law of nature is identified with fate. According to
Diogenes Laertius, Herakleitos teaches that "everything occurs
according to fate." [17] For Herakleitos the necessity of events, this
essential function of causality, is the inviolable will of a deity which
is presented as the personification of reason. It is the expression
of the absolute validity of the order in which the will of the deity
is expressed; and, as absoluteness, inviolability can appear only as
a quality of a transcendent authority assumed to exist beyond all
experience. Necessity or fate is expressed by the word εἱμαρμένη.
The verb μείρομαι signifies "to get a share." μείρομαι comes from
σμέριομαι, the root of which is smer, to allot; the corresponding
term in Latin is mereo, I merit.[18] The word expressing causal
necessity therefore originally meant "merited allotment." One's fate
is whatever is allotted to him as a reward or a punishment. It is
presumably the idea of retribution which leads to the notion of
fate as that which is allotted to one because of merit or fault,
through the inexorable will of a requiting deity. And as a matter
of fact in Herakleitos the εἱμαρμένη is the inviolability of the legal
rule, and the legal rule is undoubtedly that of retribution. The
thoroughly normative character of the universal law of Herakleitos, a norm that ought to be obeyed but which nevertheless
through folly is occasionally not obeyed, is evident in the following fragments: "So we must follow the common; yet though my
Word [λόγος = the law] is common, the many live as if they had
a wisdom of their own." [19] "Those who speak with understanding
must hold fast to what is common to all as a city holds fast to its law

(νόμος) and even more strongly. For all human laws are fed [that is, are valid] by the one divine law. The divine law prevails as much as it will, and suffices for all things, and is stronger than everything else." [20] If human laws derive their validity from the divine or universal law, it is because the divine, universal law, the inviolable law of causality, is only the projection of the human law—the legal rule—into the cosmos. This legal rule projected into the cosmos is inviolable because it is considered as the absolute will of a deity. It is the idea of natural law, in the sense of a natural legal order, that is formulated here. That this legal rule is the law of retribution is clearly expressed in the famous fragment which may be indicated as the counterpart to that of Anaximander: "The sun will not overstep his measures [that is, the prescribed path]; but if he does, the Erinyes, the handmaids of Dike [Justice], will find him out." [21] The Erinyes are the well-known demons of revenge of Greek religion, and Dike is the goddess of retribution. The Orphics call her the "Inexorable," "the judge of those who do not obey the divine law." [22] The significance for the history of scientific thought of the saying of Herakleitos lies in the fact that the inviolability of the law of causality, because of which the sun follows its path, is the compulsion of the goddess of justice, an obligation imposed upon nature by a legal rule, a normative necessity. [23] The inviolability of the universal law does not consist of the fact that it is always observed; the possibility of the sun going beyond its measures is not excluded. The inviolability consists rather in the fact that violation of the law is always and without exception punishable, because the universal law, as legal rule, is a norm laying down sanctions; this norm is, according to its tenor, a law of retribution, and as such, the unshakable will of a deity. The *logos* of Herakleitos is Dike, the goddess of inescapable revenge. [24] The inviolability of the causal law, which is so contested in modern science, originates from the inviolability which myth and the natural philosophy, which gradually evolved from it, attributed to the principle of retribution, as the substance of a divine and therefore absolutely binding will. The earliest natural science develops its natural law from this principle of retribution.

The view that the necessity which holds the cosmos together is the absolute obligation of a divine legal norm, and that this norm —the law of nature—is retribution, appears no less clearly in Parmenides than in his great antagonist Herakleitos. In order to arrive at the knowledge of this law, at truth, he sets out upon the imaginary voyage which he describes in his theoretical poem. This voyage leads him to Δίκη πολύποινος, to the "goddess of retribution." [25] She has the key to the gate through which leads the road to light, to true knowledge. Dike, the goddess of justice, is also the goddess of truth, for in this still thoroughly ethical and juridical view of the world, truth is identical with justice whose inexorableness here appears as the "unshakable heart (ἀτρεμὲς ἦτορ) of the well rounded truth."

The fundamental teaching of the Parmenidean ontology, that coming into being and passing away is only illusion, that there is only eternal unchangeable being, is expressed by Parmenides as follows: "Wherefore Dike doth not loose her fetters and let anything come into being or pass away, but holds it fast." That is Δίκη πολύποινος, the goddess of retribution. The same idea reappears later in the following form: "Moreover, it (being) is immovable in the bonds of mighty chains, without beginning and without end: since coming into being and passing away have been driven afar, and true belief has cast them away. . . . For hard necessity ('Ανάγκη) keeps it in the bonds of the limit that holds it fast on every side." Further on: "Fate (Μοῖρα) has chained it so as to be whole and immovable." [26] The hard Necessity and Fate, are identical with Dike, the goddess of retribution. The determination by the law of nature, the inviolable rule of "existence," is the "ought" of an absolute legal norm. The inviolability of the universal law is the unescapableness of retribution. It is the same idea that the poet Aeschylus expresses in his *Prometheus* when he addresses necessity, Ananke, as the "invincible power even above Zeus." "Who then is helmsman of necessity?" asks the leader of the chorus, and Prometheus replies: "The Fates three-formed and the remembering Erinyes." [27]

Retribution is also a notion, if not the fundamental notion of the philosophy of Empedokles, which is influenced by Orphic and Pythagorean elements. At the center of this philosophy lies the notion of transmigration of souls, according to which the thinker of Akragas, more a prophet than a learned philosopher, interprets his own fate. The theory of metempsychosis is here, as wherever it appears, a specific ideology of retribution. "There is an oracle of Necessity (Ἀνάγκη), an ancient ordinance of the gods, eternal and sealed fast by broad oaths, that whenever one of the daemons, whose portion is length of days, has sinfully polluted his hands with blood, or followed strife and forsworn himself, he must wander thrice ten thousand seasons from the abodes of the blessed, being born throughout time in all manners of mortal forms, changing one toilsome path of life for another. For the mighty Air drives him into the Sea, and the Sea spews him forth on to the dry Earth; Earth tosses him into the beams of the blazing Sun, and he flings him back to the eddies of Air. One takes him from the other, and all reject him. One of these I now am, an exile and a wanderer from the gods, for that I put my trust in insensate Strife." [28] It is nature itself—that is, the four elements of which, according to the teaching of Empedokles, it is composed, namely, air, water, earth, and fire—that punishes the evildoer. It is nature itself whose function is recognized to be retribution. The wrong to which the retribution is a reaction is by no means merely a social evil, an injury which one man inflicts on another man. The idea that the human soul can be embodied in other beings, in animals or plants, here leads —as, for example, in the totemistic systems—to the idea of a society embracing not only men but all other beings as well. This society is constituted by an order which subjects all beings to the same law, and, in particular, guarantees to all beings the same right to live. The fundamental norm of this order is the prohibition against killing. Thus nature apparently becomes a part of society, and the law of retribution, as a matter of course, becomes a natural law. From this law Empedokles derives the prohibition against killing animals and eating their flesh. According to Cicero [29] Empedokles taught that one and the same legal order (*unam omnium animantium condicionem iuris*) exists for all living things and solemnly proclaimed that inexpiable punishments threaten those who injure them. It seems that Empedokles considered this law of life governing men, animals, and plants, which was sanctioned by "inexpiable punishments" to be a special case of a still more general law governing the entire universe. This universal law, too, is held to be a law of retribution.

The modern notion of causality is in principle established in the writings of the Atomists, Leukippos and Demokritos. These founders of pure natural science achieved the almost complete separation of the law of causality from the principle of retribution by consistently eliminating all theological elements from the interpretation of nature and by strictly rejecting causes which are at the same time ends. As long as the world order by analogy to the social order is conceived as the expression of a more or less personal, rational, and, therefore, purposefully functioning will, the law of nature must have the character of a norm which by analogy to the social norm, the rule of law, guarantees the normal state of things by means of sanctions. The universal law must be a law of retribution. Herakleitos still regarded the law of nature in this way. But for the Atomists it had ceased to be a norm, the expression of a divine will. It became the manifestation of an impersonal objective necessity. For Demokritos does not consider the universe as constructed by some personal being.[30]

The freeing of the interpretation of nature from the principle of retribution in the philosophy of the Atomists is exactly parallel to the analogous emancipation of social theory in that of the Sophists. It was Protagoras, the contemporary of Leukippos, who taught that the specific technique of the state order which reacts to an act considered socially harmful, with a coercive act—a sanction, directed against the delinquent—is not justifiable by the religious idea of retribution, but by the rational intent of prevention. The punishment does not take place because of some obscure reason, but for a clear purpose. "No one punishes a wrong-doer with regard to and because he has committed an offense, unless one takes unreasoning vengeance like a wild beast. But he who undertakes to punish with reason does not avenge himself for the past offense, since what has been done can not be undone. He looks rather to the future, and aims at preventing that particular person and others who see him punished from doing wrong again. Whoever thinks in this way . . . punishes to deter." [31] The law of the state, like the law of nature, is freed from the myth of retribution.

However, the causal law, even in the purified form which it assumes in the writings of the Atomists, cannot entirely deny its origin. Here it is expressed by the notion of necessity, ἀνάγκη. Demokritos, according to Aetios, seems to have understood by "necessity" the blows and counterblows of the atoms which clash against one another.[32] In order to understand this formulation of physical causality, one must realize that according to Demokritos all change is only the union and separation of atoms: nothing exists but atoms which "are in disaccord with one another" [33] and crash against one another in empty space. In this manner things appear and disappear. If, as Aetios thinks, Demokritos understood necessity as blows and counterblows of atoms, this signifies that he sees causality in a phenomenon the scheme of which is action and reaction. This idea is analogous to the principle of retribution, which connects an action with its specific reaction, namely, the wrong with the punishment, the merit with the reward. The atoms strike against one another "in disaccord" just as in Herakleitos things are constantly "at war" and "are brought into harmony by the clash of opposing currents," [34] like wrong and punishment. The elements connected by the principle of retribution are opposite with respect to the direction of their action but not so far as their nature is concerned; since it is like which is requited with like. Thus according to Demokritos' law of causality, among atoms which are "in disaccord" only like can effect like. In the Hibeh Papyri [35] is found the following passage: ". . . he [Demokritos] says that in a wet substance like is [drawn] to like as in the whole creation, and thus the sea was created and all else that is . . . through combination of homogenous atoms." A fragment of Demokritos reads as follows: "Animals associate with the same kind of animals—doves with doves, cranes with cranes and the remaining animals similarly. The same is true for lifeless things as one can see in the case of grains of seed sifted promiscuously and in the case of pebbles in the surf. For in the former instance, a whirling motion of the sieve effects a separation so that lentils go to lentils, barleycorn to barleycorn, grains of wheat to grains of wheat. In the latter, the longish pebbles are driven to the longish ones, the round ones to the round by the swell of the surf as if the similarity peculiar to things created a power of attraction between them." [36] If the magnet attracts the iron it is because "like is drawn to like." "With this supposition," says Alexander Aphrodisiensis,[37] "he [Demokritos] assumes that the magnet and the iron consist of the same kind of atoms." Wrong attracts punishment which is essentially similar to it, for example, murder attracts murder (as blood revenge or death penalty); merit attracts reward which is essentially similar to it; thus the magnet attracts iron because the latter is "like" the former. When Demokritos describes the fact that a cause has an effect on a thing, by the words: the thing "suffers" the effect,[38] the idea of "suffering" punishment is in the background. Therefore it is quite understandable when Pliny [39] asserts that Demokritos recognized only two divinities: *Poenam et Beneficium,* punishment and reward, and when Aristotle [40] characterizes the atomistic law of causality thus: "They assert that nothing happens accidentally but that there is a definite cause (τὶ αἴτιον) of all which we assert happens spontaneously or accidentally." And if in Demokritos,[41] and elsewhere in the old natural philosophy, αἰτία means cause, one must not forget that this word originally meant "guilt." [42] The cause is responsible for the effect. The internal connection between the two elements of the law of causality, cause and effect, has a normative character. This normative element has not yet entirely disappeared from contemporary thinking in natural science.

II

After the victory of Christianity, the principle of an absolutely valid causality, to which there was no exception, a law inherent in nature, as developed in the atomistic theory and taken over later by Epicurus and his followers, was in danger of being lost again in the theological view of the world that prevailed in the Middle Ages. The new natural science, founded by Bacon, Galileo, and Kepler, was the first to revive it, and it remained the predominant principle for the interpretation of nature until quite recently when, in certain spheres of modern physics, it was questioned if not actually denied. If one speaks today, whether rightly or wrongly, of a crisis in this principle, one must not forget that this crisis began with Hume's famous critique of the belief in causality. Hume's objections are directed mainly against the notion prevalent at his time, that there exists between cause and effect an objective connection, a connection inherent in things themselves, an inner bond, such that the cause somehow brings about the effect. The cause does something in inducing the effect. Hence the cause is conceived of as an agent, as an active substance. Hume showed that there is in nature no causality in the sense of a necessary connection, but only a regular succession of events. The idea of a general law of causality, in accordance with which similar causes must necessarily produce similar effects, is a mere habit of thought, which, originating from the observation of regular successions of events, becomes a firm conviction. But what is the origin of the idea that the necessity of the connection between cause and effect is objective and therefore inherent in the causal events, that the cause produces or attracts the effect, that not only a *post hoc* but also a *propter hoc* exists between them? Hume's explanation is not sufficient. He says only: "having found, in many instances, that any two kinds of objects—flame and heat, snow and cold—have always been conjoined together; if flame or snow be presented anew to the senses, the mind is carried by custom to expect heat or cold, and to *believe* that such a quality does exist, and will discover itself upon a nearer approach." [43] Our mind is led by custom to expect that a certain phenomenon will always be followed in the future by the same phenomenon which has regularly followed it in the past. However, our mind is not led by custom to believe that an exception is absolutely excluded. Hume's theory is obviously influenced by the idea of customary law prevailing in England at his time. He expressly says in this connection: "Custom . . . is the great guide of human life." But custom does not constitute rules without exceptions. The idea that the connection between cause and effect has the character of absolute necessity cannot be the result of a custom or habit of thought. It very probably comes, as the development of ancient Greek philosophy has shown us, from the principle of retribution. This principle is the expression of a transcendental will independent of the men subjected to it, of a specifically objective authority which connects the punishment with the wrong, the reward with the merit by allotting the punishment "on account of" the wrong, the reward "on account of" the merit. As long as the idea of a transcendental authority endowed with reason and will subsists there can be no difference between the connection of wrong and punishment or merit and reward on the one hand, and cause and effect on the other. For in each case, this connection must be effected by the will of the authority. Thus one cannot differentiate between the law of morality and the law of nature as long as both are considered to be the will of a deity. As long as there is a belief in the existence of a transcendental authority ruling over human society as well as nature, the will of this authority is the objective tie which holds cause and effect together, even though the human mind may separate the law of causality from the principle of retribution. In transforming causality from an objectively necessary connection of cause and effect, immanent in nature, to a subjective principle of human thinking, Hume merely freed the law of causality from an element inherent in it as a successor to the principle of retribution.

Another element of the notion of causality with which modern physics takes issue is the thesis that the effect must be equal to the cause. Mach [44] has already shown this proposition, of which Robert Mayer (the discoverer of the principle of conservation of energy) had made much use, to be completely "empty." Philipp Frank [45] says: "It is a main feature of the popular notion of causality that cause and effect must somehow be equal or at least proportional. The stronger the cause the stronger the effect must be. However, a suitable means for measuring all possible causes and effects in order to be able to ascertain when a portion of a cause was equal to a corresponding portion of an effect was wanting. In the physical law that a system of bodies can increase in energy only to the extent that it takes energy from surrounding bodies, one finally saw the concrete equivalent formulation of the fact that the effect must be equal to the cause. Driesch explicitly says that 'Energy is the measure of causality.'" Frank, however, after calling attention to the problematical character of the conception of energy, emphatically maintains that from the point of view of physics it is impossible "simply to consider energy generally as the measure of causality."

The problematical character of the statement that the cause must be equal to the effect and *vice versa* is also evident in the related idea that a cause has only one effect and that an effect is traceable to only one cause. The principle of causality is considered to be essentially bipartite. Since, however, each cause must itself be considered in turn as the effect of another cause, and each effect as the cause of a further effect, each point to be causally determined lies in an endless chain of causality which has the character of a *continuum*. The phenomena indicated as cause and effect are in a direct, though not always immediately perceptible connection of events. The so-called cause merges imperceptibly into the so-called effect. "Cause and effect are," as Goethe said, "an indivisible phenomenon." That we nevertheless separate them from one another, even oppose them to one another, that we purposely isolate from the continuous chain of innumerable elements two alone as *the* cause and *the* effect which is imputed to this cause alone, is due to the age-old habit of interpreting nature according to the principle of retribution. This principle connects only a particular event, characterized as a wrong with another event, the punishment, likewise precisely determined and clearly separated chronologically from the first. The possibility of isolating these two facts from the continuous stream of events is due to the fact that both are "arbitrarily" determined and linked together by a divine or a human will, which is expressed in the norm of retribution. This method of isolating phenomena, derived from normative thinking, does not prevent the attainment of useful theoretical as well as practical results in the field of natural science, provided that these results are corrected by the realization that each effect has an infinite number of causes, each cause in infinite number of effects. Such a correction is all the more necessary since every analysis of reality shows that each effect is not only the end of a chain of causation but also the beginning of a new chain, and, at the same time, a point of intersection of an infinite number of chains. No event is dependent on one cause alone. Starting from this fact, certain philosophers have completely abandoned the notion of cause as useless and have replaced it by that of "conditions" or "components" of the event.[46] Similarly the notion of effect has been superseded by that of the "resultants." No "causalism," but "conditionism." However, it is considered necessary to indicate one of the conditions or components of an event as the "decisive" one, so that a distinction is made between the cause, as the collective notion of all conditions of an effect taken together, and the cause in the narrower sense of the "immediate" or the "decisive variation of one of the conditioning circumstances." Hence the notion of causality is not really abandoned, but only modified. What is given up is simply one of its elements, namely the idea that causality is a connection between only two facts—is bipartite—a notion which originated in the sphere of retribution. Here and here alone, is this idea incontestably appropriate—one offense, one punishment. The postulate that one ought not to be punished more than once for the same offense, that the law of retribution is exhausted by a single reaction to one fact, and thus, in a literal sense is bipartite, is expressed by the maxim: *ne bis in idem*. The criticism of the law of causality made by what has been termed conditionism aims only at its separation from the principle of retribution.

According to this principle, the two parts are connected in the sense that one must chronologically precede the other—first the crime and then the punishment, first the merit and then the reward. The two parts connected by the principle of retribution are not interchangeable. Simultaneity of the two parts is likewise inconceivable. The law of causality is, or was originally, conceived of in this way, that is, by analogy to the principle of retribution which associates its two parts in an irreversible chronological sequence. In this form of an asymmetrical principle the law of causality was considered the fundamental form of the law of nature. This idea was no longer maintainable, when it became necessary to give up the assumption of an immanent connection of cause and effect, and to replace it by the notion of a purely functional dependency.[47] Chronological sequence of phenomena was no longer an essential element of a law of nature. Functional dependency can exist even between simultaneous events. However, if there is a relationship of functional dependency between simultaneous events, they are also interchangeable. In fact, modern natural science knows of innumerable connections where no temporal difference appears between the connected elements.[48] Thus there are natural laws which do not correspond to the original scheme of causality. To be sure these connections are still frequently represented "causally," that is, as relationships of a chronologically earlier cause to a chronologically later effect. But from the standpoint of physical knowledge, functional connections between simultaneous phenomena exist. Thus the fact that a body which is thrown, follows a parabolic orbit, is explained by saying that gravity is the cause which has as effect the parabolic orbit of the body. The decisive connection, however, is that between position and acceleration as simultaneously existing elements. Boyle's law sets up a connection between the pressure and the volumen of a gas, which are two simultaneous facts, though it is customary to say that increased or diminished pressure is the cause of the diminution or the increase of the volume. The modern notion of natural law as one of functional dependency has been freed from the old notion of causality as a concatenation of two events immanently connected with one another in an irreversible chronological order. The choice is now between ceasing to identify this enlarged notion of the law with that of the causal law, since it is not desirable to speak of causality in the case of simultaneously existing events; or, in accordance with historical development, seeing in the modern natural law which comprehends the functional interdependency of simultaneous events, a modification of the law of causality. If the latter choice is made, the law of causality might be formulated as follows: Generally speaking, a specific event, the effect, occurs when another specific event, the cause, has previously occurred or occurs simultaneously. Thus the law of causality remains the fundamental form of all natural law, even though this is true only in a modified sense. This modification of the meaning of the law of causality also signifies its emancipation from the essentially asymmetrical principle of retribution.

It is assumed that the main blow to the law of causality was dealt by the recently developed quantum mechanics, the mechanics of the subatomic particles. The assumption, based on the law of causality, that mechanical processes can be predetermined if their initial state of motion is determined, proves to be useless, since in atomic physics the initial state of motion can never be fully determined. This is the "principle of uncertainty" which was discovered and formulated by Heisenberg. If one assumes predictability as the criterion of causality, as is done in modern natural philosophy, and explains an event as causally determined when it can be safely predicted, there is, according to an interpretation suggested by certain physicists and philosophers no causality in the sphere of quantum mechanics, or, at least, causality cannot be proved even when it is "objectively" given. But it is said that the causal determinateness of subatomic processes is unnecessary for arriving at physical laws for macroscopic phenomena. Such laws would not express absolute necessity, but merely statistical probability.

Reichenbach [49] interprets the crisis in modern physics, and especially in quantum mechanics, not as an issue involving the replacement of causality by statistical laws, but, as a modification of the notion of causality. It is a modification in the direction of a transition from absolute certainty to probability, a development which began in classical physics. "Every assertion of causality, applied to the prediction of a natural event, has the form of an assertion of probability." The notion of probability which is here involved is that of statistical probability. The assumption that nature is determined by the law of causality remains intact. Mere "probability" replaces the "necessity" of the previous formulation of the law of causality. The assumption that a necessary connection exists between cause and effect is replaced by the notion that this connection is only a probable one.

Whether or not the replacement of absolute necessity by statistical probability in the notion of natural law is traceable to quantum mechanics with its principle of uncertainty may be left undecided. Even before Heisenberg's discovery, if the law of causality was used to predict future events, only a calculation of probability was possible. In his *Essai philosophique sur les probabilités,* Laplace says:

We ought then to regard the present state of the universe as the effect of its anterior state and as the cause of the one which is to follow. Given for one instance an intelligence which could comprehend all the forces by which nature is animated and the respective situation of the beings who compose it—an intelligence sufficiently vast to submit these data to analysis—it would embrace in the same formula the movements of the greatest bodies of the universe and those of the lightest atom; for it, nothing would be uncertain and the future, as the past, would present to its eyes. The human mind offers, in the prefection which it has been able to give to astronomy, a feeble idea of this intelligence. Its discoveries in mechanics and geometry, added to that of universal gravity, have enabled it to comprehend in the same analytical expressions the past and future states of the system of the world. Applying the same method to some other objects of its knowledge, it has succeeded in referring to general laws observed phenomena and in foreseeing those which given circumstances ought to produce. All these efforts in the search for truth tend to lead it back continually to the vast intelligence which we have just mentioned, but from which it will always remain infinitely removed.[50]

Since it is quite impossible for the human mind, which is always infinitely remote from Laplace's absolute intelligence, to know all forces at a given moment, the human mind can foresee the future only with probability. But it can likewise explain the present by the past only with probability, since the past, too, it knows only imperfectly.

In the infinite distance between God and man, theology has

from time immemorial expressed the limitation of human beings contrasted with the infinity of God. Only God can foresee the future with absolute certainty since only God fully knows the present; and only God can fully comprehend the present since only God fully knows the past. The strict idea of causality, the absolute necessity of the connection between cause and effect, is realized only in the unlimited knowledge of God, not in the limited knowledge of man; and it makes no difference whether it is a question of determination of the future by the present or the present by the past. Transferred from the emotional to the rational this is merely the age-old idea that the law which governs the world is God's will and therefore a norm. The norm determines what is to happen in the future. Natural law, on the contrary, explains reality by seeking in the past the cause of the present event. The laws of nature by which science describes a given reality in the most general and simplest way are a result of experience, and experience is drawn not from the future but from the past. Predictability is a criterion, though by no means the only criterion, of causality, but is not causality itself. The presence of a causal nexus is proved not only by the fact that, as in an experiment, a predicted effect actually occurs, but also by the fact that the past existence of a fact assumed to be the cause of a given event can be demonstrated. The application of the law of causality to future events, an application which originated from practical necessity, is a secondary function resulting from the fact that cognition, though independent of volition and action, is placed at their service. Prophecy is no longer pure cognition but knowledge applied to technique. The future can be known from the present only on the assumption that the past, by which the present is explained, repeats itself in the future. What we grasp of the future by means of our knowledge is at bottom merely the past. If one sees the essence of the law of causality in the fact that it determines the future, even if only for a Laplacean intelligence, one confirms, perhaps unconsciously, the normative origin of the law of causality.

If the history of the idea of causality is carefully followed, the amazing conclusion is reached that, at least until Hume, the law of causality was considered as a norm, directed at nature, prescribing a definite behavior of things, since it was felt to be the expression of the divine will. The theory of Malebranche may be mentioned as a particularly characteristic example of this conclusion. He taught that on the basis of our experience we perceive no necessary connection between phenomena and no forces of causation. We observe only regular successions. As to the cause of the phenomenon that a moving ball striking against one which is not moving sets the latter in motion, he states:

Les hommes ne doivent pas juger qu'une boule agitée soit la principale et la véritable cause du mouvement de la boule qu'elle trouve dans son chemin; puisque la première n'a point elle-même la puissance de se mouvoir. Ils peuvent seulement juger que cette rencontre des deux boules est occasion à l'auteur du mouvement de la matière d'exécuter le décret de sa volonté qui est la cause universelle de toutes choses.[51]

The conformity of the behavior of things to law is interpreted as the execution of a divine command. Malebranche transfers the causal relationship which he does not find within finite things to the transcendental sphere, to God, or more accurately, to the will of God. This signifies that he conceives the law of causality to be a norm; he denotes it directly as *décret*. In this Malebranche does not differ essentially from Galileo and Descartes nor from Leibnitz, Locke, and Berkeley. Hume's real achievement does not consist in the pointing out that no necessary connection of cause and effect can be assumed on the basis of experience. That had already been ascertained before his time. It consists rather in the fact that he gave up looking for the necessity of the causal nexus in the will of God, and abandoned it together with the entire previous notion of causality. The law of causality ceases to be an expression of the divine will, a norm directed at nature. The element to which alone absolute necessity of the connection between cause and effect in reality can be attached, the transcendent will which established this objective connection, is now put aside. Nevertheless, the principle of strict causality can be maintained in modern science. To be sure, it can be maintained only if conceived of as a norm; for only a norm can lay claim to inviolability. The fact that it is not always obeyed in reality does not affect its validity. However, from the point of view of science this norm cannot be conceived of as emanating from a metaphysical authority as the expression of a divine will directed at nature; but it may be conceived of as an epistemological postulate directed at human cognition demanding to seek a connection between the phenomena observable in reality as cause and effect.[52] The fact that human cognition can fulfill this postulate only approximately, does not mean that there are exceptions to it, just as the fact that a legal norm *pre*scribing a certain behavior is not obeyed in a concrete case, that it is—as we say in a figure of speech—"violated," does not mean that it has ceased to be valid, that there is an exception to its validity. It is precisely because it is supposed to be valid that it can be considered to be "violated." Only a rule *de*scribing the real behavior can have an exception. Hence the rules by which natural science describes reality in accordance with the epistemological postulate of causality, the so-called laws of nature, may very well have exceptions and consequently may be considered to be mere statistical laws of probability. This transformation of the notion of causality is the last step in the process of its emancipation from the principle of retribution.

CAUSALITY AND IMPUTATION

I T IS usual to distinguish natural and social sciences as dealing with two different objects: nature and society. But, are nature and society really two different objects?

Nature, according to one of many definitions, is a particular order of things, or a system of elements, connected with one another as cause and effect, that is to say, according to the specific principle called "causality." The so-called laws of nature by which the science of nature describes its object, as, for instance, the statement: If a metallic body is heated it expands, are applications of this principle. The connection between heat and expansion in our example is that of cause and effect.

If there is a social science different from natural science, it must describe its object according to a principle different from that of causality. Society is an order of human behavior. But there is no sufficient reason not to consider human behavior as an element of nature, that is, as determined by the law of causality; and, so far as human behavior is conceived as determined by causal laws, a science which deals with the mutual behavior of men, and for this reason is classed as a social science, is not essentially different from physics or biology. However, if we analyze our propositions concerning human behavior, we find that we connect acts of human beings with one another and with other facts not only and exclusively according to the principle of causality, that is, as cause and effect, but according to another principle quite different from that of causality, a principle for which science has not yet established a

From *Ethics*, Oct., 1950.

324

generally recognized term. Only if it is possible to prove the existence of this principle in our thinking, and its application in sciences dealing with human behavior, are we entitled to consider society as an order or system different from that of nature and the sciences concerned with society as different from natural sciences.

II

Law is a most characteristic and highly important social phenomenon; and the science of law is probably the oldest and most developed social science. In analyzing juristic thinking, I have shown [1] that a principle different from that of causality is indeed applied in the rules by which jurisprudence describes the law, either the law in general or a concrete legal order, such as the national law of a definite state or international law. This principle has, in the rules of law, a function analogous to that which the principle of causality has in the natural laws by which natural science describes nature. A rule of law is, for instance, the statement that, if a man has committed a crime, a punishment ought to be inflicted upon him; or the statement that, if a man does not pay a debt contracted by him, a civil execution ought to be directed against his property. Formulated in a more general way: If a delict has been committed, a sanction ought to be executed. Just as a law of nature, a rule of law connects two elements with each other. But the connection described by the rule of law has a meaning totally different from that of causality. For it is evident that the criminal delict is not connected with the punishment, and that the civil delict is not connected with the civil execution, as a cause is connected with its effect. The connection between cause and effect is independent of the act of a human or superhuman being. But the connection between a delict and a legal sanction is established by an act, or acts, of human beings, by a law-creating act, that is, an act whose meaning is a norm.

This distinction cannot be made within a religious-metaphysical view of the world according to which the connection of cause and effect is established by an act analogous to a law-creating act: by the act of God creating nature. Consequently, the laws of nature, as manifestation of the will of God, have the character of norms prescribing nature a definite behavior. This is the basis on which a metaphysical doctrine of the law asserts that it is possible to find in nature a natural law. From the point of view of a scientific interpretation of the world, however, within which only a positivistic doctrine of law is possible, the distinction between law of nature and rule of law must emphatically be maintained.

The act of human behavior whose meaning is a norm may be performed in different ways: by a gesture; by spoken or written words; by a symbol or by a series of acts constituting a complicate legislative procedure; or by a custom. Using a figure of speech, we say that by such an act (or acts) a norm is "made" or "created"; in other words: the meaning of the act (or acts) is a norm. A norm "created" by an act of human behavior is a "positive" norm. Its existence consists in its validity. We describe its meaning by saying that something is "prescribed" or "permitted"; or, using a term comprising both, that something "ought (or, for the negative, ought not) to be done." If we presuppose a norm prescribing or permitting certain human behavior, we may characterize behavior which is in conformity with the presupposed norm as correct (right, good) and behavior which is not in conformity with the presupposed norm as incorrect (wrong, bad). If these statements are value judgments, the presupposed norm constitutes the value. If we presuppose a norm prescribing or permitting certain human behavior, we may define correct behavior as behavior which is in conformity with the presupposed norm; and incorrect behavior as behavior which is not in conformity with the presupposed norm. Then, we may say of a concrete human behavior that it does or does not fall under the definition of correct behavior and is, therefore, correct or incorrect behavior. But it falls under the definition only if it is in conformity with the presupposed norm. Only the statement whose meaning is that the behavior is or is not in conformity with the presupposed norm is a value judgment; not the statement that concrete behavior does or does not fall under the definition. Hence, the norm is not, as is sometimes said,[2] a definition; the norm is part of the content of a definition, the definition of correct or incorrect behavior. Definition is the meaning of an act of cognition. The acts whose meaning is a norm are not acts of cognition; they are acts of will. The function of the legal authorities is not to know and to describe law but to prescribe or permit human behavior and thus to make law. To know and to describe the law is the function of the legal science. The distinction between the function of the legal authority and that of the legal science, between legal norms and rules of law, is of great importance.

III

Since the connection between delict and sanction is established by a prescription or a permission—a "norm"—the science of law describes its object by propositions in which the delict is connected with the sanction by the copula "ought." I have suggested designating this connection "imputation." This term is the English translation of the German *Zurechnung*. The statement that an individual is *zurechnungsfähig* ("responsible") means that a sanction can be inflicted upon him if he commits a delict. The statement that an individual is *unzurechnungsfähig* ("irresponsible") —because, for instance, he is a child or insane—means that a sanction cannot be inflicted upon him if he commits a delict. Formulating this idea more precisely, we may say that in the first case a sanction is connected with certain behavior as a delict, whereas in the second case a sanction is not connected with such behavior. The idea of imputation (*Zurechnung*) as the specific connection of the delict with the sanction is implied in the juristic judgment that an individual is, or is not, legally responsible (*zurechnungsfähig*) for his behavior. Hence we may say: The sanction is imputed to the delict; it is not caused by the delict. It is evident that the science of law does not at all aim at a causal explanation of phenomena, that in the propositions by which the science of law describes its object the principle of imputation, not the principle of causality, is applied.

IV

In studying primitive society and especially the peculiarities of primitive mentality, I found that the same principle is at the basis of primitive man's interpretation of nature.[3] It is very probable that primitive man does not use the principle of causality in order to explain natural phenomena, that the idea of causality—as a fundamental principle of natural science—is the achievement of a relatively advanced civilization. For early man interprets the facts perceived by his senses according to the same principles which determine the relations to his fellow-men, that is to say, according to social norms.

When men live together with other men in a group, in their minds the idea arises that some behavior is right and some behavior is wrong; or, in other terms, that the members of the group ought to behave under certain circumstances in a certain way. It is a fundamental fact that men living in a group interpret their mutual behavior according to such norms. The earliest norms of mankind probably established restrictions on the sexual impulse and on the desire for aggression. Incest and murder within the group are probably the earliest crimes, and blood revenge the earliest socially organized sanction. At the basis of this sanction is the most primitive principle determining social life, the norm of retribution. It comprises punishment as well as reward. It may be formulated: If you behave rightly, you ought to be rewarded, that is, a benefit ought to be bestowed upon you; if you behave wrongly, you ought to be punished, that is, an evil ought to be inflicted upon you. Condition and consequence are connected with each other not according to the principle of causality but according to the principle of imputation. So far as there exists in the mind of primitive man a need for explanation at all, an event if considered to be harmful is interpreted as a punishment for wrong behavior, if advantageous, as reward for right behavior. In other terms: Harmful events are imputed to wrong behavior; advantageous events to right behavior. If such an event occurs, primitive man does not ask: What is the cause of it? but: Who is responsible for it? It is not a causal, it is a normative interpretation of nature; and, since the norm of retribution determining the mutual relations of men is a specific social principle, we may call this interpretation a socionormative interpretation of nature.

The so-called animism of primitive man, his view that not only human beings but all things have souls (are "animated"), that there exist invisible but powerful spirits within or behind the things, and that means that all things are persons—this view implies that things react toward man as human beings act in their mutual relations, that is, according to the norm of retribution, the principle of punishment and reward. It is, in the belief of primitive man, these spirits from whom misfortune as punishment and prosperity as reward emanate. If there exists in the belief of primitive man a connection between wrong behavior and misfortune as punishment, on the one hand, right behavior and prosperity as reward, on the other hand, it is because he believes that these powerful superhuman beings operate nature in this way. The essence of animism is a personalistic, and that means a socionormative, interpretation of nature, an interpretation not according to the principle of causality but according to the principle of imputation.

Hence there is in the mind of primitive man no such thing as nature in the sense of modern science, that is, an order of things connected with one another according to the principle of causality. For primitive man, that which is nature within the meaning of natural science is part of his society as a normative order, the elements of which are connected with one another according to the principle of imputation. The dualism of nature as a causal, and society as a normative, order, the dualism of two different ways of connecting elements with one another, is foreign to the primitive mind. That this dualism exists in the thinking of civilized man is the result of an intellectual evolution during which the difference between human and other beings, between persons and things —a difference unknown to primitive man—was established and the causal explanation of the relations among things was separated from the normative interpretation of the relations among persons. Modern science of nature is the result of the emancipation from a social interpretation of nature, that is to say, from animism. In a somewhat paradoxically pointed formula we might say that at the beginning, during the animistic period of mankind, there was only society (as a normative order); and that nature (as a causal order) was created by science after the emancipation from animism. The instrument of this emancipation is the principle of causality.

V

It is probable that the principle of causality has its origin in the norm of retribution.[4] It is the result of a transformation of the principle of imputation by which in the norm of retribution the wrong behavior is connected with punishment, the right behavior with reward. This process of transformation began in the philosophy of nature of the ancient Greeks. It is highly characteristic that the Greek word for cause, αἰτία, originally meant guilt; the cause is responsible for the effect, the effect is imputed to the cause, just as the punishment is imputed to the crime. One of the first formulations of the law of causality is the famous fragment of Heraclitus: "The sun will not overstep its prescribed path; if it does, the Erinyes, the handmaids of justice, will find him out." Here the law of nature still appears almost as a rule of law: If the sun does not follow its prescribed path, it will be punished. The decisive step in this transition from a normative to a causal interpretation of nature, from imputation to causality, is that man became aware that the relations between things—in contradistinction to the relations between persons—are independent of a human or superhuman will, or, what amounts to the same, are not determined by norms; that the behavior of things is not prescribed or permitted by a superhuman will. However, the complete purification of the principle of causality from all elements of animistic —that is personalistic—thinking, the establishment of the principle of causality as totally different from that of imputation, was only gradually achieved. Thus, for instance, the idea that causality means an absolute necessity in the relation of cause and effect—an idea still prevailing at the beginning of the twentieth century—is certainly a relic of the view that it is the will of an absolute, omnipotent authority which connects the effect with the cause.[5]

VI

Once established, the principle of causality is applicable also to human behavior. Psychology, ethnology, history, and sociology are sciences which deal with human behavior as it actually takes place or, what amounts to the same, with human behavior as an element of nature as a causal order. If a science dealing with human behavior is called a social science, these sciences are social sciences, but as such not essentially different from natural sciences, such as physics, biology, or physiology. They aim at an explanation of human behavior as cause and effect. To what extent they are able to reach their goal, the establishment of causal laws of human behavior, is another question. The difference between them and the natural sciences not dealing with human behavior is only a difference in degree of precision, not a difference in principle. Such a difference exists only between natural sciences and sciences which interpret human relations not according to the principle of causality but according to the principle of imputation—sciences which deal with human behavior not as it actually takes place as cause and effect in the sphere of reality but as it ought to take place, determined by norms. These are the normative social sciences, such as ethics, theology, and jurisprudence. They are not "normative" sciences in the sense that they prescribe or permit a particular human behavior; as sciences they do not prescribe or permit, they do not issue norms of social behavior; they describe social norms and social relations established by such norms. The social scientist is not a social authority: his function is cognition, his task is to know and to understand, not to regulate, society. Society within the meaning of these normative sciences is a normative order; men belong to such a society only so far as their behavior is determined by the norms of the moral, religious, or legal order. It is true that, if a normative order, especially a legal order, is by and large effective, we may make the statement: If the condition laid down in the social norm is realized, the consequence, which according to the social norm ought to take place, probably will take place; or, in case of an effective legal order: If a delict is committed, a sanction will probably be executed. But it is doubtful whether such a statement has the true character of a law of nature, like that which describes the effect of heat on metallic bodies. This question, however, may be left undecided here, for it is certain that the normative social sciences, especially jurisprudence, do not aim at such statements. They are interested not in the causal, but in the imputative, nexus between the elements of their objects.

VII

The grammatical form of the principle of causality as well as that of imputation is a hypothetical judgment (proposition) connecting something as a condition with something as a consequence. But the meaning of the connection in the two cases is different. The principle of causality states: If there is A, there is (or will be) B. The principle of imputation states: If there is A, there ought to be B. As to the application of the principle of causality to the laws of nature, I refer to the example I have already given, the law describing the effect of heat on metallic bodies: If a metallic body is heated, it is (or will be) expanding. Examples of the principle of imputation as applied in social laws are: If somebody has done you a favor, you ought to be grateful to him; or, if a man sacrifices his life for his nation, his memory ought to be honored (moral laws). If a man commits a sin, he ought to do penance (religious law). If a man commits theft, he ought to be imprisoned (legal law). The difference between causality and imputation is that the relation between the condition, which in the law of nature is presented as cause, and the consequence, which is here presented as effect, is independent of a human or superhuman act; whereas the relation between condition and consequence which a moral, religious, or legal law asserts is established by acts of human or superhuman beings. It is just this specific meaning of the connection between condition and consequence which is expressed by the term "ought."

VIII

Another difference between causality and imputation is that each concrete cause must be considered as the effect of another cause and each concrete effect as the cause of another effect; so that the chain of causes and effects is, by definition, infinite. Further, each concrete event is the intersection of an infinite number of lines of causality. The condition to which the consequence is imputed in a moral or religious or legal law, as, for instance, death for the sake of the nation, to which honor of memory is imputed; benefaction, to which gratitude is imputed; sin, to which penance is imputed; theft, to which imprisonment is imputed, are not necessarily at the same time consequences imputable to some other condition. And the consequences, as, for instance, honor of memory imputed to the death for the sake of the nation, gratitude imputed to benefaction, penance imputed to sin, imprisonment imputed to theft, are not necessarily at the same time a condition to which another consequence is imputable. The line of imputation has not, as the line of causality, an infinite number of links, but only two links. If we say that a definite consequence is imputed to a definite condition, for instance, a reward to a merit, or a punishment to a delict, the condition, that is to say the human behavior which constitutes the merit or the delict, is the end point of the imputation. But there is no such thing as an end point of causality. The assumption of a first cause, a *prima causa,* which is the *analogon* to the end point of imputation, is incompatible with the idea of causality, at least with the idea of causality implied in laws of classical physics. The idea of a first cause, too, is a relic of that stage of thinking in which the principle of causality was not yet emancipated from that of imputation.

IX

It is just this difference between imputation and causality, that there is an end point of imputation but no end point of causality —it is just this fundamental difference, that constitutes the antagonism between what is called "necessity," prevailing in nature, and what is called "freedom," essential to society, that is to say, essential to man in his normative relations to other men. That man as a part of nature is considered not to be free means that his behavior, if conceived as a natural fact, must according to a law of nature be determined by other facts as an effect by its causes. But if we interpret definite human behavior according to a moral, religious, or legal law as merit, sin, or crime, we impute the consequences determined by the moral, religious, or legal law: the reward to the merit, the penance to the sin, the punishment to the crime, without imputing the merit, the sin, the crime, to something or somebody else. It is usual to say that we impute the merit, the sin, the crime, to the person responsible for the behavior thus characterized. But the true meaning of the statement that a merit is imputed to a person is that the person ought to be rewarded for his merit; the true meaning of the statement that a sin is imputed to a person is that this person ought to do penance for his sin; the true meaning of the statement that a crime is imputed to a person is that this person ought to be punished for his crime. What is imputed is not the human behavior which constitutes the merit, the sin, the crime; this behavior cannot be separated from its subject. As far as imputation is concerned, when a morally meritorious act is performed or a religious sin or a legal crime is committed, the question is not: Who has performed or committed these acts? This is a question of fact. The moral, religious, or legal question of imputation is: Who is responsible for these acts? And that means:

Who ought to be rewarded? Who ought to do penance? Who ought to be punished? It is the reward, the penance, or the punishment which is to be imputed as a definite consequence to a definite condition, to its specific condition. And the condition is the act constituting the merit, the sin, or the crime. The imputation of the reward to the merit, of the penance to the sin, of the punishment to the crime, implies the imputation to the person, that is, to the subject of the act constituting the merit, the sin, or the crime, this subject being an inseparable part of the act as an act of human behavior. What is decisive is that the imputation, in contradistinction to causality, comes to an end in that human behavior which, according to a moral, religious, or legal law, is the condition of the consequence determined by that law: the condition of the reward, the penance, the punishment.

X

This is the true meaning of the statement that man as subjected to a moral, religious, or legal order—and that means man as a member of society, as a moral, religious, or legal person—is free. Freedom is usually understood as exemption from the principle of causality, and causality is (or originally was) interpreted to mean absolute necessity. It is usual to say: Because a human being is free (or has a free will)—and that means, according to the usual view, that he is not subjected to causal laws determining his behavior—he is capable of moral, religious, or legal imputation; only because man is free can he be made responsible for certain acts, can he be rewarded for merit, can he be expected to do penance for sin, can he be punished for crime. It is usual to assume that only his freedom—and that means his exemption from the principle of causality—makes imputation possible. However, it is just the other way around. Human beings are free because we impute reward, penance, or punishment, as consequence, to human behavior, as condition, not because human behavior is not determined by causal laws but in spite of the undeniable fact that it is determined by causal laws. Man is free because his behavior is the end point of imputation. And it can be the end point of imputation even if his behavior is determined by causal laws.

XI

The many attempts to save the "freedom of will" as the alleged fact that the human will is not determined by the law of causality, are vain and must remain vain as long as a universal law of causality is supposed to be valid and freedom of will means that human will is not causally determined. The most important attempt at harmonizing the universal law of causality with freedom of will has been made by the outstanding physicist Max Planck.[6] He presupposes the validity of a universal law of causality, according to which a fixed causal connection exists in all events of nature and of the spiritual world,[7] and considers as the decisive criterion of the fact that an event is causally determined that it can be predicted with certainty by an observer who possesses the necessary knowledge of the circumstances before the event and does not interfere in this event.[8] He admits "that it would be nonsense to speak of a universal causality if there were exceptions to it; if, in other words, the events of the soul's conscious or subconscious life, the feelings, sensations, thoughts, and also the will were not subjected to the law of causality. . ." [9] Nevertheless, he insists on the freedom of will because he thinks that the freedom of will is an essential condition of man's moral responsibility; [10] and for this reason he asserts that there is no contradiction between the assumption of a universal law of causality and the idea of a free will; that it is possible to maintain the latter "without any surrender of the assumption of a strict universal law of causality." [11] How, then, does he conciliate the universal law of causality with freedom of will? He asserts "that the law of causality on the one hand and the freedom of will on the other hand refer to totally different questions." [12] The law of causality is the answer of science to the question of the structure of reality. The "question as to whether the will is or is not free is solely a matter of the individual consciousness; it can be answered only by the ego. The notion of the freedom of the human will can mean only that the individual feels himself to be free; and whether he does so can be known only to himself." [13] It is of importance to note that Planck, in order to harmonize the law of causality with the notion of the free will, does not change the meaning of this notion but only the authority at which the question of the free will is directed. He affirms that the question is directed—if not exclusively so at least also—at the individual consciousness. That the individual feels himself "free" means that he feels his will is not determined by the law of causality, and consequently that there is an exception to this law. This, however, cannot be the content of a "feeling." That man's will is not causally determined is a "notion," as Planck correctly states, and a notion cannot be the content of a feeling; it can be only the result of a process of thinking. From a psychological point of view, it would be more exact to describe the phenomenon concerned by saying that the individual act of will is accompanied by a feeling on the basis of which the individual thinks that his will is not determined by the law of causality. This thought is either true or false; and if the universal law of causality is assumed to be valid, the thought is to be considered to be false. The feeling is misleading man's thinking. There is, of course, no contradiction between the law of causality, that is, the statement that all phenomena are causally determined, and a man's statement that he has a feeling which induces him to think that his will is not causally determined, which is a statement about a fact. However, from the fact that a man has a feeling which induces him to think that his will is free, does not follow that this thought is true. For there is certainly a contradiction between the law of causality and the content of the man's thought, and it is precisely the content of the man's thought that refers to the question of the freedom of will. The question as to whether a man has a certain feeling can, indeed, be directed only at, and be answered only by, the man's ego. But this is not the question of the freedom of will, which, even according to Planck, is the question as to whether the human will is or is not determined by the law of causality; which is not a question concerning the feeling accompanying a man's act of will but a question concerning his will and its relation to the law of causality. This question can be directed only at and answered only by objective science.

If Planck showed nothing else but the self-evident fact that there is no contradiction between the law of causality and the "feeling" of man to be free, he would contribute nothing to the very problem which is at the center of the great antagonism between determinism and indeterminism: the problem whether the human will can be conceived of—and not whether it can be felt—as not causally determined. As a matter of fact, it is this question which Planck tries to answer in the affirmative. It is, according to his own formulation, the question as to whether it is possible to gain "an *understanding* of the fact of free will and the sense of moral responsibility from the standpoint of natural science" [14] and he tries to demonstrate that the freedom of will, that is, its being not causally determined—and not man's feeling to be free—is compatible with the universal law of causality assumed by natural science. He declares that "the question as to whether the will is or is not causally determined is, in truth, a question of the viewpoint from which one approaches the problem, that is, the question of the supposition with which one judges an act of will." He admits that "the human will, viewed from an objective scientific standpoint, is causally determined," but, he asserts, "viewed from the subjective standpoint of individual self-consciousness, the human will is free." [15] This means that one and the same question may be answered in different ways if it is asked from different points of view. But if the question of free will—as Planck supposes—is the question as to whether the human will is or is not subjected to the law of causality, and that means, a question of the validity of the law of causality, it is by its very nature a question of objective science, and not of subjective self-consciousness. If, however, the question which arises from the point of view of the individual self-consciousness is the question as to what man is feeling at the moment of an act of will, or the question whether he is aware of the cause of this act, it is a question different from that of the free will, and the answer to the former questions is no answer to the latter. And then it is not the same question namely, the question as to whether the will is or is not causally determined, which may be answered in different ways from different points of view.

Planck asserts that the question as to whether the will is or is not causally determined has to be answered in the negative from the subjective viewpoint of individual self-consciousness because man can never predict his own future behavior. Planck says: "Perhaps the most impressive proof that the individual will is independent of the law of causality"—it should be noticed that in this statement there is no reference to the feeling of man—"will be found if the attempt is made to predict in advance one's own motives and actions on the sole basis of the law of causality by means of an intensified self-cognition. Such an attempt is condemned to failure, because every application of the law of causality to one's own will, and every information gained in this way, is itself a motive acting upon the will, so that the result which is being looked for is continually being changed." [16] Man as an observer of himself cannot predict his future behavior because the act of observation interferes with the object observed. But from this fact does not follow that the object of observation is not causally determined. The situation is similar to that described by the so-called uncertainty principle of quantum mechanics. As we shall see later, Planck refuses to infer from this principle that there is an exception to the law of causality or that this law has to be abandoned altogether.

Besides, Planck admits that "a complete understanding of the causal course of our past will actions, down to the most obscure motives, is entirely within the realm of theoretical possibility." [17] Only causal understanding of one's own future behavior is impossible. However, every future act of will becomes in due time a past act of will, and then the individual is no longer prevented from knowing the causes of his own act of will. To be sure, he cannot predict the act; but from this fact cannot follow that his will is not causally determined. Consequently, the human will is to be considered as causally determined not only—as Planck asserts— from the objective point of view of science, but also from the subjective point of view of the individual self-consciousness; and the view that the universal law of causality and the freedom of will are incompatible is not, as Planck asserts, based on an inadmissible confusion of two distinct points of view.

Planck compares the alleged antagonism of the objective viewpoint of science and the subjective viewpoint of the individual self-consciousness with the difference of two systems of reference in physics. "We know that any quantitative predication about a spatial-temporal event has a definite meaning only if the system of reference is indicated for which it is supposed to be valid. This system can be selected at pleasure, and in accordance with the different systems chosen the predication too will differ. Thus, if a system of reference closely connected with the earth is taken, we must say that the sun moves through the heavens, but if the system of reference is transposed to a fixed star, the sun is at rest. There is an opposition

between the two formulations, but there is neither contradiction
nor obscurity: we are simply dealing with two different ways of
looking at the matter. According to the physical theory of relativity
—which to-day can surely be counted among the definite acquisi-
tions of science—the two systems of reference and the two corresponding points of view are equally correct and equally justified,
and it is, in principle, impossible to employ any measurements or
calculations, in order to choose between them, save in an arbitrary
manner." [18] This comparison of the objective viewpoint of science
and the subjective viewpoint of the individual self-consciousness
with two different systems of reference in physics does not hold.
In physics, one and the same question: as to whether the sun is
moving and the earth is at rest, or whether the earth is moving and
the sun at rest, is answered in different ways according to the system of reference chosen. However, it is not the same question
which is answered from the objective point of view of science in a
way different from that in which it is answered from the subjective
point of view of the individual self-consciousness. There are two
questions. The first one is the question as to whether the human
will is or is not causally determined; and the answer is that it is
causally determined. The second one is the question as to whether
the individual can understand his future act of will as causally
determined; and the answer is that he cannot. This, however, does
not mean that his act of will is not causally determined. If one and
the same question, namely the question whether the human will is
or is not causally determined, is asked, the answer given from the
objective viewpoint of science is exactly the same as the answer
given from the subjective viewpoint of individual self-consciousness, provided that this question can be addressed at all to this consciousness.

Another, no less fallacious, argument of Planck to demonstrate
the compatibility of the causal law with free will is the statement
that it is logically impossible to apply the law of causality to the
human will so far as this will is part of one's own ego, and the ego,
as subject of cognition, is inaccessible to any—therefore also to a
causal—cognition. "There is a point, a unique point, in the large
and immeasurable world of nature and mind which practically and
logically is and always will be inaccessible to every science and consequently also to every causal consideration. This point is one's

own ego." [19] "The impossibility of conceiving one's own will as subjected to the law of causality . . . has its reason in logic. . . . So far as we act as subjects of cognition we must renounce any purely causal understanding of our own present ego. Here is the point where the freedom of will maintains its position and from where it cannot be displaced." [20] However, the human will is a psychic phenomenon and as such accessible to psychological research, as any other psychic phenomenon, by observation of one's own psychic experience as well as by observation of the psychic experience of others. Such observation can be guided by no other principle than that of causality. The statement that the human will is free is meaningful only if it refers to the will as an objective psychic phenomenon, to the ego as an object, not to the ego as the subject, of cognition. That the ego as subject of cognition is not accessible to causal cognition is true; but it amounts to the tautology that the subject of cognition is not the object of cognition.

XII

The dogma of the freedom of will seems to be supported by the development of modern physics, especially by the results of quantum mechanics where the assumption of a universal law of causality meets with serious criticism. Even before the discovery of this new field of physics, it could be argued that there is in reality no strict causality, because an event is to be considered as causally determined if, on the basis of an accurate observation of the preceding events, it can be predicted; but due to the insufficience of our senses and the inevitable inaccuracy of our observations resulting therefrom, there is no event in reality which can be predicted with absolute certainty. However, in opposition to this view, the principle of strict causality can be maintained by referring it not to the reality as given immediately to our senses, but to the ideal picture of the world constructed by the science of physics. Physics, says Planck, "substitutes a new world in place of that given to us by our senses or by the measuring instruments which are used in order to aid the senses. This other world is the so-called physical world picture. It is merely an intellectual structure. To a certain extent it is arbitrary. It is a kind of model or idealization created to avoid inaccuracy inherent in every measurement and to facilitate exact definition." [21] "While the prediction of any event in the sense world is always subject to a certain inaccuracy, all the events of the physical world picture happen in accordance with certain definite laws which can be formulated so that they are causally determined." [22] However, there is in quantum mechanics a phenomenon that seems to escape this interpretation. It is the so-called uncertainty relation, originally formulated by Heisenberg. This relation states among other things that "measurement of an electron's velocity is inaccurate in proportion as the measurement of its position in space is accurate, and *vice versa.*" [23] The reason is that "we can determine the position of a moving electron only if we can see it, and in order to see it we must illuminate it, i.e., we must allow light to fall on it. The rays falling on it impinge upon the electron and thus alter its velocity in a way which is impossible to calculate. The more accurately we desire to determine the position of the electron, the shorter must be the light waves employed to illuminate it, the stronger will be the impact, and the greater the inaccuracy with which the velocity is determined." [24] That means that the object of observation is changed by the very act of observation, however accurate this observation may be. It constitutes a causal interference in the process observed, and thus makes insight in the causal nexus of the observed phenomenon impossible. A number of physicists, among them Heisenberg and Bohr, draw from this impossibility the conclusion that the behavior of the individual electron can be predicted only with a certain degree of statistical probability, that, consequently, it cannot be interpreted as subjected to the law of causality, that that law does not apply in this case, that there is no strict causality in the reality of nature, that the so-called laws of nature are merely laws of probability exposed to exceptions. Some physicists and philosophers are going even so far as to assert as the result of the uncertainty principle that nature is not, as classical physics assumed, governed by laws, hence a world of order and as such understandable, but intrinsically and in its elements neither subject to law nor understandable.[25] Other physicists and philosophers, however, reject this conclusion. Planck, for example, says that this abandonment of the law of causality "rests upon a confusion between the world of senses and the physical picture of the world"; and he comes to the result that "there is fully as rigid a determinism in the world picture of quantum physics as in that of classical physics." [26]

The principle of strict causality can be maintained also by interpreting it as an epistemological postulate, that is, as a norm directed at human cognition demanding to seek a connection between the phenomena observable in the world of senses, to conceive these facts as cause and effect, and thus to explain reality. Such a postulate presupposes, of course, as a working hypothesis that reality is fit for such an interpretation. As a norm, the principle of causality is neither true nor false, the question is only whether it is useful. There can be no doubt that it has been proved to be so, that in applying it, human cognition has succeeded in transforming the chaos of sensual perceptions into a meaningful kosmos. It stands to reason that this postulate can never be completely fulfilled, for the human senses are insufficient and this insufficiency can never be overcome even by the best instruments. Consequently, human knowledge of the world of senses must always remain within certain limits, the development of natural science having the character of an infinite, never-ending process.[27] This fact, however, cannot affect the validity of the epistemological postulate of causality. If, in a concrete case, as in that of the uncertainty relation or the self-observation of a present act of will, the postulate cannot be fulfilled, this nonfulfillment must not be interpreted as an exception to its validity, just as the nonobservance of a moral or legal norm prescribing a definite human behavior does not constitute an exception to its validity. The norm continues to be valid in spite of its nonobservance; if the norm would not be considered valid it could not be considered to be not observed. A norm *pre*scribing a certain behavior does not allow exceptions; only a rule *de*scribing something does so. In other words: If the working hypothesis that the phenomena of reality can be interpreted as cause and effect proves to be, by and large, fruitful in scientific experience, the fact that in certain cases it does not apply is not a sufficient reason to abandon this hypothesis. If the principle of causality is conceived as an epistemological norm or if it is conceived as a law describing its object, but referred not to the world of senses but to the ideal world picture of the science of physics, its strict validity is beyond question. If, on the other hand, it is conceived of as implied in the laws by which natural science according to its present status describes the world of our senses, these laws of nature may be considered to be merely statistical laws of probability which allow exceptions.

In order to maintain the strict validity of the principle of causality it is not necessary to accept—as, for example, Laplace did [28]—the metaphysical assumption of an ideal, because omniscient, spirit or intelligence which knows all past and present events, which is capable of abstaining in its observation from interfering in the object observed, and hence can foresee with absolute certainty and accuracy all future events. Planck, too, has recourse to the assumption. He abandons his attempt at maintaining the strict principle of causality by referring it to the ideal picture of the world constructed by physics, for this picture "is due to our imagination and is of a provisional and changeable character, it is an emergency concept hardly worthy of a fundamental physical notion," [29] an "anthropomorphical" idea.[30] For this reason "the question arises whether it might be possible to endow the concept of causality with a more deep and direct significance by making it independent of the introduction of an artificial human product." [31] This, he thinks, can be done by the assumption of "an ideal intellect having complete knowledge of to-day's physical events in all places" and hence able to predict all future physical events,[32] of "an ideal spirit having full knowledge of the action of the natural forces as well as of the events in the intellectual life of men, a knowledge extending to every detail and embracing present, past, and future." [33] "The actual impossibility of predicting even a single occurrence accurately in classical as well as in quantum physics appears to be a natural consequence of the circumstance that man with his sense organs and measuring instruments is himself part of nature, subject to its laws and confined within its limits, whereas the ideal intelligence is free of all such limitations"; [34] which means that this ideal intelligence must be imagined as existing beyond nature, and that means in a transcendent sphere. If it is not subject to the laws of nature, the principle of causality does not apply to it. Thus, the metaphysical assumption of an ideal spirit leads to the paradoxical result that in order to maintain the universal law of causality an exemption to this law must be assumed. Besides, the ideal spirit is no less a product of human imagination than the ideal world picture of physics, and has certainly a much more anthropomorphic character than the latter. It is, seen from a scientific point of view, nothing but the hypostatized personification of the normative postulate to interpret natural phenomena as cause and effect, on the basis of accurate observation, without interfering in the observed object; and as such hypostatization it is not very different from the idea of an omniscient and omnipotent, transcendent God. That Planck's assumption of an ideal and transcendent intelligence is essentially influenced by religious feelings follows from the statement: "We must take care not to regard the ideal spirit as ranking with ourselves; we have no right to ask it how it acquires the knowledge enabling it to predict exactly future events, since such inquisitiveness might well meet with the reply: 'You resemble the spirit which you can grasp, you do not resemble me,' " [35] a quotation from Goethe's *Faust* and referred to by Planck to emphasize the fundamental difference between the human and the transcenscendent intelligence. Planck says: "To understand the causality of creative works of genius an intelligence of an incredibly high and even divine order is requested: but in principle I can see no objection to such an assumption. Before the eyes of God even the loftiest human intellects are like rudimentary structures." [36] To justify his assumption of the ideal spirit, whose identity with God he admits, Planck finally declares that it is due to "devotion to science" which is "a matter of faith"; [37] and that means religion. As to the relation of science and religion, he says: "Religion and natural science are fighting a joint battle in an incessant, never relaxing crusade against scepticism and against dogmatism, against disbelief and against superstition, and the rallying cry in the crusade has always been and always will be: 'On to God.' " [38] It is evidently this belief in God which is behind Planck's assumption of the ideal, transcendent intelligence and of the freedom of will. The two assumptions are in close connection with each other, so far as God as well as the human will are conceived of as a *prima causa*, a first cause, not determined by another cause. It is precisely on account of his capacity of being, in his acts of will, a first cause that man in theological speculation can be described as the image of God.

To conciliate the freedom of will with the universal law of causality is impossible if freedom of will means exemption from causality governing natural reality. However, the assertion that the will is free, if correctly understood, does not refer to the sphere of natural reality but to the sphere of validity of moral or legal norms. For, the freedom of will is essentially connected with moral and legal responsibility, and that means with imputation. There is no such thing as responsibility in natural reality. Responsibility is constituted by a normative order such as morality or law. The electron is not responsible for its being reflected or not reflected upon its impact on a crystal, for it is not considered to be under a moral or legal order. Hence no conclusion whatsoever can be drawn from a situation in quantum mechanics to the question of the freedom of will.[39] This concept has not the negative meaning that the human will is not causally determined, but the positive meaning that the human will, and consequently the human behavior caused by this will, is the end point of a normative imputation.[40]

XIII

If human behavior, in order to be a possible object of imputation, would have to be considered as exempted from the law of causality, causality and freedom would be, indeed, incompatible. Hence the apparently insurmountable conflict between the school of determinism and the school of indeterminism. However, there is no such conflict if we understand the true meaning of the statement that man as a moral, religious, or legal person is free. The alleged opposition between necessity, prevailing in nature according to the principle of causality, and freedom, prevailing in society according to the principle of imputation, loses, it is true, a great deal of its acuteness if the meaning of causality should be reduced from that of absolute necessity to that of mere probability. But even if causality were to mean absolute necessity, and imputation freedom, the one would by no means exclude the other. There is no contradiction between so-called determinism and so-called indeterminism. There is nothing to prevent the human mind's subjecting human behavior to two different schemes of interpretation. If interpreted according to laws of nature—and that means if interpreted as part of nature—human behavior is to be conceived as an effect determined by preceding causes. From the point of view of this interpretation, there is no such thing as freedom in the sense of exemption from causality, whether causality means absolute necessity or mere probability.

We may, however, and actually do, interpret human behavior according to social norms, that is to say, moral, religious, or legal laws, without the assumption that this behavior is exempted from causality. No determinist seriously requires that a criminal shall not be punished and a hero not be rewarded because the commission of the crime and the performance of the heroic deed are causally determined. He agrees with the punishment of the criminal and with the reward of the hero, that is to say, with the imputation of the punishment to the crime, of the reward to the heroic deed, in spite of the fact that the crime as well as the heroic deed is determined by the law of causality. Punishment and reward are provided for only because it is assumed that the fear of punishment can causally determine men to refrain from committing a crime, and that the desire for reward can causally determine men to perform a heroic deed. The imputation of punishment and reward presupposes the assumption of a possible causal determination of human behavior. If man is free because he is the end point of imputation, causality is not only not incompatible with imputation implying freedom—and that means with regulation of human behavior by norms connecting reward with merit and punishment with crime—but indeed the principle of causality is presupposed by such regulation constituting imputation and thus the freedom of man.

To reconcile the idea of freedom, prevailing in society as a normative order, with the law of causality, prevailing in nature as a causal order, it is not necessary to have recourse to the metaphysical-religious view which is at the basis of indeterminism. Such reconciliation is possible within the field of rational science if we recognize imputation as a principle different from, but analogous to, that of causality, the one performing in the social sciences what the other achieves in the natural sciences. This seems to be a satisfactory solution of an old problem. It is the dissolution of the sham problem of an allegedly indissoluble antinomy between natural necessity and social freedom. What seems to be a contradiction between two philosophies, fundamentally different and irreconcilable with each other, a rational-empirical and a metaphysical view of the world, is in truth the parallelism of two different ways of cognition, both rational and empirical, of two different methods by which cognition connects the elements of its objects with one another, the one being completely compatible with the other: the dualism of causality and imputation.

XIV

The principle of imputation—this term used in its original meaning—connects two acts of human behavior with each other: the behavior of one individual with the behavior of another, as, for instance, in the moral law providing reward for merit or in the legal law providing punishment for crime; or the behavior of one individual with other behavior of the same individual, as, for instance, in the religious law providing penance for sin. In all these cases the human behavior prescribed by the social norm is conditioned by human behavior. The condition as well as the consequence is an act of human behavior. But social norms may refer not only to human behavior but also to other facts. A social norm may prescribe or forbid certain behavior which has a certain effect, and social norms may prescribe or forbid the behavior of an individual conditioned not only by other behavior of the same individual or the behavior of another individual but also by facts other than human behavior. There are even norms prescribing human behavior conditioned only by such facts. If, for example, a social norm forbids murder, that is, intentional killing, that which is forbidden is the behavior of an individual which has for its effect the death of another individual. The behavior of a murderer is exactly the same as the behavior of a man who attempts to kill another but whose attempt has not the intended effect. The difference which exists between murder and mere attempt of murder is not a difference in the behavior of the delinquents but a difference in the effect of their behavior. The one has, and the other has not, the death of a man as its effect; and death is not human behavior but a physiological process. A norm may prescribe that, if a man causes by his behavior material damage to another, he ought to repair the damage; or a norm of primitive religion may prescribe that in case of an epidemic, a human sacrifice ought to be offered to the gods. The damage and the epidemic are not facts which have the character of human behavior.

It should further be noted that norms may refer to individuals without referring to their behavior. The sanctions provided for by legal norms are to be directed against individuals. But no behavior of the individual against whom the sanction is directed may be among the conditions of the sanction. This is the case when an individual or individuals are made responsible for a delict committed by another, especially if collective responsibility is established; that is to say, that individuals are to be punished not because they have committed a delict but because they belong to the group to which the delinquent belongs. In these cases the individual against whom the sanction is directed is only the object of the behavior of another individual, that is, of the individual who executes the sanction. The responsible individual is not the subject of any legally relevant behavior.

XV

If, in the statement that under certain conditions certain behavior ought to take place, the conditions are not or not only human behavior and if the connection between the conditioning fact and the conditioned human behavior is designated as imputation, this term is used in a wider sense than it was originally. For the consequence is imputed not or not only to human behavior, and that means—expressed in the usual terminology—the consequence is not or not only imputed to a person, but to facts and circumstances.

There are even social norms which seem to prescribe unconditionally or, what amounts to the same, under all circumstances, certain human behavior. These are norms providing for an omission, such as the moral norms: you shall not lie, you shall not kill, you shall not commit adultery, and the like. If these norms had really the character of categorical norms, then it would not be possible to describe the social situation constituted by these norms in a statement connecting two elements as condition and consequence; then the principle of imputation would not apply. But the social norms prescribing omission are not categorical norms. That positive actions cannot be prescribed unconditionally because a definite action can be performed only under definite conditions is self-evident. But also omissions cannot be prescribed unconditionally. Otherwise, they could be complied with or violated unconditionally, which is not the case. An individual cannot lie, commit theft, murder, or adultery always and everywhere, but only under definite circumstances. If moral norms prescribing omissions established unconditional, that is to say, categorical, obligations, an individual during his sleep would fulfill these obligations—sleeping would be an ideal state from the point of view of morality. The condition under which the omission of an act is prescribed in a norm is the sum total of all circumstances under which the act is possible. Besides, in empirical society there are no prohibitions that have no exceptions. Even the most fundamental norms, such as not to lie, not to kill, not to take a man's property away without his consent, are valid only with important restrictions. There are circumstances under which it is not prohibited to lie, to kill, to take away another man's property without his consent. This shows that all social norms, not only those prescribing a positive action but also those prescribing an omission, provide for certain behavior only under definite conditions and that any norm establishes between two elements a connection which can be described by a statement to the effect that under certain conditions a certain consequence ought to take place. This is the grammatical form of the principle of imputation in contradistinction to that of causality.

SCIENCE AND POLITICS

REALITY AND VALUE

I T IS a commonplace to assert that science should be independent of politics. By this one usually means that the search for truth, which is the essential function of science, should not be influenced by political interests, which are the interests concerned with the establishment and maintenance of a definite social order or a particular social institution. Politics as the art of government, that is to say, the practice of regulating the social behavior of men, is a function of will and, as such, an activity which necessarily presupposes the conscious or unconscious assumption of values, the realization of which is the purpose of the activity. Science is a function of cognition; its aim is not to govern but to explain. To describe the world is its object. Its independence of politics means in the last analysis, that the scientist must not presuppose any value; consequently he has to restrict himself to an explanation and a description of his object without judging it as good or bad, that is, as being in conformity with, or contrary to, a presupposed value. This implies that the statements by which a scientist describes and explains the object of his inquiry must not be influenced by values in which he himself believes. Scientific statements are judgments about reality; by definition they are objective and independent of the wishes and fears of the judging subject because they are verifiable by experience. They are true or false. Value judgments, however, are subjective in character because they are based, in the last analysis, on the personality of the judging subject in general, and on the emotional element of his consciousness in particular.[1]

From *American Political Science Review*, Sept., 1951.

The principle of excluding value judgments from the field of science seems to have an exception. It is frequently maintained that there is one value which science must presuppose, namely, truth, and that there is consequently one value judgment which a scientist may legitimately pronounce, the judgment that something is true or false. However, truth is not a value in the same sense as are the values at the basis of political activity, such as, for instance, individual freedom or economic security. The judgment that something is true or false is essentially different from the judgment that something is good or bad, which is the most general formula of a value judgment. Truth means conformity with reality, not conformity with a presupposed value. The judgment that something is true or false is the ascertainment of the existence or non-existence of a fact; and such a judgment has an objective character insofar as it is independent of the wish or fear of the judging subject and is verifiable by experience of the senses, controlled by reason. That the statement "Iron is heavier than water" is true, and that the statement "Water is heavier than iron" is false, can be demonstrated by experiment; and the one is true and the other is false, even if the judging subject for some reason or another should wish the contrary. On the other hand, the statement that a certain social organization guaranteeing individual freedom but not economic security is good, and consequently better than a social organization guaranteeing economic security but not individual freedom, is not a statement about a fact; it cannot be verified by experiment and is neither true nor false. Rather, it is valid or invalid. As a value judgment (i.e., a judgment about individual freedom and economic security as values), it must not be confused with the statement that most men actually prefer individual freedom to economic security, which indeed is a statement about a fact, and may be true or false. If the statement that most men prefer individual freedom to economic security is false and the statement that most men prefer economic security to individual freedom is true, the latter statement logically excludes the first one; but it does not exclude the value judgment that individual freedom, although not preferred by most men, is a higher value, and hence "better," than economic security. Judgments about values cannot contradict judgments about reality. Indeed, only if their meaning is such that they cannot contradict or affirm judgments about reality are they value judgments in the specific sense of this term. In this sense, reality and value are always two different spheres.

However, the terms "value" and "value judgment" are frequently used in another sense. Such is the case when the statement that something is an appropriate means to a certain end is considered to be a value judgment. The meaning of such a statement is that something, as a cause, is able to bring about a certain effect, which is supposed to be an end. The statement refers to the relationship between cause and effect; and it is just this relationship between facts that constitutes a specific reality, the reality of nature. Natural science describes its object as real by applying the principle of causality—that is, by statements that under a given condition a specific consequence certainly or probably will occur.[2] These statements are the so-called laws of nature. The statement that something is an appropriate means to an end is true or false; and in order to be true it must be verifiable by experience. If the statement that a communistic organization is "good" means only that it is an appropriate means to bring about economic security for everybody, and if the statement that a capitalistic organization is "bad" means only that it has not this result, neither statement is, in itself, a value judgment in the specific sense of the term. Both statements are judgments about reality; and, if they are classified as value judgments, such value judgments are not different from judgments about reality, but only a special type of such judgments, and hence not to be excluded from the sphere of science. However, the statement that something is an appropriate means to a certain end preserves its scientific character only so long as its meaning is that *if* something is presupposed as an end, something else is an appropriate means; the scientific statement must not imply that something *is* an end. Therefore a scientist may legitimately state that communism is an appropriate means, *provided* that economic security for everybody is presupposed as an end. But he transgresses the field of science when he states that economic security for everybody *is* an end, or *the* end, of social life; for science can determine the means, but it cannot determine the ends.

The statement that something is an end is not identical with the statement that an individual, especially the judging subject, or several individuals want it. The latter is a statement about a fact, about the actual state of mind of human beings. If by "end" that which an individual actually desires is meant, the term signifies the intention of the individual, the purpose that he is actually pursuing. But in its specific sense the statement that something is an end, for instance, the statement that economic security for everybody is the end of social life, expresses the idea that something—here economic security for everybody—*should* be pursued as an end even if it is not actually pursued. In this sense, the concept of "end" is identical with that of a "right end." The statement that something should be done or, what amounts to the same, that men should behave in a certain way, expresses the meaning of a *norm* prescribing this behavior. Hence the statement that something is an end in the sense of a right end is equivalent to the statement that it is prescribed by a norm. A norm claims, according to its meaning, objective validity. (Whether this claim is founded, we shall see later.) Hence, in the statement that something is an end in the sense of a right end, the term "end" has an objective meaning. It does not merely signify the end pursued by a definite individual. In this sense "end" means "value"; and in this sense a norm constitutes a value. To put it another way, only as a statement about what should be done in accordance with a norm presupposed to be valid, is the statement that something is an end a value judgment in the specific sense of the term, in contradistinction to a judgment about reality as a statement about what actually is done or probably will be done. Only if the judging subject presupposes a norm prescribing something as valid, is his judgment that something is or is not in conformity with this norm a genuine value judgment; only then does he approve or disapprove the object of his judgment.

In this respect we must distinguish between an end which may be considered as a means to a further end and an ultimate end, or, what amounts to the same, a value constituted by a basic norm, that is, as a supreme value. The statement that something is an end is a value judgment in the specific sense of the term only when referring to an ultimate end (as a judgment about a supreme value), not to an end as a means to a further end. Only then is it impossible for the statement to contradict a judgment about reality. To the question "Why is a particular value judgment or a particular norm valid?" the answer can be only another value judgment or another norm, never a judgment about reality—the ascertainment of a fact; and thus the question must lead to a judgment about a supreme value or to a basic norm. To the question "Why should a child honor his parents?" the correct answer is not "Because God has commanded children to honor their parents," but "Because we should obey the commands of God, who has ordered children to honor their parents." But to the question "Why should we obey the commands of God?" there is no answer. To obey the commands of God is an ultimate end— a supreme value, the content of a basic norm. The statement that science can determine the means, but not an ultimate end, is equivalent to the statement that science must not presuppose the validity of a basic norm. Scientific statements about appropriate means can be made only as conditional propositions: *if* a basic norm constituting an ultimate end is presupposed to be valid, then something is an appropriate means. That is to say, then, as a cause, it is able to bring about as an effect that which is determined as an ultimate end by a basic norm, presupposed as valid —not by science itself but by the acting individual, who intends to bring about this effect.

It is important to be aware that within a rational process referring to the relationship of means to ends, the assumption of an ultimate end is inevitable. Without such an assumption it is not possible to interpret the relationship between cause and effect as one of means and end. The reason that this is not self-evident is that most men are not conscious of the necessity for such an assumption. If, for instance, someone declares democracy to be a good, or the best, form of government, his explanation may be that democracy is the only form of government by means of which the greatest possible degree of individual freedom can be brought about. This explanation implies that he considers the guarantee of individual freedom as the end of government. To the question why he considers individual freedom to be an end, he will probably answer that it is because all men wish to be free. As a statement about a fact, this answer is highly problematical; and even if the statement were true, it is not an answer to the question. Why democracy is a good form of government is not a question of what end men actually pursue, but one of what they should pursue, of what is the right end to be pursued by men. Hence, the correct answer to the question of why democracy is a good form of government is, "Because men should be free"; and this answer means that freedom is a supreme value. This value judgment may seem so self-evident to the judging subject that he is not conscious of it as the fundamental presupposition of his judgment about democracy.

Since the judgment about individual freedom, or economic security, or something else presupposed as an ultimate end or supreme value does not allow a justification by a further value judgment, the only question that may be asked with respect to such a value judgment concerns the fact that one individual presupposes freedom, another security, and a third something else as a supreme value. It is a psychological question, that is, a question about reality, rather than one about value. Inquiry into this problem can hardly be pursued beyond the ascertainment that the choice among the different presuppositions is in the last analysis determined by the personality of the judging subject in general and by the emotional component of his consciousness in particular. A man with strong self-confidence may prefer individual freedom, whereas one suffering from an inferiority complex may prefer economic security. If a man has strong metaphysical inclinations and if fear of death makes him believe in the immortality of his soul, concern for the fate of his soul in the other world may cause him to consider the so-called spiritual values, the "welfare of the soul," more important than the so-called material values; whereas a man of more rationalistic habits of thought, with an unhampered desire to enjoy his earthly life, will consider the material values as the only ones that count. In this sense, judgments about ultimate ends or supreme values are, in spite of their claim to an objective validity, highly subjective. They thus differ from judgments about reality, which—being verifiable by experience and completely independent of the personality of the judging subject, particularly of his desires and fears—are by their very nature objective. This objectivity is an essential characteristic of science; and because of its objectivity, science is opposed to politics and must be separated from it; because politics is an activity ultimately based on subjective value judgments.

SCIENCE OF POLITICS AND "POLITICAL" SCIENCE

The principle of objectivity applies to social science as well as to natural science, and in particular to so-called political science. The object of political science is politics—the activity directed at the establishment and maintenance of a social order, especially the state. In describing the phenomena concerned, the political scientist must, of course, take into consideration the values which men presuppose in their political activities. But in doing so he has to restrict himself to ascertaining the fact that the establishment and maintenance of the different political systems presuppose different values as ultimate ends, and to finding out these different values which are at the bases of the different systems; in describing the systems, he himself must not presuppose the one or the other of these values; he must not consider the norm constituting the value as valid—that is, as binding upon himself. In other terms, he must neither approve nor disapprove of the object of his analysis lest his work, instead of being a science of politics, become a "political" science in the sense of an instrument of politics. Then it is no science at all but a political ideology.

The separation of science from politics, which means abstention from value judgments within a science whose object is, so to speak, impregnated with value judgments, is not so paradoxical as it seems; it merely is necessary to admit that ascertaining the fact that men are consciously or unconsciously determined in their political activities by definite value judgments is quite different from endorsing these value judgments. It cannot be denied that it is much more difficult to separate social, and especially political, science from politics than to comply with this postulate in the field of natural science. But the latter is by no means immune from the danger of being politicized. It is well known that the Church tried to suppress the Copernican theory, not because it could be proved false, but because it endangered the authority of the Holy Scripture and thus the authority of the Church. There is no sufficient reason for differentiating between natural and social sciences regarding the postulate of separating science from politics.

Those who deny the legitimacy of this postulate with respect to political science accept—at least in part—one of the most characteristic principles of Marxian philosophy: the dogma that science cannot be separated from politics because science is only part of the "superstructure" of an economic (and that means, according to this philosophy, a political) reality, and consequently is never really more than a political instrument. This dogma denies the possibility of an independent science. But the splendid development of modern natural science may be attributed largely to its emancipation from political powers, and especially from the power of the Church. It is a characteristic feature of this political power that it assumed authority over science. The fact that in the past natural science *has* been able to achieve complete independence is due—it is true—to a powerful social interest in its victory, an interest in that advance of technique which only a free science can guarantee. Social science does not lead, or does not yet lead, to such direct advantage afforded by improvement of technique as physics and chemistry produce on the acquisition of engineering knowledge and medical therapy. In social science there is still no influence to counteract the overwhelming interest that those residing in power, as well as those craving for power, have in a theory pleasing to their wishes—that is, in a political pseudoscience, which is nothing but a political ideology. If such a political science cannot free itself from politics, there will never be a real political science.

Although science must be separated from politics, politics need not be separated from science. It stands to reason that a statesman, in order to realize his ends, may use the results of science as a means. Science in general and political science in particular may furnish these means, and only science can furnish the appropriate means; but, as pointed out, it cannot determine the ultimate ends of politics. However, to admit that these ends are in the last analysis based on subjective value judgments seems to be too difficult for those who—for political reasons—look for an absolute justification of the political system which they try to establish or to maintain. If they are not willing to find such a justification in religion, they try to get it from science. This tendency, too, is characteristic of Marxian philosophy, which claims to establish a "scientific" socialism. True science, of course, refuses to be a substitute for religion and cannot but destroy the illusion that judgments of value can be derived from cognition of reality, that values are immanent in the reality which is the object of scientific study. The view that value is immanent in reality is a characteristic feature of a metaphysical-religious (and this means nonscientific) interpretation of nature and society. It can consistently be maintained only if it is assumed that both are the creation of God as the personification of the absolute good. This view leads inevitably to the insoluble problem of theodicy, that is, to the unsurmountable contradiction of a reality which, as the creation of God, is to be considered good but in which, nevertheless, evil is also immanent. The view that value is immanent in reality, if maintained by an antireligious, antimetaphysical theory of society (as, for example, by the positive philosophy of Comte or the economic interpretation of history by Marx) is without any foundation.

NORMATIVE SCIENCES

The postulate of the separation of science from politics presupposes that the object of science is reality, that scientific statements are statements about reality as opposed to value judgments in the specific sense of the term. There are, however, sciences, or disciplines usually considered to be sciences, such as ethics and jurisprudence, the object of which seems not to be reality but values. They describe norms constituting values, and in this sense may be called "normative" sciences. Morals, the object of the one, and law, the object of the other, are indeed systems of norms, or normative orders, determining a definite human behavior by prescribing or permitting such behavior. In order to consider them as sciences, we must take into consideration the fact that there are two different kinds of norms, just as there are two different kinds of value judgments: there are positive norms, which are created by acts of individuals, and norms that are not created in this way, but are only presupposed in the minds of the acting and judging individuals. The act by which a norm is created may be performed in different ways: by spoken or written words, by a gesture, by conventional symbols, and the like. The norms of a positive moral order may be established by the sermons or writings of a religious founder or by custom, that is, by the habitual behavior of the members of a social community; the norms of positive law may be established by custom, by acts of legislation, by judicial decisions, by administrative acts, or by legal transactions. The acts by which the norms of a positive normative system are created are always facts manifested in the external world, perceptible to the senses. The followers of Christ could hear the voice of their master when he, in the Sermon on the Mount, ordered them to love their enemies. We can read the Holy Scripture reporting this as a fact. We can also read a statute imposing upon us the obligation to pay taxes. As soldiers, we can hear the command of our superior officer ordering us to do or to forbear from doing something, and, as drivers of cars, we can see the green traffic light permitting us to cross an intersection. To say that a norm is created by a fact, is a figure of speech. The norm is the specific meaning of the fact, and this meaning, not perceptible by our senses, is the result of an interpretation. To interpret the meaning of a fact as a norm is possible only under the condition that we presuppose another norm conferring upon this fact the quality of a norm-creating fact; but this other norm, in the last analysis, cannot be a positive norm. Thus what Christ ordered us to do in the Sermon on the Mount are norms binding upon us only if we presuppose that Christ is the supreme moral authority, and to do this means that we presuppose a norm that we should obey the commands of Christ. But this norm is not, as are the commands of Christ, a positive norm, that is to say, the meaning of a fact, a norm-creating act performed in space and in time, but rather a norm the validity of which is only presupposed in our mind.

The difference between a positive and a nonpositive norm is particularly clear in the field of law. The fact that a man orders another man to pay a certain sum of money is interpreted to have the meaning of a norm issued by the one and binding on the other, and not an attempt of a gangster to extort money from another, if the one issuing the order is considered to be an organ of the community, a tax officer for instance, acting as authorized by a statute. The act by which the statute has been adopted that confers on the official his authority, has the meaning of a binding norm only if it is performed in a way determined by the constitution. But the historically first constitution has the character of a binding norm only if we presuppose a norm that we should behave as those who established the constitution ordered us to behave. If we do not suppose that the fathers of the constitution had their authority from God, this norm is a basic norm. It is not established, as was the constitution itself, by the acts of human beings; it is only presupposed by those who want to interpret certain human relations as legal relations, or as relations determined by legal norms. This presupposition, however, is not arbitrary. As a matter of fact, we presuppose that we should behave as those who established the constitution ordered us to behave, if the legal order established on the basis of this constitution is by and large effective. This is the principle of effectiveness implied in the basic norm.[3]

Jurisprudence as a *science* of law has positive norms for its object. Only positive law can be the object of a science of law. This is the principle of legal positivism as opposed to the natural-law doctrine, which pretends to present legal norms not created by acts of human beings but deduced from nature. To deduce norms from nature, that is to say, to consider nature as a legislator, presupposes the idea that nature is created by God and is thus the manifestation of his will, which is absolutely good. Hence the natural-law doctrine is not a science but a metaphysics of law.[4] Positive law may be national law, the law of a definite state based on its constitution and created by law-making acts of legal authorities instituted by this constitution; or international law created by custom, that is, the habitual practice of the states, based on the presupposition that the states should behave as they regularly behave—which presupposition is the basic norm of international law. But the norm on which the validity of a positive legal order is based is, as a matter of fact, a nonpositive norm, and the principle of legal positivism can be maintained only as restricted by this fact. This restriction, however, does not abolish the opposition between legal positivism and natural-law doctrine. The basic norm of a positive legal order— in contradistinction to the substantive norms of natural law prescribing a definite human behavior as in conformity with nature (and that means as just) and prohibiting a definite human behavior as contrary to nature (and that means as unjust)—has a merely formal character. It serves as a basis for any positive legal order, regardless of its conformity or nonconformity with natural law; and it has, within the science of law, a merely hypothetical character. The statements by which the science of law describes its

objects as positive norms have the character of conditional propositions. As a science, it cannot state absolutely that individuals or
states are obliged or entitled by legal norms to behave in a certain
way. It ascertains only that *under the condition* that the basic
norm conferring on the fathers of the constitution a law-making
authority is presupposed as valid, are individuals obliged or entitled, by legal norms based on the constitution, to behave in a
certain way; and only that *under the condition* that the basic norm
instituting the custom of states as a law-creating fact is presupposed
as valid, are states obliged or entitled, by legal norms created by
custom, to behave in a certain way. A science of law cannot itself
presuppose either of these basic norms as valid, nor can it decide
that any nonpositive norm is valid. To ascertain the validity of the
nonpositive basic norm of a positive legal order is beyond the
sphere of a science whose object is this positive legal order.

Positive legal norms can be the object of a legal science because
the existence—and this means the validity—of a positive norm
is conditioned by the existence of facts. These facts are the acts by
which the legal norm is created, such as a custom, a legislative, judicial, or administrative act, a legal transaction, together with the
effectiveness of the total legal order to which the norm belongs. In
describing its object as norms, the science of law refers to these
facts; and the positivity of the law consists just in the relation to
these facts. If it is assumed that norms prescribing or permitting
specific human behavior (implying also acts of state) constitute a
value, and that consequently the statement that the human behavior (or perhaps the act of state) is or is not in conformity with
a norm of positive law (that is, is legal or illegal) is a value judgment, it must be remembered that this value is not opposed to
reality. Such a value judgment is—like a judgment that something
is an appropriate means to a presupposed end—not a judgment
essentially different from a judgment about reality, but a special
kind of judgment about reality. The statement that a certain
human behavior (or a certain act of state) is legal or illegal may
be true or false; it is verifiable by experience. Such a statement is
possible only with respect to a definite national, or the international, legal order. The statement, for instance, that it is illegal
under a definite national law not to fulfill a promise of marriage is
false if within this legal order there is no norm attaching a sanction

to the nonfulfillment of a promise of marriage; and it is true only if there is such a norm. There exists such a norm only if it is created in accordance with the constitution which is at the basis of that law, and this constitution is valid only if the legal order established on it is by and large effective. These are facts which can be ascertained by the science of law, just as facts can be ascertained by the science of nature. Hence the statement that norms are the object of the science of law does not mean that the object of this science is not reality. It means only that this object is not a natural reality as described by natural science. But the object of legal science may be characterized as legal reality. The difference between natural reality and legal reality is that legal reality as described by legal science consists of facts which have—under the condition that the validity of the basic, nonpositive, norm is presupposed—a specific meaning: the meaning of positive norms.

Natural science describes its object as real in statements that under certain conditions (causes), certain consequences (their effects) necessarily or probably take place. These propositions are, as pointed out, the so-called laws of nature, which are laws of causality. Causality is not a force immanent in reality; it is a principle of cognition, the specific instrument by which natural science describes its object. Since norms determine human behavior, the science of law, in describing the law as a set of norms is also describing human behavior; but it does not describe it as it takes place as cause and effect in natural reality. It describes behavior as it is determined, that is, prescribed or permitted, by legal norms. The statements by which the science of law describes its object are not an application of the principle of causality; they do not have the meaning of the laws of nature, although they have the same grammatical form. They are propositions connecting a condition with its consequence, but this connection has another meaning than that expressed in the laws of nature. Their meaning is not that under a certain condition a certain consequence actually, that is, necessarily or probably, takes place; but that under the condition of certain human behavior, other human behavior as consequence *ought* to take place. These statements are the rules of law. In the rule of law that "If a man commits theft, another man ought to punish the thief," the punishment is not described as the effect or the theft as the cause. The term "ought" expresses the specific

meaning of the connection between condition and consequence
established by a legal norm (a prescription or permission) as different from the connection between cause and effect. It may be designated as "imputation." It is the principle according to which the
social sciences, the object of which are norms determining human
behavior, describe their object. It is the principle which, in the
field of certain social sciences, such as ethics and jurisprudence, corresponds to the principle of causality in the field of natural sciences.
It is necessary to remember, of course, that when the principle of
imputation is applied, and when it is stated that under the condition of certain behavior, other behavior *ought* to take place, the
term "ought" has not its usual moral, but a purely logical, meaning. It designates, like causality, a category in the sense of Kant's
transcendental logic.[5]

SCIENCE OF LAW AND POLITICS

If the propositions by which the science of law describes its object
are called "rules of law," they must be distinguished from the legal
norms described by the science of law. The former are instruments
of the legal science, the latter are functions of the legal authority.
In describing the law by rules of law, the science of law does not
exercise the function of a social authority, which is a function of
will, but the function of cognition. Although the legal norms issued
by the legal authority may be considered as constituting a specific
value, namely the legal value, the rules of law are not judgments
of value in any possible sense of this term, just as the laws of nature
by which the natural science describes its object are not value judgments. If the statement that something is or is not in conformity
with a legal norm may be classified as a value judgment, it is such
a judgment only in the same sense as is the judgment that something is an appropriate means to a presupposed end—that is to
say, it is a value judgment not in the specific sense of this term
as essentially different from a judgment about reality, but rather a
special type of judgment about reality. As such it is, by its very
nature, not incompatible with a science of law, just as the judgment that something is an appropriate means is not excluded from
the science of nature. But as the result of a peculiarity of positive

law of which we shall speak later, even the judgment that something is legal or illegal has no place within the science of law.

The judgment that something is legal or illegal must be distinguished from the judgment that something is just or unjust. These two judgments differ from each other in the same way as do the statements that something is an appropriate means to a presupposed ultimate end and that something is an ultimate end. If the statement that something is an appropriate means and the statement that something is legal are considered to be value judgments, they are, as pointed out, at the same time judgments about reality; whereas the statement that something is an ultimate end and the statement that something is just, are genuine judgments of value, essentially different from judgments about reality. Their meaning is not that something is or is not in conformity with a positive norm, but that it is or is not in conformity with a nonpositive norm. Consequently they are excluded from the field of science—of nature or of law.

The only nonpositive norm that the science of law may take into consideration—not as its object but as a condition of its statements describing its object—is the basic norm of the legal order which is its object. The specific function of the basic norm of a positive legal order constituting the legal value, is to serve as the ultimate source of law, that is, as the reason for the validity of the constitution of a legal order; and the constitution is that positive legal norm (or set of norms) which regulates the creation of the other norms of the legal order. Hence the basic norm of a positive legal order has, as pointed out, a merely formal character; it does not constitute a substantive value as, for example, the nonpositive norm that men ought to be free, or that men ought to live in security—which constitute the value that we call "justice." In fact, the positivity of the law consists in that its validity does not depend on its conformity with justice, but in that it is created in a definite way determined by the basic norm, and that it is, by and large, effective. A positive law may be just or unjust; the possibility of being just or unjust is an essential consequence of its being positive. The judgment that something is legal or illegal, as pointed out, necessarily refers to a definite legal order valid for a certain space and at a certain time. What is legal according to one legal order

may be illegal according to another. In this sense, the value constituted by positive legal norms is always a relative value. But the
idea of justice, in its specific sense, designates an absolute value,
constituted by a nonpositive norm claiming to be valid everywhere and at all times, a substantive norm with an unchangeable
content.[6] Even if the statement that something is just or unjust
means that it is or is not in conformity with a norm of a positive
moral order established by custom or by the commands of a religious founder, it is excluded from the field of a science of law. For
the validity of such a positive normative order depends on a basic
norm different from the basic norm of positive law, which is
the only condition under which the science of law may describe its
object as a set of valid norms constituting the specific legal value.

Other values, especially the value of justice, which is the specific
value according to which the positive law as the legal reality may
be evaluated, are properly called "political values" in order to
distinguish them from the legal value. The differentiation of law
and politics means the differentiation of two normative systems.
When politics is opposed to law, the term "politics" is used in a
narrower sense than in the postulation of the separation of natural
science from politics, where politics means any normative system
whatever. The postulation of the separation of the science of positive law from politics means that the legal scientist, in describing
his object, must refrain from political value judgments as judgments referring to norms other than norms of positive law,
especially from evaluating his object as just or unjust. It is not for
the legal scientist but only for the legal authority to prefer something as just to something as unjust.

But although the science of law can and must be separated from
politics, that is to say, although the legal scientist must refrain
from political value judgments, the law-making process, which is
the function of the legal authority, cannot be separated from
politics. For this function is determined not only by legal norms
but also by norms of another normative system which, in order to
distinguish them from law, are, as pointed out, called "political."
It is a peculiarity of the law to regulate its own creation.[7] Just as
the constitution regulates the creation of statutes or institutes custom as a law-creating fact, statutes and rules of customary law

regulate the creation of individual norms by the courts in the judicial decisions. In creating a norm, the legal authority applies a higher norm determining the creation and the content of the lower norm. But because a norm can determine the creation and the content of another norm only to a certain extent, the norm-creating authority always has a certain degree of discretion in his norm-creating function. So far as his norm-creating function is left to his discretion, the legal authority may be, and actually is, determined by other than legal norms—and *so far* his function has a political character; whereas it is a legal function so far as it is determined by legal norms. Normally, the legislative organ is legally bound by the constitution only with respect to the law-making procedure. The content of the norms to be created by the legislative organ is only exceptionally determined by the constitution. This is the case when the constitution prohibits or prescribes a certain content for these norms, for example, when the constitution prohibits restriction of religious freedom. So far as the legislative function is not determined by the constitution, the legislator may be, and actually is, determined by political principles, especially by his idea of justice. He may prefer one regulation to another in the same field because he considers the one to be just, the other to be unjust.

The legal scientist does not have the choice between accepting or rejecting the law, as established by the legislator, on the basis of his judgment about what is just and unjust. The scientist has to describe the decision of the legislator as the existing law, whether he considers it in conformity or not in conformity with what he considers to be justice. He may only examine whether the norms created by the legislative organ are or are not in conformity with the positive norms of the constitution, and the result of this examination is in the last analysis the objective ascertainment of a fact, not a subjective value judgment. But even the statement by the legal scientist that a statute is or is not constitutional, is of no legal importance. For the question as to whether a statute is or is not constitutional is not to be decided by the science of law, but by the legal authority on which the law confers this power. The same applies to a judicial decision with regard to the function of a court. It is normally much more closely determined by a higher legal norm—a statute or a rule of customary law—than is the legislative function by the constitution. But there is always a wider or narrower sphere of discretion left by the higher legal norm to the law-creating function of a court, and within this sphere of discretion the judicial decision may be, and actually is, determined by norms other than those of positive law. In creating an individual norm by the judicial decision, the court has always the choice between different decisions which are possible within the framework of the general norm determining the judicial function. The court may prefer the one to another because it considers the one to be just and the other to be unjust. But the legal scientist has no such choice. He has to take the decision rendered by the court as the existing law, valid for the concrete case. He may examine whether the judicial decision is or is not in conformity with the general legal norm to be applied by the court, and may come to the conclusion that it is or is not legal. But this judgment—in the last analysis a judgment about a fact—is legally irrelevant. For the decision on the question as to whether the decision of a court is legal or illegal is not within the competence of the science of law, but is within that of the legal authority on which the law has conferred this power.

The application of the law by a legal authority, as well as the description of the law by the legal scientist, implies an interpretation of the law. To interpret a legal norm is to find its meaning. It is a requirement of legal technique that a legal norm shall be formulated as clearly as possible, so that its meaning is unquestionable. However, since legal norms are mostly expressed in human language, and human language is frequently ambiguous, this requirement can only approximately be complied with. Hence, very often more than one meaning can be found in a legal norm. The doctrine that a legal norm has actually only one meaning and that there is a scientific method which enables us always to find this single correct meaning of it, is a fiction used by traditional jurisprudence in order to maintain the illusion of legal security.

There are, of course, different methods of interpretation. One is an interpretation according to the intention of the lawmaker or according to the wording of the legal instrument; another is a historical or a logical interpretation; and a third is a restrictive or an extensive interpretation. If the law itself does not prescribe one of these methods, each of them is applicable and may lead to a result different from that of another. Even if one method of interpretation is obligatory, it may furnish different and contradictory meanings. In applying a norm, the legal authority chooses one of these meanings and thus attributes to it the force of law. This may be called an authentic interpretation, although in traditional language this term is used only to designate a legal norm the express purpose of which is to interpret another, previous norm, not the interpretation implied in the application of a norm. The choice of one of the several meanings of a legal norm by a legal authority in its law-applying function is a law-creating act. So far as this choice is not determined by a higher legal norm, it is a political function. For the choice between the different meanings of a legal norm, if not determined by a higher legal norm, may be, and actually is, determined by norms other than legal, and this means by political norms. Hence the authentic interpretation of the law by a legal authority may be characterized as a political interpretation. On the other hand, the task of a legal scientist interpreting a legal instrument is to show its possible meanings and to leave it to the competent legal authority to choose in accordance with political principles the one which this authority thinks the most appropriate. In showing the possibilities which the law to be applied opens to the legal authority, the legal scientist scientifically serves the law-applying function; and in revealing the ambiguity, and thus the necessity for improving the wording, he serves the law-creating function in a scientific way. If the legal scientist recommends to the legal authority one of the different meanings of a legal norm, he tries to influence the law-making process and exercises a political, not a scientific, function; if he presents this interpretation as the only correct one, he is acting as a politician in the disguise of a scientist. He is veiling legal reality. But science has to unveil reality; only political ideologies try to veil it. Hence the scientific interpretation of the law, which is the interpretation of the law by a legal scientist, may be characterized as a legal interpretation—in contradistinction to the interpretation applied by a legal authority. By preferring one of several possible interpretations to the exclusion of the others, the latter offers what may be characterized as a political interpretation.

The "Legal" and the "Political"

The distinction between a legal and a political function as the distinction between a function determined by legal norms and a function determined not by legal but by political norms, is often of considerable importance. A typical example is the problem of recognition of a community as a state, or of a body of individuals as the government of a state. The fact that traditional doctrine does not distinguish between a legal and a political recognition has caused the confusion prevailing among the writers who have treated this problem. According to some writers, recognition has only a declaratory character—it has no legal consequences. Hence a community is a state, and a body of individuals a government, if each fulfills the requirements of international law, regardless of whether the community or the government is or is not recognized as such by the governments of other states. According to other writers, recognition has a constitutive character, which means that it has essential legal consequences. They assert that a community is a state and a body of individuals the government of a state, only when recognized as such by the governments of other states, and only in relation to the recognizing states. But, in truth, recognition is both a constitutive and a declaratory act; or, more precisely formulated, the act called recognition comprises two functions—a legal function which is constitutive and a political function which is declaratory.

Recognition of a community as a state or of a body of individuals as the government of a state means, in the first place, the ascertainment of the fact that a community is a state or that a body of individuals is the government of a state. This recognition is determined by norms of general international law, which stipulates the conditions under which a community is a state and a body of individuals the government of a state. Hence this recognition, as a function determined by the law, is a legal function and may be called legal recognition. The ascertainment of a legally relevant fact always has a constitutive character, since in the realm of law a fact to which the law attaches legal consequences exists legally only if ascertained in the way the law prescribes. International

law confers upon the governments of the states the power to ascertain the existence of the facts "state" and "government" in the
sense of international law. Hence the legal recognition of a community as a state or of a body of individuals as the government of
a state has a constitutive character, just as the decision by which a
court ascertains that a definite individual has committed a definite
crime is by its very nature constitutive, so far as the individual is a
criminal and hence punishable only if the court has ascertained this
fact. However, by recognition is meant not only the act by which
the existence of the facts "state" or "government" is ascertained,
but also the act by which the government of a state expresses its
willingness to enter into the normal relations with the recognized
community or government. This act is not determined by norms
of general international law; it is left to the discretion of the
existing states, who may for any reason enter, or refuse to enter,
into the normal relations with another state or with the government of another state. This act may be—and actually is—determined only by political principles, and hence it may be called
political recognition, in contradistinction to the legal recognition.
So far as it has in itself no legal consequences, it is not constitutive and so far has merely a declaratory character. Usually both
functions, the legal and the political recognition, are combined
in one and the same act called "recognition," which, with respect
to its legal function is constitutive, and with respect to its political
function is declaratory.

Although the distinction between "legal" and "political" is useful and necessary, it is capable of misuse fully as harmful and ob-
jectionable. Such misuse is, unfortunately, quite frequent in the
traditional theory of law. A characteristic case is the distinction between two branches of national law, one of which is opposed as
"political" law to the other as "legal" law, or law in the strict and
genuine sense of the term. This is the significance attributed to the
traditional dichotomy of law into public and private law, the
definition of which concepts is one of the most controversial of
questions. Whatever the difference between so-called public law
and so-called private law may be, it certainly does not consist—as
the distinction between a political and a nonpolitical law pretends
—in the fact that public law is "law" in a lesser degree than private
law. In this sense, law cannot be "political." Law being by defini-

tion opposed to politics, a political law is a contradiction in terms. The fact that so-called public law regulates the organization of the state and the competence of its organs, that is political matters, is no reason to assume that this law is, as law, inferior to private law regulating the economic and family relations among the subjects of the state. The attempt to minimize the legality of public law (as compared with private law) by defining public law as the regulation of the relation between the state and its subjects, as a relation of superiority and inferiority and hence a "power" relation, and by defining private law as the regulation of the relation among the subjects of the state, as a relation among equals and hence as a nonpower or a true "legal" relation, has been proved again and again to imply a logical fallacy. The state as a legal person can be conceived of only as subjected to the law like all other persons; and a relation between legal persons established by the law can be conceived of only as a legal obligation or a legal right one person has in relation to another. It can, therefore, not be conceived as a "power" relation but only as a legal relation, that is to say, as a relation between subjects equally subjected to the law establishing the obligation or the right, whatever their content may be. If the doctrine that public law is "political" law and as such less law than private law, has in spite of the contradictions demonstrated by its critics, been obstinately maintained by many writers, it is still not based on scientific grounds. The insensitivity of its proponents to logical contradictions shows that the purpose of this doctrine is not to describe the law in an objective and consistent way, but to furnish an ideology justifying nonobservance of the law. If public law, especially the norms regulating the jurisdiction of the organs of the state, is not law in the strict sense of the term, the government is not bound by these norms as a private subject is bound by the law. The government may then always act as it considers it politically expedient, even if such action is not authorized by the law. The doctrine that public law has a political and not a strictly legal character is not a scientific theory; it is a political ideology.

Closely connected with this doctrine is the frequently advocated view that the constitution of a state, or the constitution of an international community laid down in a treaty, is not a legal but a political instrument, which, consequently, must be interpreted not juridically but politically. An instrument is legal if it contains legal

norms establishing legal obligations and legal rights. Hence there
cannot be the slightest doubt that the constitution of a state or the
constituent treaty of an international community is a legal instrument. The only question is whether they are at the same time also
political instruments. If the answer is affirmative, it is certainly not
based on the content of the instruments, which by its very nature is
law and nothing but law—constitutional law in one case and international law in the other. The instrument in question may be
called political only with respect to the purpose of the law it contains. But if it is admitted that the purpose of a state constitution
or a treaty constituting an international community is "political"
such an admission does not alter the fact that this purpose is to be
achieved by law as the only and specific means; otherwise the establishment of a constitution would be superfluous. The political
purpose by no means deprives the instrument of its legal character.
There is no legal instrument which has not an extralegal purpose,
because the law, seen from a teleological point of view, is always
a means and not an end. That a loan contract has an economic
purpose, and therefore can be designated as an economic instrument, has not the slightest effect on its legal character. Hence the
political or economic purpose of a legal norm cannot exclude a
juridical, that is, a legal, interpretation, all the more since a legal
interpretation includes—as pointed out—all possible interpretations of a legal norm. But the view that a constitution is a political,
not a legal, instrument, evidently has the same tendency as the
doctrine that public law is political, not legal law: it tries to
justify actions of the organs of the state or of the international community which no possible interpretation of the constitution war-
rants.

The same tendency is involved when an unconstitutional action
of the organ of a national or an international community is justified by the statement that this organ is not a legal, but a political,
agency. In view of the fact that the function of any organ of a
legal community is legal so far as it is determined by the law, and
political so far as it is not determined by the law but left to the
discretion of the organ, each organ is at the same time a legal and
a political organ. But the function of some organs is much more
closely determined by the law than that of others; consequently,
in the exercise of their function, they have much less discretion,

and hence political character in much lesser degree, than the others. Most courts are so restricted, while most administrative organs are not. But this rule has important exceptions. There are courts which have a far-reaching discretion and administrative agencies whose functions are very much restricted by administrative law. Who can deny that, for example, the Supreme Court of the United States is not only a legal but—in this sense—to a great extent also a political agency? There is no organ of a legal community to which the law does not leave at least a certain degree of discretion in the exercise of its function, and hence no organ that is a legal, and not at the same time a political, agency. But however wide the sphere of discretion may be which the law leaves to an organ in the exercise of its function, this function can be conceived of as exercised by an organ of the legal community only if it is performed within the discretion conferred upon the organ by the law; that is, if the function is in conformity with the law.

One of the worst cases of abuse of the distinction between the legal and the political is its ill-famed but widespread application to international disputes. There are, it is argued, two kinds of disputes —those referring to legal matters and those referring to political matters. The former, as legal disputes, are justiciable; the latter, as political disputes, are not. That is to say, only legal, but not political, disputes can be settled by the application of international law and hence by decisions of international tribunals. If it were true— as this doctrine pretends—that there are disputes to which, because of the nature of their subject matter, existing international law cannot be applied, the distinction between legal and political disputes would be justifiable. But there are no such disputes. For any dispute consists in the claim of one party that the other party is obliged to behave in a certain way, and in the rejection of this claim by the other party. In this respect there are only two possibilities. Either the existing international law establishes the obligation disputed by the parties or it does not. In both cases, existing international law is applicable to the dispute. In the first case the dispute has to be decided in favor of the plaintiff; in the second case, in favor of the defendant. In the first case the international tribunal, in applying existing international law, has to decide that the defendant is obliged to behave as the plaintiff claims; and in the second case, likewise applying international law, it must decide that the defendant is not obliged to behave as the plaintiff claims, that this claim has no basis in international law and that, consequently, the defendant is legally free to behave in this matter as he pleases. This freedom is legally guaranteed; for it is a principle of every legal order that what is not legally forbidden to the subjects of the legal community constituted by the legal order, is legally permitted to them. In applying this principle to the case, the tribunal applies existing law. Hence there is no dispute to which the existing international law is not applicable, and no dispute which, for this reason, is political and therefore not justiciable.

It may be, however, that the application of existing international law, although logically possible, is from one or another point of view politically unsatisfactory. This means that according to norms other than those of existing law, the dispute might be settled in another way than it has to be settled according to existing law—for example, that it might be decided not for the defendant, but for the plaintiff. But the judgment that the application of existing law to a dispute is unsatisfactory, is a value judgment of a highly subjective character; what is unsatisfactory to one party may be very satisfactory to the other. Nevertheless it is not excluded that the parties to a dispute agree to submit to the decision of an international agency competent to decide the dispute according to norms other than those of positive international law, especially according to norms of justice or equity. Then this agency is legally authorized to create new law for the case at hand. Its decision is a legal decision, binding upon the parties. So far this dispute, too, is a legal dispute. But the content of the decision—just as the content of the decision of a legislative organ—is determined by nonlegal norms. Such a dispute differs, it is true, from a dispute to be decided according to preëxistent law. But the difference does not consist in the fact that the one can, whereas the other cannot, be decided according to preëxistent law which, because of the nature of the subject matter of the dispute, is not applicable. The difference consists in the fact that, though the preëxistent law is applicable in both cases, one of them, on the basis of a legal agreement, is to be decided according to new law. The doctrine that there are nonlegal, or political, disputes, not justiciable because of the inapplicability of existing international law, misinterprets that which from a nonlegal point of view is an inadequacy by labeling it a legal impossibility. Its purpose is not to interpret the law in an objective way but to justify the attempt to exclude the application of existing law, in contradiction to its scientifically ascertainable meaning. The doctrine thus is not a scientific theory, but an instrument of politics.

The misuse of the distinction between the legal and the political is one of the most effective, although not the only, means employed to confound the science of law with politics. To avoid the mingling of these two heterogeneous spheres is as essential for the preservation of the scientific character of jurisprudence as the separation of science from politics is a vital condition for the existence of all independent science.

NOTES

WHAT IS JUSTICE?
(Pages 1–24)

1 Plato, *Laws,* 662b.
2 See, "Platonic Justice," pp. 82 ff.
3 Matthew V:38, 44.
4 Luke XVIII:29, 30.
5 Luke XIV:26.
6 Matthew V:45, 48.
7 1 Corinthians III:19.
8 1 Corinthians II:1 ff.
9 Philippians III:9.
10 Galatians V:6.
11 Ephesians III:19.
12 See "The Idea of Justice in the Holy Scriptures," pp. 72 ff.
13 "Zur Kritik des sozialdemokratischen Parteiprogramms," aus dem Nachlass von Karl Marx, *Neue Zeit* IX–1 (1890–1891), p. 567. See my *The Communist Theory of Law* (New York: Frederick Praeger, 1955), pp. 34 ff.
14 Immanuel Kant, *Grundlegung zur Metaphysik der Sitten,* I. Abschnitt.
15 Aristotle, *The Nicomachean Ethics,* 1129b.
16 *Ibid.,* 1107a, 1106a, 1105b.
17 *Ibid.,* 1133b.
18 See "Aristotle's Doctrine of Justice," pp. 110 ff.
19 See "The Natural-Law Doctrine Before the Tribunal of Science," pp. 137 ff.

20 Thus the relativistic doctrine of justice, essentially connected with legal positivism which does not recognize the existence of an absolute justice, is frequently made responsible for the totalitarian state. The Protestant theologian Emil Brunner says in his work *Justice and the Social Order* (London and Redhill: Lutterworth Press, 1945), the totalitarian state is "the ineluctable consequence" of "a positivism void of faith and inimical to metaphysics and religion" (p. 16). This statement is in open contradiction to the fact that the ideal state of Plato, the prototype of a totalitarian state, is the consequence of his antirelativistic doctrine of ideas which, aiming at absolute values, culminates in the assumption of an absolute good implying absolute justice. See "Platonic Justice," pp. 82 ff. and K. R. Popper, *The Open Society and Its Enemies* (London: G. Routledge, 1945), I, *passim* and pp. 89 ff. If there is a relationship between the philosophy of values and politics, the autocracy of the totalitarian

state, political absolutism, is connected with the belief in absolute values, whereas democracy and its essential principle of tolerance presupposes a relativistic view. See "Absolutism and Relativism in Philosophy and Politics" (pp. 198 ff.).

However, Brunner is not very consistent, since he is forced to admit (p. 57): "The Church, which to-day protests, and rightly so, against the oppression it suffers at the hands of the totalitarian State, would do well to remember who first set the State the bad example of religious intolerance by using the secular arm to safeguard by force what can only spring from a free act of the will. The Church should always bethink itself with shame that it was the first teacher of the totalitarian State at nearly every point." This is certainly true; but only because or in spite of the fact that the Church does not teach "a positivism void of faith and inimical to metaphysics and religion" but just the contrary: the belief in absolute justice.

Brunner's work is a justification rather than a refutation of relativism. His doctrine of absolute justice based on "the Christian faith" (p. 8) starts from the thesis: "Either there is a valid criterion, a justice which stands above us all, a challenge presented *to* us, not *by* us, a standard rule of justice binding on every State and every system of law, or there is no justice, but only power organized in one fashion or another and setting itself up as law" (p. 16). Brunner thinks he can find the law of absolute justice in a divine order of creation, which he characterizes as the "Christian law of nature," in contradistinction to the natural law of the rationalistic school of Pufendorf, Thomasius, etc. (pp. 80 ff.). However, after maintaining that the belief in an absolute, divine justice, the recognition of the Christian law of nature as an order different from and possibly opposite to the positive law is indispensable in order to stop the disintegration of the idea of justice by the relativistic positivism, he admits—and this is the result of his doctrine of absolute justice, the Christian law of nature—that all positive law is only "relatively just" (p. 17). That means that he recognizes a relative justice in addition to the absolute justice. This, however, is a contradiction in terms. If a normative order does not correspond to the absolute justice it is unjust and, hence, cannot be just, even not relatively just. There cannot be beside a relative justice an absolute justice, just as there cannot be an absolute justice beside a relative justice. This is confirmed by Brunner who admits that it is an error to assume "that a law of the State must not be obeyed if it conflicts with the law of nature, and hence is unjust"; otherwise, the law of nature would mean "an intolerable menace to the system of positive law." "No State can tolerate a competition of this kind presented by a second legal system. The laws of the State actually obtaining must possess a monopoly of binding legal force; the law of nature must claim no binding legal force for itself if the legal security of the State is to remain unshaken" (p. 87). A law of nature which has no binding force cannot be that "standard rule of justice binding on every State and every system of law" which, according to Brunner's statement on p. 16, is the essence of absolute justice opposed to the relative justice advocated by legal positivism. A law of nature which has no binding force is no normative order at all; for the existence of such an order is its binding force. Brunner justifies this astonishing turn to relativistic positivism by referring to the reformers, who "in their profound respect for the authority of the State and positive law" "took their stand clearly on the side of positive law, only granting to the law of nature the function of a criterion" (pp. 87 f.).

That only the relatively just positive law and not an absolutely just law of nature is legally binding, is exactly the doctrine of relativistic legal positivism. This doctrine, it is true, does not recognize a law of nature even as a criterion, because such a recognition implies the possibility of justifying positive law; and legal positivism, as a science of law, refuses to justify positive law.

In his doctrine of justice, Brunner makes ample use of this possibility. What he proclaims as the content of the absolutely just law of nature: state, family, individual freedom, private property, are the essential institutions established by the positive non-communist legal orders of our time. Hence these legal orders are proved to be, at least in principle, in conformity with the Christian law of nature. Only communism is according to this doctrine in contradiction to the absolute, divine justice. However, the communist state which, as a totalitarian state, is declared to be "a monster of injustice" (p. 17), "the acme of injustice" (p. 137), is—since it is after all a state—finally recognized as "an ordinance of God, a divine institution" (p. 69). For "even the unjust State is still a State" (p. 174), its legal order as "a certain order of peace, however brutal," has a certain degree of justice (pp. 174 ff.). That means: Brunner's doctrine of absolute justice is compelled to attribute even to the law of the communist state a relative justice. Hence, there is, according to this doctrine, from the point of view of justice, no essential difference between this law and the law of the capitalist states, since their law too, as a positive law, is only relatively just.

A doctrine of absolute justice directed against relativistic positivism in view of the evident contradictions in which it is entangled, cannot claim to be taken seriously from a scientific point of view, even if it would not declare that its purpose "is not primarily theoretical but practical, as all theological work should be" (p. 8).

THE IDEA OF JUSTICE IN THE HOLY SCRIPTURES
(Pages 25–81)

[1] See "The Natural-Law Doctrine Before the Tribunal of Science," pp. 137 ff. and my *The Political Theory of Bolshevism* (Berkeley: University of California Press, 1949), pp. 14–19.

[2] *Dr. Martin Luthers Werke. Kritische Gesamtausgabe. Briefwechsel* (Weimar: Hermann Böhlaus Nachfolger, 1938), VIII, 643.

[3] For Scripture quotations I used (1) *The Complete Bible, An American Translation;* the Old Testament translated by J. M. Powis Smith and a group of scholars, the Apocrypha and the New Testament by Edgar J. Goodspeed (University of Chicago Press, 1939); and (2) *The Holy Bible.* Revised Standard Version (London and New York: Thomas Nelson & Sons, 1953).

In some quotations I changed the word "Lord" to "Yahweh" and the word "righteousness" to "justice."

[4] J. G. Frazer, *Folk-Lore in the Old Testament* (London: Macmillan, 1919), III, 304 ff.

[5] In Ezekiel XXIII:4 we read that Yahweh made two sisters, Oholah and Oholibah, his wives. The name of the one signifies Samaria, that of the other Jerusalem.

[6] George F. Moore, *Judaism* . . . (Cambridge: Harvard University Press, 1927), II, 251 ff.

[7] The unsurmountable antagonism which exists between the idea of justice of the Old Testament (that is, the principle of retribution), and the justice taught by Jesus (that is, the principle of love), was recognized as early as the beginning of the second century by Marcion. As a consequence of this antagonism Marcion denied that Yahweh, the God of the Jews, who created the world and governed it as supreme legislator and judge in accordance with the justice of retribution, could be identified with the God, father of Jesus, who was unknown to the Jews and who is neither the creator of this evil world nor its legislator or judge—qualities incompatible with his essence: love. Marcion emphatically rejected the Old Testament and tried to restore a pure Christian Gospel by eliminating from the New Testament the Jewish elements. See Adolf von Harnack, *Marcion. Das Evangelium vom fremden Gott* (Leipzig: J. C. Hinrichs, 1921), pp. 27 ff. and Hans Jonas, *Gnosis und spätantiker Geist* (Göttingen: Vandenhoeck & Ruprecht, 1934), pp. 173 ff.

[8] Moore, *op. cit.,* p. 119.

[9] Robert Eisler, *The Messiah Jesus and John the Baptist* (London: Methuen, 1931), pp. 334 f. interprets Jesus' answer, "Pay the emperor what belongs to the emperor and pay to God what belongs to God" to mean: "Throw Caesar's, that is,

Satan's money down his throat, that you may then be free to devote yourselves wholly to the service of God." Eisler correctly relates this statement of Jesus to his saying, "You cannot serve God and the mammon," "Mammon being the whole system of money and credit, which, like some rival god and the author of all evil, is the real temporal 'lord of this world.' . . . He who no longer possesses money, uses money, or wishes to use money, need pay no more taxes to Caesar."

10 It is true that, according to John XIX:11, he said to Pilate: "You would have no power over me unless it had been given you from above." But none of the Synoptic Gospels contains a similar statement.

11 Hugo Gressmann, *Der Ursprung der isaelitisch-jüdischen Eschatologie* (Göttingen: Vandenhoeck & Ruprecht, 1905), p. 193.

12 B. Duhm, *Das kommende Reich Gottes* (Tübingen: I. C. B. Mohr, 1910), pp. 33, 34.

13 August Freiherr von Gall, ΒΑΣΙΛΕΙΑ ΤΟΥ ΘΕΟΥ (Heidelberg: C. Winter, 1926), p. 324.

14 Quoted according to *The Apocrypha and Pseudepigrapha of the Old Testament in English*, ed. by R. H. Charles (Oxford: Clarendon Press, 1913).

15 Gall, *op. cit.*, p. 242.

16 Gressmann, *op. cit.*, p. 288.

17 Charles Guignebert, *The Jewish World in the Time of Jesus* (New York: E. P. Dutton, 1939), pp. 109, 116 f.

18 E. C. Dewick, *Primitive Christian Eschatology* (Cambridge: University Press, 1912), p. 11.

19 R. H. Charles, *Immortality* (Oxford: Clarendon Press, 1912), pp. 7 ff.

20 Guignebert, *op. cit.*, pp. 114 f.

21 *Ibid.*, p. 114; Adolphe Lods, *La Croyance à la vie future et le culte des morts dans l'antiquité israélite* (Paris: Fischbacher, 1906), I, 225.

22 Gall, *op. cit.*, p. 426; Johannes Weiss, *Die Predigt Jesu vom Reich Gottes* (Göttingen: Vandenhoeck & Ruprecht, 1900), p. 111.

23 Gall, *op. cit.*, p. 312.

24 Dewick, *op. cit.*, pp. 69 f., 83.

25 Emil Schürer, *Geschichte des jüdischen Volkes im Zeitalter Jesu Christi*, 4th ed. (Leipzig: J. C. Hinrichs, 1907), II, 579 ff., 641 f. Cf. also: Joseph Klausner, *The Messianic Idea in Israel* (New York: Macmillan, 1955), p. 414.

26 Cecil John Cadoux, *The Historic Mission of Jesus* (New York and London: Harper, 1941), p. 219: "Jesus speaks at times about the life of men beyond the grave . . . He also speaks still more frequently of the approaching cataclysm, when apparently for the whole race at once an entire set of new conditions would by the Coming of the Kingdom be introduced. In speaking of both the two spheres . . . Jesus uses very largely the same set of technical terms and ideas . . . We have no option but to accept . . . this strange fusion of apparently disparate topics."

27 This is the correct translation of the words ἐντὸς ὑμῶν, not: "within you" (as Goodspeed also translated). The latter translation has been used as an argument for the purely spiritual character of the Kingdom of God as taught by Jesus. But even if ἐντὸς ὑμῶν means "within you," i.e. in your heart, the Kingdom of God Jesus had in mind cannot be interpreted as a transcendental sphere lying outside the empirical world: only the just will enter the Kingdom, that is to say those who have the right inner attitude. Robert Eisler in *The Messiah Jesus and John the Baptist*, pp. 344 ff. tries to prove that the words of Jesus: The kingdom is ἐντὸς ὑμῶν are "an echo of Deuteronomy XXX:14": "But the word is very near you; it is in your mouth and in your heart, so that you can do it," and quite compatible with his idea of the Kingdom of God as a "political, moral, and religious state of people here on earth."

28 Joseph Klausner, *Jesus of Nazareth* (New York: Macmillan, 1929), pp. 398 ff. See also Hermann Gunkel and Leopold Zscharnak, eds., *Die Religion in Geschichte und Gegenwart*, 2d ed. (Tübingen: J. C. B. Mohr [Paul Siebeck], 1930), IV, 1819 f.

According to Klausner, there was at the time when Jesus lived in the belief of the Jews a distinction between the "Messianic age," "days of happiness and prosperity, both material and spiritual," and the "world to come" "wherein is neither eating nor drinking, nor fruitfulness, nor begetting of children, nor trafficking, nor jealousy, nor strife, but 'the righteous shall sit with crowns on their heads and enjoy the brightness of the Shekina [the divine presence].' " The "Messianic age" precedes the "world to come." Since "the poor and downtrodden and afflicted, the lost and strayed, the ignorant and social outcasts whom Jesus gathered around him" could not be attracted nor satisfied with spiritual promises only, Jesus "was compelled to hold out an earthly ideal also, more particularly since he, too, was addicted to the beliefs and ideas of his race and age." Cf. also Klausner, *The Messianic Idea in Israel*, pp. 408 ff.

29 Weiss, *op. cit.*, pp. 15, 123.

30 Max Radin, *The Trial of Jesus of Nazareth* (Chicago: The University of Chicago Press, 1931), pp. 46 ff.

31 Theodor Zahn, *Kommentar zum Neuen Testament* (Leipzig: A. Deichert'sche Verlagsbuchhandlung, Nachf., 1908), "Das Evangelium des Johannes," IV, 626.

32 Weiss, *op. cit.*, p. 105.

33 *Ibid.*, p. 119.

34 T. Francis Glasson, *The Second Advent* (London: The Epworth Press [Edgar C. Barton], 1945), pp. 127 ff., 130.

35 Joseph Klausner, *From Jesus to Paul* (New York: Macmillan, 1943), pp. 562 ff.

PLATONIC JUSTICE
(Pages 82–109)

1 *The Republic*, 518–519.
2 Cf. my essay "The Platonic Love," *The American Imago*, III (1942), 1–110.
3 *Laws*, 836.
4 *Symposium*, 202.
5 *Ibid.*, 209.
6 *Epistle II*, 314.
7 *Republic*, 459.
8 *Ibid.*, 602.
9 *Laws*, 662–666.
10 *Ibid.*, 644.
11 *Phaedo*, 114.
12 *Meno*, 86.
13 *Ibid.*, 81.
14 *Republic*, 330–331. This passage is generally overlooked.
15 *Ibid.*, 505.
16 *Ibid.*, 337.
17 *Ibid.*, 434.
18 *Ibid.*, 435.
19 *Ibid.*, 506.
20 *Epistle VII*, 341.
21 *Epistle II*, 313.

ARISTOTLE'S DOCTRINE OF JUSTICE
(Pages 110–136)

1 Aristotle, *The Metaphysics*, 981b. Translations used: Hugh Tredennick, Loeb Classical Library (London: 1936) and *The Works of Aristotle*, ed. by W. D. Ross, 2d edition (Oxford: 1928), VII.

2 *Ibid.*, 982b.
3 *Ibid.*, 1026a.
4 *Ibid.*, 1003a.
5 *Ibid.*, 1069b.
6 *Ibid.*, 1012b.
7 *Ibid.*, 1072a.
8 *Ibid.*, 1072b.
9 *Ibid.*, 1072b.
10 *Ibid.*, 1074b.
11 *Ibid.*, 1074b.
12 *Ibid.*, 1075a.
13 *Ibid.*, 1075a.
14 *Ibid.*, 1075a.
15 *Ibid.*, 1075b.
16 Aristotle, *The Nicomachean Ethics*, transl. by H. Rackham, Loeb Classical Library (London: 1926) and *The Works of Aristotle*, ed. by W. D. Ross (Oxford: 1925), IX.
17 *Nicomachean Ethics*, 1094a.
18 *Metaphysics*, 982b.
19 *Ethics*, 1094a.
20 *Ibid.*, 1094b.
21 *Ibid.*, 1096b.
22 *Ibid.*, 1096b.
23 *Ibid.*, 1096b–1097a.
24 *Ibid.*, 1095b.
25 *Ibid.*, 1097a.
26 *Ibid.*, 1097b.
27 *Ibid.*, 1097b.
28 *Ibid.*, 1095b, 1096a.
29 *Ibid.*, 1097b.
30 *Ibid.*, 1097b.
31 *Ibid.*, 1098a.
32 *Ibid.*, 1098b.
33 *Ibid.*, 1101a.
34 *Ibid.*, 1101a.
35 *Ibid.*, 1102a. Later, Aristotle characterizes virtue as "disposition" (1106a). In answering the question as to "what species of disposition" virtue is, he says: "Excellence or virtue in a man will be the disposition which renders him a good man and also which will cause him to perform his function well." This definition, too, is tautological. Since "virtue in a man" is identical with goodness as a man's quality, the definition amounts to the statement that the goodness of a man is the disposition which renders him a good man and causes his work to be a good work. Of the same type is the statement: "Inasmuch as moral virtue is a disposition of the mind in regard to choice, and choice is deliberate desire, it follows that, if the choice is to be good, both the principle must be true and the desire right, and that desire must pursue the same things as principle affirms. . . . The attainment of truth" in so far as "practical intelligence" is concerned, "is the attainment of truth corresponding to right desire," (1139a). That means: the choice (i.e. deliberate desire) is good if it is right—which means: if it is good. Another statement of the same kind: "To like and to dislike the right things is thought to be a most important element in the formation of a virtuous character" (1172a).
36 *Ibid.*, 1129b.
37 *Ibid.*, 1094b. Although Aristotle presents his ethics as a department of politics (1094b) and characterizes politics as "the most authoritative science" whose purpose is "the knowledge of the supreme good," as a science which "lays down laws as to what people shall do and what things they shall refrain from doing" (1094b), he

states in the second book of his *Ethics:* "our present study, unlike the other branches of philosophy, has a practical aim (for we are not investigating the nature of virtue for the sake of knowing what it is, but in order that we may become good, without which result our investigation would be of no use)" (1103b), thus confusing ethics, as the science of morals, with its object, that is, morals as a normative order. It seems that he denies the possibility of describing this object in terms of general rules. For he says that "the whole theory of conduct is bound to be an outline only and not an exact system, in accordance with the rule we laid down at the beginning [referring to the statement quoted in the text] that philosophical theories must only be required to correspond to their subject matter; and matters of conduct and expediency have nothing fixed or invariable about them, any more than have matters of health. And if this is true of the general theory of ethics, still less is exact precision possible in dealing with particular cases of conduct; for these come under no science or professional tradition, but the agents themselves have to consider what is suited to the circumstances of each occasion, just as is the case with the art of medicine or of navigation" (1104a). If, as Aristotle asserts, "scientific knowledge is a mode of conception dealing with universals and things that are of necessity" (1140b), and if ethics cannot describe its object in terms of general rules because "action"—the object of a theory of morals—"deals with particular things" (1141b), ethics is not only no science but altogether impossible. For what else could a "theory" of morals present but general rules indicating that under certain conditions a certain human behavior ought to take place? And how can an acting individual know how to act morally in a concrete case if he does not know a general rule prescribing a definite conduct under definite conditions, identical with those under which he is acting? What the acting individual has to decide for himself is only the question as to whether the conditions determined by the general norm exist in his case—he has to decide the *questio facti*, not the *questio juris* (the latter is the question how to act if his action is to be considered as morally good, i.e., in conformity with a general rule of morals). The value judgment that a concrete action is morally good or morally bad consists in nothing else but in the judgment that it is or is not in conformity with a general norm presupposed by the judging subject as valid. As a matter of fact, Aristotle presents in his *Ethics* many general rules of morals, thus when he states that "to seek death in order to escape from poverty, or the pangs of love, or from pain or sorrow, is not the act of a courageous man, but rather of a coward" (1116a); or: "Falsehood is in itself base and reprehensible, and truth noble and praiseworthy" (1127a). The fact that some general rules are valid only with certain exceptions means that there is a conflict between two general rules and that, therefore, the one is restricted by the other, as Aristotle shows in *Ethics*, IX, 1.

38 *Ibid.,* 1106b.

39 *Ibid.,* 1106a.

40 *Ibid.,* 1105b.

41 *Ibid.,* 1108b.

42 *Ibid.,* 1109a.

43 *Ibid.,* 1106b.

44 *Ibid.,* 1107b.

45 *Ibid.,* 1107a. In another connection we read: "The middle states of character are in excess as compared with the defective states and defective as compared with the excessive states, whether in the case of feelings or of actions. For instance, a brave man appears rash in contrast with a coward and cowardly in contrast with a rash man; similarly a temperate man appears profligate in contrast with a man insensible to pleasure and pain, but insensible in contrast with a profligate" (1108b). Hence virtue may be not only a mean but also an excess as well as a deficiency. But there are virtues and vices to which, according to Aristotle's express statement, the *mesótes* doctrine does not apply at all. "Not every action or feeling however admits of the observance of a due mean. Indeed the very names of some essentially denote evil, for instance malice, shamelessness, envy, and, of actions, adultery, theft,

murder. All these and similar actions and feelings are blamed as being bad in themselves; it is not the excess or deficiency of them that we blame. It is impossible therefore ever to go right in regard to them—one must always be wrong" (1107a). Among the virtues to which the *mesótes* doctrine is not applicable, temperance and justice are mentioned: "Just as there can be no excess or deficiency in temperance and justice, because the mean is in a sense an extreme, so there can be no observance of the mean nor excess nor deficiency in the corresponding vicious acts." Nevertheless, later the *mesótes* doctrine is applied to temperance as well as to justice.

46 *Ibid.*, 1106a, b.

47 *Ibid.*, 1109a.

48 *Ibid.*, 1109b.

49 *Ibid.*, 1107a.

50 *Ibid.*, 1143a.

51 Cf. n. 37 and quotation n. 50.

52 The fact that Aristotle's ethics in determining the moral value, that is, virtue, presupposes the established social order, results also from his assertion that moral virtue is not the product of instruction, but of habit. "We become just by doing just acts, temperate by doing temperate acts, brave by doing brave acts. This truth is attested by the experience of states: lawgivers make the citizens good by training them in habits of right action" (1103b). If we, without previously being instructed by an ethical theory, can act morally and can become virtuous by acting morally, the moral action can only be that action which is usually considered to be such. The habit which makes a man virtuous can only be that habit by which the moral order actually prevailing in his society is maintained, the positive moral order under which he is actually living. The reference to the positive law is highly characteristic. Not only because here its concordance with morals is presupposed as self-evident, but because the law produces the desired disposition of man to act in conformity with the law not through instruction but by attaching to the contrary behavior specific sanctions. The "habit of right action" becomes possible only after the positive law prescribing this action has been established. Similarly, the habit of moral action is possible only if a positive moral order is established; and just as the right action is the one prescribed by positive law, the moral or virtuous action at which Aristotle's ethics is aiming is the one prescribed by the positive moral order presupposed to be valid at a certain time and in a certain place.

53 *Ibid.*, 1129a.

54 *Ibid.*, 1129a.

55 *Ibid.*, 1130b.

56 *Ibid.*, 1130a.

57 *Ibid.*, 1129b.

58 *Ibid.*, 1129b.

59 *Ibid.*, 1129b.

60 *Ibid.*, 1131a.

61 *Ibid.*, 1131a.

62 *Ibid.*, 1132a.

63 *Ibid.*, 1131a.

64 *Ibid.*, 1131b.

65 *Ibid.*, 1132a.

66 *Ibid.*, 1132a.

67 *Ibid.*, 1132b.

68 *Ibid.*, 1133a.

69 *Ibid.*, 1132b–1133a.

70 Cf. quotation n. 66.

71 *Ibid.*, 1133b.

72 *Ibid.*, 1133b.

73 *Ibid.*, 1155a.

74 *Politics*, 1253a.

75 This essay is not dealing with the question as to whether and to what extent Aristotle's philosophy contains a natural-law doctrine. For Aristotle does not identify natural law with justice. In the *Nicomachean Ethics* (1134a) a distinction is made between "natural justice" (*physikón dikaion*) and "legal justice" (*nomikón dikaion*) as between two kinds of "political justice." Political justice "is found among men who share their life with a view of self-sufficiency," that is to say, within the state. "For justice exists only between men whose mutual relations are governed by law" (1134a). By a rule of natural justice Aristotle understands a norm "that has the same validity everywhere and does not depend on our accepting or not"; by a rule of legal justice a norm "that in the first instance may be settled in one way or the other indifferently, though having once been settled it is not indifferent" (1134b). But such a norm, too, represents "justice." Aristotle does not say that a norm of positive law, if it is not in conformity with natural justice, is not to be considered as valid; nor does he indicate the requirements a norm must fulfill in order to be in conformity with natural justice. Although he asserts the existence of natural justice, this concept does not play an essential part in his *Ethics,* of which only a few lines are devoted to this problem. Besides, the assertion of a "natural justice" is hardly compatible with the statement made in connection with the doctrine that moral virtue is the product of habit: "it is clear that none of the moral virtues is engendered in us by nature, for no natural property can be altered by habit" (1103a).

76 *The City of God (Civitas Dei)*, Bk. XIX, chap. 21.

77 *Ibid.*, Bk. IV, chap. 4.

THE NATURAL-LAW DOCTRINE BEFORE THE TRIBUNAL OF SCIENCE
(Pages 137–173)

1 Hugo Grotius, *De Jure Belli ac Pacis,* Bk. I, chap. i, sec. 10.

2 *Ibid.*, Prolegomena, sec. 12.

3 Thomas Hobbes, *Leviathan,* Part I, chap. xv.

4 Samuel Pufendorf, *De Jure Naturae et Gentium,* Bk. II, chap. iii, sec. 20.

5 See "Causality and Imputation," pp. 324 ff.

6 See "Value Judgments in the Science of Law," pp. 209 ff.

7 See "Causality and Retribution," pp. 303 ff.

8 See my "Naturrecht und positives Recht: Eine Untersuchung ihres gegenseitigen Verhältnisses," *Revue Internationale de la Théorie du Droit,* II (1927–1928), 71 ff.; and my *General Theory of Law and State* (Cambridge: Harvard University Press, 1945), pp. 389 ff.

9 For instance Grotius, *op. cit.*, Prolegomena, sec. 39: "The principles of that law [the law of nature], if only you pay strict heed to them, are in themselves manifest and clear, almost as evident as are those things which we perceive by the external senses; and the senses do not err if the organs of perception are properly formed and if the other conditions requisite to perception are present." The view that the principles of natural law are self-evident is in open contradiction to the fact that there is not, and never was, agreement about these principles among the followers of the natural-law doctrine. Pufendorf, *op. cit.*, Bk. II, chap. i, sec. 7, admits that "among men there are as many minds as there are heads and to each one his own way seems best." Nevertheless he maintains (Bk. I, chap. iii, sec. 3) "that, in the faculty of apprehension and in the judgment there is inherent a natural rectitude, which does not allow us to be misled in moral questions, if proper attention be paid to them." But if no "proper" attention is paid? This is actually possible. The real view appears in the following statement (*loc. cit.*): ". . . if we do not wish to destroy all morality in actions, we must at any hazard maintain that the understanding of man is by nature sound, and that upon sufficient inquiry it apprehends clearly, and as they actually

are, the matters which present themselves to it. And further, that the practical judgment, at least as concerns the general precepts of natural law, cannot be so corrupted that it may not be held responsible for any evil actions that come from it, on the ground that they proceeded from an insuperable error or ignorance." That means that error or ignorance about the principles of natural law, although actually not impossible, does not exclude responsibility. The well-known rule that ignorance of the positive law is no excuse is simply applied to natural law.

10 It is significant that the doctrine according to which positive law is superfluous, even harmful, to society, was advocated by the founder of theoretical anarchism, William Godwin, in his famous *Enquiry Concerning Political Justice* (London: 1793), and that Godwin was not a follower of the natural-law doctrine. When he says that "law is an institution of the most pernicious tendency" (*ibid.*, II, 771), he refers to positive as well as natural law. He expressly rejects two fundamental principles of the natural-law doctrine: that man by his very nature has certain rights—he says that the idea of man and the idea of right are "incompatible" with one another (*ibid.*, I, 112 f.)—and the idea of the social contract. "It is impossible for any government to derive its authority from an original contract" (*ibid.*, I, 149). He attacks the very foundation of the natural-law doctrine when he states: "We know too little of the system of the universe, are too liable to error respecting it, and see too small a portion of the whole, to entitle us to form our moral principles upon an imitation of what we conceive to be the course of nature.—It is an extreme error to suppose that the course of nature is something arbitrarily adjusted by a designing mind" (*ibid.*, II, 692).

11 Thus, for example, Philip Melanchthon in his work *Ethicae Doctrinae Elementorum Libri Duo* (1560) answers the question as to whether written laws are necessary as follows: "Many ignorant people clamor stolidly that there is no need of written laws and that cases should be decided according to the natural judgment of those presiding [*ex naturali judicio eorum qui praesunt*, which may be freely translated: 'by application of the principles of natural law by those in government']. But we ought to know that this barbaric opinion must be rejected and that people must be taught that written laws are preferable and should be heeded with love and respect." *Opus Reformatorum*, Philippi Melanthonis Opera (Halle i. S.: Schwetschke, 1850), XVI, 234–235.

12 Pufendorf, *op. cit.*, Bk. II, chap. iii, sec. 14.

13 *Ibid.*, sec. 15.

14 *Ibid.*, Bk. VII, chap. i, sec. 11.

15 *Ibid.*, sec. 8.

16 *Ibid.*, Bk. VII, chap. ii, sec. 1.

17 *Ibid.*, Bk. VII, chap. i, sec. 11.

18 The real and the ideal nature of man are mixed up in the statement of which parts have been quoted above. It runs as follows: "After the preceding remarks it is easy to find the basis of natural law. It is quite clear that man is an animal extremely desirous of his own preservation, in himself exposed to want, unable to exist without the help of his fellow-creatures, fitted in a remarkable way to contribute to the common good, and yet at all times malicious, petulant, and easily irritated, as well as quick and powerful to do injury. For such an animal to live and enjoy the good things that in this world attend his condition, it is necessary that he be sociable, that is, be willing to join himself with others like him, and conduct himself towards them in such a way that, far from having any cause to do him harm, they may feel that there is reason to preserve and increase his good fortune" (Bk. II, chap. iii, sec. 15).

19 Hobbes, *De Cive*, chap. xiv, sec. 10.

20 Hobbes, *Leviathan*, Part II, chap. xxvi.

21 *Loc. cit.*

22 Samuel Pufendorf, *Elementorum Jurisprudentiae Universalis Libri Duo*, Definition XIII, sec. 6.

23 Pufendorf, *De Jure Naturae . . .* , Bk. VIII, chap. i, sec. 2.

24 Pufendorf, *Elementorum* . . . , Definition XIII, sec. 18.

25 Pufendorf, *De Jure Naturae* . . . , Bk. II, chap. iii, sec. 11.

26 Hobbes, *Leviathan*, Part I, chap. xv.

27 Hobbes, *The Elements of Law*, ed. by F. Toennies (Cambridge: University Press, 1928), p. 57.

28 *Ibid.*, p. 150.

29 Hobbes, *Leviathan*, Part II, chap. xxvi.

30 Pufendorf, *De Jure Naturae* . . . , Bk. VIII, chap. i, sec. 5.

31 *Ibid.*, Bk. VII, chap. iv, sec. 2.

32 Pufendorf, *Elementorum* . . . , Observation V, sec. 21.

33 Hobbes, *Leviathan*, Part I, chap. xv.

34 Pufendorf, *Elementorum* . . . , Definition XVII, sec. 1.

35 *Ibid.*, Definition VIII, sec. 2.

36 Hobbes, *The Elements of Law*, p. 86.

37 Grotius, *op. cit.*, Bk. I, chap. iv, sec. 1.

38 *Ibid.*, sec. 2.

39 *Ibid.*, sec. 7.

40 Pufendorf, *De Jure Naturae* . . . , Bk. VII, chap. viii, sec. 4.

41 *Ibid.*, sec. 5.

42 *Loc. cit.*

43 *Loc. cit.*

44 John Locke, *Second Treatise of Civil Government*, chap. xviii, secs. 203–204.

45 *Ibid.*, chap. vii, sec. 87.

46 *Ibid.*, sec. 89.

47 *Ibid.*, chap. xix, sec. 240.

48 Immanuel Kant, "Die Metaphysik der Sitten," in *Gesammelte Schriften*, herausgegeben von der Kgl. preussischen Akademie der Wissenschaften (Berlin: Georg Reimer, 1907), VI, 320.

49 See the passages quoted in my article "Naturrecht und positives Recht," cited above, n. 8.

50 Hobbes, *The Elements of Law*, pp. 87 ff.

51 *Ibid.*, pp. 89 ff.

52 Locke, *op. cit.*, chap. xi, sec. 135.

53 *Ibid.*, sec. 137.

54 J. J. Rousseau, *Contrat Social*, Bk. I, chap. iv.

55 Locke, *op. cit.*, chap. vii, sec. 90.

56 *Ibid.*, chap. viii, sec. 95.

57 *Ibid.*, sec. 99.

58 Sir Robert Filmer, *Patriarcha*, chap. ii.

59 *Ibid.*, sec. 5.

60 *Ibid.*, sec. 6.

61 *Ibid.*, sec. 10.

62 Grotius, *op. cit.*, Bk. II, chap. ii.

63 Richard Cumberland, *De legibus naturae* (London: 1672). English translation: *A Treatise of the Laws of Nature* (London: 1727).

64 *Ibid.*, chap. i, sec. 21.

65 *Ibid.*, chap. vii, sec. 2.

66 *Ibid.*, sec. 9.

67 *Loc. cit.*

68 Locke, *op. cit.*, chap. xi, secs. 138, 139.

69 *Code de la Nature ou Le véritable Esprit de ses Loix*. Republished in *Collection des Economistes et des Réformateurs Sociaux de la France*, by E. Dolléans (Paris: 1910).

70 A. Lichtenberger, *Le Socialisme au XVIIIe siècle* (Paris: F. Alcan, 1895), p. 114.

71 Dolléans, *op. cit.*, pp. v ff., and Kingsley Martin, *French Liberal Thought in the Eighteenth Century* (London: E. Benn, 1929), p. 243.

72 Dolléans, *op. cit.*, p. 23.

[73] *Ibid.*, p. 17.
[74] *Ibid.*, p. 36.
[75] *Loc. cit.*
[76] *Ibid.*, p. 13.
[77] *Ibid.*, p. 37.
[78] *Ibid.*, p. 39.
[79] *Ibid.*, p. 16.
[80] *Ibid.*, p. 84.
[81] *Loc. cit.*
[82] *Ibid.*, pp. 85 ff.
[83] A Russian translation and commentary of Morelly's *Code de la Nature* was published in 1940.
[84] Dolléans, *op. cit.*, p. 57.
[85] *Ibid.*, p. 103.
[86] First published in 1830.
[87] First published in 1855.
[88] The resemblance of Comte's positive stage of mankind and Plato's ideal state was first shown by Adolf Menzel in his excellent essay *Naturrecht und Soziologie* (Vienna: C. Fromm, 1912), p. 38. Menzel shows that the sociology of the nineteenth century, in spite of its opposition to the natural-law doctrine, has exactly the same character as the latter. It is the presentation of political postulates in terms of a law of evolution.
[89] Auguste Comte, *Cours de philosophie positive*, 2d ed. by E. Littré (Paris: 1864), VI, 50 ff. (For the English translation I used *The Positive Philosophy of Auguste Comte*, transl. by Harriet Martineau [London: 1853].)
[90] *Ibid.*, VI, 50 ff.
[91] *Ibid.*, p. 48.
[92] *Ibid.*, p. 440.
[93] *Ibid.*, pp. 439 f.
[94] *Ibid.*, p. 457.
[95] *Ibid.*, pp. 494 ff., 497.
[96] *Ibid.*, p. 454.
[97] *Ibid.*, p. 482.
[98] Auguste Comte, *Système de politique positive* (Paris: L. Mathias, 1851), I, 156.
[99] Comte, *Cours de philosophie positive*, VI, 511.
[100] *Ibid.*, p. 516.
[101] *Ibid.*, V, 446; VI, 169.
[102] *Ibid.*, pp. 434, 436.
[103] Herbert Spencer, *The Principles of Sociology*, sec. 270.
[104] *Ibid.*, sec. 259.
[105] *Ibid.*, sec. 260.
[106] Herbert Spencer, *The Principles of Ethics*, sec. 369.
[107] *Ibid.*, sec. 7.
[108] *Ibid.*, sec. 54.
[109] *Ibid.*, sec. 8.
[110] *Ibid.*, sec. 9.
[111] Spencer, *Principles of Sociology*, sec. 260.
[112] Spencer, *Principles of Ethics*, sec. 48.
[113] *Ibid.*, sec. 343.
[114] *Ibid.*, secs. 272, 283.
[115] *Ibid.*, sec. 331.
[116] *Ibid.*, sec. 301.
[117] *Ibid.*, sec. 343.
[118] G. W. F. Hegel, *The Philosophy of History*, transl. by J. Sibree (New York: The Colonial Press, 1899), p. 9.
[119] *Ibid.*, p. 39.

120 *Ibid.*, p. 10.

121 *Ibid.*, p. 25.

122 *Ibid.*, p. 30.

123 *Ibid.*, p. 13.

124 *Ibid.*, p. 14 f.

125 *Ibid.*, p. 457.

126 *Ibid.*, pp. 9, 13.

127 *Ibid.*, p. 15.

128 *Ibid.*, p. 457.

129 *Science of Logic;* transl. by W. H. Johnston and L. G. Struthers (London: Allen and Unwin, 1929), II, 68.

130 *Ibid.*, p. 70.

131 *Ibid.*, p. 67.

132 G. W. F. Hegel, *Philosophy of Right,* transl. by S. W. Dyde (London: G. Bell, 1896), sec. 257 f.

133 *Ibid.*, sec. 258.

134 *Ibid.*, secs. 258, 331.

135 *Ibid.*, sec. 347.

136 *Ibid.*, sec. 354.

137 *Ibid.*, sec. 358.

138 *Ibid.*, sec. 359.

139 Karl Marx, *Capital* (London: Swan Sonnenschein & Co., 1901), p. xxx.

140 See Friedrich Engels, *Herr Eugen Dühring's Revolution in Science* (London: M. Lawrence, 1935), *passim.*

141 Friedrich Engels, *The Origin of the Family, Private Property and the State* (New York: International Publishers, 1942), p. 158. For the references, see my *The Political Theory of Bolshevism* (Berkeley: University of California Press, 1948), pp. 10 ff.

142 Plato, *The Laws,* II, 663.

A "DYNAMIC" THEORY OF NATURAL LAW
(Pages 173–197)

1 See "The Natural-Law Doctrine Before the Tribunal of Science," pp. 137 ff.

2 University of Chicago Press, 1953. Since Wild thinks that Plato is the founder of the natural-law doctrine (p. 73), his defense of Plato is, in the main, a defense of this doctrine.

ABSOLUTISM AND RELATIVISM IN PHILOSOPHY AND POLITICS
(Pages 198–208)

1 See my *Staatsform und Weltanschauung* (Tübingen: I. C. B. Mohr [Paul Siebeck], 1933).

2 See my *General Theory of Law and State* (Cambridge: Harvard University Press, 1945), pp. 419 ff.

3 Bertrand Russell, *Philosophy and Politics* (London: Cambridge University Press, 1947), *passim.*

4 See "Platonic Justice," p. 109.

5 See "Aristotle's Doctrine of Justice," pp. 112 f.

VALUE JUDGMENTS IN THE SCIENCE OF LAW
(Pages 209–230)

1 Ralph B. Perry, *General Theory of Value* (New York: Longmans, Green, 1926).

2 See Wilbur M. Urban, "Value and Existence," *Journal of Philosophy*, XIII (1916), 463. See also my essay "Die Rechtswissenschaft als Norm- oder als Kulturwissenschaft," *Schmollers Jahrbuch für Gesetzgebung, Verwaltung und Volkswirtschaft im Deutschen Reich*, XL (Leipzig: 1916), 1181 ff.

3 Juristic value judgments referring to the norms of international law and the relation of this law to national law will not here be given a special treatment.

4 Sometimes a judgment asserting that an object is an appropriate means for a certain end or purpose, is designated as a value judgment. The "value" here consists in the relation of means to end. Since this relation is a relation of cause and effect, the "value" is here of an entirely objective nature. An object is "purposeful" if it is suited to bring about a certain effect which is regarded as an end. It can be objectively established whether or not the object is so suited. To establish it is a pure judgment of fact. Quite different from the judgment that something is an appropriate means for a certain end is the judgment that something ought to be recognized as an end, an ultimate end, which is not in itself a means for a further end. This judgment implies the assertion of a norm. If the existence of this norm cannot be objectively verified, the judgment is a subjective value judgment.

5 This parallelism between ideology and reality is analogous to the psycho-physical parallelism, but radically different from that between ideological "superstructure" and social (economic) reality which Marxists assume. See my *The Communist Theory of Law* (New York: Frederick Praeger, 1955), pp. 1 ff.

6 See "What is Justice?", pp. 1 ff.

7 See "The Natural-Law Doctrine Before the Tribunal of Science," pp. 137 ff.

8 From the point of view of normative jurisprudence, only one legal order exists: the universal order comprising both international law and the various national legal orders based thereupon. See: "Pure Theory of Law and Analytical Jurisprudence," pp. 283 ff.; also: my *General Theory of Law and State* (Cambridge: Harvard University Press, 1945), pp. 328 ff.

THE LAW AS A SPECIFIC SOCIAL TECHNIQUE
(Pages 231–256)

1 "Wherever there is society, there is law."

2 Ovid, *Metamorphoses*, i, 89–93. "Golden was that first age, which, with no one to compel, without a law, of its own, kept faith and did the right. There was no fear of punishment, no threatening words were to be read on brazen tablets; no suppliant throng gazed fearfully upon its judge's face; but without judges lived secure." (Transl. by Frank Miller, Loeb Classical Library, London: 1916.)

3 See my *The Political Theory of Bolshevism* (Berkeley: University of California Press, 1948) and *The Communist Theory of Law* (New York: Frederick Praeger, 1955).

4 Frederick Engels, *The Development of Socialism from Utopia to Science*, "The People" Educational Library, I (New York: 1892), 24.

5 *Ibid.*, p. 26.

6 Exodus XX:5.

THE PURE THEORY OF LAW AND ANALYTICAL JURISPRUDENCE
(Pages 266–287)

1 See my *General Theory of Law and State* (Cambridge: Harvard University Press, 1945) and *Principles of International Law* (New York: Rinehart, 1952).

2 The problems of justice and natural law are more extensively discussed in "What is Justice?", pp. 1 ff. and "The Natural-Law Doctrine Before the Tribunal of Science," pp. 137 ff.

3 I consider the most characteristic American representatives of sociological jurisprudence to be those men who are more commonly known as American legal realists.

4 The first edition was published in 1832, under the name of *The Province of Jurisprudence Determined;* much new material was added in later editions. All references in this essay are to the fifth edition, published in 1885, hereafter cited as "Austin."

5 Austin, 88

6 Austin, 89 ff.

7 Austin, 395.

8 Austin, 444.

9 Austin, 395.

10 Austin, 220.

11 E.g., Austin, 101.

12 Austin, 220.

13 Austin, 263.

14 Austin, 224.

15 Austin, 172 ff.

LAW, STATE, AND JUSTICE IN THE PURE THEORY OF LAW
(Pages 288–302)

1 Mr. Bergman raises the objection to the Pure Theory of Law that defining the concept of law as a coercive order ". . . is begging the question. How does one know at the outset that what is termed 'positive law' is 'law' at all? It would be more fitting to call such rules 'positive norms.' " But what if these norms present themselves as "law?" Mr. Bergman refuses to call them law because he understands by law only law that is just. Since the Pure Theory of Law does not pretend that its definition refers to just law but only to what usually is and always was termed law, since the Pure Theory of Law is not interested in knowing whether the law as defined by it is law in the specific sense Mr. Bergman uses this term, there is obviously no begging of the question. See my *General Theory of Law and State* (Cambridge: Harvard University Press, 1945), pp. 15 ff. and my *Law and Peace in International Relations* (Cambridge: Harvard University Press, 1942), pp. 3–11.

2 See "The Law as a Specific Social Technique," pp. 231 ff.

3 Mr. Bergman rejects the view that sanction is essential to the legal norm, by the statement that he believes that "might cannot make law." This is just the above mentioned confusion. If he would analyze the phenomenon he calls "might," he would probably be more cautious in his statements about the relationship between law and might. See the chapters "Psychic Compulsion" and "Motives of Lawful Behavior" in my *General Theory of Law and State,* pp. 28 ff.

4 Thus Mr. Bergman says, "A community arises wherever two or more persons have interests in common."

5 Plato, *Laws*, II, 661 ff.

6 See my *Der soziologische und juristische Staatsbegriff*, 2d ed. (Tübingen: J. C. B. Mohr [Paul Siebeck], 1928); and my *General Theory of Law and State*, pp. 181 ff.

7 Mr. Bergman does not agree with the statement that the law regulates its own creation, because he understands by law justice. The Pure Theory of Law has never maintained that justice regulates its own creation or that the positive law regulates the creation of justice. But it can hardly be denied that the process by which positive law is created—legislation, judiciary—is regulated by positive law.

8 Mr. Bergman erroneously maintains that the Pure Theory of Law identifies the state with the law. I never maintained that the highly decentralized social orders of primitive and international law constitute states.

9 Since Mr. Bergman does not see that the law regulates its own creation, he sticks to the usual saying, the law is the creature of the political community. Hence he defines the law as "the means by which the political community endeavors to realize its paramount interest in maintaining the peace and order of the area." That the law has the purpose of maintaining peace is true, but that does not constitute an element of the definition of the law concept. The question is by what means peace is maintained when it is maintained by the law. If we eliminate the maintenance of peace from this definition as not essential and if we substitute for "community" the order constituting the community, Bergman's definition amounts to the meaningless statements: the law is the means by which the law endeavors to realize the law.

10 This is the answer to Mr. Bergman's categorical statement ". . . there cannot be a pure theory of law."

11 That a statement about reality is based on the perception of our senses does not, of course, mean that such a statement is true because men believe in it, as Mr. Bergman asserts in order to prove that there is no difference between value judgments and statements about reality, since both are "subjective." The statement that the sun revolves around the earth was not true although men believed in it; men believed in it because they erroneously thought it was true. If a statement were true because men believe in it, then two contradictory statements were true at the same time if there were people who believed in the one and also people who believed in the other. This would imply the abandonment of logic. Mr. Bergman seriously maintains that "truth is what man believes," and that the objectivity of his belief is "its prevalence in the community . . . whether the belief concerns a physical fact or a moral evaluation." Consequently he denies the difference between belief and knowledge, which implies the denial of any difference between religion and science. In this respect, I am afraid, Mr. Bergman has proved too much. But in another respect, too little. His doctrine implies that a subjective value judgment assumes objectivity if the judging subject is a community. He speaks of "community belief," of a community's concept or sense of justice, as if the community were the judging subject. What is meant is that individuals belonging to the community, or the majority of those individuals, have the same subjective value judgment. However, the fact that many individuals render the identical value judgments, cannot change the character of the judgment. Mr. Bergman confuses the objectivity of a judgment with the frequency of the act of judgment. Besides, by substituting for the individual the personified community as judging subject, nothing is won. As there are many different communities, there are many different "community beliefs" or community value judgments, especially many different community judgments about what is just. In one community a socialistic, in another an individualistic ideal of justice prevails. Then the question arises, which of these different ideals is the right one. And to this question, Mr. Bergman's philosophy has no answer.

12 See "The Natural-Law Doctrine Before the Tribunal of Science," pp. 144 ff.

13 Rousseau, *Social Contract*, Bk. II, chaps. 1–3.

14 *Ibid.*, Bk. IV, chap. 2. This is an open contradiction. In order to attenuate this impression Rousseau does add: ". . . this presupposes indeed, that all the qualities of the general will still reside in the majority. When they cease to do so, whatever side a man may take, liberty [and that means justice] is no longer possible." If the

will of the majority is not necessarily in conformity with the general will, and a monarch as well as a popular assembly or a parliament may issue true law, or fail in expressing the general will, how can Rousseau say that the vote of the majority "always" binds the rest, that the general will is "found by counting votes," and that to be in the minority "proves" one to be mistaken about what the general will is? As a matter of fact, Rousseau's *Social Contract* owes its tremendous success to the fact that it has been understood as a justification of democracy based on the principle of majority will.

It is interesting to note that the dualism of the "general will" and the "will of all," of true law and positive law, is paralleled by the dualism of the true will of an individual and his actual will. In order to maintain the fiction that an individual who voted against the bill adopted by the majority is still free, although bound by a will that is evidently not his own, Rousseau goes so far as to say that to be in the minority means not only to have a false opinion about what the general will is, but also to have expressed a will which is not one's own will, one's true will. If I vote against the majority and "if my particular opinion had carried the day, I should have achieved the opposite of what was my will." The true will of an individual—but not his actual will—is always in conformity with the general will. Only the individual might not know what the general will is and consequently what his own will is. The individual truly "wills" something that he does not know. It is at the price of such fantastic fictions that the positive law—in this case the positive law of democracy—is identified with justice.

15 Savigny, *System des heutigen Römischen Rechts* (Berlin: Veit, 1840), I, 35.

16 Savigny, *Vom Beruf unserer Zeit für Gesetzgebung und Rechtswissenschaft,* 3d ed. (Heidelberg: 1840), p. 49.

17 *Ibid.,* p. 43.

18 Leon Duguit, *L'Etat, le droit objectif et la loi positive* (Paris: A. Fontemoing, 1901), p. 16.

19 *Ibid.,* p. 426.

20 Mr. Bergman, too, identifies law and justice. He terms "law" only the just law and suggests for unjust law the term "fiat." Consequently the organs of the state, the government, does not make law, but it may make "fiat." "Law" is created by the "articulate majority." But what is the "articulate majority"? If it is the majority of those who, in accordance with the constitution, participate in the popular assembly, or the majority of the elected members of parliament, just law would be identical with democratically created law, and Mr. Bergman's doctrine would be a rather naive identification of justice with democracy. But Mr. Bergman is not as naive as that. He does not define his "articulate majority" as the constitutional majority of a democratically organized community. What he has to say positively of this creator of true law is only that "in any given community the population may be divided between those who articulate [through action or through words] their thoughts and those who do not"; and that "at any given time within a given political community the articulate majority is a precise group, but the society of men has not yet developed measurements fine enough to locate and register this moving force in the body politic." Mr. Bergman is quite right when he admits that the articulate majority "is a nebulous concept at best." But although it is not possible to "locate" and to "register" the articulate majority, this uncontrollable entity is declared by Mr. Bergman to be "the voice of the community" and the organs of government are only "its ears." The government has to "identify" the rules of law issued by this nebulous authority and to "administer them." Since it is impossible to prove that a law issued by the government is not in conformity with that issued by the nebulous law-maker, there must be an assumption in favor of the former. And that is just what Mr. Bergman expressly declares: "the presumption of course is always that the government will follow the law which the community [meaning the "articulate majority"] has established and that, as a consequence, the normative expression of the government will correspond to the normative expression of the community," that is, to the true law

emanating from the "articulate majority." Mr. Bergman's "articulate majority" is a very primitive, democratically dressed revival of the *solidarité sociale* of the French sociological school.

CAUSALITY AND RETRIBUTION
(Pages 303–323)

[1] See my *Society and Nature* (Chicago: Chicago University Press, 1943).

[2] This principle is in most cases designated by the term "reciprocity." I prefer the term "retribution" because it expresses better the social and especially the moral and legal character of the principle.

[3] Karl Joel, *Geschichte der antiken Philosophie* (Tübingen: I. C. B. Mohr [Paul Siebeck], 1921), I, 239 ff.

[4] Aristotle, *Physica*, Bk. III, iv, 203b.

[5] Karl Joel, *Der Ursprung der Naturphilosophie aus dem Geiste der Mystik* (Jena: E. Diederichs, 1906), pp. 66 f.

[6] Aristotle, *De anima*, I2, 405a, 19.

[7] Aeschylus, *Agamemnon*, 750 f.

[8] Hermann Diels, *Die Fragmente der Vorsokratiker*, 5th ed. (Berlin: Weidemann, 1934), Fr. 25.

[9] See John Burnet, *Early Greek Philosophy*, 3d ed. (London: A. and C. Black, 1920), pp. 54 f. Burnet says "the current statement that the term ἀρχή was introduced by him [Anaximander] appears to be due to a misunderstanding."

[10] Diels, *op. cit.*, Fr. 1; Burnet, *op. cit.*, p. 52.

[11] Wilhelm Capelle, *Die Vorsokratiker* (Stuttgart: A. Kröner, 1953), p. 75.

[12] Werner Jäger says, that the law whose idea is expresesd in the fragment of Anaximander is the law of the "polis," the Greek city state (*Paideia*, transl. by Gilbert Highet [Oxford: Basil Blackwell, 1939], p. 159).

[13] Diels, *op. cit.*, Fr. 53; Burnet, *op. cit.*, p. 136.

[14] Diels, *op. cit.*, Fr. 80; Burnet, *op. cit.*, p. 137.

[15] Capelle, *op. cit.*, p. 127.

[16] Diels, *op. cit.*, Fr. 1; Burnet, *op. cit.*, p. 133.

[17] Diogenes Laertius, IX, 7.

[18] Emile Boisacq. *Dictionnaire étymologique de la langue grecque* (Heidelberg: C. Winter, 1916), p. 621.

[19] Diels, *op. cit.*, Fr. 2; Burnet, *op. cit.*, p. 139.

[20] Diels, *op. cit.*, Fr. 114; Burnet, *op. cit.*, p. 139; Capelle, *op. cit.*, p. 136.

[21] Diels, *op. cit.*, Fr. 94; Burnet, *op. cit.*, p. 135.

[22] Capelle, *op. cit.*, p. 39.

[23] In Euripides's *Medea*, 410–411, the law of gravity appears as a legal norm. The order of nature and the legal order are identical. In consideration of Medea's criminal plans the chorus says: "Upward aback to their fountains the sacred rivers are stealing; Justice is turned to injustice, the order of old to confusion" (*Tragedies of Euripides*, in English verse by Arthur S. Way [London and New York: Macmillan, 1894], I, 78).

[24] The inviolability of the universal law as the unshakable will of a deity of justice whose function is retribution, is to be found also in the Babylonian epic of creation.

[25] Diels, *op. cit.*, Fr. 1. Burnet, *op. cit.*, p. 172 translates: "Avenging Justice."

[26] Diels, *op. cit.*, Fr. 8; Burnet, *op. cit.*, pp. 175 f.

[27] Aeschylus, *Prometheus*, 531–532.

[28] Diels, *op. cit.*, Fr. 115; Burnet, *op. cit.*, p. 222.

[29] Cicero, *De re publica*, III, xi, 19.

[30] Plutarchi Stromat., 7, in Hermann Diels, *Doxographi Graeci* (Berlin and Leipzig: W. de Gruyter, 1929), p. 581. See Capelle, *op. cit.*, p. 415.

31 Plato, *Protagoras*, xiii, 324.

32 Aetios, I, xxvi, 2, in Diels, *Doxographi Graeci*, p. 321. See Capelle, *op. cit.*, p. 418.

33 Simplicius, *De caelo*, p. 294, 33 Heiberg. See Capelle, op. cit., pp. 396 f.

34 Diogenes Laertius, IX, 7; see Diels, *Die Fragmente* . . . , Fr. 10.

35 *The Hibeh Papyri*, ed. by B. P. Grenfell and A. S. Hunt (London: Egypt Exploration Fund, 1906), Part I, xvi, 62 f.

36 Diels, *Die Fragmente* . . . , Fr. 164.

37 Capelle, *op. cit.*, p. 410.

38 According to Aristotle, *De generatione et corruptione*, I, vii, 323b.

39 Pliny, *Natural History*, II, 14, in Diels, *Die Fragmente* . . . , II, 103.

40 Aristotle, *Physica*, Bk. II, iv, 196a.

41 Diels, *Die Fragmente* . . . , Fr. 83.

42 Jäger, *op. cit.*, p. 159.

43 David Hume, *An Enquiry Concerning The Human Understanding*, ed. by L. A. Selby-Bigge (Oxford: Clarendon Press, 1894), p. 46.

44 Ernst Mach, *Die Mechanik in ihrer Entwicklung* (Leipzig: F. A. Brockhaus, 1897), pp. 443, 496.

45 Philipp Frank, *Das Kausalgesetz und seine Grenzen* (Wien: J. Springer, 1932), pp. 136 f.

46 Max Verworn, *Die Frage nach den Grenzen der Erkenntnis* (1908), pp. 15 ff., 44; Fritz Mauthner, *Wörterbuch der Philosophie* (München und Leipzig: G. Müller, 1910), "Bedingung," "Konditionismus," "Ursache."

47 Mach, *op. cit.*, p. 402, says: "The law of causality expresses the mutual dependence of phenomena. The particular reference to space and time in the formulation of the law of causality is not necessary because our spatial and temporal relations amount to the mutual dependence of phenomena."

48 E. Zilsel, "Ueber die Asymmetrie der Kausalität und die Einsinnigkeit der Zeit," *Die Naturwissenschaften* (1927), XV, 280 f.

49 H. Reichenbach, "Das Kausalproblem in der Physik," *Die Naturwissenschaften*, XIX (1931), 713 f.

50 Pierre Simon Marquis de Laplace, *A Philosophical Essay on Probabilities*, transl. from the sixth French edition by F. W. Truscott and F. L. Emory (New York: I. Wiley, 1917), p. 4.

51 Nicolas Malebranche, *De la recherche de la verité*, ed. by M. F. Bouiller (Paris: Garnier, 1879), I, 319.

52 See "Causality and Imputation," pp. 324 ff.

CAUSALITY AND IMPUTATION
(Pages 324–349)

1 See my *General Theory of Law and State* (Cambridge: Harvard University Press, 1945), pp. 45 ff., 92.

2 Felix Kaufmann, *Methodology of the Social Sciences* (London: Oxford University Press, 1944), pp. 48 ff.

3 See "Causality and Retribution," pp. oo ff.

4 *Ibid.*

5 See my *Society and Nature* (Chicago: University of Chicago Press, 1943), pp. 249 ff.

6 His essays discussing this problem are included in Max Planck, *Vorträge und Erinnerungen* (Stuttgart: S. Hirzel, 1949); they are entitled "Kausalgesetz und Willensfreiheit" (pp. 139–168); "Die Kausalität in der Natur" (pp. 250–269); "Vom Wesen der Willensfreiheit" (pp. 301–317); and "Determinismus oder Indeterminismus" (pp. 334–349). An English translation of the second essay appears in Planck, *The Philosophy of Physics* (New York: W. W. Norton, 1936); of the third essay in Planck, *The Universe in the Light of Modern Physics* (London: Allen and Unwin, 1937).

7 *Ibid.*, p. 302.

8 *Ibid.*, p. 302.

9 *Ibid.*, p. 303.

10 *Ibid.*, pp. 301, 309.

11 *Ibid.*, pp. 267, 302.

12 *Ibid.*, p. 267.

13 *Ibid.*, p. 267.

14 *Ibid.*, p. 302. Italics mine.

15 *Ibid.*, p. 338.

16 *Ibid.*, p. 267.

17 *Ibid.*, p. 307.

18 *Ibid.*, p. 311.

19 *Ibid.*, p. 163.

20 *Ibid.*, p. 164.

21 *Ibid.*, p. 255.

22 *Ibid.*, p. 256.

23 According to the description of Planck, *ibid.*, p. 259.

24 *Ibid.*, p. 259.

25 P. W. Bridgman, "The New Vision of Science," *Harper's Monthly Magazine,* CLVIII (March, 1929), 443 ff.

26 Planck, *op. cit.*, p. 260. Also other physicists, above all, Einstein, have never abandoned the principle of strict causality. Recently, Louis de Broglie, who previously had joined Heisenberg and Bohr, also expressed serious doubts about the doctrine that in quantum mechanics the principle of mere probability must be substituted for that of strict causality. He says: "La question qui se pose est finalement de savoir, Einstein l'a souvent souligné, si l'interprétation actuelle . . . est une description 'complète' de la réalité, auquel cas il faut admettre l'indéterminisme et l'impossibilité de représenter les réalités de l'echelle atomique d'une façon précise dans le cadre de l'espace et du temps, ou si, au contraire, cette interprétation est 'incomplète' et cache derrière elle, comme les anciennes théories statistiques de la Physique classique, une réalité parfaitement déterminée et descriptible dans le cadre de l'espace et du temps par des variables qui nous seraient cachées, c'est à dire qui échapperaient à nos déterminations expérimentales." He concludes: "L'interprétation purement probabiliste de la Mécanique ondulatoire a certainement depuis un quart de siècle rendu des services aux physiciens, parce qu'elle les a empêchés de s'enliser dans l'étude de problèmes très ardus et difficilement solubles . . . et leur a ainsi permis de marcher résolument dans la voie des applications qui ont été nombreuses et fructueuses. Mais aujourd'hui le pouvoir explicatif de la Mécanique ondulatoire, telle qu'elle est enseignée, paraît en grande partie épuisé. Tout le monde le reconnaît et les partisans de l'interprétation probabiliste eux-mêmes cherchent, sans beaucoup de succès, semble-t-il, à introduire des conceptions nouvelles encore plus abstraites et plus éloignées des images classiques . . . Sans nier l'intérêt de ces tentatives, on peut se demander si ce n'est pas plutôt vers un retour à la clarté des représentations spatiotemporelles qu'il faudrait s'orienter. En tout cas, il est certainement utile de reprendre le problème très difficile de l'interprétation de la Mécanique ondulatoire afin de voir si celle qui est actuellement orthodoxe est vraiment la seule que l'on puisse adopter" (*La Physique quantique restera-t-elle indeterministe?* [Paris: Gauthier-Villars, 1953], pp. 21 f.).

27 It seems that Planck also accepts this interpretation of the principle of causality. He says (*op. cit.*, pp. 268 f.): "It is true that the law of causality cannot be demonstrated any more than it can be logically refuted; it is neither true nor false; it is a heuristic principle; it points the way, and in my opinion it is the most valuable pointer that we possess in order to find a path through the confusion of events, and in order to know in what direction scientific investigation must proceed, so that it shall reach useful results. . . . Science does not mean an idle resting upon a body of certain knowledge; it means unresting endeavor and continually

progressing development towards an aim which the poetic intuition may apprehend, but which the intellect can never fully grasp."

28 See "Causality and Retribution," p. 320.

29 Planck, *op. cit.*, p. 264.

30 Max Planck, *Der Kausalbegriff in der Physik.* English edition: Max Planck, *Scientific Autobiography and Other Papers* (New York: Philosophical Library, 1949), p. 144.

31 Planck, *Vorträge und Erinnerungen*, p. 264.

32 *Ibid.*, p. 265.

33 *Ibid.*, p. 267.

34 *Ibid.*, pp. 265 f.

35 *Ibid.*, p. 266.

36 *Ibid.*, p. 311.

37 *Ibid.*, p. 266.

38 *Ibid.*, p. 333.

39 Bridgman, as pointed out, considers as a consequence of the uncertainty principle that the law of cause and effect must be given up and that "the universe fades away from us by becoming meaningless"; he expressly declares that this statement does not imply "that there really is something beyond the verge of meaning" (*op. cit.*, p. 451). Of the effects which this revolution of science may have he says: "The immediate effect will be to let loose a veritable intellectual spree of licentious and debauched thinking . . . The man in the street will, therefore, twist the statement that the scientist has come to the end of meaning into the statement that the scientist has penetrated as far as he can with the tools at his command, and that there is something beyond the ken of the scientist. This imagined beyond, which the scientist has proved he cannot penetrate, will become the play ground of the imagination of every mystic and dreamer. The existence of such a domain will be made the basis of an orgy of rationalizing. It will be made the substance of the soul; the spirits of the dead will populate it; God will lurk in its shadows; the principle of vital processes will have its seat here; and it will be the medium of telepathic communication. One group will find in the failure of the physical law of cause and effect the solution of the age-long problem of the freedom of the will . . ." It is of importance to note that even a radical indeterminist in the field of physics, like Bridgman, refuses to see in the uncertainty principle a support of the dogma of the freedom of will.

40 Planck seems to admit that the freedom of will is not a problem of natural science but of ethics. He says (*Vorträge* . . . , p. 312): "We have thus been led to the discovery that the causal cognition fails us precisely at the point which is of the chief importance for the conduct of life. Neither science nor self-knowledge can perfectly inform us how we will act in a given future situation. A different guide is needed for this end . . ." This guide is ethics. But ethics as a science whose object is morals, that is, a system of norms, does not and cannot inform us how we will act in the future, and Planck—in contradiction to his just-quoted statement—does not expect this result from ethics. He continues: "A guide not acting on the understanding but, immediately, on the will, by providing us with rules of conduct for given situations [is needed]. It follows that science requires a complement for the gap it has left. This complement is ethics, which adds to the causal 'must' the moral 'ought,' and places by the side of pure cognition the judgment of value which is strange to causal consideration." If ethics is supposed to fill the gap in science—and "science" can mean in this connection only natural science—it must act on the understanding, it must be a kind of science, although different from natural science applying the principle of causality. If by "ethics" a guide is meant which acts on the will by providing us with rules of conduct, the object of the science of ethics, that is, morals (or mores) as a system of norms, is substituted for ethics. Planck, as many other writers, confuses the one with the other. He says: "It is true that ethics is not based on science; but on the other hand, it cannot

wholly detach itself from science, and must certainly not enter into conflict with it. Thus ethics has, and also has not, much in common with science." Ethics as a *de*scription of morals or mores *is* a science and as such has something in common with natural science, although it differs from it precisely by the fact that it does not apply the principle of causality but the principle of imputation. Morals or mores, a system of norms or *pre*scriptions, the object of ethics, has nothing in common with science; just as the world of senses—the object of natural science—has nothing in common with science. Neither ethics as a science nor morals or mores as the object of this science can enter into conflict with science; and if natural science assumes the validity of a universal law of causality, ethics cannot maintain that within its object an exception to this law appears. The confusion of ethics as a science with its object, that is, morals or mores as a system of norms, prevents Planck from conceiving the correct relationship between natural science and ethics, as a social science, and, consequently, from a satisfactory solution of his problem: the compability of the principle of causality with the idea of the freedom of will.

SCIENCE AND POLITICS
(Pages 350–375)

1 See "Value Judgments in the Science of Law," pp. 209 ff.
2 See "Causality and Imputation," pp. 324 ff.
3 See "Value Judgments in the Science of Law," pp. 221 ff.
4 See "The Natural-Law Doctrine Before the Tribunal of Science," pp. 141 f.
5 See "Causality and Imputation," pp. 331 f.
6 See "What is Justice?" pp. 1 ff.
7 See "The Pure Theory of Law and Analytical Jurisprudence," p. 279.